AFRICA
WO/MAN
PALAVA

Women in Culture and Society

A series edited by Catharine R. Stimpson

Chikwenye Okonjo Ogunyemi

AFRICA WO/MAN PALAVA

The Nigerian Novel

by Women

THE UNIVERSITY OF CHICAGO PRESS • CHICAGO & LONDON

CHIKWENYE OKONJO OGUNYEMI is professor of literature at
Sarah Lawrence College.

The University of Chicago Press, Chicago 60637
The University of Chicago Press, Ltd., London

©1996 by The University of Chicago
All rights reserved. Published 1996
Printed in the United States of America

05 04 03 02 01 00 99 98 97 96   5 4 3 2 1
ISBN (cloth):   0-226-62084-0
ISBN (paper):   0-226-62085-9

Library of Congress Cataloging-in-Publication Data

Ogunyemi, Chikwenye Okonjo.
    Africa wo/man palava : the Nigerian novel by women / Chikwenye
Okonjo Ogunyemi.
            p.   cm. — (Women in culture and society)
    Includes bibliographical references and index.
    ISBN 0-226-62084-0. — ISBN 0-226-62085-9 (pbk.)
    1. Nigerian fiction (English)—Women authors—History and criticism.
    2. Women and literature—Nigeria. 3. Women in literature. I. Title.
    II. Series.
    PR9387.4.O38   1996
    823—dc20   95-37391
                                                                          CIP

This book is dedicated to all those, past and present, immersed in the struggle for Nigerian freedom.

Contents

Foreword

Chikwenye Okonjo Ogunyemi is a Nigerian literary critic in exile who now lives and works in the United States. By choice and raw necessity, she speaks the cultural and natural languages of three continents: Africa, Europe, and North America. These experiences and talent provide the ground for *Africa Wo/man Palava: The Nigerian Novel by Women,* a ground-breaking book.

The focus of *Africa Wo/man Palava* is eight Nigerian women novelists: Flora Nwapa, Adaora Ulasi, Buchi Emecheta, Funmilayo Fakunle, Zaynab Alkali, Eno Obong, Ifeoma Okoye, and Simi Bedford. Known too little in the United States, they are "griottes," women who take on the role of "entertainer, teacher, social critic, ideologue, and wise but despised mother" (3). They also self-consciously weave the yarns of language to create the cloth of a text.

Inexorably, the history of Nigeria has shaped the careers of these novelists and their relations to their native land. In the nineteenth-century, the British colonized Nigeria, the setting of very old, powerful, traditional cultures and societies. In 1960, after being divided into three regions (Eastern, Western, and Northern, in addition to the capital of Lagos), Nigeria gained independence. In 1963 it became a republic. However, only three years later, in 1966, a series of coups occurred, followed by the terrible 1967–1970 Civil War. Since then, for better and worse, civilian and military governments have ruled Nigeria.

Born in the 1930s, three of the novelists of whom Ogunyemi writes—Nwapa, Ulasi, and Emecheta—were comparatively young during the transition from colonial to post-colonial Nigeria. Indeed, Nwapa published her earliest novel in 1966, the year of the coups, the first African woman to publish a novel in English in England. Although the other five writers—Fakunle, Alkali, Obong, Okoye, and Bedford—hail from different parts of Nigeria, they all belong to the next generation. They grew up and matured in the post–Civil War period. Their narratives, Ogunyemi writes, "signify" upon those of the older generation and mark "the shift from the colonial to the contemporary world, the rural to the urban, the illiterate to the educated . . . No longer are they compelled to tell the sagas of their ancestors, . . . since their three predecessors have accomplished that duty" (288).

Constructing a detailed map of the work of these eight novelists, Ogunyemi reveals three great, overarching, linked ambitions. To achieve them, she draws on a wide repertoire of ideas about literature from European, African, African-American, and feminist critics. Her first ambition is to explore the African vernacular novel, an intercultural and interlingual "maze" of Igbo, Yoruba, Pidgin, and English. Usefully and lucidly, she shows how fiction adapts such complex African concepts as "*Chi/Ori*," from the Igbo "*Chi*" and the Yoruba "*Ori*," which refers to many phenomena, among them "a powerhouse lodged within the individual" (36).

Ogunyemi's second ambition is to establish a literary tradition comprising vernacular African women novelists. Doing so, she adapts Alice Walker's concept of "womanism" and woman-centeredness to an African context. Located in sacred space, on the land, in the marketplace, and in the household, the figure of the mother is central to this genre.

Directly but carefully, Ogunyemi explores the relationships among women and between women and men. On the one hand, conventional gender roles are hard on women. If a woman is a native in her father's house, she is a slave in her master's/husband's house. Moreover, the woman writer (and critic) is often ignored and discouraged. On the other hand, conventional gender roles are complementary, assigning gender-specific values, activities, roles, and powers to women. Living with and through such contradictions, the "womanist" novelist both speaks out against oppression and seeks reconciliation between women and men.

Finally, Ogunyemi's third ambition is to show how women writers might participate in the task of creating a genuinely democratic Nigeria. She asks what difference women's voices might make in nation-building. Poignantly and openly, she questions how an African feminist might name herself and speak, especially under the duress of a military regime.

Uniting these themes is the concept of "palaver," which Ogunyemi feminizes and inflects as "palava." One of the several meanings of "palaver" is that of a country's conversation, its discourse. Giving both pleasure and sociopolitical guidance, the African "wo/man palava" writes in the vernacular about women and their worlds to a nation giving birth to itself—often agonizingly.

Today it is fashionable to mock the word "multiculturalism." Ogunyemi's work shows how foolish and myopic this derision can be. To be sure, both she and the novelists of whom she writes are deeply aware of a tragic, ferocious multiculturalism that is a consequence of colonialism and ethnic warfare. Yet these women also articulate a fertile multiculturalism that permits several tongues to speak at once. The blood of this multiculturalism is not that of war but of birth. Shaped boldly and artfully, these several tongues become the matrix of a literature that is at once traditional and original; Nigerian, African, and international. Ogunyemi fervently hopes that these tongues can become the matrix of a nation that sustains rather than damages its children and citizens.

CATHARINE R. STIMPSON
Director, Fellows Program
MacArthur Foundation

Acknowledgments

I am deeply indebted to the following who indefatigably played the role of *awon iya wa* during the labor to put this together: Rowland Abiodun, Anne Adams, Sarah Allen, Bolanle Awe, Rhonda Cobham-Sander, Barbara Elsbeth, Sallee Lavallee, Mary O'Gorman, Dayo Ogunyemi, Omolola Ogunyemi, Ngozi Okonjo-Iweala, Isidore Okpewho, Elfie Raymond, Marie Umeh; to Amherst College (through a Copeland Fellowship), Sarah Lawrence College (through a Hewlett-Melon grant), and the University of Ibadan (through a travel grant), for generously providing financial assistance; and to my students at Barnard College, Sarah Lawrence College, University of Calabar, and the University of Ibadan for the intellectual challenge.

Introduction
Firing Can(n)ons:
Salvos by African Women Writers

You don't fire cannons when an ordinary man dies. Cannons can be seen only in wealthy men's houses. Cannons are the sign of greatness. . . . Boom! boom! boom! . . . Now, the shooting of the cannon did not only announce the death of a great man, but also announced that the great man's ancestors had dealings with the white men, who dealt in slaves.

Flora Nwapa, Efuru (1966)

To turn away from, to step outside the white hermeneutical circle and into the black is the challenge. . . .

Henry Louis Gates, Jr., The Signifying Monkey (1988)

How long can a woman wait for a man?

Zaynab Alkali, The Stillborn (1984)

The limited response Rhonda Cobham-Sander and I received in 1986 when, as coeditors of a special issue of *Research in African Literatures,* we called for papers on writings by African women was eye opening. As reading involves seeing, hearing, speaking, and tasting, among other necessary abilities, we were reminded that African women go unseen, unheard, and unheeded, since novels written by them and about them are still generally ignored by readers and critics. Nevertheless, the women novelists writing for an adult audience are numerous and insightful. Not only do they fill in the gaps in men's texts, instituting presences where there had been absences, their refined version establishes a thrillingly authentic, African voice, which resonates with every new text. From the multicultural and dynamic West African coast there are such influential novelists as Flora Nwapa, Ama Ata Aidoo, Buchi Emecheta, Adaora Lily Ulasi, Funmilayo Fakunle, Zaynab Alkali, Ifeoma Okoye, Simi Bedford, Eno Obong, Mariama Ba, and Aminata Sow Fall; from the restive and diverse East Africa, Grace Ogot, Muthoni Likimani, Asenath Bole Odaga, Miriam Khamadi Were, and Rebeka Njau; from apartheid Southern Africa, Bessie Head, Miriam Tlali, Lauretta Ngcobo, Tsitsi Himunyanga-Phiri, and Tsitsi Dangarembga; from the Islamic northern Africa, Nawal El Saadawi and Assia Djebar. These women are the established novelists whose works are accessible to an English reading public.

The Igbo say, *A di a ju nni na nkpuchi.* "One does not reject food still covered in a dish," since it might turn out to be delicious and nutritious if uncovered and eaten. This principle problematizes the fact that the African novel by women has not been sampled. African women writers are concerned, angry, confused, constrained, disenchanted, and sometimes even apathetic about the poverty, anarchy, and inequities caused by indigenes and outsiders in Africa. In spite of these diverse and, sometimes, ambivalent emotions, the women writers usually exhibit a sense of social responsibility in their writing. They believe in change for the sake of progress, not simply as a passing fashion to destabilize society. While walking this tightrope, these authors tend to be restrained: their novels quietly serve as a manifesto, a vision, and a warning to African men and women that change is critical and inevitable. Their novels compellingly demonstrate to the world the painful repercussions from the imbalance in international arrangements; psychically, their novels energize as juju, talismanically unleashing verbal power, while providing, at least for the African woman, a needed weapon and occasional sanctuary in a just cause.

The 1986 and 1988 awards of the Nobel Prize in Literature to Wole Soyinka of Nigeria and Naguib Mahfouz of Egypt have brought international acclaim to African literature with its masculinist orientation. The unusual attention has increased pressure for meaningful dialogue along gender lines. Their sisters' stories must also be recognized, for women writers, overshadowed by these and other literary giants such as Chinua Achebe of Nigeria, Ngugi wa Thiong'o of Kenya, and Sembene Ousmane of Senegal, are infrequently read and rarely taught in African schools.

Up until now, there has been a dearth of theoretical and critical material on African women's literature. Two of the five books devoted entirely to African women writers that have appeared were authored by men: Lloyd W. Brown's *Women Writers in Black Africa* (1981) gallantly tackles controversial feminist issues from the viewpoint of the male feminist, while Oladele Taiwo's *Female Novelists of Modern Africa* (1984) glosses over them. The third book, *Ngambika: Studies of Women in African Literature* (1986), a collection of essays edited by Carole Boyce Davies and Anne Adams Graves, illuminates as it seeks to carry out the double burden of theorizing and examining women's images in men's and women's writings. Another collection of essays, *Nigerian Female Writers: A Critical Perspective* (1989), edited by Henrietta Otokunefor and Obiageli Nwodo, ambitiously analyzes, in 160 pages, the works of twenty women writing in different genres in Nigeria. While Florence Stratton's *Contemporary African Literature and the Politics of Gender* (1994) insightfully reads women's texts, a sizable portion of the book is devoted to rereading well-known male texts, giving them further exposure at the expense of works by unknown women writers.

The present book deviates from the paths painstakingly cleared by Davies and Graves, Otokunefor and Nwodo, and Stratton. I propose a vernacular theory as a background to understanding twenty-eight novels by eight established Nigerian women writers writing for the adult world. The novelists are Flora Nwapa, Adaora Lily Ulasi, Buchi Emecheta, Funmilayo Fakunle, Ifeoma Okoye, Zaynab Alkali, Eno Obong, and Simi Bedford.

The current resistance to read women's texts is a carryover from colonial educational practice. Critics, teachers, and administrators of the patriarchal school, reinforced by conservative women, have legitimized this stance in the intellectual arena, regarding the novels as feminist and Western and therefore irrelevant in the current sociopolitical context. Trivializing the texts is an old ploy, a cover for an inability or unwillingness to confront the socioeconomic questions and institutionalized injustice raised by women's subversive texts. In writing the hitherto unwritten, in voicing the hitherto unspoken and unspeakable, the women writers have, wittingly or unwittingly, fashioned a political agenda. The different strata of governmental authority in Nigeria, the Nigerian peoples themselves, and the international readership are willed to address issues of oppression raised in the texts, which also grapple with controversies in contemporary culture traced to their traditional roots. Reinstating women in government and harnessing women's potential for the progress of the continent would acknowledge the power of women, the neglect of which partially accounts for Africa's, and so Nigeria's, instability and declining status.

As writers with a cause, women are playing the transformational role of the griotte as entertainer, teacher, social critic, ideologue, and wise but despised mother. Christopher Miller (1990, 178) captures the versatility of the griot's art in contemporary culture by hypothetically replacing the oral medium with the written. Since griots traditionally are male or female, my use of the feminine form, *griotte*, is to figure in the female dimension, which is usually suppressed. As griottes, the women writers cause imperceptible shifts in established discourses. Griots serve as vital links between men and women, "participat[ing] as women while remaining men," as Sory Camara so adroitly put it (see Miller 1990, 263). A slight reversal is pertinent here: the women writers, as privileged and responsible Nigerian daughters, participate in the discourse, like men, while remaining true to their womanhood. This gender crossing underscores the productiveness of complementarity.

In a talk at the Universität Bayreuth on July 15, 1986, Anne Adams compared the African woman's text with the *lappa*, the most important item in the African woman's wardrobe. The simple two or three yards of fabric is versatile: it can be used as a dress, a blanket, a pillow, a curtain or screen, a mattress or mat, a sheet, a bed cover, a tablecloth, an umbrella, headgear, a baby carrier, a sling, a wall decoration, or an *aju* to cushion and protect the head from the load it carries. Its commonplaceness ensures its position as a symbol of African womanhood. Women use it often; men use it also, during the day and invariably at night to cover themselves. Women's novels, like the *lappa*, are intended primarily for women who mostly bear burdens, yet they are indispensable for communal use.

African novels written by women, as counternarratives, fascinate with their inherent contradictions as they reveal strength and weakness, beauty and ugliness, ambiguity and clarity, in unfolding the politics of oppression. They attempt to provoke wo/men into reassessing their position in society. Men can personalize the concerns raised as they see male characters manipulated by authors who place them in lordly, as well as demeaning, situations. Though the portrait of men as impotent and irresponsible, dependent on women for nurturing and support, might be unacceptable to a masculinist, it is necessarily diagnostic. Yet, the women writers are not run-of-the-mill feminists, for they occasionally depict women as oppressors. In a discursive universe, with the community attempting to navigate the treacherous waters separating men from women, as well as women from women, the literate from the nonliterate, the haves from the have-nots, the urban from the rural, the adult from the young, the military from the civilians, the rulers from the ruled, women writers have taken the important first step of stating the problems to be addressed and negotiated by those interested in effecting an African rehabilitation. An intricate black aesthetics still prioritizes the giving of pleasure, integrally related to the artist's honing her sociopolitical acuity toward commitment and progress. Thus, the issues emerge as women's stories, left untold or hitherto distastefully told by men, now set down in writing to counter the ephemeral nature of women's traditional orature.

What, then, is behind the *lappa*? How should women view it? And men? In uncovering most novels by Nigerian women, the first striking observation is the pervading female atmosphere, which is accentuated by female characters caught in the maze of national concerns. Different types appear: the matriarch; the divinely inspired or Mammywata character presented as an independent woman; the energetic rural or urban woman; mothers (biological and social); and the occasionally passive victim. The writer touches on national issues, colonial and postcolonial politics, and the dynamics of male-female relationships. Some characters move toward integration within the community. The writer's concern for improving the quality of Nigerian, not just women's lives, marks her politics. Genuinely democratic, her ideology is integrative rather than singularly adversarial, as it is child directed and community centered rather than self-oriented or solely woman centered. She warns against disintegration, as she is conscious of the complexities of African history and culture. She dramatizes woman's moves for negotiating for a place in the tackling of problems peculiar to emergent nations. Women's vision complements men's patriarchal view, both providing an enriched encounter with African literature.

Though often restrained and tentative, women's texts contain political innuendoes, as well as criticism of failure in the domestic and public domains. Thus, they serve as the public conscience. By writing at all, the writers problematize what I call the Igbo *kwenu* syndrome, which is the tendency to erase or ignore dissidence, put women or younger people in their place, generate anonymity, and preempt profundity in situational analysis by turning an audience into yes men for easy solidarity. As daughters who belong, the women also cry, *kwenu,* insisting on being heard as they seek affirmative action.[1] Women or other minority voices can disagree without being disagreeable, a factor that is usually ignored, driving opposition, no matter how slight, underground. This provides fertile soil for alienation. Male critics, such as Femi Ojo-Ade in his early "feminist" phase, castigate women for fighting against the mentality of total subordination under patriarchy. Such men consider resistance self-defeating, anti-African, and feminist. Feminism has been presented as offensive, and, therefore, no respectable African woman writer openly, actively, and consistently associates herself with the ideology. Nigerian women writers, in particular, do not view the twentieth-century problem as "woman palava," that is, simply, feminism. Rather, their perspective encompasses all oppressed people, men included; as a human problem, the Nigerian dilemma must be resolved by the collaborative efforts of men and

1. For example, see Toyin Akinosho's negative review of Ifeoma Okoye's *Men Without Ears* in a Nigerian newspaper: "For *Men Without Ears,*" *The Guardian* (May 8, 1985): 9. The article reflects male hostility or contempt for women's texts. He feels that Nigerian writing must be at an all-time low for *Men Without Ears* to have won a national award. It is curious that Akinosho, a geol - ogist, was acceptable to *The Guardian* to make such controversial pronouncements; perhaps the choice was deliberate.

women, rather than being treated as gender specific. In the texts, women are most often featured because the majority of the oppressed are women, limited by too many children or disturbed by not having any. The texts are arresting points in a harsh landscape of indigenous and foreign misrule, which have been identified as a prelude to vast social transformations.

In a symbolic gesture to inaugurate change, in 1966, as the salvos that precipitated the civil war in Nigeria were being fired, Flora Nwapa, the first African woman to have a novel published in English, in Britain, discharged her opening round in *Efuru* in an undeclared battle of the sexes. Since the cannon is a power that destroys even as the canon excludes, erasing the potential for a commonweal, Nwapa has had to deal with can(n)ons in the novel, to create a more conducive atmosphere. Hers are warning shots to institute a new beginning; her friendly fire is an instructive oxymoron to expose the tensions and contradictions inherent in the writing. Women writers after her have intuitively followed her model, sensitive to its salvific undertow in their counter-discourse. However, since there are many "men without ears," as Ifeoma Okoye brazenly declares in the title of one of her novels, men and women appear not to have heard the shots. Already, the disease has metastasized, with grave consequences inside and outside Nigeria. Behind this failure to hear and hiding "behind the clouds," again as Okoye ironizes the malady, lie paralyzing arrogance and fear of real and imagined impotence, be it sexual or political, that must be openly named in order to be treated—for self-understanding and the restoration of a sense of honor and discipline for the benefit of all.

Continued collaboration between inept and corrupt black leaders and white men has partly exacerbated the problems of colonialism and postcolonialism, restricting African females to a woman's space. That segregation keeps the continent underdeveloped. It would be distorting the facts, however, to put all the blame on the white man's coming, for the controversy is steeped in contemporary representations of myth and is rooted in geography. Nwapa's Uhamiri, the owner of the Lake, and Okita, the Great River which flowed into her, "were supposed to be husband and wife, but they governed different domains and nearly always quarrelled. Nobody knew the cause or nature of their constant quarrels" (Nwapa 1966, 201). In these geographical and psychoanalytical terms, Nwapa addresses the power clashes that eternally plague gender relationships. Re-membering the history enables Bessie Head/Elizabeth to recover her health and strength by uncovering all in "a question of power," Mariama Ba/Ramatoulaye to write "so long a letter," Tsitsi Dangarembga/ Tambu to psychoanalyze colonial childhood and other "nervous conditions," and African women to find oppressive subterfuge in "the joys of motherhood" with Buchi Emecheta/Nnu Ego.

With Biafra, to continue the analogy, clearly a dead-end destination, Emecheta has called for a cease-fire. To move beyond the adversarial gridlock, the African literary academy must democratize its policies and act as midwife for the true literature of the people, representing African wo/men and children, for the people, that is, audiences composed of wo/men as well as children, by the people in their integrality. Such a move will make ripples in Rebeka Njau's pool and spur on Sindiwe Magona's and our "children's children" to exclaim triumphantly with Lauretta Ngcobo: "And they didn't die. . . ."

"How long can a woman wait for a man?" Alkali asks with tongue in cheek, as she is obviously not waiting for any man. She is neither playing the role of the victim, nor, paralyzed with the binary opposition of the center-periphery model, does she consider women as passive creatures waiting to be inscribed upon. Like Alkali, Nigerian women have always had a stand, though beset by numerous oppositions set up within and without. Indeed, they are not standing still but are already on the course, participating in the discourse without waiting for a formal invitation.

As the epigraphs implicate issues of imperialism, (post)colonialism, culture, and gender constructs, this book will focus on these aspects. In writing this book, my intention is to contribute to the democratization process by producing a literary theory to provide insightful readings of Nigerian women's novels. To be on firm ground, I will start with the familiar, in my mothers' houses, as it were, in Nigeria, theorizing in the vernacular, that is, communicating in a language that is Nigerian. Such a language is bound to be interlingual and intercultural, traversing Igbo, Yoruba, Pidgin, and English as they are manifested in the novels under consideration. These cultures have impacted each of the writers to some degree.

As Houston Baker (1984) and Henry Louis Gates (1988) explain, the vernacular incorporates the notion of the slave born in "his" master's house as well as that which is native, that is, indigenous to a place. Since the master is sometimes the father, Kwame Appiah's (1992) "In my father's house" is implicated; so also is the notion of Jesus' Father's house with its many mansions in John 14:2. In all these instances, the vernacular state is clearly a maze. The condition of being "native" is the state of being born in some master's house/land—that is, the fatherland—from which it is extremely difficult to be liberated. With the current international arrangements on immigration, constraints are placed on those divorcing their father(land) to seek adoption elsewhere. Even when they succeed, their original father keeps haunting them,

7

as he causes them to be excluded by being categorized as immigrants. Apparently, nativity is central to conceptualizing the vernacular, a crucial point that Baker, Gates, and Appiah gloss over, in spite of their anxiety to incorporate gender theory. Since woman is always at the center of any nativity, I wish to place woman, from the perspective of motherhood and mothering, at the center of this discourse from which they exiled her. Interestingly, woman is not only a "native" born in her father's house, but is born again as a "slave" in her master/husband's house. The colonial—or so-called postcolonial—situation overdetermines woman's already native, slavish position by further enslaving her, controlling her very life and economics from a distance she cannot traverse geographically or psychically. If birth is the core of woman's vernacular condition, the source of her cruel predicament, perhaps privileging birth or a rebirth of the nation can be a maneuverable moment in the discourse to set her free, by turning the notion of birth around on itself. Consequently, to establish a theory under the rubric of vernacularism, in which womanist theory is obviously implicated, I will explore woman's space to (dis)cover women in an attempt to explain their place in the household and in the public; hypothesize the nature of women's vernacular discourse; and then analyze the texts generated from this burgeoning but indeterminate background, thereby returning women from obligatory exile to legitimize their position in our parents' house.

According to Baker,

> Ordinarily, accounts of art, literature, and culture fail to acknowledge their governing theories; further, they invariably conceal the *inventive* character of such theories. Nevertheless, all accounts of art, expressive culture, or culture in general are indisputably functions of their creators' tropological energies. When such creators talk of "art," for example, they are never dealing with existential givens. Rather, they are summoning objects, processes, or events defined by a model that they have created (by and for themselves) as a picture of art. Such models, or tropes, are continually invoked to constitute and explain phenomena inaccessible to the senses. Any single model, or any complementary set of inventive tropes, therefore, will offer only a selective account of experience—a partial reading, as it were, of the world. While the single account temporarily reduces chaos to ordered plan, all such accounts are eternally troubled by "remainders." (1984, 9–10)

The Nigerian novel by women is a crucial "remainder" not accounted for in many African discourses, especially the theory of decolonization, since we are still very much colonized economically and culturally, most tellingly in the language we have chosen for writing about and generating literary discourse. Baker's and Gates' vernacular theory will serve as a fine model for determining the principles controlling this body of work. Motherhood or mothering will serve as the central trope for a literary theory of the novel under consideration. Motherhood/mothering engenders numerous connecting threads, resulting in an intricately woven *lappa* with patterns replicated with slight variations, as with the Yoruba *aso ebi*. The slight deviation in uniformity (difference) stimulates interest to the keen eye without upsetting it too much, since the project is still grounded in the familiar—that which is repeated and modified. One can refer to this as the commonplaceness of refined vision.

So central are children in the African consciousness that many women's texts usually have a woman on the cover, with the inevitable child firmly strapped to her back, as if the child is part of her body or clothing. *Omo la 'so,* the Yoruba say, and *Nwabundo,* according to the Igbo; the child is indeed clothing and shade, to protect the mother from harsh exposure to the elements or people's unkind eyes and words. The Nigerian woman is "mummy," always somebody's mother, even as she is mummified. She doesn't feel any resentment at this extension of her individuality, nor should she. It differs from being merely somebody's wife, a status entailing the loss of one's name and locus concomitant with exposure to further exploitation.

The covers of *Ngambika* and *Behind the Clouds* convey the same maternal spirit. A variation in the cover is a woman with the child, with another one tagging on to her *lappa,* and, for good measure, a girl (*titi* in pidgin)[2] walking by her side. The woman and the girl are overburdened, carrying produce or water for domestic use or sale in the market. Needless to say, the girl is expected to follow her mother's unwavering footsteps, if no one intercedes. The womanish girl is a living criticism of the system that assumes she too must be exploited and overworked. The cycle of poverty might be broken, if she goes to school long enough to obtain the wherewithal to sustain a fulfilling motherhood. The dual burden of a double career foregrounds Davies' and Graves' theory of woman calling out for help to balance the load she has been carrying alone, for Zora Neale Hurston's metaphor of the black woman as the mule of the world in *Their Eyes Were Watching God* still has international repercussions and implications. Emecheta has oftentimes used slavery as a trope in many of her novels, in consonance with this black tradition.

2. *Titi* (from tit, teat, breast) is pidgin for girl. This word stresses a girl's biological destiny and the nurturing role expected of her in society. In contrast, a boy is referred to as *bomboy* (cf. bomb and tomboy), always under pressure and free to play around.

Equally arresting is the 1910 picture of two identically dressed women, used as the cover for *All the Women Are White, All the Blacks Are Men, But Some of Us Are Brave* (Hull, Scott, and Smith 1982). Though both women seem to mirror each other, a closer look reveals differences. The idea of being similarly dressed is a carryover from Nigeria. The Yoruba refer to identical clothing as *aso ebi,* "cloth for kin." *Aso ebi,* the "uniform" worn by friends and/or kin to identify those who belong from outsiders, particularly at crowded affairs like weddings, funerals, chieftaincy inaugurations, or political gatherings, is important in Yoruba psychosocial consciousness. It engenders group identity, solidarity, a sense of being special. In spite of the general impression of sameness in the *aso ebi,* there are always distinctions in the total effect of each person's outfit, creating individuality in uniformity through choice accessories and poise of carriage.

Gates' theory about literary signifying is pertinent to my clothing analogy: "When one text Signifies upon another text, by tropological revision or repetition and difference, the double-voiced utterance allows us to chart discrete formal relationships in Afro-American literary history. Signifyin(g), then, is a metaphor for textual revision" (1988, 88). *Aso ebi,* that is, the signifying of one person upon another through textile revision, the generating of a spirit of togetherness, has become a burgeoning practice in other parts of Nigeria. It enhances our perception of the diversity in uniformity that is a concomitant feature of Nigerian life and the Nigerian novel by women. *Aso ebi,* then, is a metaphor not only for textual revision but helps establish womanism as a tradition and a code for communal solidarity.

The following patterns emerge: (1) the myth of Osun as primary mother bringing up her son single-handedly, a role which prepares her to become the mother-at-large, caring for the world. Closely linked with Osun is the myth of Odu. Odu is the divine mother who contains oracular secrets. The oracle is the divine word that is uttered to her child, that is the propitiate, who must become engaged in a personalized, interpretive process for psychic development; (2) the Mammywata, the childless mother, in her postmodernist existence, caring for all her devotees; (3) the *Chi/Ori,* represented in her interiority as the divine mother lodged within; (4) the *Omunwa/Iyalode* in her politicoeconomic role as the mother without; (5) the *Ogbanje/Abiku*'s mother as the jinxed caregiver; and, finally, (6) the propensities of women as a matricentric force. I will examine the principles governing motherhood, in an attempt to explain some issues raised, in praxis, with the genesis of the Nigerian novel by women.

In the next chapter, I will explore women's place in Nigerian discourse in the Nigerian household, as it were, to establish the nature of women's struggle and how the forces within and without (that is, among women themselves, among Nigerians, and among women in the international arena) impact the writing. Drawing from the vernacular, I place motherhood at the center, using its many manifestations as tropes to formulate a theory which will give privileged access to reading the Nigerian novel by women (and, perhaps, other black writers). Finally, and importantly, in part 2, I will work out a theoretical analysis of the novel, concentrating on the novels of each writer to trace a Nigerian women's literary tradition.

This book is part of the literary fallout from the explosive 1929 Igbo *Ogu Umunwanyi*, usually translated as the "Women's War," a neat category that suggests that the problem is over and done with. Since *ogu*, "fight," as opposed to *aya/agha*, "war," is the operative word, I prefer to translate *Ogu Umunwanyi* as the women's struggle, or rather, in the contemporary discursive space, the ongoing Africa wo/man palava. The women in southeastern Nigeria were belatedly fighting to return to their precolonial space. The harsh psychosocial realities of colonialism and post–World War I debilitating health and economic situations drastically changed women's perennial struggle against the eruptions of masculinism, to include new, oppressive phenomena. These debilitating manifestations covered British totalitarianism, racism, classism, ethnicism, the downgrading of indigenous languages, virulent forms of sexism, religious orthodoxy, and economic control. Although these oppressive sites have undergone some changes under postcolonialism, in 1995, they still largely remain with us, in spite of the lessons of the Nigerian civil war of 1967–1970. They are areas African womanism addresses. This book enters the lists to face some of the issues that bind and separate us—women and men—as represented by the undying, restless spirits of *ogu umunwanyi*.

The struggle is often self-deprecating for women. As Trinh Minh-ha (1989) puts it, "Women writers are both prompt to hide in (their) writing(s) and feel prompted to do so. As language-stealers, they must learn to steal without being seen, and with no pretense of being a stealer, for fear of '*exposing the father*'" (19; my emphasis). This innate fear of exposing the father speaks to women's complicity in maintaining the status quo, a point dramatized in Emecheta's *The Joys of Motherhood* (1979). Nnu Ego's readjusting of Nnaife's falling *lappa* in that crucial moment of his final emasculation, threatening to expose further his nakedness and powerlessness as he climbs into the police van, is epiphanic. It is a graphic trope for women's complicitous cover-up of male impotence in failing to respond effectively to aggressive colonialism and continued postcolonial chaos in a timely fashion. Excluding women from the sites of power has taken and continues to take its toll.

11

In writing into the Nigerian discursive space, I, too, stand accused of complicity in my own ambivalence in controlling the floodlight while dealing with the "enemy" within and opening up the floodgates against the enemy without. One grapples with the shame of defeat, of failing to protect home and country. Following the colonial debacle, one must not be careless or fight too hard, as Hurston's Janie Killicks Starks Wood did, killing all her men.

Overt male disrespect of women is psychologically explicable: as my people in Ogwashi-Uku say, *Onye nwa okuku lu ike k'ona tugbu,* "The chicken takes on an enemy it can defeat." Women, especially wives, become obvious targets of male frustration. Nonetheless, covert male reverence for women is apparent in their affection for mothers and sometimes for daughters (particularly when a daughter is referred to as *nnee,* "mother"). This is a vestige of earlier and continued codependency of the sexes. Its asexuality underscores the trope of colonialism as rape, the likely victim being the sexually active wife rather than one's aged mother or prepubescent daughter.

In this anomalous situation, Nnu Ego's unwitting gesture of betrayal to the women's cause in the face of colonial humiliation is a far different response from Janie's soft killing of her husband, Joe Starks, whom she strips stark naked in *Their Eyes Were Watching God* by Hurston. Janie openly states that Joe no longer has anything down there, thereby appropriating power with his demise. Nnu Ego, on the other hand, tries to cover her husband's something, a final abdication of power (however little), which ends with self-destruction after her lifelong search for affirmation through father, husbands, and sons.

For whom and to whom do African women then write or tell their stories? Ideologically, African womanism's inherent ambivalence toward feminism is related to questions of style and authority. Feminism's feisty spirit predisposes it to use the headlines, the exposé, personal and public. This propensity for confrontationally "telling all," the African woman critic has no authority or inclination to adopt, since her target audience (African wo/men) are not her primary audience. The Western audience, with its numerical superiority and spending power, reads the foreign language in which she writes, creating a rupture in the competing audiences. The notion of an invasive addressee, who should be an eavesdropper/voyeur now turned primary audience, is part of the postcolonial dilemma Edward Said addressed in his *Orientalism* (1978). Therefore, the African woman critic bites her tongue, distrusting her pen and computer as she speaks and writes.

Since, as silent observer or even reluctant participating oppressor, Western women have historically gained and still gain from African (post)colonialism, the result has been resistance in writing simultaneously to us and them. The revolt of the complicitous African woman writer against hostile Africans, amicable Westerners, and sterile theory necessitates a shift as she uncovers, while mystifyingly covering up, the African situation.

PART ONE

Kwenu: A Vernacular Theory

Chapter One
An Excursion into Woman's (S)(p)ace

All women are witches.
> Ifa verse

In anything we do,
If we do not guarantee the place of women,
That thing will not succeed.
> Ifa verse, trans. Abiodun (1989)

I traded; but without success.
Then I took to painting Uli;
And the gift of song came to me.
> From the Igbo, trans. Obiora Udechukwu

If you call Africa woman woman
Africa woman no go gree
She go sa a ay
She go say
A be lady o.
> Fela Anikulapo-Kuti

Lemoine-Luccioni would have us believe that only by stopping the struggle for autonomy and assuming our difference can women protect Man from the ultimate apocalypse. Saving the world would seem to be up to women.
> Alice Jardine, *Gynesis* (1985)

Sociocultural factors impinging on women's lives are clear pointers to a country's progress. Examining such Nigerian indicators will help to contextualize the novel by Nigerian women. Why is motherhood so central in the texts? What is the destiny of the childless woman? How does the syndrome of obligatory motherhood impact culture, political ideology, and, ultimately, writing? What follows is an attempt to address these and other issues in an overview of the woman's world, from my perception as an informed insider who has observed what being a correct Nigerian woman entails. I believe that the paradox in Nigerian thinking of elevating motherhood while degrading wifehood is leading, inexorably, to the breakdown of marriage and the family, a situation that exacerbates current national tensions reconstructed in text after text.

When tragic circumstances or outright failure defy logic, the immersed subject moves toward the supernatural, seeking help from the other world that, in Nigeria, is coterminous with the earthly. Invariably, the difficulties become resolved. This approach to problem solving in the personal and domestic spheres is so commonplace that it has affected people's attitudes, often breeding complacency. The other world is increasingly becoming one's richer relations, and, ultimately, the federal government. When these are in dire straits, they, in their turn, are expected to seek outside help. The central government in the postcolonial period has had to depend economically on cocoa, groundnut, palm oil, oil, and, now, its borrowing power, to enable it to provide the largesse. This enormous chain of dependency at the personal and governmental levels involves an eternal search for what might be referred to as the "Big Mama." She is, in principle, the benign witch,[1] who keeps providing essentials and attempts to resolve problems. She is psychologically satisfying. A setback ensues from mismanaging her gifts and failing to cultivate the mother within, to maintain a balance between material and spiritual well-being.

Achebe captures this aspect of the national predicament through Okonkwo in *Things Fall Apart* (1958). Macho and sexist, Okonkwo is permanently in a state of denial about his feminine side, even as he unconsciously searches for his alien(ated) mother. Substituting his favorite daughter for her as a palliative, he finally thrives when he finds the maternal source: when circumstances force him to live with his mother's relations. Achebe expresses the essence of maternal affection succinctly: "A man belongs to his fatherland when things are good and life is sweet. But when there is sorrow and bitterness he finds refuge in his motherland. Your mother is there to protect you" (123). Once Okonkwo abandons her and journeys back to his fatherland, his life ends tragically, when he confronts the harsh face of colonialism, unprotected by the maternal principle. I believe that, like Okonkwo, Nigerian men, no matter how macho they may appear to be, are unconsciously waiting for women to release them from the trap of the fatherland, the suicidal trappings holding them captive in their father's house. Even the legendary tortoise, in dire straits, always finds a way out of his dilemma. The men have turned turtle; they need

---

1. The English word *witch*, with its negative connotations of woman's inordinate power for evil or her alluring sexuality, fails to convey the positive nuances of its equivalent in Nigerian usage. I use the oxymoron "benign witch" in an attempt to convey woman's supernatural power and her willingness, as mother, to use it for reward or chastisement.

the maternal principle to help to turn them back up, to reinstate them, so that all can act concertedly for the country's progress. The general Nigerian confidence in juju's efficacy, while psychologically sound, reflects the ethics of dependency—the belief that the all-powerful mother, with her supernatural juju, will make everything all right. To accomplish this feat, women need extra empowerment, perhaps the powers ascribed to witchcraft through verbal acuity.

When the female subject in the epigraph changes her career midstream, drifts from the crass commercialism of the stressful outer world to commune with and seek protection from the divine mother within her and without, she becomes blessed, triumphing artistically and spiritually. To counter disempowerment, the older woman often seeks and acquires mystic powers; in local parlance, she becomes a witch, often dwelling on the edge of town. In the role of the witch, she is perceived as wicked, if she attacks her enemies as a defensive strategy; or, she is seen as a true mother, if she protects her people, especially successful men who are particularly vulnerable, since they are exposed to the evil eye in their public position. She accomplishes her talismanic duties unobtrusively, rarely flaunting the power she is expected to use for the good of her family, community, or nation. Girls imbibe this lore because women rarely question female self-effacement, accepting the idea that men should be supported for the commonweal. The lesson that needs to be passed on is that a strong community is born only when support is mutual, and strong women are not chased to the periphery. Women also need to be mothered. Stanlie James (1993, 45) observes cogently that different forms of mothering "may serve as an important Black feminist link to the development of new models for social transformation in the twenty-first century." Mothering and othermothering, as James refers to some aspects of the black phenomenon, are parts of an indigenous system that has buoyed up the community. It will be instructive to examine it closely.

Men fear the secret ways women manage to survive in spite of great hardships. Part of traditional female empowerment among the Igbo is connected with *uli* rituals. Using *uli* is an experience in transformative power. As a cosmetic, it is similar to camwood or henna in enhancing one's own or another woman's beauty, writing on woman's body, as it were. As an art form, it parallels drawing in ink, painting on a blank wall, composing literature. In short, *uli* is woman's writing on the wall, emphasizing its spiritual qualities. *Uli* painting/writing conditions one to worship the divine within, enabling the individual to express sororal or maternal feelings toward others. Just as *uli* is useful for interior decorating, to mark the artistry of a caring woman, it is also

19

necessary for decorating public shrines, to inspire the community to commune with its gods. This symbiotic relationship with the shrine underscores its morally formative thrust. By encoding on the shrine walls cryptograms such as the fearsome snake with its effortless motion and quietness, the self-gratulatory lizard with its phenomenal feats, the leaf with its nutritive or curative potential, or the tricky tortoise with its eternal triumphs, women teach a lesson on transformations, the power of indeterminacy, the state of becoming, and the human links with nature which we must respect and maintain, even imitate. With their cryptographic powers, women learn and emulate nature's protean qualities osmotically, as should men, for the commonweal. The shift from one's self to another, from the domestic to the public, from the mundane to the sacred, from the human to other aspects of the environment, from painting to singing or writing, illustrates woman's versatility and the possibility of generating order, hope, and healing in the community.

By making marks on one's body, wall, or paper, the artist/writer distinguishes herself. She likes to make things work, oftentimes deciding against using her creative power destructively. Painting-singing-writing demonstrates a positive commitment to the people, as it involves celebrating, criticizing, and molding the culture for public good. According to the Igbo, *nke onye bu nke onye,* for surely, "a thing of one's own remains one's own," which gives the possessor the right to praise or criticize it to improve and insure its value.

An examination of some myths which have engendered such an attitude will illuminate the writers' mind set. This is in keeping with what Chinweizu, Onwuchekwa Jemie, and Ihechukwu Madubuike (1983, 3) refer to as "Afrocentric discourse," in elucidating the African text. Specifically, Houston Baker's and Henry Louis Gates' "vernacular theory" also provides appropriate models for reading black texts. Baker's thoughts on vernacularism have far-reaching implications, some of which apply to the Nigerian situation. For example, we refer to our own mother tongues as vernacular. Enslaving, tentacular vestiges of colonialism merge effortlessly with the indigenous, in contemporary emanations of some myths and other social phenomena. All provide viable ideas for formulating a woman-centered vernacular theory to generate a sophisticated reading of Nigerian women's texts.

In the following sections, I explore the myths of water deities, particularly as exemplified in Osun's story, subsumed under the divination text, Odu, which serves as metafiction. I move on to the emergence of the colonial Mammywata and then examine the emergent figure of woman as mother in her spiritual, care-giving, political, and other contemporary roles. Woman's diversified, unspecific, but vital maternal responsibilities determine her politics, ideology, and writing in a very cultural specific fashion. These complicate the writer's contribution to women's (inter)national discourse.

The Myths of Osun and Odu: Aesthetics, Creativity and the Secrets of Verbal Authority

Osun's story in Yorubaland and numerous, analogous water goddess myths—such as Ugwuta's Ogbuide, Ibuza's Oboshi, Nnobi's Idemili, Ogwashi-Uku's Obida, in Igboland—are prevalent throughout riverine Nigeria.[2] As a working hypothesis, Osun can be considered interchangeably with Idemili, Ogbuide, Obida, Oboshi, and other water deities who populate the religious waterscape. The vastness of Osun's domain and the intensity of her worship in spite of Christianity warrants my concentrating on her commonplace myth. Fascinatingly, as with most oral tales, it keeps varying with each teller.

In one oral version, Osun, charged with (re)production, was the lone female among seventeen *orisa* sent by Olodumare, the supreme deity, to establish the world. Since they disrespected her by failing to consult her to make the colony function smoothly, she withdrew from them. In the ensuing postcolonial crisis, the world suffered from the repercussions of the quarrel for, during her strike, she did not permit rain to fall. The drought caused chronic shortages in diverse areas of the productive process, even though, quite tellingly, she was pregnant, a condition which served as her ace. Isolated, she continued to ply her vocation of hair plaiting by the river named after her, firmly establishing her autonomy. As Osun is both *orisa* and the essence of the river without which there would be no civilization, the male *orisa* were panic stricken. They appealed to Olodumare for help to right matters. The supreme deity ordered them to reconcile with Osun, who, as hair plaiter, holds a crucial portfolio as she is also in charge of aesthetics and fate, which is *ori* in Yoruba, the word that doubles for head, the seat of reason (Abiodun 1987a, 78) and one's destiny. For success and harmony, woman's place in the scheme of things had to be guaranteed. In the ensuing negotiations, she promised that, if she had a son, he would act as a mediator between her and them, but if she had a daughter, she would have added support in maintaining her difference, and

---

2. Nwapa portrays Ogbuide fictionally as Uhamiri in *Efuru* and *Never Again*, while Emecheta deals with Oboshi in *The Bride Price*, where one of the characters goes "to placate their Oboshi river goddess into giving her babies." Both religious concepts are identical with the principles of Osun worship. See also Amadiume (1987) for her comments on Idemili, the river goddess, especially 27–29.

there would be an impasse. The male *orisa*, marvelling at the magic of the womb, stunned by the silence of the womb which they could not hear, the darkness of the womb which they could not read, the mystery of the womb which they could not decipher, prayed fervently for a son. I believe this prayer instituted in the Nigerian psyche the obsession for children, especially male children, a malady Marie Umeh refers to in conversation as being "son-struck." The conciliatory moves became fruitful when Osun gave birth to the male child Osetura, the name the *babalawo* use for Esu (Idowu 1962, 81). Still autonomous and different, Osun had saved the world.

Like any son, Osetura/Esu, for Osun, is a reminder of pain and gender difference (hence the possibility of his being a mischief maker) as well as a sign of joy and mediation, a complex relationship that partly accounts for the tortuousness of gendered discourse. Also, "With the *ase* (authority to effect a change or make things happen) at creation to a major female *orisa* such as Osun, women—especially those already past menopause—are believed to possess a form of noiseless and concealed power that they can use to accomplish any desired goal. And, because such a goal may be constructive or destructive [in order to rebuild], elaborate annual festivals like the *gelede* are held in parts of western Yorubaland to placate and acknowledge the power of women, who are known in such contexts as *awon iya wa* (our mothers)" (Abiodun 1987a, 72). Likewise, our mother Osun is still worshipped in the major Yoruba towns along her river banks, to ensure fertility, health, and wealth for her devotees.

There are many exasperating silences in the story of the relationship between Osun and the male *orisa*, and the inventiveness or silence of the raconteuse has left the gaps unbridged. For example, how did Osun become pregnant? What really caused the rupture between her and the other *orisa*? Why did they become so awkward with her? Why would she, if she had a daughter, keep her away from them? Why was she willing, if it were a son, to let him commune with them to indicate that she did not mind being reconciled? Why did they pray so fervently for a son?

The conflict engendered the concept of wo/man *palava*, that is a problem, partly gender based, involving men and women. With Osun's pregnancy shrouded in mystery, one can hypothesize that she is hermaphroditic. Another possible interpretation is to regard her as a black Madonna, who has experienced an immaculate conception. The other *orisa* must have been envious of her unique power to control, through reproduction, the source of survival and progress in the community, an idea occasionally echoed in some of the novels. Her ability to do what they cannot do is crucial. In damage control, the desire for a harmonious community entails that each individual, male or female, must be enabled to contribute that difference, without flaunting it, to ensure dynamism in apparent unity.

One can posit yet another hypothesis. Perhaps the story is silent in parts because of the storytellers' reluctance to be sexually explicit—evading themes of incest, rape, or adultery—particularly as the myth is sometimes narrated to children. From this viewpoint, Osun was "used" by her brother *orisa,* one or more of her colleagues, who unwontedly impregnated her.[3] To cover up the embarrassing moment of a pregnancy resulting from rape within the familial circle, or, in a chaotic situation without the benefit of a modern paternity test to work out a DNA fingerprint to identify the father-to-be, the pregnancy of an unwilling female can be euphemistically referred to as virginal.

Situating Osun in an international crossroads, Bolanle Awe (1985) reads her as the Yoruba version of Venus/Aphrodite. Parts of Osun's story and Osetura/Esu indeed appear similar to the myths of Isis/Hera and Horus, Ceres/Demeter and Proserpina/Persephone. The themes of beauty, love, sexuality, rape, immaculate conception, fertility, grief, separation, mediation, and reconciliation are interconnected motifs recurring in Yoruba, Egyptian, Greek, Roman, and Christian myths. The protagonists are all variations on the theme of the great, ancestral mother in a hostile universe. Her greatness lies in her policy of containment of her anguish for the good of all.

Such an attitudinal gesture is not to be equated with martyrdom. As primal mother, Osun implants in her daughter the will to produce while facing the challenges of a woman's life: the tensions emanating from the two sexes not working harmoniously together and woman's strategic withdrawal, that is, exile, to recoup her losses. In *Isara,* the fictionalized biography of his father, Soyinka explores the pain and benefits of being an exile or, as he put it, an ex-ile, s/he who is away from (Latin *ex*) home (Yoruba *ile* or community), playing an interlingual game to arrive at a multiculturally enriched English concept. Pronounced with a different tone, *ile* also means soil, land. In this context, *ex-ile* can be conceived as being out of touch with the solid ground, that is, with reality, taking leave of one's senses, as in madness, aerial flights of fancy, frenzy. Being an *ex-isle,* that is, away from one's island or element, can be likened to a fish out of water. *Ex-aisled* recaptures the original confusion between *isle* and *aisle;* it reminds us of the satisfaction in walking down the *aisle* and the trauma woman experiences when her man walks away from a marriage, turning her into an *ex.* Emanating from Osun's ordeal, the women's

---

3. The pidgin word "used" implies carnal knowledge; it is appropriate here, with the mixture of its nuances in pidgin and standard English.

novels capture these tumultuous emotions, particularly the fact that Nigerian women have been in exile in not participating with the running of the country politically.

Specifically, in Osun's instance, *ex-ile* conveys the essence of separation from the norm, her withdrawal from the *orisa* community, and the establishment of the primal matricentric family, which Nigerian women mimic especially in polygynous households. In the event of a son, she needed to keep her option for a return open; she also needed a mouthpiece to make her exile less traumatic. Through her son, she participates vicariously in the world where men make the decisions, even if they need women to effect them for harmony. Osetura/Esu as mediator or errand boy inevitably has a split personality to accommodate his mother's agenda and the wishes of the male *orisa*. He complicates matters occasionally by mischievously pursuing an independent agenda of his own. The woman novelist is, simultaneously, an incarnation of Osun, the rebellious reproducer, as well as of the child Osetura/Esu, the mischievous mediator, who is sometimes referred to as "genderless, or of dual gender" (Gates 1988, 29). The paradox partly accounts for the ambivalence in the novelist's so-called feminism, her playing the devil's advocate. Clearly, the strong undertow in the myth is Osetura/Esu; s/he is the umbilical cord linking the male with the female, creating an undercurrent in Osun's exile, the essence of Nigerian female ideology. Reconciliation is central to this ideology. Nigerian women's fiction replicates the cyclical motions, especially the desire for a settlement; these are echoes of the original *orisa* negotiations after Olodumare mandated postcolonial harmony.

Osun's pregnancy is the original statement of the power of women's fecundity and creativity, a tour de force synthesizing the biological, by producing a child, and the literary, by providing us with an excellent account illustrating eternal verities. She is the archetype of the female Nigerian men, admiringly or despairingly, refer to as "Africa woman," a complex pidgin phrase insinuating toughness as well as achievement. Osun's estrangement from the other *orisa* serves as a paradigm for the nature of gender relationships in Nigerian society; men refer to it as woman *palava.* Some equate it with feminism, that is, women's rebellion, in Nigerian understanding, in not keeping to a woman's place from where they can help men, if called on to do so. To me, the phenomenon is best represented as Africa wo/man *palava,* since both sexes are inevitably embroiled in it.

As if she were writing specifically about Osun qua river, Trinh Minh-ha (1989, 126–27) reminds us that "Great Mother is the goddess of all waters, the protectress of women and of childbearing, the unweary sentient hearer, the healer and also the bringer of diseases. She who gives always accepts, she who wishes to preserve never fails to refresh. Regenerate. . . . No water, no birth, no death, no life." Woman's tears recall the pain of the *palava* meaning trouble, even as they illustrate the crucial part played by water in life. The following translation of a Yoruba incantation is cautionary as it captures the potentially divisive gender situation imagistically:

> When the weather is blazing-hot
> It is the fan [Osun's insignia] that pacifies it.
> When the fire is glowing,
> We use water to quench it.
> Sweeping past, fire is chasing water,
> Sweeping past.
> If fire chases water,
> And does not turn back,
> Propitiation is the answer
> Sweeping past, fire is chasing water.
> The glow of fire
> Fire should not chase its glow
> Into the river.
>   (Abiodun 1989, 12; source: Pa Adeniji)

Predictably, all did not go well with the endeavors of the *orisa*, since they lacked Osun, the quintessential female principle to maintain a balanced world. In the ensuing postcolonial chaos, as soon as they rectified their error of omission and openly acknowledged and revered her, she became willing to inject that catalytic female power, without which household and state affairs rarely have a propitious ending. The concept of Osun confirms the notion of merging the ameliorating qualities of water and womanhood for survival and progress. As Abiodun put it, "The power of women appears to be similar to that of water, with which most female deities are associated. Water is an active ingredient in the Yoruba preparation of ero 'a softening agent/medicinal preparation' as also is the fluid from a snail and the oil from red palm kernels. . . . [E]ro . . . is capable of normalizing, negating, or rendering impotent any other power, life, or substance. Here, like water, ero operates noiselessly and unceremoniously. Such is the nature of the power of 'our mothers' as represented in their praise-names" (1989, 11–12).

It is not surprising that in Yoruba culture, a first daughter is *owo ero* (Abiodun 1989, 7), like water, a softening agent. At the birth of a child, the caretakers are greeted, *e ku owo l'omi*, "greetings for your hands being in water," in recognition of the constant use of water in hygiene to make the neonate stay on this side of the divide. Civilizations emerge on the banks of rivers that are full of life to support the people, while women pass on the culture through their interaction with the children in the domestic sphere. People swear by the waters of Africa (the Igbo refer to the phenomenon as *ikwu iyi—iyi* is a curse and also a stream) to demonstrate patent honesty, since they risk being swallowed by the waters if they are lying.

Water is life giving, yet, one can drown in it. It is purificatory, medicinal, spiritually healing. Still waters serve as mirror for looking at and into one's self. Water can be soft or hard. It can boil or freeze. It can be drunk to quench one's thirst or voided to cleanse the body. Woman's cooking provokes the watering of the mouth. As Fela Anikulapo-Kuti points out in one of his popular lyrics, "Water no get enemy." Ideally, "Woman no get enemy"; goodwill should take care of hostilities. Identification with water is a mark of flexibility, the gradual erosion of opposition. Bodies of water represent stability in the face of instability. Water lacks strength yet is powerful, a paradox applicable to women.

Water softens Earth (the Igbo goddess Ala/Ani) to make it yield, a sorority which ensures subsistence. Men also want women to act like Ani, conserving, reproducing, and sustaining life. Women can achieve these ends not necessarily by blindly following so-called tradition, but by modifying it to cope with the exigencies of modern-day existence. Rivers have been known to dry up, creating the hardships of a nomadic existence. The sparse water supply in parts of Africa, droughts, and encroaching deserts draw out women's tears, which go unheeded as fiery men continue to rule. The have-nots become endangered. As Nigeria is on the threshold of the twenty-first century, the need for clear choices is apparent. She can imitate the *orisa*, by seeking reprieve through female mediation, for women's texts are utterances, cooling waters in the fiery national discourse. "Utterances," according to Henry and Margaret Drewal (1990), "as expressions of the spiritual inner self of an individual, possess *ase*, the power to bring things into an actual existence" (5). The women's novels have this extraordinary power; magically, they have brought the plight of the Nigerian underclass to world attention, acting as an agent for change.

Osun's story encapsulates several principles: motherhood, gender problems, woman's independence, fe/male interdependency, woman's career, economics, aesthetics, domesticity, sustenance, fertility to insure the future, interest in the environment, quarrel and mediation, *siddon look* tactics, that is, "sit down and cogitate," a belligerent form of pacifism. Every woman's story is a variation of this crucial tale. Osun inspires woman to be a mother with a career, to bring order in the face of anarchy, to engage in debate across gender lines, to cancel oppositionality. She affirms female independence. The many roles Osun undertakes serve as a model for female versatility, providing us with a course in female ontology. Since Osun is in charge of destiny, like a creator or writer, she controls the human plot for each individual. Mutability is its essence, for as editor she not only creates and recreates, she encourages us to do so, for self-enhancement. Such fluidity is consonant with her moral and psychological growth in the face of overwhelming odds. Her *siddon look* tactics provides grounds for the *bildungsroman,* for sitting down and looking on in silence do not imply vacuousness. The pause makes room for development, especially with the refusal to be complicit in one's oppression. The period of withdrawal engenders secret ways of thriving. Osun's concentration on beautification holds possibilities for metamorphosis. As a river, her nature constitutes the paradox of change or motion in the face of sameness. As a pregnant female she obeys arithmetical laws of multiplication and addition, while being cognizant of the pain of subtraction and division in difficult relationships with the male *orisa.* In this state of flux, the constant is the self, the uncompromising development of self-reliance in an ever-changing world.

Such self-reliance is female agency at its best. In her dilemma over her isolation, she does not give way to depression, wringing her hands despairingly. Instead, the wealthy *orisa* busies herself, using her hands to create beauty by plaiting hair. She thereby exemplifies for women the need to control beauty, the psychological soundness of controlling one's looks for one's self-satisfaction and not necessarily for male benefit. In changing her looks, she magically changes how she looks at life. By plaiting hair, she weaves her destiny, establishing that one's life is one's primary responsibility.

Osun's story is metafiction; it predates Gates' account of Esu in *The Signifying Monkey,* which I am signifying on. Esu's story must be retold in order to acknowledge female presence at the beginning of black discourse. This presence is greatly enhanced by the fact that the 256 principal verses of the Yoruba divination text known as Odu is female in essence, since Odu doubles as the wife of the divination *orisa,* Orunmila/Ifa, according to one myth, or of Obatala, the creating *orisa* (Gleason 1987, 303). The crucial point about her intimate connection with divination and creativity through her wifehood is usually unmentioned.

In spite of being supplanted, *Igbo odu* remains her "sacred grove"; it serves as a suitable place for spiritual composure, inspiration, composition, and well-being. *Igbo,* "grove," marks the denseness, the complexity, the unknown elements and surprises inherent in Odu. *Igba odu* is "Odu's calabash," the "sacred container of Ifa itself" (Gleason 1987, 303). Odu, as the Word, ultimately encapsulates every story that can ever be told. According to Gleason, the calabash "symbolizes cosmos—earth and covering sky. It is also an icon of secrecy, of the primal egg" (301). The female packaging of the rounded calabash as womb/egg establishes Odu as she who reproduces everybody's story or fortune. The idea of containment puts the female at the center of all discourses; male resistance in according the female such power is apparent in the continued effort to make Odu Ifa's insignificant other. Nonetheless, Odu is the secret text even as she conceals the text. The diviner known as *babalawo*, that is, ironically, "father has secrets" (Bascom 1991, 81) is trained to reveal her secrets to the inquirer, who, while personally interpreting the text, maintains contact with the maternal principle, which provides psychological stability. The futile attempt to displace Odu through the continual appropriation of her power is sexism at the basics. The onslaught continues with Odu's secret texts published in books and in recent attempts by computer programmers to package her as software. As of now, she and Ifa keep resisting, preferring the privacy of the calabash to the accessibility and volubility of the computer and the great, wide information highway.

The male initiate training to become a *babalawo* grapples with the secrets, literally reading in the dark in an attempt to establish an inquirer's destiny. His accuracy certifies the initiate's expertise as a would-be diviner. In this scheme of things, women are inexcusably barred from becoming diviners (Bascom 1991, 81). William Bascom affirms that "There are numberless recitals, dealing with every sphere of life, which [initiates] have to memorize by listening to a senior 'Babalawo.' These recitals are called 'Odu'. . . . Every sphere of life has an 'Odu' applicable to it" (21). Osun, like all the other deities, is intimately connected with Odu, since Osun's story is part of the Odu corpus. Odu, therefore, is metafiction, the mother-text par excellence. She is the primal text that contains and generates all possible texts. Since the 256 leading verses of the Odu keep multiplying by 16 at different levels, a thought that is quite dizzying in and of itself, the continuous engendering of texts is a mark of Odu's prolificity as "primal mother" (Gleason 1987, 303). As a result, her entire corpus is unending and unfathomable, an encyclopedic, intricate, authoritative, information retrieval system. Odu encapsulates the riddle that contains all possible riddles as well as their solutions or interpretations. Since Odu is a wife, it is apparent that Yoruba divination or its metaphorical extension, Nigerian literature, especially Nigerian literature by women, and its exegesis are collaborative efforts rather than gender divisive. Together with Osun's constant reaching out through Osetura/Esu, these primal mothers exemplify the Nigerian woman novelist's conciliatory agenda, even as they demonstrate gender division of labor for the common good. In particular, women's writing derives ultimately from the Odu matrix, with each novel speaking to its predecessors. Each speech praises, criticizes, reiterates, refines, and/or extends its antecedent. Women's writing is equivalent to Odu in its oracularity, especially in the telling of stories that should be interpreted for our edification. It is a gift with magical potential. As such, it is secretive, calabash-like, womb-like. Its words serve as seeds or eggs or nuclei from which texts emanate. With her eternal verities, Odu shifts into the contemporary scene in women's writing, from where she discreetly effects her hidden agenda: as primal mother, to catalyze each individual to become involved and personally come to grips with the problem of living. Osun, the marine goddesses, and Odu underwent some colonial transformation, giving rise to the Mammywata phenomenon, which I will now examine.

The Mammywata Myth as Gendered Insurance

Colonialism impacted some of the minor water deities, causing them imperceptibly to undergo a sea change. Their anglicization was, perhaps, necessitated by the people's attempt to grapple with the trauma of defeat and the daily humiliation of being ruled and "pacified" by a few British officers, who seemed to lead a charmed existence. The embattled experience of being colonized and disinherited in their fatherland called for a change of tactics. Since armed confrontation had failed them, they resisted by employing other indigenous strategies combined with mimicking the enemy. Their modified attitude engendered the Mammywata phenomenon. The people needed an edifying concept to erase their impotence and establish well-being; the idea of the Mammywata was to serve that purpose. She became recognized as one unifying deity wherever Pidgin English is spoken in Nigeria, especially in riverine areas, where European influence permeated.

Mammywata was endowed with European qualities while still retaining some of the attributes associated with local water deities; Idemili, for example. Ifi Amadiume (1987, 100) observes that Idemili's "importance was also indicated by the epithets applied to her. . . . *Oke Nwanyi*—the great lady; *Eze Nwanyi*—female king; *Idemili Ogalanya Ngada*—Idemili with huge baskets of riches; *Nwanyi Odu Okpa*—a woman wearing ivory anklets; one who roofs her house with zinc, so that nothing can destroy her; *Ono na mba, mba n'akwalu akwa*—one who is worshipped abroad; *Eze onyili Mba*—the unconquerable one; *Agadi nwanyi, nmuo nwelu okwu na ano na mpata*—old woman! Deity who has a shrine! Woman who sits on a special stool for *ozo* titled men!" Thus, Idemili is female but acts like a male, like the griotte. As far away as

South Africa, the same idea is known among AmaXhosa as "Mamlambo, the River Woman whose dangerous beauty drew people into the depth of her magnetic eyes, sucked them into the world deep under the river, where she made her home" (Magona 1991, 9).

According to Nwapa (1991), Mammywata worship evolved with the birth of the colonial representative's daughter of color.[4] Biracial children started appearing on the colonial scene as a result of liaisons between Europeans and local women. Besides the spiritual approach for dealing with the enemy, fathers saw the additional advantage of giving their daughters in marriage to colonial officials, many of whom were single or came without their wives. Typical in-law politics meant that the children from these liaisons, as blood ties, could mediate between Nigerians and the ruling colonial world, going so far as to establish some intimacy. Many women, supported by their kinsmen, did make use of such advantageous connections, which were validated through custom or modification of custom.

The biracial child as a go-between, acting as the power broker between the exclusive or even sacrosanct world of the colonialist and the native world of her mother, was playing the role of Esu, or, to go further afield to the United States, had the trappings of the "tragic mulatto." However, not beset by virulent racism, because of the minority population status of whites in Nigeria, she evolved into a magic mulatto, a fortunate Midas whose intervention meant economic progress for her "native" half of the family. Rather than being ostracized for her difference, the magic mulatto was much admired for her golden beauty, which modified distinctive European features, thereby making them more acceptable to the Nigerian eye. The emerging figure of the Mammywata encapsulated the perception of the biracial girl as the epitome of beauty and the bringer of the good things of life. Mammywata gradually became synonymous with beauty, biracial or not. The original qualities associated with Osun, especially beauty and wealth, had now become linked with the mulatto, and, in an easy extension, Mammywata. Devotees extended her portfolio by appealing to her for health, well-being, peace, and fertility. However, praying to Mammywata, who was considered childless, to give children to the barren seems inexplicable with its inherent contradictions. However, it must be remembered that children are synonymous with wealth, in traditional cultures.

4. In her presentation, "Priestesses and Power Among the Riverine Igbo," for the conference, "Queens, Queen Mothers, Priestesses and Power: Case Studies in African Gender," held at The Schomburg Center (April 8–11, 1991), Flora Nwapa suggested that Mammywata became prevalent with the births of "mulattoes."

Some of the colonialists did come with their wives, who did not have or did not bring their children with them on the colonial adventure. The colonial wife without a visible career was perceived as rich and idle, living in the best house, pampered by servants who catered to her every whim. Childless, though powerful and autocratic, all qualities which became invested in the evolving Mammywata, she had to be obeyed.

For Nigerians with tightly curled hair, which stays neat once combed or plaited, the white woman's constant need to comb her long, silky hair to keep it tidy was fascinating, even if, with familiarity, it was to appear obsessive. This trait was also transferred to Mammywata. Osun, the career hair plaiter, presumably beautifying other women by plaiting their hair, now coexisted, in the folk imagination, with a self-involved Mammywata perpetually combing her thick hair, the symbol of fertility. With such preoccupations, Mammywata, like her colonial model, had no time for children, and remained childless. Again, like her colonial model, the altruistic colonial wife who could sometimes be seen busying herself with the well-being of the natives, devotees saw Mammywata in a similar role, though often, in desperation, they begged her for children, vestiges of prayers to precolonial deities. Clearly—or, perhaps, not so clearly—Mammywata epitomizes the childless woman who mothers the community at large, since she has the resources for such a purpose. Thus, she easily becomes the model for the childless mother in the Nigerian novel.

While motherhood is currently a mixed blessing for the Nigerian woman, the childless but powerful woman or the woman without a man remains an anomaly, an enigma, fearfully witchlike. Childlessness is considered tragic, providing an irresistible attraction to writers. In his play *Song of a Goat,* J. P. Clark uses infertility as a trope to demonstrate how male sterility tragically keeps woman from experiencing her fullest potential. The couple in the drama never face their problem together, each dissembling as s/he seeks a way out of a sterile relationship. Clark's is yesterday's story as told by a man. Revising this, Okoye gives today's version in her novel *Behind the Clouds.* After tortuous and humiliating experiences in their bid to produce children, the man and the woman in this novel are finally able to address the hitherto unmentionable: they actually tackle the predicament of male impotence, demystifying the problem with a Western approach. The infertile man receives medical treatment for the benefit of all, a postcolonial message that is politically empowering in its scientific approach to an agonizing health issue. Aidoo also handles the theme of sterility in *The Dilemma of a Ghost* (1965) and *Anowa* (1970), Nwapa in *Efuru* (1966) and *Idu* (1970), Ulasi, cursorily, in *Many Thing Begin for Change* (1971), Emecheta in *The Joys of Motherhood* (1979), Fakunle in

31

Chance Or Destiny? (1983), and Eno Obong in *Garden House* (1988). The frequency of the theme is remarkable, as it appears in other texts. Aidoo encodes it in *Anowa* as the fruitlessness, for Africans, of the slave trade, and in *Dilemma* in the difficulties Pan-Africanism faces in bearing fruit, owing to cultural misunderstandings between Africans and African-Americans. Unproductiveness in varied spheres of life is a bane to be lamented. Writers are anguished about African impotence, particularly treacherous leaders and the economic and technological dependence on self-serving people rapaciously looting the entire continent. Childlessness provides a point of departure for the writer. As a metaphor, childlessness conveys the late coming of women to the writing scene and the dearth of writing by women. Since boys were given preferential treatment in acquiring Western education necessary for producing Western-style literature, woman's silence in this new literary scene was inevitable.

Commenting on the issue of the oppression of women as related to childlessness, Abena Busia writes, "Although we must fight the battle to stop both the discrimination, in some communities, against childless women and the tyranny of the necessity to bear children, in particular sons, for most African women the place of mothering still remains central" (1988, 9). The childless woman often finds a way out of her predicament, as women were to do in the field of writing. Among the Igbo, as late as the 1920s, when a wealthy woman could not have children of her own, she could marry another woman to bear children for both of them to parent, a marital arrangement Ifi Amadiume (1987) refers to as "female husband." Though this situation appears to have lesbian overtones, the couple did not explore the sexual side of their relationship, since the wife had a male lover for bearing children whom the biological father could not legally claim. The British banned this system with their colonial marriage laws, wiping out a tradition that had stood childless women in good stead and had smoothed the bitter edge of patriarchal marriage. The childless woman who has the opportunity to mother has Mammywata as a model. She epitomizes Nigerian women, who, without written texts of their own, have finally found, in the writers, surrogate mothers to produce child-texts to air their viewpoint.

Even though her oxymoronic existence accentuates vestigial tensions, writing the childless mother into the text is a revolutionary act acknowledging her. Equally revolutionary is appropriating the image of Mammywata as a model for the childless mother. Beautiful, single, rich, independent, powerful, and childless, she thrives in her domain, an idea that is ahead of its time. In the cultural and literary milieus, Mammywata is figured as performing a maternal function in the society at large, though she has no child of her own.

Anybody willing to follow her rules can become her child; voluntary motherhood is every woman's lot.

Christianization, the presence of the white woman on the national scene, and the emergence of the Western-educated Nigerian "woman" who aspired to become a "lady" by mimicking white ways, a predilection Fela critiques in the lyric reproduced as an epigraph to this chapter, gave rise to a new elite.[5] The Nigerian lady, with her processed hair and wealth, enhanced the myth, making it viable in the religious domain. Even if the Nigerian lady does not freely comb her hair, as the white woman or Mammywata does, for fear of ruining her waves and curls, like them, she possesses riches, which she can bestow upon her poorer relatives, and she can afford the wherewithal to transform herself into a beauty. With a career involving intellectual pursuits rather than physical work, it is easy to obtain a high income with the leisure and power to go with it. In short, she is a Mammywata clone.

Mammywata demands obedience, trust, and hard work, in return for her gifts. Male association with Mammywata or the educated lady is turbulent, because she exists in a different world, literally and metaphorically. Since Mammywata's dwelling in water provides her with the facility to appear and disappear at will, men call her fickle. Sometimes, men equate her with the woman playing hard to get, for she is, indeed, hard to get. With superhuman panache, she enchants the stubborn male to his destruction, because, in the inevitable gender power tussle, he usually loses. Her pidginized name is a warning to men of the alluringly destructive power of Western culture with its ideology of liberation, contradicted by insidious examples of black enchainment. As a benefactress, however, she brings untold fortunes to devotees, while remaining as enigmatic as ever. Men and women seek her out to their peril, if they are not immersed in her laws; yet they stand to gain tremendously, if they respect her ways. The Nigerian musician Victor Uwaifo stresses this rule of thumb. He expresses its spirit in his popular song "If You See Mammywata," counseling his audience not to run away but to take advantage of an encounter with Mammywata, protected by an armor of prosperity. His advice doubles as a plea for the educated woman to be accepted rather than feared, as is often the case, for her alleged argumentative disposition.

Usually alone, Mammywata loves reflecting on herself, stressing her introspective nature, individuality, and self-sufficiency. Since she dwells in water well stocked with mirrors, she constantly looks at her own reflection. This in-

---

5. For a detailed discussion of this aspect of colonialism in the cultural sphere, see Michael Echeruo's *Victorian Lagos* (1977).

tense, female, self-directed gaze replaces the customary, demeaning male gaze; the look inward uplifts woman. With its emphasis on spirituality, the mirror in the water rather than on the wall revises the European fairy tale and the myth of Narcissus. The rich Nigerian woman mimics these refined myths in her relationship with men—be it father, husband, lover, colleague, or son— male characters who also feature prominently in the Osun myth. Indigenous as well as anglicized myths thus provide her with adequate insurance against any enemy, including postcolonial ideologies. As modes of enlightenment, the myths' penchant for education, aesthetics, and partaking of power and riches forms the essence of a women's literature. However, the goal is rarely equality in the Western sense but complementarity. One is glibly informed that God did not make the fingers equal but designed them to function together as a body of people should.

In addition to writers appropriating Osun and Odu as primal mothers in their prolificity, their envisaging Mammywata characteristics as a model for the Nigerian barren woman is as mollifying as it is inclusive. Though the entire Mammywata figuration may not be totally desirable in a country where so much premium is placed on having children, at least it recognizes the anguish of the childless woman, and dramatizes ways to come to terms with it. In grappling with such a complex situation, the women novelists, especially Nwapa, have used Mammywata as a prototype, which, astonishingly, predates that moment in the feminist evolution when theorists strove to erase the notion of obligatory motherhood.

Collectively and severally, the myths not only serve as paradigms for fiction by Nigerian women; the writer also incarnates Mammywata, bestowing the beauty and riches of her artistic accomplishments on her audience with a price: that men and women listen to a new tune and create a meaningful space for women, childless or not, for national progress. Writing in a partially Western context, the writer projects herself into the texts as a Mammywata figure, hence the proliferation of such characters in the novels. Mammywata becomes a sign of resistance to woman being praised only for motherhood. The writer demonstrates the desire of women to communicate with men, an outreach essential for carrying on the discourse. The importance of conflicting discourses is not always in arriving at a consensus, though it is marvelous if such a goal is attained. Rather, such debates keep people connected and their opinions current, as they question the nature of the fingers in the societal pie or, as Nigerians would put it, examine the sand ruining our *garri*, the Nigerian staple. It is more emotionally healthy to interact than to remain silent and perhaps precipitate civil disturbance. Such interaction also exists on the psychological plane with the individual's dramatic response to the inner life as exemplified in the Igbo concept of *Chi* or the Yoruba *Ori*, in which self-regard evolves into self-reliance.

Chi/Ori, or, the Mother Within

The Dog's *Ori* helps it to cut through the bush.
Thunder uses *Ori* to split the Iroko tree.
Every Deer grows a pair of horns through *Ori*.
With its *Ori*, Fish swims without mishap in water.
Owawa, Rat's *Ori* helps it to go through caves.
Ori precedes man,
It also guides him,
Ori plans good things for its owner.

Abiodun, "Verbal and Visual Metaphors"

Igbo cosmology is similar to the Yoruba in many aspects. With Idemili and Osun as water deities receiving supplications and prayers through rituals performed in the open, these superhuman mothers function differently from the more private human mothers. Equally superhuman is illumination sought through Odu; once properly propitiated through Ifa, her spouse (Afa in Igbo), her generative world of words fabricates a text tailored to suit the devotee in a divining session. Information accessed from this matrix is further personalized through interpretation, providing a subtext to the living drama which precipitated the devotee's dire need for en-*lighten*-ment. The Mammy-wata model, on the other hand, seems to narrow the gap between the suppli-cant and the maternal other, since Mammywata exemplifies the use of resources without and within. The Igbo *Chi* and the Yoruba *Ori* modify the discursive forces, encouraging the individual to become discerning and to glean steadfastly information on the systemic ordering of life. *Chi* and *Ori* convert the religious discourses constructed around the worship of the deities into a psychological discourse, while still retaining vestiges of the religious.

Women's power is predicated on the belief that, openly acknowledged or not, a feminine force determines the important phases of each individual's life. This gives rise to the worship of and dependence on the mother, the most loyal female that one can have. On the personal level, the relationship with the mother extends into the concept of *Chi/Ori*; as with the mother, one owns one's *Chi/Ori*, as the epigraph indicates. Ownership implies some element of control, for *Chi/Ori* is the *quidditas* inside the human body, that part that can-not be detected but that we know is there. It is essence, innateness, instinct, genetics, luck, endowment, destiny, empowerment; it is the caretaker and caregiver installed within. It is everywhere in the body.[6] *Chi/Ori* breeds dependency as well as self-reliance. Fetishizing *Chi/Ori* as an object of worship expresses people's difficulty in being weaned from the mother.

Chi/Ori is recognized as a powerhouse lodged within the individual, a recourse accessible, in danger or crisis, to the owner willing to use it. Accessing this power ensures individuation. Conceptualizing and internalizing *Chi/Ori* as an enabling agency are basic in training the mind in stress management. Gradually, the individual gains control by constructing a discourse in which, uncannily enough, s/he still relies on the *Chi/Ori*, that is, a part of the self. As *Chi/Ori* dwells within, she is manipulable. With Osun delegated to guide the *Ori*, it gradually dawns on the individual that *Chi/Ori* is the mother within— a treasure, always beautiful, always precious, always dependable, always already there. Yet, she never cramps one's style.

In the mind's eye, *Chi/Ori* represents the individual's quintessence, the creator god's unique, or personalized, gift ensconced within, facilitating the accomplishment of difficult tasks because she is always accessible, always willing to help. As the primary mediating deity, *Chi/Ori* labors to engender the psychological moment efficacious in reaching one's goal, particularly in a time of stress. Though she provides so much security, one inevitably rebels when goals diverge or she appears too slow. With patience, it becomes clear that she is billed as a supportive system. She eases the painful individuation process necessary for maturity. Disrespect to one's *Chi/Ori* may result in total despair, because *Chi/Ori* can punish the owner; treating *Chi/Ori* as a familiar and developing an intense relationship with her can produce a psychologically well-adjusted person.

Igbo speech acts in a critical moment are replete with spontaneous outbursts of feeling to one's *Chi* for protection or intercession. For example, when in a crisis, a Christian's eyes might be said to be looking up to God; by contrast, an Igbo person, Christian or not, in a similar crisis would be advised to watch his or her *Chi*, as in *Nebechi*, which doubles as a name. In trouble, one exclaims in Igbo, *Chim o*, "O, my *Chi*," or, in Yoruba, *Ori mi o*, "O, my *Ori*," ingratiating oneself with the talismanic *Chi/Ori* to come to the rescue. *Chi* may be construed as the adrenaline needed before taking to the playing field. The paradox in this game is that *Chi* wards the individual even as the individual, consciously or unconsciously, determines the extent to which *Chi* is to

---

6. When I asked different people where they think their *Chi* resides in their bodies, the responses included the head, the throat, the heart, the chest, the breast (the same word, *obi*, is used for heart, chest, and breast in some Igbo dialects), and the stomach.

participate in the unfolding process of the game of life. Open recognition of *Chi's* diversely crucial functions becomes manifest in the proliferation of *Chi*-names among the Igbo. An inherently subversive sign, the *Chi*-name resists Christianization, as it partly contributes to the ambiguity in contemporary Christianity. This causes people, unwittingly, to resort to many gods, with *Chi* and the Christian God juggling for priority in crisis.

Chinua Achebe in "Chi in Igbo Cosmology" (1976), Donatus Nwoga in *The Supreme God as Stranger in Igbo Religious Thought* (1984), and Rowland Abiodun in "Verbal and Visual Metaphors: Mythical Allusions in Yoruba Ritualistic Art of *Ori*" (1987b) assume theoretically that *Chi* and *Ori* as essences are male. In praxis, they appear to be maternal principles, as attested to by the nature of their owners' expectations of them. That the female Osun is charged with *Ori* clues us into the nature of the en-*gender*-ing of personal power. Erasing *Chi/Ori's* femaleness results in masculinizing the internal, psychological discourse, paralleling what goes on fruitlessly in national dis-courses. Resistance generates a crisis in spirituality on the personal level, and, in the public, as women notice their erasure in private and public lives, they counter it openly and subversively, to the nation's detriment.

The link between the supplicant and the *Chi/Ori* compares with that of the infant and the mother. It promotes dependency in the immature, which evolves gradually into the self-reliance we recognize as maturity. The suppli-cant ingratiates himself or herself to her, as a child would to the mother, for the sweets of life. S/he demands, expects, and usually receives the wherewithal to survive and develop. The epigraph above captures graphically the eternal state of dependency in the cosmology, though the supplicant unconsciously expects that the *Chi/Ori* will provide the basic needs for success. When these are not satisfied, for whatever reason, the supplicant assiduously appeals to her. S/he worships her, if need be, for continued well-being. If she is tardy, the supplicant cries to her peremptorily, because she knows, even before it is stated, what her ward's needs are.

In the Yoruba pantheon, the stiff competition *Ori* faces from four hundred other *orisa* vying for favor from the supreme god, Olorun (Abiodun 1987b, 263) conjures up polygyny at its grimmest and suggests co-wifely rivalry. The Yoruba refer to the commonplace syndrome in the polygynous household as *orogun*, the Igbo as *ekwolo nwunye di*. *Ori's* calculated antics of abasing the self in total submission (ibid.) are the ploys of the "sweet" woman. The artistic representation of *Ori-inu* as a "geometricized cone" seems to be, metaphori-cally, the breast when a woman is prone. *Ori's oriki*, praising her as "The one-with-the-umbrella-shaped-body-that-rolls-freely-on-its-side" (265), sounds like the breast or like a fat woman abasing herself in Yoruba fashion to obtain her heart's desire. It could also be the agitated breast in motion or the breast manipulated by an eager, suckling baby. Abiodun unwittingly confirms the point about *Ori* being female when he writes:

> The task of choosing a good *Ori* in heaven is not easy since all are conical in shape and look exactly alike. The Yoruba solution to this dilemma is the kneeling nude female figure holding her breasts in *Iroke*. . . . The female intervenes on behalf of humanity to ensure the selection of good *Ori,* which must be chosen and 'received kneeling down' *(Akunlegba).* A man's kneeling is not as potent and as sacred as that of a woman. Here is *Ikunle-abiyamo,* the-kneeling-of-the-pains-at-childbirth. Linked to the greatest act of reverence that man can give to the *orisa* are the special qualities and position of women as those through whom all have come into the world. . . . *Ori* [i]s the source of all good things. Conversely, it is also over *Ori* that we should give thanks for everything we have received [as people, especially Nigerian men, invariably do to their dead mothers with their lavish funerals]. (Abiodun 1987a, 266)

Nwoga (1984, 64–65) applies the *Chi* concept to the literary context: "Buchi Emecheta, the novelist, who is from Ibusa in Bendel State, uses this same conceptualization of chi in her novels. Though in her earlier fiction she was satisfied with the concept of chi as 'personal god' (e.g., in *The Slave Girls* [*sic*], 28), she later identifies the chi with the olo uwa and that really is the underlying framework of the novel *The Joys of Motherhood.*" Not only does Emecheta write herself into the text with her autobiographical slant, she also incorporates the ancestor as *Chi.* Since the body is a shrine for the *Chi,* writing about *Chi* is enshrining it and the body in print. *Chi* represents the writer's foremothers in oral literature as well as her muse.

Achebe informs us that *Chi* holds "the central place in Igbo thought of the notion of duality" (1976, 133). *Chi* relates to the adult in a manner similar to that of the mother to her child at the preoedipal stage. "Onye kwe chie ekwe. (If a man agrees, his chi agrees)" (135). The mutuality benefits and strengthens the individual. Though *Chi* is powerful, she seeks consonance with her owner; she protects her ward against enemies, nurtures, and supports him or her emotionally, all maternal duties in a gendered division of parenting. The following *Chi*-names attest to this support system.

"Chika (chi is supreme); Chibuzo (chi is in front) [Chi as a guide] . . . are only a few examples of the large number of names that show the general primacy of chi over mankind. Chinwuba asserts chi's special responsibility for increase and prosperity [like Osun and Ori]; Chinwendu, its power over life; and Chikadibia, over health." Achebe's *Chi* is thus ubiquitous and superordinate; she can easily be equated to the child's expectation of the mother. He continues: "A few other names suggest this role of chi as the great dealer out of gifts: Nkechinyelu and Chijioke, for example . . . [in contrast with] Obu etu nya na chie si kwu, which we often hear when a man's misfortune is somehow beyond comprehension and so can only be attributable to an agreement he himself must have entered into, at the beginning, alone with his chi. . ." (ibid.). Like the mother again, *Chi* sometimes withholds a gift lovingly, denying the child what s/he mistakenly believes would bring extra comfort. This apparent contradiction creates a gap that one can explore for beneficial ends. For the less mature, the gap instead results in depression or catty remarks. When a father dissociates himself from his troublesome children by making wry remarks to the unfortunate mother, referring to them as the woman's children, he rejects them. The children belong to the man if and when they succeed but rarely when they fail. Unfortunately, many women also subscribe to this distorted view of family life, which can be considered as an extension of the techy relationship between *Chi* and the owner.

Though mother and child, like the *Chi* and the supplicant, are not always in accord, this does not sever their relationship. Sometimes discord makes the relationship even more intense, as they experience difficulties together and grow to know each other better. Achebe's analysis of the metaphysical can be used to complete the picture in the literary field: "In a general way we may visualize a person's chi as his other identity in spiritland—his spirit being complementing his terrestrial human being; for nothing can stand alone, there must always be another thing standing beside it" (131). This is the mother-child dyad expressed in metaphysical terms.

If Mother is substituted for *Chi* in the following names, the psychoanalytical implications become quite clear. *Chinelo*—Mother thinks or determines (the course of action); *Chinwe*—Mother owns; *Chinye*—Mother gave; *Chienye*—Mother always gives; *Chiwehogo*—Mother has brought or will bring kindness; *Chika*—Mother is supreme; *Chima*—Mother knows all; *Chimalogo*—Mother acknowledges kindness; *Uchechi*—Mother's mind [is inscrutable]; *Chidozie* or *Chiedozie*—Mother has made (or makes) reparations; *Chinagolu*—Mother defends one's innocence; *Chinua(lumogu)*—Mother, defend me or Mother defends me; *Chinweizu*—[one proposes], Mother disposes; *Chinweike*—Mother has power; *Chiemeke*—Mother has done very well; *Chidumbi*—Mother lives with me; *Chinonso*—Mother is near; *Chimuanya*—Mother is awake, so deeply consoling for the sick or distressed. These are a few of the commonplace, male and female names in Igbo culture. With my substitution, the nature of Igbo psychology in relation to *Chi* and mother becomes clearer. This dependence on the *Chi*/mother or the female is a subtext that requires conscious unraveling. The interdependence between the sexes must be acknowledged to institutionalize, formally, a change in attitude toward women, to give them the respect and dignity needed for the constructively harmonious relationship that we had once upon a time.

As the child matures, the *Chi* becomes more remote as the mother becomes the other. During development, the child/adult in difficulty begins to appeal to additional sources of support. The boy gradually identifies with his father, moving away from his mother's sphere, if progress is smooth. The girl is thrown closer to the mother because of gender-centered socialization processes. Later, *Chi* has a place, becoming internalized as well as externalized, readily available for consultation. *Chi* as an inner energy is a moving spirit. People envision her dynamically, literally wandering from one part of the body to another to energize the individual for intellectual, emotional, and physical functions.

As the child grows into adolescence, s/he seeks the mother sporadically. The connection is similar to that between people and the social mother in the public domain. Roman Catholics, in their intense relationship with Mary, will understand the closeness. In spite of this intense drive for the Mother, the Nigerian male is unwilling to face the phenomenon or to accept that it exists. Rather than face his own dependence, he regards woman as contemptible or a lot of trouble, or as a constant source of quarrel *(wahala,* or its synonym, *palava);* this negative socialization stems from a desire to be macho and a privileging of all things male.

In manhood, the Nigerian male seeks a wife who will perform all the functions of his mother and more. He still cherishes the role of the child in this relationship, quite often not living up to his position as husband and/or father. When his wife complains, he seeks support from other women/wives, hence the predominance of polygamous/polygynous Nigerian men. When these women do not sustain him, he returns to his mother, if she is still alive, or he seeks his *Chi/Ori* or any other god/gods from whom he demands satisfaction, just as the child demands satisfaction from his mother. *Chigbolum*— "*Chi* protects me" or "*Chi*, defend me"—sums up this dependency; it is the cry of the desperate child to its mother.

From a literary perspective, *Chi* as inspiriting muse gives the writer the courage and determination to institute, identify with, or counter a discourse. Traditionally, it is the mother who teaches the child to express the self in words and to develop the tactics to cope successfully in conflict, hence the primacy I accord the *Chi* as mother. In a literary tradition with intertextual connections, each text's *Chi* distinguishes its uniqueness, for "Ofu nne n'amu, ma ofu chi adeke . . . one mother gives birth [to many children], different chi create" (Achebe 1976, 137). This concept may be extended to different works by one artist; diversely inspired and conceived, they are different and are differently received despite their common origin. According to Achebe, "every act of creation is the work of a separate and individual agent, chi, a personified and unique manifestation of the creative essence" (139). *Chi na eke* is *Chi* who creates and/or divides, as Nwoga correctly insists. In essence, *Chi* is comparable to a woman who bears children and/or divides the largesse among them. Nwoga does not trace the divisiveness implicated in his insistence; it is individuality at its worst, sabotaging a consensus of opinion.

In Igbo cosmic wisdom, *Chi* is also conceptualized as dwelling in the sun, hence the connection with the dawn. Nwoga's point about *Chi* as the beginning of a new day is worth quoting at length. According to Nwoga,

> [Jeffrey] explores the relationship between chi as personal god, chi as "Supreme Being" and chi as "sun." . . . He also relates the usual word for sun in Igbo, anyanwu (translated as "the eye of anwu"), to the Jukun equation of sun as supreme being with the name anu, to the Egyptian equation of Ra and Iunu as the sun god. Jeffrey's exploration would lead one to the hypothesis that both chi and anwu are words for the same thing/concept but derived from different sources. While the Igbo have emphasized the god meaning of chi and the sun meaning of anwu, occasionally the meanings interlace so that the sun meaning of chi emerges in the pattern of chi worship and the god meaning of anwu, emerges in the pattern of Anyanwu worship. (1984, 73–74)

I may add that, when one is at one's best, *Chi* is the sunshine within, almost turning one into a super being. To the child, the mother is the morning sun that shines on her/him specially; she is also the supreme being to be adored as a bountiful provider. The scorching, afternoon sun that drives one to look for shade presents the reality of dissonance, even as the possibility of a cooling off is in the horizon with the setting sun.

As a "child-text" (see Suleiman's contrasting concept: 1985, 369), the contemporary novel by Nigerian women opens a new chapter in African literature, illuminating it like the morning sun. Like *Chi* as dawn, the novel brings enlightenment for a new beginning to cancel oppressive, exclusive ways. The

41

girl's name, *Chiadik'ofo*—"the day is never the way it is at dawn"—profoundly expresses the constancy of change. In the literary context, this implies political change in our relationship with the outside world; it also involves the transformations that Nigerian men and women need to undergo in order to function optimally in the twenty-first century. The woman's text is Nigeria's *Chi*: the morning sun with its hope, the afternoon sun with its bite, the evening sun with its beauty, its softness, its playfulness, willing us to accommodate, to change as it does, before it dissipates its energies, to begin again the following morning.

In Igbo ritual, though *Chi* might reside somewhere in the sky, in a crisis, *Chi* can be brought down at dawn, through the intercession of a priest. A devotee can build a personal shrine for worship. Contemporary belief conveniently enshrines the *Chi* within, eliminating the inconvenience of getting a priest to act as intercessor. The supplicant performs the ritual spontaneously in an exercise of spiritual affirmation or prayer. It has also taught people the uses of intercessory prayers, which draw many others into the circle, as in *Chi* worship. *Chi* is thus the projection of one's self, for inner strengthening, and also the light within, which illuminates the dark recesses of one's life. Intimacy with her stabilizes the individual and the nation.

Chi and *Ori* obviously are complex figures within the Nigerian cosmology. "In most areas," Nwoga observes, "chi remains a pure abstraction of the alter ego, that counterpart of man which satisfies the structural conception of reality as dualistic. . . . Among the West Niger Igbo the same concept of chi as the person who has reincarnated in the individual is also prevalent" (1984, 64). Nwoga explains further: "The deceased who is believed to be reborn in the new child is generally called the child's agu or chi. A man's chi is the alter ego of the person concerned, whose present life must be supervised, ruled and guided by the circumstances of the agu's or chi's life in his or her previous world existence. For example, if one's chi was killed or kidnapped at Ibusa, the child would be forbidden to go to Ibusa. . ." (178). *Chi* or the reincarnation of an ancestor, as conceived here, partially accounts for heredity in genetics and projection in psychiatry; *Chi* as mater is thus not only biological but a socializing parent, for each West African is blessed with many mothers, as Ama Ata Aidoo constantly reminds us in her works.

Each storyteller, having learned by listening as a member of different audiences, is inspired by her *Chi/Ori* to tell a story. Since telling is unpredictably risky, the Igbo raconteuse invokes creative/protective spirits at the beginning of her storytelling, that is, the moment of departure into storyland, closing the session with the remark that she has safely returned from the imaginative world in spiritland. The audience welcomes the teller back from the hazardous journey to the land of the living. The writer expects such a reception from her readers. Writing, like storytelling, is intercessory, with the artist melding the group's artistic gifts and collective experience to present the novel to those willing to read or listen. Pleasing everybody is impossible because individuals react differently to the light or heat of the sun.

Nwapa, as the first woman novelist, incorporates all these nuances associated with the *Chi*. In many ways a foremother, Nwapa is a pathfinder or *Chinedu* (*Chi* who guides). She resembles her mother, who was the first woman in Ugwuta in eastern Nigeria to obtain the Standard Six primary school certificate. The diploma and Nwapa's first novel, *Efuru,* are symbols of their entrance into a Western way of life. Following the steps of one's mother, one's ancestor, one's foremother, is praiseworthy. In writing *Efuru* rather than narrating it orally to a live audience, Nwapa was setting down the words in print that she might have spoken, were the medium Igbo and not English. Like her mother, she has a text to show for her endeavors, with the added difference that the words inscribed on hers are her very own.

Just as a kind benefactor may be referred to as one's *Chi,* so a writer who precedes another can serve as her *Chi,* smoothing the path for those who follow. The later writer incorporates her predecessors' experience with hers, signifying on them, as Henry Louis Gates puts it, away from Harold Bloom's (1973) theory about male anxiety generated by the predilection toward canonicity with its power. Confidence replaces anxiety, because of the relative ease in following in somebody's footsteps and partaking of the collective literary heritage. When the predecessor is still living, she becomes a mother/sister. Operating in a primarily oral culture, once the text is in the public domain, questions of copyrighting, plagiarizing, or anxiety are nebulous, as the material is available for anybody to use. The anonymity of oral literature makes the laws associated with the print culture inoperative in Nigeria. The flexibility of oral cultures generates variants of a text. The writer is part of a long chain in reincarnating texts. She inherits the past, learns from it, then leaves her own distinctive stamp on the corpus, thus helping to establish a tradition.

Chi catalyzes one to speak out, preceding activism. Ekwefi (Okonkwo's second wife in Achebe's *Things Fall Apart*), in dealing with Okonkwo's shooting at her, whimpers to her friend, Chielo, the priestess of Agbala: "I cannot yet find a mouth with which to tell the story." Chielo quickly consoles her: "Your chi is very much awake" (Achebe 1958, 34). Being dumbfounded about physical or verbal abuse is commonplace with Nigerian wives. Fortunately, women's *Chi* has finally encouraged her daughters, if not her sons, to write and broadcast woman's harrowing story that the fictional Ekwefi could not tell or could only tell one woman friend. Nwapa's Efuru speaks for Achebe's Ekwefi, even as Nwapa speaks to Achebe and her other male predecessors, countering their discourse. The later Achebe, with his concern for the woman's position in national life, as exemplified in his *Anthills of the Savannah,* demonstrates that he has been listening to the women.

Perhaps the Nigerian woman's problems are compounded by socializing practices, if we believe Nancy Chodorow's (1978, 75) statement that "exclusive and intensive mothering as it has been practiced in Western society does seem to have produced more achievement-oriented men and people with psychologically monogamic tendencies." It would then seem that the numerous mothers that the Nigerian child is blessed with reproduce the carefree, polygamous male, ever craving the diverse female attention he had enjoyed in childhood. The numerous mothers also seem to prevent him from assuming domestic responsibility for himself and his children, since he perceives the caring for people as women's duty. On the flip side, if the Nigerian male is polygamous, many Nigerian women must be, too, since the ratio of women to men is less than two to one, and if all the women were monogamous, then there would not be enough women to service all polygamous male needs. Emecheta explores this concept in her most recent novel *Kehinde* (1994), as Nwapa had done in *One Is Enough* (1981).

With *Chi/Ori* at the center of Nigerian thought, it is predictable that motherhood and mothering and the different patterns they unfold would be central to the Nigerian female text. Through them, women writers apotheosize mothers, since motherhood is considered respectable by both men and women. Even Emecheta's overworked Nnu Ego, the most joyless of mothers, at the end of *The Joys of Motherhood* becomes an ancestral goddess, who, while exercising her maternal powers, ironically refuses to use them to grant her devotees' prayers for children. Women writers consistently create spheres of female influence, depicting women as mothers in families, boarding schools, universities, offices, the marketplace, business, and war, to show female power or, occasionally, the lack of it, with its disastrous consequences. These motifs capture matricentricity in Nigerian culture.

The *Chi* has learned to thrive in English, as her ward has succeeded in doing. To achieve her political, sociological, and aesthetic ends, the writer has appropriately feminized the *Chi* to serve as a metaphor for female control, as in the portraits of Nwapa's and Emecheta's strong, female characters. *Chi* is really a female principle closely related to one's destiny; dependence on woman for reproduction, difficult as it may seem to accept, is man's destiny. *Chi,* as guardian spirit, upholds her dependent psychologically. In short, she represents all those maternal and ethical principles that strengthen one's moral consciousness. *Chi* leads people toward transcendence. Worshipping the ·*Chi* and the ancestors in African traditional religions is salutary; they guarantee spiritual solace, a concept that has been imposed on Christian practice.

The conflation of these sociological and metaphysical dimensions in approaching one's *Chi/Ori* in modern praxis has some bearing on the role of woman as conceived by the writers. The novelists represent female power through strong, neomythical, protean characters whom one can link with *Chi/Ori*. Uhamiri in Nwapa, Oboshi and Presence in Emecheta, Osun in Ulasi, personal ethics in Okoye, *Ori* in Fakunle, Mammywata in Eno Obong and Alkali, and "Watersprite" and Grandma in Bedford double as guardian angel/*Chi/Ori* for the individual and for the entire community. Though man might cynically comment on women's trouble-making possibilities by saying, "Woman na palava," he can name his child *Chinedu*, "*Chi* keeps guiding," or exclaim, *Ori mi, ma je nsi osi*, "My *Ori*, don't let me go astray." These are spiritual affirmations of a maternal force for daily empowerment.

Omunwa/Iyalode; or, The Mother Without; or, The Daughter-of-the-Soil

> My father spoke again: "In our culture, few people are raised by their real parents. Your real mother carries you for nine months, but think of those who carry all our troubles, who feed us, who comfort us as we grow up. Those women are our mothers too."
>
> Buchi Emecheta, *Kehinde*

If my hypothesis of *Chi/Ori* as the mother within is valid, then the Igbo *Omunwa* and her Yoruba counterpart *Iyalode* can be constructed as the mother without. Closely tied to this concept is the unspoken assumption of woman as a "daughter-of-the-soil," with its responsibilities and perquisites, since an outsider cannot legitimately become an *Omunwa* or *Iyalode*. The notion of daughter-of-the-soil parallels the prevalent Nigerian idea of "son-of-the-soil," with its vernacularism and patent sociopolitical privileges, especially the emotional assurance of belonging as an indigene born on his father's soil.

In contemporary indigenous culture, *Omunwa* and *Iyalode* are analogous, governmental positions, filled by an illustrious, older woman who is politically recognized by being formally installed to minister as mother in the public domain. The predisposition to have a mother take control within and the political and psychological necessity to have a woman function as mother

45

without, meaningfully supervising the community even under many phases of (post)colonialism, speak to a deep-rooted need in Nigerians for a stable infrastructure with women caretaking. The cogent force for continuous, open reassurance stems from the honorific role attached to motherhood by men and the piety they show to their menopausal mothers. These are women who have ceased to function visibly as wives and are now utterly devoted to their sons, their daughters having left home for their husbands' houses. Interestingly, these emotions are never verbally articulated, though they are apparent in actions. While the younger woman writhes in the servility attached to wifehood, the older woman relishes the newfound power over her son's household and the community. Part of her authority derives from people's fear of her alleged occult power. I must add that anybody who lives to an old age in our harsh environment no doubt has some innate powers.

It is no surprise that in the adult world, motherhood is held in such high premium and, for women, becomes so validating that, if a majority of women desired to have power as a collective rather than as individuals, motherhood and its perquisites would be the easiest route to perform a coup de grace on the entire populace. The power of motherhood instills the desire, to the last Nigerian woman, to have children for self-esteem. This desire is an immutable, ideological point where Nigerian women part company with those Western feminists who decry the notion of anatomy as destiny or make speeches against obligatory motherhood. As the Nigerian playwright Tess Onwueme so clearly enunciates in her 1992 play *Go Tell It to Women,* only a poor strategist, in seeking power and equality, would discountenance the power she already indisputably has, neglecting to exploit it to access more recognition and exercise more power in the body politic. An equally important source of power not fully explored, politically, is the claim of daughterhood, since women have fathers, many of whom can be won over to the women's side by their daughters.

Since Nigerian women are so numerous and have not been coopted as a body on a national scale, their diversity, internecine feuds, and busyness prevent them from using these advantages to act concertedly for their own political advancement as a group rather than as individuals. The strain to survive and care for others either as mother or daughter or wife leaves them little energy or time to organize. What takes a physical and emotional toll on women is the current recession, caused by international inequalities, poor Nigerian management, not to mention the unnerving nature of life under military rulers. Among other shortcomings, the military collude with the West to strip us economically through corrupt practices and unconscionably large military budgets.[7] We are battered women with no shelter to run to, always on the road to recovery, because we are in an anomalous position in which we never make contact with our violators; so far removed are the military sons-of-the-soil and their foreign collaborators from the sites of the hardships they help to create. Consequently, in spite of the powerful, national image of motherhood, the paradox of exercising power without having power is such that the country gets away with its failure to acknowledge its debt to women and to utilize productively the expertise of more than half of its most industrious human resources. In other words, sons and daughters, not just some sons, must have their rightful place to usher in Nigerian postmilitarist modernity.

The Nigerian sociologist Kamene Okonjo suggests that "the absence of women from meaningful political representation in independent Nigeria can be viewed as showing the strength of the legacy of single-sex politics that the British colonial masters left behind" (1976, 58). What is the precolonial legacy that the British attempted to erase, and how does its vestigial manifestation operate in the contemporary postcolonial setting?

With the image of the Big Mama so deeply entrenched in the Nigerian psyche, rural people would be lost, like their urban counterpart, if they did not have the Mother in the public domain. Okonjo has illuminatingly described the Public Mother as a vital force in the social and political life of the Igbo in midwestern Nigeria. The women are under the wing of their representative, the symbolic figure known as the *Omu. Omu,* or the full form, *Omunwa* (childbearer-cum-nurturer)—that is, she through whose agency reproduction is assured—doubles as an honorific title for the woman leader and as a greeting for all daughters.[8] In using this greeting, man unwittingly acknowledges indebtedness to woman for her reproductive and reproducing roles, expressing his innate craving for ceaseless mothering, even in adulthood. Placed on a pedestal in public, the *Omu* or *Yeyeoja* (another Yoruba equivalent)

---

7. Most third-world countries devote a majority of their budgets to the military, a great deal of it spent on buying outmoded equipment from the West.

8. Woman is not only expected to be her children's mother. She is also expected to nurture others in the extended family and in public. She usually accepts the burden. Rebelling against the idea brings notoriety, and people would generally refer to such a person as a witch, of the wicked variety.

In many Nigerian cultures, the man's house also belongs to his mother, so the wife remains, in a sense, an outsider. This is why the mother-in-law, the butt of many jokes on American TV comedy programs vis-à-vis the man who owns the house, appears silly to a Nigerian because there is no basis for a wife's mother to dominate in her daughter's household. The quarrel is usually between the man's mother and his wife.

serves as woman's role model.[9] Woman's selflessness and concern for all those under her implies that mothers/daughters are rarely mothered.[10] In urban areas, the need for women to act as mothers in public results in the older woman being called "Auntie" or "Mummy" or "Mama" by total strangers, casting women in a role in which they are constantly expected to display responsibility. (See, for example, Emecheta, 1994, 59.)

In dealing with the place of the *Omu* from a sociopolitical perspective, Okonjo observes that there are usually two monarchical lines in Igbo towns and villages west of the Niger. They are "the male obi, who in theory was the acknowledged head of the whole community but who in practice was concerned more with the male section of the community, and the female omu, who in theory was the acknowledged mother of the whole community but who in practice was charged with concern for the female section" (1976, 47). The *Omu* also exercises her authority when an *Obi*, the male ruler, has to be installed. In the mundane running of the community, she is in charge of the marketplace, controlling the mores of the community of women from that economic stronghold. This public division of authority—father and mother or son and daughter—replicates the familial, which, as we will see, the federal military government under Ibrahim Babangida tried to mimic.[11]

The historian Nina Mba has noted a similar process among the Yoruba in the concept of the *Iyalode* (the Mother-at-large) and *Iyaloja/Yeyeloja* (the Mother-at-the-market) (1982, 7–8). Both functionaries share the duties carried out by the *Omu*. The *Iyalode* is often called on to deal with intractable situations. Chosen on merit, because of her personality, wealth, and achievement, she is held in high esteem by men and women. In practice, she epitomizes motherhood and daughterhood, for she is also the guardian and moving spirit of the land. Through her, every woman becomes legitimized in an affirmative caretaking role with its built-in rewards. This system is a model for the woman writer who envisages writing or the literary marketplace also

9. These are political and spiritual women leaders who supervise conduct in the marketplace. Omu is Igbo, Yeyeoja her Yoruba counterpart.

10. The Igbo saying *e mu nwa g'eli e zi,* "she who bears the child will also eat," is usually uttered when a woman/mother wishes to affirm her humanity and her needs (as distinct from those of her children), in times of stress.

11. Ideally, following Igbo dyarchy, a more democratic equivalent would be to have two elected legislative houses, one male, to represent men, and the other consisting solely of women, to represent women. Such a political arrangement would begin to free women from bondage in the masters' or fathers' houses, scrapping the current farce that goes for democratic representation worldwide. The alternative would be to ensure legally that each constituency is represented by a man and a woman.

as an agency for change or as a place to acknowledge the already changed—for better or worse.

For the *Omu/Iyalode*, the marketplace is central to the performance of her duty. The marketplace is a women's space where she exercises her political acumen, her ethical and ethnic control, and her economic power. For the ordinary woman, the marketplace has developed into a legitimized social space with economic and political potential. Educated or illiterate, women need the marketplace to enable them to perform their duties efficiently; every single town has a marketplace to service the community.

As I envisage it, the marketplace as women's public space is a metonym for colonial space in which the colonized (for the purposes of this postulate, women), though at the center, ultimately have minimal control, since the colonizers (that is, the men) have already disempowered them with their insistent gaze directed to undermine woman's potential economic power. Stephen Slemon puts the notion nicely, when he writes that the "silencing of otherness is inscribed into the colonial encounter" (1988, 17). This dispossession of the people at the center, again centered in women's texts as characters and market women, creates a tension, as women try to break the restrictions imposed on them. The erection of borders where they did not exist before is the heretical sign of colonialism and divisiveness, not good neighborliness. Rupture along gender lines, rather than a parallel working-together, becomes the colonial heritage. Reinstating a modified form of complementarity will move us into the twenty-first century.

With the marketplace as the site where the butcher, the fishmonger, the hair plaiter, the grocer, the cosmetologist, the seamstress, the fabric trader, and the food seller, to name but a few purveyors, thrive, each has a niche. The market combines, into one gigantic whole, what, in the Western world, has been compartmentalized and masculinized under capitalism into the departmental store, the bookstore, the grocery store, the hairdressing salon, the restaurant, the designer establishment, and the drug store. Onitsha Market in eastern Nigeria, as the biggest marketplace in West Africa, prides itself in being able to meet every single need, Western or indigenous. The saying goes that, if one's need is not met in this marketplace, it can never be met anywhere else.

From the foregoing discussion, it becomes apparent that the center-periphery model, where the periphery is totally victimized and disempowered, is not very useful. If oracles are anything to go by, one's destiny can always be modified with hard work. With this given, it is clear that the rejection of the victim mode causes women to continue to struggle because there is something tangible to be gained.[12] There must then be a vortex with many centers vying for power within it. In this disarray, some centers are more powerful than others, oftentimes causing collisions/coalitions; for example, the coups and the different women who emerge with the latest military victors or, perhaps, survivors.

The power of the mother, located in the matricentric, validates by its being perceived as different from other types of power. It is similar to the federal government's overwhelming power that comes to almost naught globally, though it is to be reckoned with in the African international context. The Igbo say that *onye ni maro onye kaa nwulu anwu*, "one who does not recognize his/her superior is dead," thereby legitimizing some form of hierarchization. Internalizing such notions makes the fight for equality, particularly along gender lines, an uphill task once one is satisfied with some power.

The power inherent in black women coming together, as in the marketplace, was palpable in the curiosity expressed by the White House during the international conference held at the Massachusetts Institute of Technology, entitled "Black Women in the Academy: Defending Our Name, 1894–1994." This interest demonstrates that even black women must have some power, or at least some potential, in the intellectual marketplace, but we do not know it; neither do we know where it is located, or how to harness it to improve black life. Increasingly for black women, as mothers and daughters, we have become aware that the violence of our catch-22 situations must be confronted. The focus has to be on securing a better life rather than engaging in the violence of a futile struggle for liberation from something, only to find one's self beleaguered by something else; or, the struggle to be equal to somebody, only to find us all tyrannized by somebody else. The White House understands the vernacular relationship of black women from all over the world to it as a symbol of black bondage.[13] Genuine difference will ultimately lie in who participate in

12. Women are usually scolded by sympathizers if they moan too long following some disaster, that is, in Igbo, *i kutopu aka*—the hanging of one's hands in despair, as if they are paralyzed. One is not allowed to remain alone or permitted to continue in a state of inertia, except, perhaps, in cases of insanity.

13. It is interesting to note that, at the MIT conference, a panel of four Nigerian women, two Igbo and two Yoruba, rose to defend African women and the imperialist inscriptions on their bodies in clitoridectomy or infibulation. They lambasted Western fetishization of African genitalia, e.g., Sara Bartmann, the "Hottentot Venus," who "was displayed for five years, until she died, in Paris, at the age of twenty-five. . . . Her sexual organs were then given to the Musée de l'Homme in Paris—where they are still on display" (Giddings 1992, 445) and Alice Walker's *Possessing the Secret of Joy* (1992) with its infamous French connections. These Western displays are fortuitously or deliberately designed to avert the gaze that should be riveted on the interna-

the meaningful running of the white houses that affect governments all over the world. Black women are in the marketplace for a part of the big white house and would like to retouch it with some of Ralph Ellison's invisible man's magical paint.

I am deeply indebted to the late Bessie Head for pointing out the social, economic, psychological, and political importance of the marketplace. Prioritizing the marketplace impacts literary theory and the reading of the Nigerian novel by women. As we sat down relaxedly in Calabar's Watt Market during her 1982 visit to Nigeria, this lonely South African writer, who was weighed down by not being nurtured as a daughter in her exile in Botswana, was thrilled that the market women identified with her when they addressed her in Efik. When she merely smiled in return, they spoke Igbo, assuming that she did not understand Efik. Next, they tried Pidgin English, and they were able to reach her. She realized that she was being included in their circle, and she had miraculously ceased to be an outsider, the painful position she had to bear in South Africa and Botswana. Erasing the feeling of unbelonging, as Joan Riley names the phenomenon, was exhilarating for Bessie. Her *siddon look* tactics had paid off, even if this was a temporary belonging.

The marketplace, traditionally located at the center of town, is not only the heartbeat of woman, but also of the community. As a meeting ground, it trades on goodwill, embracing men, women, and children without difficulty. It is a symbol of the type of society that the womanist writer-mother envisages: a spirit of freely coming together and working together. Woman is at the center of the marketplace, which folklore regards as a microcosm of the world: the Igbo say, *uwa bu afia*, "the world is a market," accommodating all kinds and conditions of people. As the center for transactions, control of this space is crucial in power politics. As a place where one can come and go freely, transact business with little or no discrimination, and where the main desire of the founding mothers is for decent behavior, the marketplace is a prototype of a

---

tionally engendered poverty that traps African women and their children. It is poverty and, according to the World Bank (1992), the lack of clean water (a simple commodity a little money can buy), with attendant illnesses and deaths from diarrhea (44–49), not the imagined lack of sexual satisfaction following female circumcision that make African women and their children the most wretched people on earth. What the panel found offensive was that Walker discountenanced all the visible signs of squalor and wretchedness that she encountered on her so-called journey through Africa, while she was enthralled by the invisible wounds, signs of women's misguided exercise of power. I believe that female circumcision can be stemmed by the education of girls, and boys, were resources available for training Africans in anatomy and modern midwifery. I should add that a couple of African-American women walked out of the session in anger, demonstrating that there is no one ideological viewpoint among black women.

womanist haven. Here, a woman can obtain economic independence, the crucial basis for erasing dependency and instituting complementarity rather than the disruptive notion of equality. With their colonial and postcolonial experiences, Nigerians are cynical about the limits of European ideologies, as equality in Europe was rounded out with rabid colonialism in Africa: equality as touted by feminists seems like a clear case of déjà vu. The market as a place or an economic idea is therefore important in the Nigerian woman's text. From a magical viewpoint, the text, like the market, has the potential to institute personal and communal metamorphoses in making all citizens sons- and daughters-of-the-soil, not only for sharing the largesse. They must also serve as a medium to take in and nourish the seeds for genuine modernization.

The proximity of the marketplace to the palace grounds demonstrates its political importance. Ostensibly, the closeness was originally necessitated by the need to protect women against outside invaders; in reality, men closely monitor the women more for internal security. The nearness makes consultation between the ruler and the women leaders easy, facilitating the collecting of fees and gifts for the king, the "father" of all. In a subsistence economy, where money rarely changes hands, the importance of the market with its monetary exchange is of the utmost interest to those in control. As the local stock exchange, the marketplace determines, by its size, the position of a village or town in that local government or in the country. The thriving market is an index of a wholesome people and effective rulers.

The marketplace is an important crossroads, where people meet to obtain provision from an incredibly rich source for the culinary arts and day-to-day living. In the sometimes intimate atmosphere of the market, a clique of women, for example, hair plaiters, can discuss their difficulties, husbands, male relations, put them in proper perspective, and, by speaking out, work through their problems therapeutically. Since each woman has some horror story that sometimes gets exaggerated in the telling, this support system trains women to endure hardships even as they pursue their careers. It is not unusual to hold political palavers in the market because of the accessibility to crowds. This is invigorating and politically expedient for women, the market constituting a source that the social reformer can easily tap.

The marketplace also has its own tension. With its crowds, it serves as an entertainment center, while offering the individual anonymity and publicity simultaneously. It frequently doubles as a backdrop for initiation and other rituals, when the sacred and the profane intersect. In dynamics, it embraces opposites: open yet so secret, humming with accord in spite of differences. Realizing the potential of the market to women, men try to encroach on this space, to prevent it from being overwhelmingly female with all the power that it confers on women, apart from men.

History has bequeathed memorable women traders to us. The legendary Madam Tinubu is prototypic. From the April 1988 discussion during the conference at the Women's Research and Documentation Center, Institute of African Studies, University of Ibadan, Nigeria, the participants established that this Mammywata-like, rich but childless slave dealer outlived four husbands. With a private army of men, Madam Tinubu operated openly in and between Abeokuta and Lagos, acting as an important broker among the British, the Lagosians, and the Egba in the tortuous nineteenth-century diplomacy and power politics of what would become western Nigeria. Under contemporary scrutiny, the fact that she acquired her wealth from the slave trade is troubling, while some women scholars find her lack of a clear-cut feminist agenda problematic. However, in nascent Nigerian history, she has caught the female imagination as an incarnation of Osun. She, as well as the numerous anonymous successful women traders, serve as models for many strong and sometimes amoral characters in the Nigerian novel by women: Nwapa's Efuru, Idu, and Amaka; Emecheta's Ma Palagada, Adaku, and Kehinde; Eno Obong's Mayen and Alhaja Sherifat are their fictional progeny, whose impact is beginning to modify the received versions of history.

Apotheosized, Madam Tinubu's maternal presence graces Tinubu Square, guarding the center of indigenous, commercial life in Lagos. This childless mother, with her strong, daughterly Egba roots, obviously served as a political foremother to many Nigerian women.

The 1929 debacle is an example of the effect of her role as fundamental mother in modern Nigerian politics. Known in Igbo as *Ogu Umunwanyi*—that is, the Women's Struggle, or, as it is currently referred to in historical circles, the (Aba) Women's War—it was organized by market women who were feeling the pinch of global depression through their British tax/taskmasters and their Nigerian underlings. The widespread skirmishes involving women throughout southeast Nigeria showed the economic importance of the marketplace and its political clout in having women organized, even in a dangerous venture. *Ogu Umunwanyi* has been inspiriting, serving as a subtext for many novels, including especially Nwapa's *Efuru*, Emecheta's *The Slave Girl* (1977), and Ulasi's *Who Is Jonah?* (1978b).

Madam Tinubu and especially *Ogu Umunwanyi* were crucial in shaping Mrs. Funmilayo Ransome-Kuti's political development. Mrs. Kuti, like Madam Tinubu, was Egba, operating within and beyond the ancient city of Abeokuta and Lagos. She was clearly acting the role of the dauntless daughter by deploying a female army of committed market women adversely affected by the post–World War II economy. The humiliating aftermath, as the British controlled the population by the usual show of brutal force to end the *Ogu Umunwanyi*, must have influenced Mrs. Kuti's strategy to attack the Nigerian chiefs, who were British henchmen, rather than engage in an open confrontation with the well armed, ruthless colonial government.

Tactically steering the politics away from mere personality clash between her and the Alake of Egbaland implicit in a palace coup, she fomented a large-scale civil disobedience with her market women's army, paralyzing the Egba kingdom in 1947. Her action influenced the colonial government's indirect rule policies, as the women reiterated the point that their southeastern predecessors had made and that women continue to make: there should be no taxation without adequate governmental representation. Democracy is not democratic, without women's full participation: we need two houses to represent us—one made up of men, the other of women from all walks of life. Kuti's sway in an identical geographical location as Madam Tinubu's has caused scholars to ponder why Egbaland produced two generations of illustrious daughters. One can conjecture that Egbaland's reputation in producing efficacious juju was crucial in sustaining women in crises to succeed in achieving their political goals. The novelists are daughters of these gifted women. Like their foremothers, the novelists counter the continued erasure of women in the postcolonial public arena by making issues that adversely impact women an important, though not the only, focus of their works.

With the economy at the center of these battles, it is obvious that trading has possibilities for women. Trading as a means of exchange, social intercourse, and economic growth, inspires female independence. Market mothers are independent women with tremendous influence not only in the marketplace but also, as we have seen, in Nigerian politics and in decision making, when they do decide to participate. For example, there was swift governmental submission in Benin and Ibadan, the capitals of Bendel and Oyo States, respectively, when, in the 1970s, some market women, angered by government's insistence on their paying taxes before children could be registered for school, threatened to go naked, and, horror of horrors, let the children be cursed for seeing their mothers naked. As the threat reminded the rulers of the 1929 Women's Struggle and the 1947 Egba Women's Rebellion, the officials scurried off to amend their educational and tax policies. Without being asked, the governments ordered the police to check food prices, escalated by idle middle men trying to obtain a hold in the local economy.

The Ugwuta or Onitsha market woman with her trading acumen, the "petty trader" who sells odds and ends to make ends meet, the body seller who caters for a special male need for her own economic benefit, and the new big-business woman/contractor are in the marketplace, controlling a sizable part of the national economy. Women in Nigeria do have some power, but they have no idea how to harness and extend it to their political advantage.

The movement from petty trading to the big business of contracting deals is in keeping with the growing sophistication in female ranks that is captured in the novels dealing with contemporary urban life: Nwapa's *One Is Enough* and *Women Are Different* (1986), Emecheta's *Destination Biafra* (1983a), and Eno Obong's *Garden House*. Women have also become enriched through increased legitimate or criminal participation in the oil business and the drug world. They also battle against sexism, which continues to thrive not because of female economic dependency but because people misread it as part of an immutable tradition and do not recognize that it limits women's capabilities and achievement and retards the country's development.

Countering the outer, restrictive, patriarchal milieu, the marketplace provides female networking of the utmost importance. With its rules and regulations that call for compliance by all market women, the space is structured, in spite of its apparent chaos. Teeming with female vitality, nowhere else is there such a concentration of women as buyers or sellers reinforcing each other by their sheer numbers. As a place of work, a home away from home for the seller, and a respite away from home and the workplace for the buyer, the well-organized market is a place where many women want to be. It is no surprise that women tend to spend too long a time there for its added emotional benefits in good economic times. The general concern for trading, in the texts, demonstrates the writers' recognition of its political uses. Female camaraderie, the communion between strangers, the exasperation at being cheated, or the delight at making a bargain make it an excursion that woman willingly undertakes. She readily initiates her daughter to participate in a gathering where people are relatively free.

To harness this ancient power from the marketplace, women in contemporary politics need a leader as influential as the *Omu/Iyalode* is in the traditional setting. Since women already have a space in private, and they also traditionally have a space in the public, the idea is to turn these traditional spaces into new ones, following the examples of revolutionary mothers in literature and history. In other words, the strategy is to use what we already have to begin to change the Nigerian body politic. Women do not want to become men. The gender division of labor and responsibility is not controversial, as long as each person's contribution as daughter or son, wife or husband, is recognized and rewarded at home and in the public.

Such reasoning influenced women's acceptance of the ideas of the former first lady of Nigeria, Maryam Babangida, about better life for rural women. As a daughter from Asaba, which has institutionalized woman's public role, Maryam Babangida acted as if she was the *Omu* of Nigeria. In her role as first lady, she effectively controlled the domestic sphere, particularly the female half of the population, while her husband, as military president, had the arsenal to run the government and limit male opposition. Her book *Home Front* (1988) is, in a sense, a manifesto of this governmental style. It also serves as a metaphor for the gruelling battle that soldiers' wives, or women generally, face at home daily without their husbands. The scarcity of necessities, such as water, energy, food, shelter, schools, family planning, health care, and transportation, are some of the areas where women endure incredible hardships that do not facilitate accomplishment of their duties. The daily battle is so enervating that women have little energy left to pursue things political or pleasurable. In the circumstances, fighting for women's rights is not just preposterous; even discussing it abstractly shows signs of insensitivity to human deprivation. In spite of these odds, women have to design a unique agenda, if their particular needs are to be genuinely met by the patriarchal government that should be mellowed through women's meaningful participation. Better life for rural women was Maryam Babangida's solution, an idea now signified on by the current first lady, Mrs. Abacha. In a very crucial sense, Maryam Babangida complemented her husband by controlling women, since rebellion from that unarmed source could spell disaster.

In a scintillating study of the Chilean military situation that throws much light on the management of women under military rule, Maria Helena Valenzuela (1991, 102) writes: "Volunteer work has been fundamental in implementing and maintaining the [military] dictatorship. It has fulfilled a constituency function, working from the base, acting as a chain transmitting small favors and benefits to its members, even becoming its own political government party." The thrust of Maryam Babangida's efforts at mobilizing women from the grass roots is thus similar to Lucia Hiriart's ingenious control of Chilean women under the military regime of her husband, General Pinochet. In cultures of terror sanctioned by a military or pseudodemocratic aegis, woman is grateful for a safe place, however cramped or peripheral it may be. Unfortunately, Maryam Babangida's volunteer work became complicated with the massive corruption she built into it; and, with her arrogance and need to exhibit power, she unwittingly generated disaffection, as women began to notice the lack of substance in her political actions. However, she was a catalyst and had set something in motion.

In hindsight, therefore, Maryam Babangida's *Home Front* can be read as a manifesto for domesticity, for women not to seek political power but to be satisfied once the domestic sphere is manageable; women are invariably silenced with bribes or governmental handouts.[14] The fundamental limitation with military regimes is that women (and civilian men) can never participate meaningfully, since they are not armed and therefore cannot defend themselves. They can only resist by deliberately working inefficiently, thereby creating anarchy as Nigerians did during colonialism. The problem with this form of resistance is that it soon becomes a permanent way of life, crippling the country under Abacha since 1994.

This is why Emecheta's war novel—*Destination Biafra*—is so subversive when she makes her female protagonist an officer in the army. Where *Destination Biafra* calls women to arms, *Home Front* responds by appealing to women to battle things out in the home. Ironically, Emecheta, the Ibuza daughter whose home town is within walking distance of Maryam Babangida's Asaba, wearily locks horns with her, in a quarrel that demonstrates the

14. It is fortuitous that, at this juncture, the First Lady of Nigeria, Maryam Babangida, would speak cursorily to the issues raised by the women's agenda in her book *The Home Front: Nigerian Army Officers and Their Wives*. The thrust of the book, as the title hints, is the "ideal" of the sensible wife, who complements her busy, patriotic husband. The anti-intellectual, military stance of the government appeared slightly diffused by the writing, although the fanfare and the display by moneyed interest groups that accompanied the launching of the 74-page book were cause for embarrassment and concern about the nature of Nigerian hegemony. For whatever her achievement is worth, Maryam Babangida is the first First Lady to venture into the realm of writing, as well as to attempt to realize some of her thoughts in praxis. Her dynamism and activism have created a woman's sphere in the public domain and brought the possibility of mobilizing women for change through her Better Life for Rural Women program. In other words, she has dared to take the first step toward realizing the woman novelist's dream of destroying the retrogressive Nigerian oppressive system by attempting to liberate the lowliest in the society.

The Nigerian situation is comparable to that of the consciousness-raising role of the Tanganyika African National Union (TANU) during the restive colonial days. TANU succeeded in achieving independence for Tanzania in part by its use of the palaver with traditional writing in Kiswahili. The political party socialized adults, stressing "the injustices of colonialism [read oppression/sexism], and showing the possibilities that lay ahead. This had to be done cautiously because of the restrictive legislation and the meagre resources at the party's disposal" (Katoke and Ndagala 1979, 65). One can only hope that, with more girls going to school, women's writing in Nigeria will be equally effective, and that women's liberation will have a more auspicious ending than TANU's in the postindependence era. Gains in women's education will have tremendous repercussions in Nigeria and throughout the continent, since almost 50 million Nigerian women stand to profit from it.

complexities of the palaver: the simple truth that contemporary women have neither a united front nor a common agenda.

It is also ironic that Maryam Babangida was based in Lagos, from where she made her forays into the poverty-stricken interior to a captive audience awed by her expensive clothes from another world. She becomes Mammywata incarnate. Kristin Mann reminds us of the revolutionary role of Lagos: "Many developments in the second half of the nineteenth century, then, created opportunities for Lagos women to redefine their relationships with husbands or elders in ways that gave the women new freedom and thus greater control over their labor and resources. Women struggled to take advantage of these opportunities" (1991, 703). It is thought provoking that, after one hundred years of working out this new freedom in Lagos, Maryam Babangida would enjoy its advantages yet go to the rural regions of Nigeria to help to perpetuate the second-class citizenship of women under her husband's military rule. Liberation can never come from a source economically and politically linked with a corrupt, self-serving military government. The mere thought is sheer madness.

We believe that if a mad person goes to the marketplace, s/he will never be cured. This is perhaps because once the person is seen as mad, s/he remains so in people's perception, as the antics or violence exhibited remain indelible in the public mind. Maryam Babangida has been in the marketplace of public opinion, and she acted strangely. It became apparent that her form of governmental madness is incurable; her rule, with its complicity with the military, is a warning to women not to assume that equity or healthy complementarity will automatically be achieved through women's administrative control. Though it was good riddance, her departure made women motherless.

The orphan is usually told that the mother has gone to the marketplace, to spare the child the pain of coping with the death of just one mother, since other mothers readily take the place of the deceased. This is not a lie where the marketplace is believed to be accessible to those from spiritland. Orphaned by the departure of Maryam Babangida, who had so much potential were it not for the corrupting forces and the arrogance of power, other women role models, such as the teacher or the student, must replace her to sell ideas about liberation from the shackles of illiteracy. Nigerian modernity hinges on how nonliterates, especially women, finally become formally educated. The modern extension of the marketplace as a liberating space in the lives of women has shifted to the school, particularly the girls' boarding school, which stands for enlightenment, as Zaynab Alkali demonstrates in *The Stillborn* (1984) and *The Virtuous Woman* (1987).

The other writers are also concerned with the reformatory possibilities of the modern school, because of its importance in the emergence of the new Nigerian woman; this is the thesis of Nwapa's *Women Are Different*. What the marketplace does for women, education can now do for the emergent woman. Education provides woman with the essentials for seeking and holding onto freedom. As freedom does not come easily, in more recent times, the schools have led to the development of "bottom power," the pidginized version of erotic power, and to the emergence of the "cash madam" phenomenon, that is, a class of wealthy women, usually educated, who know how to wheel and deal in the contemporary world. Emecheta has explored this phenomenon in *Double Yoke* (1982a), Nwapa in *One Is Enough* and *Women Are Different,* Eno Obong in *Garden House,* Okoye in *Behind the Clouds,* and Fakunle in *Chance or Destiny?* The school is part of the system parents and the government use to boost women's morale, yet control them as we see in the unfortunate development in Bedford's *Yoruba Girl Dancing* (1991). Criticizing or panegyrizing the alma mater as a focal point in female development demonstrates the value the writers place on the importance of the school in their own lives. The novelist's text as a literary marketplace replicates this dynamic, communal atmosphere; it can be equally influential for the exchange of ideas to enable and empower women. Liberation will come through the agency of educated mothers. By conflating traditional maternal power with the influence exerted by contemporary educated women, they will, through sheer numbers, make a tremendous difference; people will recognize the advantages of complementarity when half of the national work force becomes more contented.

American feminist theorists Nancy Chodorow, Dorothy Dinnerstein, and Adrienne Rich would frown at the reductionist view implicit in such a perception of woman's role as mother and/or daughter. However, these speculative uses of motherhood and daughterhood depend on cultural needs. They compare with the visions of the Swedish woman, Ellen Key. Cheri Register (1982, 609) summed up Key's viewpoint quite succinctly: "One of the challenges left to modern feminists, Swedish and otherwise, is to envision, as Key tried to do, a complete social transformation that would put motherhood at the center of public life." As Okonjo and Mba have demonstrated, the ideal is structured into the indigenous dyarchical system, which, unfortunately, has been displaced at the center by "democracy." Negativism toward democracy is a sign of the people's resistance to an alien system that was never Nigerianized. The adverse treatment meted out to the opposition in the democratic process, particularly where that opposition consists of an ethnic "minority" large enough to be reckoned with, puts democracy into constant peril in Nigeria. The result has been instability. Key's vision speaks to the current Nigerian position: "In practical terms, Key saw 'social motherliness' offering a use for the maternal inclinations of women without children. As an ideal, she saw in it the power to transform a society beset by exploitation, war, and sexual hypocrisy. . . . Women's experience of 'motherliness' had as a 'natural consequence . . . an immediate feeling for everything weak and in need of help, everything growing and becoming'" (Register 1982, 605). This type of arrangement, which can involve women with children and clearly takes the childless woman as daughter into consideration, speaks to the Nigerian situation, where informal adoption of children from large families keeps such women fulfilled in their maternal roles. The Yoruba address an unknown woman, childless or not, as *Iya*, or *Mama*. This implies that every woman can be legitimately recognized for her potential in a country so torn apart.

Nigeria has not progressed in part because of a lack of genuine female authority in the contemporary public arena, such as we have seen utilized in Israel, Sri Lanka, India, Great Britain, the Philippines, Pakistan, Canada, and other countries. Nigeria also needs strong women leaders in the top echelons of power, to infuse the sense of purpose at the national level as it is in the traditional, particularly through a genuine, democratic revolution. Unfortunately, traditional female power is already being eroded by being looked on as anachronistic. Oppression by men and children militates against women's political activism. One may add that caring for military men in power, plus the subject male population, seems so debilitating that it is difficult to combine this private work with a public one. How do women recuperate enough to keep going in this miasma of poverty and disrespect, since there are more wives than there are menopausal mothers, the women who have earned some authority through people's fear of their superhuman power?

With the thrust of these novels being the portrayal of woman's space, one of the problems that the Nigerian woman writer faces clearly is the erosion of her power as writer. Though power is always relative, the writer is a matriarch in her own right. Is the writer's power as limited as Adrienne Rich perceives the control of the African-American matriarch? "Needless to say," she comments in *Of Woman Born: Motherhood as Experience and Institution* (1977), "the black woman's 'power' as 'matriarch' is drastically limited by the bonds of racism, sexism, and poverty. What is misread as power here is really survival-strength, guts, the determination that her children's lives shall come to something even if it means driving them, or sacrificing her own pride in order to feed and clothe them" (202). These words can be applied to the Nigerian woman, who uses the marketplace to stretch herself for the benefit of her family, especially her children. Unfortunately, Rich fails to see that the strength exhibited by strong women, in spite of sexism and poverty, is the domestic power that has aided black families everywhere to avert annihilation. Sons recognize and exploit it for their own uses. Few Nigerian women depend solely on their husbands to bring up their children, the way the middle-class or upper-class Western woman does. The Nigerian woman rears her children and educates them to be independent as well as to help relations. Woman thus exercises a great deal of ingenuity and power, to ensure that her children (and indirectly her country) succeed. Woman's effectiveness in this sphere must be sung, not played down, since she does not particularly care for the type of power that makes men so monstrous.

Power comes in all sorts of ways and should not be trivialized if it comes in gender-specific forms. There is a distinction "between power as domination and control over others and power that is creative and life-affirming" (Hooks 1981, 84). Motherly and daughterly power, partly derived from the marketplace, is in the latter category; it keeps the world going as the other triggers misery and war. It exhibits strength and responsibility toward the needy who appear in its orbit, the powerful stuff of which philanthropy is made. Female power is and should always be different from male power; it is needed for world progress. We must always remember that "Sexism has never rendered women powerless. It has either suppressed their strength or exploited it. Recognition of that strength, that power, is a step women together can take towards liberation" (Hooks 1981, 93). Occasionally, however, even one's child can exploit such strength to render woman almost powerless, as we will see in the *ogbanje/abiku* phenomenon.

The *Ogbanje/Abiku* Complex: Mother as Jinxed Care Giver

In poor countries, including Nigeria, "*Diarrheal diseases that result from con-taminated water kill about 2 million children and cause about 900 million episodes of illness each year* . . . frequent diarrhea . . . can leave a child vulnerable to illness and death from other causes."

The World Bank (1992)

[I]t seemed to me that Bukola was one of the denizens of that other world where the voice was caught, sieved, re-spun and cast back in diminishing copies. Amulets, bangles, tiny rattles and dark copper-twist rings earthed her through ankles, fingers, wrists and waist. She knew she was *abiku*. The two tiny cicatrices on her face were also part of the many counters to enticements by her companions in the other world. Like all *abiku* she was privileged, apart. Her parents dared not scold her for long or earnestly.

Soyinka, *Ake*

Our country is an abiku country. Like a spirit-child, it keeps coming and going.

Okri, *The Famished Road*

In Nigeria, where infant mortality is high because of malaria, diarrhea, sickle cell anemia, and other preventable diseases, people recognize the symptoms, and the *dibia/babalawo* have herbal remedies for the diseases. The real source of apprehension is death that cannot be ascribed to any obvious cause, bringing in a mystical dimension that keeps parents worried. The West, too, has inexplicable deaths, such as what is now popularly referred to as SIDS—sudden infant death syndrome—or nameless viral infections. To cope with these mysterious deaths, Nigerians take solace in the *ogbanje/abiku* myth. The conviction that a dead child is reincarnated, then returns from a contiguous world to be born again by its mother, deeply consoles the grieving woman. The catch is that the wayward child may once more choose to die, thereby establishing a cyclic time, which leaves the bereaved profoundly baffled at an apparently ineluctable fate. The resolve to arrest the traumatic birth-death-rebirth cycle institutes a deadly struggle between mother and child. The condition limits the joys of motherhood. As a discursive field, the *ogbanje-abiku* phenomenon is fundamental; it stems from a metaphysical dimension and can be understood in this context. The Igbo *ogbanje* and the Yoruba *abiku* are identical myths with slightly differing manifestations determined by the cultural imperative.

Ogbanje refers to the iconoclast, the one who runs back and forth from one realm of existence to another, always longing for a place other than where s/he is. It also refers to the mystical, unsettled condition of simultaneously existing in several spheres. Conceptually, the power inherent in the *ogbanje* erases natural and artificial boundaries that are drawn to systematize the cosmos. Metaphorically, one can read *ogbanje* as the road of life, with its constantly changing scenes, unforeseen twists, surprises, and disappointments. This road which leads one to the other place, that is, to expectations and different phases of existence, always ends in death. The mystique of the time and space traveler, transcending human restraints, stands as the ultimate sign of liberation. Crossing boundaries that intersect others, *ogbanje* opens up the cosmos for a glimpse at the possibilities of becoming. The magic clearly encapsulates a sense of urgency, for the restless, prescient spirit, privy to arcane knowledge in various realms, acts bizarrely. Precocity, curiosity, and prematurity (especially the inexplicable desire to die before one's parent) endow this spiritual carrier with a multiple consciousness. Its complex imaginary remains superior to that of the ordinary individual (Osundare 1989, 99). However, the gift, which separates the *ogbanje* from others, is lodged in a seemingly disease-ridden body that is psychically primed and more knowledgeable, cosmically, than the parents'.

Endowed with extraterrestrial authority but cursed with a fragile constitution, the lonely *ogbanje* needs constant parental attention, to the neglect of other healthier children. Not only is s/he prone to illness, s/he is liable to succumb to other forms of danger, precursors of an early death. Death before the parent, one of the most harrowing experiences a parent may have to bear, is always a prospect with the *ogbanje*, to deflect which the mother becomes enslaved to the whims and caprices of her plaintive child.

Though *ogbanje* conceptually overlaps *abiku*, the latter privileges death in its figurations. *Abiku* is one who is born to die. *Abiku* cryptically and presumptuously poses the rhetorical question, "Is it death?" However it is viewed, *iku*, 'death,' is prioritized. As the condition refers to a living being, death, then, is alive, if not well. Since every human being is born only to die, the concept ironizes even as it begs the issue of mortality. To set apart a group of children, perceived to desire an untimely death, only to ostracize them and/or treat them specially, sends out mixed signals. This is noticeable in the repertoire of names designated for such children in Igbo and Yoruba. The Igbo names Ogbanje, Ojemeta (Did s/he start journeying today?) and Udene (Buzzard, Vulture) and Yoruba ones such as Kokumo (S/he didn't die again), Igbekoyi/Igbokoyi (the forest/grave has rejected this; *igbe*, "feces" is a synonym for *igbo*, "forest") speak to their parents' anguish.[15] The thinking behind such ugly naming is to shame the children as a deterrence to dying. Since children are multiply named, they can truly earn their alternate, beautiful names and be addressed as such when they finally choose to live.

The adult position generates a hysterical note in blatantly referring to death. A patently self-fulfilling, prophetic tone suffuses the parent-child drama, grimly compromising their perception of life. Since the parent has no intention of letting the child precede him or her to the other world, that is, the ancestral world, a tug-of-war ensues. At the site of this struggle is a reversal of power in favor of the child, who effects transitions effortlessly. S/he is metasyncretic and as such, has conquered Death, controlling multiphasic discourses.

The *ogbanje/abiku* complex, as it impacts the child's relationship with the parent(s), is comparable to its Oedipal counterpart in Western tradition.

15. African-American naming of fictional characters appears to reflect this thinking. Gloria Naylor's Buzzard in *Mama Day*, Shit in *Linden Hills*, Wild Child in Alice Walker's *Meridian*, and Toni Morrison's Sixo and Seveno in *Beloved* and Viole(n)t and Wild in *Jazz* are telling examples.

Freud's construct is limited by its derivation from the European nuclear family, which has no clear equivalent in the Nigerian context. We must therefore account for what Baker (1984, 10) refers to as "remainders," in formulating theory. What goes on in a single-parent family, especially one with a woman at the head? What hypothesis covers the extended family or the polygynous household where a woman controls her own small unit with occasional reference to father(s) who are often absent? In a culture where each child has multiple mothers because of intricate networking among women who spontaneously care for the children, how do we establish neat parent-child relationships?

These fundamental differences necessitate an alternative account, to provide privileged access to the Nigerian woman's text. Appiah cautions:

> It is exactly because they can have little difficulty in understanding what Soyinka [and, I might add, his sister writers] says that Europeans and Americans must learn to be careful in attending to his purposes in saying it. For there is a profound difference between the projects of contemporary European and African writers: a difference I shall summarize, for the sake of a slogan, as the difference between the search for the self and the search for a culture. . . . In the world of authenticity, Freud stands as a giant witness to the impossible pain of discovering one's inner, deeper, more real, *simpliciter* one's *authentic,* self. (1992, 74, 75)

In their intriguing poems, each entitled "Abiku," Wole Soyinka and J. P. Clark, in their separate ways, not only "search for a culture" but successfully inscribe a tradition. In his "Abiku," Soyinka startlingly voices *Abiku*'s complaint and resistance, rather than speak to the issue from the viewpoint of the mother, who is stereotypically martyrized. In contrast, Clark privileges the adult perspective, nuanced to raise points much closer to the *ogbanje* agenda.

At the site of biological motherhood, where woman should be at her most resourceful and powerful, lurks a great drama in which the child thwarts the mother. This twist in the parent-child discourse enervates the woman and comes to signify her ultimate powerlessness, since she depends on something beyond herself and out of her control for access to authority. For the Nigerian woman, this undecidability replaces the Oedipal, or, perhaps, complements it, as Soyinka seems to imply in the line, "The god's swollen foot." In the struggle, the mother is at her most vulnerable, challenged by her disloyal child, even as she uses money, pleading, anger, desperation, love, tenderness, care, and faked indifference, a formidable arsenal to keep her child. This drama is usually seen from the mother's viewpoint with the child silenced. What has *Ogbanje/Abiku* got to do with it?

I acknowledge my debt to Niyi Osundare, whose illuminating analysis of Soyinka's poem opens up *Abiku*'s multivalent meanings, engendering theoretical possibilities. From Soyinka, the uneasy parent-child relationship can be read as a trope for the resistance inherent in Africa's colonial condition, which parallels the tensions in slavery and/or racist milieus in the United States and elsewhere. *Abiku,* as a worldwide, black problem, extends to postcolonialism, which partly touches the politics of the black prisoner.[16] In each metamorphic phase, the white man and the black man are latched onto one another, each bearing a burden.[17] However, *Abiku* is a paradox; with the displacement of whites by blacks fronting for them, he is at once the colonizer and the colonized, the jailer and the prisoner, powerful and powerless.[18] Theoretically, *Abiku* creates limitless choices and has the innate power to cancel out an aspect of his condition to emerge whole. As the colonizer, *Abiku*'s air of superiority and aloofness marks his difference and longing for that other place where he would much rather be. Also, in spite of being a minor or being in the minority, he exercises power disproportionately. Belonging culturally to that other world, he is uncommitted to the present, merely interested in the material advantages to be garnered from those he lords over. On the other hand, the images of circles, entrapment, and imprisonment, as well as violence on and violation of *Abiku*'s body, are overdetermined patterns etched on his personality. *Abiku* counters with a traitorous plan, in an attempt to gain independence and control from the demonizing mother, or the mother country, as the case may be. The points of contention are population and economic control, the institution of gerontocracy as opposed to democracy, the intolerance of difference, and the validity and urgency to inaugurate children's (the colony's) rights to a separate existence, which the parent must make viable.

Next, we are confronted with the mother's sickening commitment in not letting her offspring go. The mother-child dyad degenerates into a mutually

16. In Nigeria, the prison system still retains its colonial premise: it houses criminals and those in political disfavor.

17. The feminists and womanists are yet to establish a counterdiscourse to incorporate the invisible black woman and the absent white woman.

18. Soyinka's *Abiku* is male as line 11 of the poem clearly indicates. Though Bukola, the *abiku* character in Soyinka's *Ake* is a girl, she is hardly significant in the childhood autobiography. The central figure is Wole, who must be read as *abiku:* not only is he in constant danger, and makes his mother apprehensive, he is constantly crossing boundaries, and the book ends with his anticipated journey to another colonial world without traveling shoes.

destructive relationship: as the Yoruba say, *Eni ti o ba bi 'mo, omo ni o pa a; eni ti ko bi, oro omo ni o pa a,* "she who bears a child, the child will be the death of her; she who bears no child, not having a child will be the death of her." Reciprocity in treachery and the threat of death lurk in the relationship, as encapsulated in Soyinka's poem. This analogy befits the nation states that emerged in Europe in the eighteenth and nineteenth centuries, with their slave trading and colonizing adventures. The mother-child connection thus extends beyond the familial, to cover national and international relations.

In a culture where a child is normally seen but not heard, by taking the unusual position of the child advocate in representing *Abiku*'s viewpoint, Soyinka puts the hitherto unspoken at the center of the discourse as he addresses the prime fact of the terror of death for everybody except *Abiku*, who has mastered Death. This mastery of death sets *Abiku* apart because death is part of his name and condition; indeed he is the undead or "the living dead" (Osundare 1989, 99). In the transition from "innocence to authority" (Soyinka 1989, 18), and at the moment of recognition of his inherent power, *Abiku*'s arrogance becomes painfully strident, and naturally so. While *Abiku* laments his present condition as prisoner, imagining and relishing the carefree existence and liberties of the other place, he can be construed as a jailer, since he jinxes and thereby restricts all those committed to him, especially his mother, who is doomed to dote on him.

This Yoruba perspective counters the European part of the poem, especially the Oedipal reference to "the god's swollen foot," which can also be read as Esu's uneven feet. The crippled foot belies the notion of *Abiku* as wanderer or traveler or *wakajugbe,* the restless walker on an endless journey.[19] For Nigerians, the last reference is telling, as it can be equated with the frequently advertised British whiskey, Johnny Walker, still going strong since its calculated in-*toxic*-ating beginnings in West Africa. Traveling is also usually undertaken to better one's lot. Canceling temporal, spatial, and artificial boundaries by traveling to engender infinite possibilities is liberatingly *Abiku*'s metier. Si-

19. The idea of *abiku* as "wanderer child" is captured by Toni Morrison (1987) in her character Beloved; the name marks the mother's adoration of the troublesome child. Beloved also wants to be loved in a very real sense, not violated. To buttress the girl's private agenda, as distinct from the racist implications of American capitalism, Morrison utilizes *Beloved* to question the violence with which parents handle or are driven to treat children in the name of love. Seeking for a cool, clean, clear place, the *abiku* roams from the ordinary sphere to the other world, replicating the writers' imaginative sweep. I have cited *Beloved* to show the possibility of extending the reading to other, non-Nigerian, black texts, especially those involving mother-child relationships. Richard in Wright's *Black Boy* (1945) is another fascinating example.

multaneously old, young, "ageless," and waiting to be born, while belonging here, there, and everywhere, *Abiku* emerges as the archmagician and master creator, a shape shifter adept at playing many roles. To Osundare (1989, 99), "The enigma of *Abiku* is that he is a grand fusion of time past, time present and time future. He is a living dead who imports death into the future," a summation that encapsulates Emecheta's fiction, especially her novel, *The Slave Girl*, and her been-toism—her living abroad while concentrating on Nigeria in her writing. Osundare refers to *Abiku*'s "godlike arrogance and his superiority over ordinary mortals. In fact, he is accorded treatment meant for a god, propitiated with goats and cowries, feared (but hardly revered) for his supernatural power over time, death and decay" (ibid.). In the case of Emecheta's enslaved *ogbanje* character, the orphaned Ojebeta is constantly journeying through time, space, and different cultures, as her name indicates. Emecheta sets up this received notion only to deconstruct it, as we shall see in Part 2.

J. P. Clark's "Abiku" is a textual *ogbanje/abiku* in its repetitious naming, thematic affirmation, and refinement of and departure from Soyinka's poem. Clark's "Abiku" is an excellent case of signifying, in Gates' theoretical conceptualization of the vernacular term. *Abiku* itself as a status or condition epitomizes "rememorying," to borrow Toni Morrison's word in *Beloved* for the notion of returning to the past and reconstructing it for contemporary uses. With reiteration and revision, one establishes a tradition of newness as an agency for progress. This idea is in consonance with the fact that *Ogbanje* retains an original core, in spite of the repetitions. The refinement in Clark's version captures the difference between the concepts of *abiku* and *ogbanje*. This complexly nuanced perspective is not surprising, since Clark is Ijo, a riverine people who associate with both the Igbo and the Yoruba.

Writing from the viewpoint of a seemingly neutral adult, Clark appeals to *Abiku* for compassion on the mother. He stresses the restlessness, urgency, the plurality of vision; these are all implicit in *ogbanje*, that is, "one who runs all over the place," from here to there, to everywhere. Death is never mentioned, though it serves as the context for appealing to *Ogbanje*. *Ogbanje* as traveler and pluriculturalist is truly African: a product of an unmapped territory, s/he is an outsider and an insider, an earthling and otherworldling, with riverine connections. Rich yet poor, free yet bound, marked yet whole, *Ogbanje*'s indeterminacy engenders mischief. Hierarchies collapse as *Ogbanje* forces an adult in a gerontocratic society to abase himself by appealing to a child. It is distracting for the child to place itself at the center of the discourse. The attendant rupture causes adults to perpetrate violence on *Ogbanje*, as part of a communal exorcism necessary to keep the child in one place. At the end of the ordeal, *Ogbanje* becomes liberated, and the adults, too.

Soyinka's *Abiku* is defiantly macho to the end, leaving the final lines of the poem open ended. As a fiendishly wasteful shapechanger, he constructs "mounds from the yolk," which is nourishing for the young, but deadly for the adult, with its cholesterol. Clark, on the other hand, effects closure by referring to the tired mother's milk. The milk nourishes not just *Ogbanje* but other children; by structuring in sibling rivalry, Clark recognizes the fact that the other children are always envious of the egocentric *Ogbanje*. He disempowers the aberrant child, to restore parental authority, even though it is a shadow of its original self. Clark's *Ogbanje* is not gender specific, a refinement in the narrative construct which recreates its complexity. Rather than focusing solely on the rupture caused by *Ogbanje*'s fickle nature, Clark shifts attention from *Ogbanje* to the other children and mother at the end of his poem. This shift is crucial for restoring a semblance of order. Yet, knowing that misery and chaos are constants in Nigerian life as symbolized in *ogbanje*hood, the last lines appear to be a resolution. Soyinka's, on the other hand, reiterates the indeterminacy of life, which is what *Abiku* represents, after all. Ominously, for woman, the nightmarish cycle ends only with the mother's demise, for *ogbanje*hood is not limited to childhood.

The Igbo scholar and writer Catherine Acholonu treats the late Nigerian poet Christopher Okigbo as an *ogbanje* archetype. Like Soyinka and Osundare, she privileges the male in her analysis, though in praxis, the phenomenon is linked more with girls than boys, who are more likely to die earlier than girls. Since girls are less valued than boys, the father is invariably absent from the site of struggle, preoccupied with other matters and members of his large, polygynous household. In a world riddled with physical and emotional suffering, the "shallow grave" hurriedly dug for the *ogbanje* girl is an apt metaphor for unrecognized potential or for the fate of being interned, both appalling destinies for women, as Florence Stratton (1988) infers in reading Emecheta. The woman writer uses such tropes and plots to protest her novel's mixed reception, in spite of her talent. To counter outright hostility, the eight women novelists to be considered have to be tricksters. They sometimes play games with their subtexts, like "the seven *ogbanje* girls, who brandish their beauty to attract suitors while concealing the fatality of their existence" (Acholonu 1989, 109).

The Igbo Acholonu associates the *ogbanje* with "talent," "violent death," and "reincarnation" (104), while the Yoruba Niyi Osundare, also a scholar and a writer, links *abiku* with "infant mortality," "supplications," and divinity (1989, 97). These embody the multiple perspectives of Nigerian writers. In their imaginary, the *ogbanje/abiku* emerges as a trope for the writer writing in a European, instead of a Nigerian, language. Those lacking fluency in English have no access to this foreign world. Alienated from his/her emotional language, the inspired writer suffers a profound loss, even as s/he arranges English words in their infinite possibilities. Though s/he Nigerianizes the English, s/he becomes imperceptibly bewitched by English word power, which diminishes facility in the less-used Nigerian language. The situation of the writer is analogous to the condition of other Western-educated Nigerians or of those Africans whom Appiah refers to as europhone (1992, 54), the elite, lured by the attractions of a different world. They act like outsiders, looking in to assess their mothers' house, sometimes sympathetically, at other times in disgust. The educated, in their elitism, like the *ogbanje/abiku*, having enjoyed life elsewhere, have no energy to invest in putting their mothers' houses in order. It is easier to complain about the disorder, or to remain in exile, no matter the cost of this temporary abode where s/he is sometimes taunted to go home.

Also, *ogbanje/abiku*'s spirit of adventure parallels the free-roaming nature of a text. This creative spark is enriched by the mother's strong bond and unwitting collaboration in refusing to let go of her fractious child. By leaving an inscription on the child's body to recognize a return, the parent turns the *ogbanje/abiku* into a text to be reproduced, refined, and reissued, each edition slightly different from its predecessor while retaining enough of the original to identify it as part of a tradition. The writing on the body is a mark of despair and identity, a magical attempt to contain mutability and cultural pluralism, which the *ogbanje/abiku*, as other, represents. The writing is also the distinguishing mark that prevents the europhone from being assimilated in the Western world. *Ogbanje/Abiku*'s tortuous evolution resembles the tedious writing process: the labor in producing the text, the editing, the author's anxiety for the book to remain in print and to be accessible and favorably received. As tragic subtext, Soyinka graphically encodes the mother-child dyad in the image of the treacherous snake, tellingly reinforced with the spider. The latter reference dramatizes, in a compelling fashion, the inevitable separation of the spider from its young, fleeing from the web of adult entrapment. Readers and critics, as well as librarians and teachers, form a corps for communal parenting of the text, since no single person can successfully parent a child or completely master a text.

Though the text *(Ogbanje/Abiku)* must lead an independent life away from the author (parent), as Roland Barthes, who had elaborated the idea, insists in "The Death of the Author" (1977), the original umbilical connection somehow remains in the reader's or critic's memory, affecting, even if tangentially, the text's reception. This is particularly so as most Nigerian writers in English are alive and well or only recently dead. Severing the link between Barthes' necrotized author and her/his text is not so easily effected as his theorizing the Oedipal killing of an already dead author indicates. In the roller coaster life, the author is also a text. *Ogbanje/Abiku,* in its textual denseness, is open to multiple readings, while, as Soyinka's nutcracker, *Abiku* magically assumes the role of interpreter to reveal textual secrets, the kernel of an oracular message. *Abiku*'s conflicting roles would appear to encapsulate Foucault's concept of the author in his "What Is an Author?" (1977). The fundamental writer, reader, and critic coalesce into the mercurial *Ogbanje/Abiku.* Ironically, one problem in Nigeria has been that not too many people read, except when they are forced to: for examinations. This hostility toward the written word kills the author.

The frenzied *ogbanje/abiku* management and the capricious child-wielding power in several worlds correspond to the author's attempt to invent a world out of the chaos of the past and the present, the rural and the urban, the illiterate and the literate, in an attempt to construct an uncertain future. *Ogbanje*'s confusing and confused agenda makes Clark plead, "No longer then bestride the threshold," a prayer that the Marxist feminist scholar Ogundipe-Leslie could prescribe for the uncommitted writer wavering between tradition and feminism. Clark's specific appeal, "Then step in, step in and stay," counters *Ogbanje*'s outsiderly critical stance. Its troubling posture is as unsettling as the parochial male perception that palava is gender specific rather than a Nigerian problem involving men as much as women. Clark, however, appears to be mispleading: *Ogbanje*'s inexorable fate, even as s/he inadvertently punishes others, is also that of a victim in a tortuous drama. Like all who blame *Ogbanje/Abiku,* Clark fails to see that, once conditions are satisfactory, *Ogbanje/Abiku* will have no compelling reason to protest against this world or to long for the other.

The *ogbanje/abiku* and the onlookers, as sometimes happens between the writer and her audience, appear to have a clash of visions. Like the writer, the *ogbanje/abiku* is a fractious spirit, unwilling to tolerate the intolerable, weighing chances in this world and the other idyllic realm, intent on effecting some change. On the other hand, the mothers, as well as the onlookers—used to hardship and unwilling to put up any resistance to things that are the way they have always been—search for affirmation with kindred, suffering spirits, questioning the child's apparent rebellion. In this abnormal power struggle, the people who should be in control cede a little of their power, desperately focusing on the special child to will the wanderer to stay, to be ordinary. Nurturing the talented child, especially an educated daughter with eyes set on other worlds, is equally frustrating. At some level, they finally realize that she is their saving grace, hence the veiled admiration and open hostility toward the unyielding writer, the irrepressible palava woman who strategically involves the outside world with the trouble within by writing about it in a foreign language. Yet it is this encoding of a mystery in a language with no vocabulary to accommodate it that is the most frustrating aspect of theorizing *ogbanje/abiku.*

The gaze into a different world, Western in the case of the writer, is as forbidding as the vision of the metaphysical is problematic. The frequency of death of children at an early age in a crises-ridden milieu invariably drives women to seek help from the occult world, as the writer, in desperation, courts world opinion. For the black woman, one constant has been the terror of losing a child through means almost as devastating as death (e.g., separation through slavery, travel, foreign acculturation/education, drugs, imprisonment, sickness, or any evil force that comes between mother and child or the writer and her world). Dependence on the *dibia/babalawo* (conjurer) to work magically to root out the problem is expedient, as the troubled mind seeks solace in miracles. As these scenarios form motifs in the texts, the writer or her alter ego appears as *ogbanje/abiku,* focusing on the predicament. The writer's courage in exposing a postcolonial malaise separates her from the rest of the conservative female community. With her reputation established through the grapevine, she is treated specially, showered with attention, and almost apotheosized by the appreciative; others see her dissidence as cynical despair.

The *ogbanje/abiku*'s ethereal quality is recognized specifically by the mother; she also occasionally glimpses the earthiness. As we have seen, this seesaw existence, with its many dizzying manifestations and expectations involving the mother, extends to a support system within the community at large. Since the ritual performed by the *dibia/babalawo* to make the child stay is public rather than private, the community has a crucial part to play and has a vested interest in the outcome. One can liken the involvement to a conference on the literary writer: the exorcism provides an occasion to criticize, affirm, direct, and encourage, thereby demonstrating the importance of the celebrant to the community. Cessation of the *ogbanje/abiku* state is manifested in ambiguity rather than in clarity of vision, an open-endedness fancied by some writers who see life as complex figurations with no pat answers.

By referring to Okigbo as *ogbanje,* Acholonu explores this aspect of the writer's work quite convincingly. Okigbo immolates the writer in him, to affirm his ideological rebellion against an intolerable government. That rebellion takes the form of participating in a civil war; his involvement ends with the poetry of his untimely death, while his written poetry lives on to speak for him. Such an analysis can be extended to the women writers, who, in their intimacy with their own children, rebel against the pain of child loss, the lack of fulfillment in child bearing and the condition of woman. Interchanging the contradictory roles of the mother and the *ogbanje/abiku,* the victim and the victimizer, enriches the writing. The woman writer's commitment to writing is charged with unusual stress and pain, since her politics is more complex and her future more uncertain than those of her male counterpart.

Just as the mother somehow survives the anxiety of her untenable position in a culture that values children and just as she is invalidated by her *ogbanje/abiku* child, so the woman writer endures the mixed reception accorded her work. The anguish of mother and child during and after parturition is an abbreviated statement of the pain of the Nigerian condition. The woman's current cry echoes the past, punctuating the fresh horror of the *ogbanje/abiku's* imminent departure from an unchanging miasma of wretchedness. By depicting the hardships women bear, the writer captures the agony of this terrible place that fosters many partings. The text becomes almost reassuring, an ideal way that a woman wants her child to be, in the circumstances—something textually frozen yet linked with her and bearing her stamp of authenticity. Even if it has a mind and life of its own, its precarious existence confirms the horrors of third worldism, without giving up all hope.

The beleaguered writer must occasionally be radical, like the *ogbanje/abiku,* refusing to accept the status quo to get to the bottom of things. "To be radical?" quotes Alice Jardine, "It's the power to criticize even when it's not the right moment" (1985, 260). In the Nigerian context, there is never a right moment. Radicalism is the courage to raise palava in spite of the fact that men will either remain silent or treat the issues derisively, their ploys for retaining male advantages. For the writer as *ogbanje/abiku,* it is the ability to say "no" to demeaning aspects of third-world life, as manifested in its poverty, whether or not those who contribute to the terrible situation are occasional allies—particularly white women or black men, in an international context. These allies cannot always be relied on to determine the agenda, for the very obvious reasons of their conflict of interest. In the turmoil, the mother/author emerges as the jinxed care giver, hardly effective in her no-win situation. For the critic of a text or of life or of a life, there can never be a right moment to register one's discontentment; relief comes from having performed a maternal duty in pinpointing lapses to ensure development.

Unacknowledged interdependency in the colonial predicament is one such bewildering area. The postcolonial quandary, which corresponds to the aftermath of slavery; the post/colonial subject; the prisoner; the black woman; and the person discriminated against are variously constituted by racism, sexism, and technologism. The conflation of these abject conditions is skillfully handled in Emecheta's oeuvre, and with the utmost clarity in *The Slave Girl, The Joys of Motherhood, Destination Biafra,* and *Kehinde.* In *The Slave Girl,* though Ogbanje Ojebeta, the heroine, develops into a woman, she remains confined in the role of the titular girl, who is orphaned, enslaved, married, and continues her tedious life in a country sliding into colonialism without people being conscious of it. Yet, to survive as a colony, a slave, or a woman entails tremendous exertion of effort; extending this to turn the oppressive situation around is almost miraculous. Though the oppressor depends on the victim's output of energy for his comfortable existence, he exerts great pressure to keep this fact unarticulated. Instead, he constantly makes it known, and he is believed, that the slave depends on the master, the woman on the man, the mother on having a child, the colonized on the colonizer. He draws sharp lines to enable him to polarize, his construction an agency for control. However, the demarcations are occasionally blurred, and positions are constantly being modified in a play of mutual interdependency for resistance is inevitable.

In the *ogbanje/abiku* complex, the mother is inexorably drawn to the position of her troubling child. Sullen and silent, both are embroiled in a destiny that controls them. They are pawns in an endless game whose rules they once knew or vaguely know. The distractive *ogbanje/abiku* is charismatic, a reincarnation of a predecessor, and part of a chain of discontented spirits looking for a livable existence. S/he is palava, without which life would be dull and without any progress. S/he comments on the inhospitable Nigerian environment, hostile for children, women, and others handicapped in numerous ways. The *ogbanje/abiku* jolts the community into action, just as the woman's text unsettles readers, driving them from complacency to anxiety, forcing them to confront the evil that spirits children from their beloved parent or prevents the underclass and underprivileged from experiencing contentment as mothers, as people.

Sometimes woman does derive joy from her children, as we shall see in the next section. However, the *sweet* mother usually coexists in the *bitter* wife, splitting woman's personality. With women outliving their husbands, the widow soon experiences a life gone *sour,* as she is usually accused of causing her husband's demise. If she is fortunate enough to survive the travails of widowhood or lives long enough to be acknowledged, she emerges seasoned, and earns her own *salt.* The mystical power that had enabled her to escape being consumed after being tasted/tested, as is the destiny of woman, and then to outlive her exploiters, earns the older woman the respect and authority grudgingly bestowed on her. She is the mother par excellence.

A Taste of Women in Nigeria: The Sweet Mother, the Bitter Wife, the Sour Widow, the Salt of the Earth

Though the *ogbanje/abiku* phenomenon is commonplace, women allocate quality time to revel in the joys of motherhood. For example, in celebrating the birth and development of the *dada* and twins, the Yoruba provide emotionally enriching moments for the mother and her children. *Dada* is the special child whose hair snarls into dreadlocks, in spite of its being combed. Sango, the awful *orisa* of thunder, is renowned for his dreadlocks, making it imperative for his male devotees to mimic him by braiding their hair. He is the patron of the *dada*. The magical power lurking in the *dada*'s locks, comparable to the biblical Samson's, deters people from casually touching such hair; parents dare not cut it without performing prescribed rituals. The tangled hair generates a fertile imagination. It arouses fear in the onlooker (as in the case of the unshorn Mau Mau fighters) and remains a sign of power and a complex fate. When a parent decorates such hair with cowrie shells or coral, she acknowledges the importance of hair in one's destiny. People therefore hold the hair, even that already cut, as something sacred, since the enemy can psychologically incapacitate its owner through the occult use of discarded or harshly managed hair. As hair emanates mysteriously from within, women have learned from Osun to dispose of it carefully, just as the women writers, more often than not, tactfully unveil their inspirational material to circumvent hairsplitters.

Ibeji, "twins," and *iyabeji*, "mother of twins," are equally regarded with awe. Reputed to have the highest twin rate in the world, with one set of twins for every forty births, the Yoruba revere twins (Halliburton and Canady 1994, 106). The first twin to emerge is Taiwo, the second, Kehinde, and these names are not gender specific. In Yoruba cosmic thinking, Taiwo is considered the pathfinder, sent ahead by Kehinde to examine the world. For this spiritedness, some regard Taiwo as superior to Kehinde, the one who brings up the rear. For being circumspect, others consider Kehinde worthier. Because of their unusualness, and to ensure that they stay, the *babalawo* usually prescribes that the *iyabeji* go begging. This ritual eliminates all hostile spirits, while making provisions for the family, since people are very supportive of the dancing *iyabeji*, admiring and praying for her and her twins. The general aura of goodwill energizes and empowers them. To reciprocate, *iyabeji* often celebrates with ritual *saara*, offering children dishes made of cowpeas/black eye peas, such as *moin-moin, akara,* and boiled beans with stew as the pièces de résistance, because beans are the twins' favorite food. Children love and envy twins for being a constant source for mouth-watering *saara* get-togethers. Twinhood is, therefore, intriguing: it gives rise to conjectures about their duality, mystical power, clear sightedness, and charmed existence. Thus, it is foolhardy to cross twins, because it means double trouble.

With the *dada* and twins, the mother basks in the reflected glory of her offspring. She and her children share the joy of playing crucial roles, for being a biological mother remains the most fulfilling aspect of a Nigerian woman's life. I have not yet heard of a Nigerian woman who planned never to bear children, if she has the ability to do so. Without any doubt, as when women and men cooperate, together, twins and the *dada* constitute a formidable force for good. They are always welcome to swell the ranks and strengthen the power of the family.

How then do we reconcile the Nigerian position with Gallop's (1987) assertion in "Reading the Mother Tongue: Psychoanalytic Feminist Criticism" that "the institution of motherhood is a cornerstone of patriarchy" (322)? Nigerian women have obviously not become so radical in their politics as to deny themselves the few joys of motherhood, just to spite patriarchy. In fighting patriarchy, the objective should not be to kill off the species by refusing mothering and motherhood, for the majority of women are still sustained by their closeness to their offspring.

Prince Nico Mbarga captured the intimacy of the mother-child pair when he hit the Nigerian airwaves in 1977, with his tune "Sweet Mother," publicly recognizing woman's ordeal as mother. The tune's unceasing popularity shows that Mbarga touched a cord in this nation of predominantly polygynous households upheld by unsung women. His affirmation of filial love in the words, "I no go forget you . . . for the suffer wey you suffer for me," validates the mother, entrenching, for woman, the ultimate (black)mail—the bitter Nigerian wife must be on her best behavior as mother, for the sake of her child. The nation has also rewarded educated women by structuring into the system fully paid maternity leave before and after parturition. After the resumption of duty, women are also allowed free time, fully paid, to go home to nurse their babies. This makes it easy for the woman to become a "sweet mother."

Ogundipe-Leslie (1987, 6) dissects this female predicament by questioning the stereotype with its insistent conformism to have children without complaining. She would efface "the figure of the 'sweet mother,' the all-accepting creature of fecundity and self-sacrifice." If this were possible, the uncelebrated, childless wife, one of the most embittered of all women, would have a happier place. At the initial stage of reshaping Nigerian women's politics, however, it appears strategically unwise to adopt a Western feminist attitude toward the mother by casting out woman's only means to power, no matter how limiting. Abena Busia (1988, 9) reminds us of the indispensable role of the mother: "In matrilineal societies, the mother is the key to the political, spiritual, and even economic foundations of the society—a fact which has implications beyond the individual or even the family, and extends itself to the cohesion and survival of the group." The importance of the mother is clearly not limited to matrilineal cultures, for, in the polygynous, woman is forced willy-nilly to head her own unit for communal good.

The ensuing bond in the Igbo *umu nne* (the children of one mother) is stronger than that of *umu nna* (the children of one father) who did not suckle the same breast, the symbol of affection and loyalty to the mother. Filomina Chioma Steady (1981, 7) couches the idea somewhat differently: "The bond between the mother and child surpassed all other human bonds and transcended patrilineal rules of descent." Unfortunately, this bond displaces her as wife, as a persona, in the patriarchal community.

Thus, a daughter is considered an extension of her paternal grandmother rather than of her own mother.[20] This attitude encourages man to revere his mother and to love his daughter in a biological connection that excludes his wife, the focus of the male-female struggle. This explains the husband's aloofness toward the wife and creates the silent, invisible wife. The double vision of woman as loving mother and hateful wife is a contradiction that women must sort out in the palaver. She must move from the backyard or the outhouse, where traditional architecture confines her, to the front, in an effort to be herself in her own right; the easiest route forward appears to be education, as educated women are among the most recognized in the country.

Nigeria has conditioned women not to complain about the burden of mothering, lest they be considered unnatural or, worse still, lose their children because of a negative attitude about what should be considered a blessing. In some cultures one does not count the number of children a woman has, lest they die. Emecheta circumvents such limitations by addressing the issue of excessive births that perpetuate poverty or helplessness. Her Nnu Ego, fighting a

---

20. The Yoruba name a daughter born shortly after the death of a paternal grandmother Iyabo, Iyamide, Yetunde, Yejide, or Yewande (Mother has returned), and a son born shortly after the death of a paternal (grand)father Babatunde or Babajide (Father has returned). The mother's family tree never features in the naming ceremony, since it is uprooted by marriage.

losing battle with her seven surviving children, is an exceptional character whose numerous children destroy her, providing a sharp contrast to the more plausible Nigerian story whose heroine, the indefatigable Emecheta herself, triumphs though her husband abandons her with five children in London.

The been-to Emecheta, much more anglicized than the other writers, might agree with Dorothy Dinnerstein (1976, 21) that the female problem "has limited their opportunity . . . to contribute to those aspects of the growth of our species' cumulatively pooled achievement that change the gross, overt shape of our shared reality: to make history." Though this observation depends on a limited view of history that excludes the essential factor of reproduction, the validity of daily experience, and the contribution of ordinary people, its political thrust is clear. Women in Nigeria possess the will, and some have acquired the entrepreneurial skills, to collaborate with men to make "history." Those involved in modern leadership roles are too few, an unfortunate situation that the literary texts have thrust into our consciousness. Women need education to mobilize, fill in the numerous gaps available in an evolving society, and then slide into public roles, one hopes, to provide an anodyne in the society.

The view from the home reveals men as dependent, needing women's services, which older mothers ensure that they receive by monitoring wives. In the contemporary international scene, woman appears, "mothering men, whose weakness makes her feel strong, or mothering in the role of teacher, doctor, political activist, psychotherapist" (Rich 1977, 246). Nigerian women have to take advantage of their numbers in order to expand their areas of influence. For example, women can efficiently handle education (not only teaching but other vital aspects of the industry), become efficient health care managers, be informed about their role in the economy, and be actively engaged in diplomacy not only as ambassadors' wives. The mobilization of rural women for progress should not depend solely on Dodan Barracks or Aso Rock, the presidential manor; it should be a female desire. It should be entrenched in a female, cooperative system depending on constant sororal interaction and support, as traditionally practiced and as we see displayed among the women in crisis in Emecheta's *Destination Biafra*. Female extension workers who already live or are willing to live in the rural areas can serve as role models of how women can structure their immense energies to enhance productivity and societal development.

Nancy Chodorow, the object-relations theorist, and Dinnerstein postulate that if mothering is not left as the exclusive preserve of women, that is, if men and women participate equally in parenting, the female psyche will begin to change so that women will not necessarily feel and receive psychological gratification from mothering or single parenting as they do now. In their vision, the ideal society will provide a situation where mothering is not thrust on or left solely to women in the public and private spheres, but men and women will share the duties and pleasures of parenting to create a more psychologically balanced society. This will release women for other spheres of activity beyond mothering. For the Nigerian woman this is debatable. At the state she is in now, she would prefer to be given the wherewithal to make her parenting successful and empowering rather than have man share the parenting, eroding the space that gives her authority. Chodorow's and Dinnerstein's theories fail to tackle the harrowing problem of incest, which arises from unhealthy intimacy between father and daughter in the confining nuclear family—not to mention child sexual molestation in the school system. No Nigerian woman would want such horrors to proliferate, aggravating our already precarious national situation.

Moreover, since the Nigerian mother shares mothering with other women, her attitude toward parenting is radically different from that of her Western counterpart. The hot climate reduces the daily burden considerably. Her skill in using her simple technology of strapping the child to her back with the *lappa* frees her to go about her business while the child is secure. Once a child is out of the woman's body, like a text in the public domain, the child/text ceases to be the special preserve of the mother/writer and becomes a "property" in the public domain. Therefore, the Nigerian woman does not mind parenting; in fact, she looks forward to it as something meaningful in a very harsh world. Furthermore, she hardly ever parents single-handedly, even in the big cities. Her support network—which consists of her mothers (mother, grandmother, aunts, sisters, mothers-in-law, and women-in-law), friends, co-wives (either in her polygynous household or in the extended family), maids and children old enough to participate in communal parenting—is so broadly based and works so satisfactorily that male help would be considered intrusive.

The preoccupation of the writers with mothering and motherhood is in consonance with a deeply felt need by Nigerian women. Fulfillment lies in having a viable career to sustain the primary role of motherhood, to ensure that all is well with the family. This contrasts with Alice Jardine's Western feminist cynicism about women's salvational role in the final epigraph to this chapter. Now that the family and country are a shambles, many Nigerian women, as mothers and daughters, see themselves as an important part of the rehabilitative process. They have traditionally been involved in the remediation of behavioral problems in the family and community because of their high investment in their children. Unfortunately, many of them do not understand the international ramifications of the current system, hence their failure to grapple with it effectively.

On the one hand, Nigerians deny the constraints of motherhood, counting on divine intervention to facilitate child rearing. Motherhood is envisaged as a source of joy and fulfillment to women. Some proverbs, on the other hand, emphasize its tedium. Taking off from where Nwapa ended *Efuru*, Emecheta queries the facile assumptions of contentment in *The Joys of Motherhood*, where she examines the burdens of motherhood. Living in isolation in England with the task of raising five children single-handedly, she had firsthand knowledge of the hardships of motherhood without the support system built into parenting in Nigeria. Exile is the hard mother who disciplined Emecheta. From this harsh experience, she sees motherhood as a burden, in a way a woman living in Nigeria does not. Emecheta foregrounds her views on motherhood by underscoring the Yoruba philosophy about children and/or parenting. The no-win paradox is cryptically expressed in the proverbial *Omo bibi, ejo, aini, oran,* "Childbearing is palavering, childlessness, tragic." Parenthood/nonparenthood evokes word power, instituting discourse. This knowledge drives the Nigerian woman to want children so as not to be left out of the sites of power. The child can therefore be said to be the Nigerian woman's destiny. In this catch-22 situation, to be a mother or not to be a mother is not even the question, since every woman, childless or not, seems determined to raise children and nurture people. The problem is this: How are the women to care for all the people?

Coming from a predominantly oral culture where the text is aural rather than visible, where children belong to the community with the mother as one of the caretakers, where a woman refers to other people's children as "my children," it is interesting to hear Emecheta talk possessively about her books as her children, angrily personalizing hostile reception. The practice of copyrighting stories and books, referring to them as one's children, and also claiming real children as one's own stems from a Western anxiety for possession and individuation. It differs from the anonymity of orature, with the storyteller acting as a medium, transmitting the story, which is part of the public repertoire. No woman is an island with her child, though each child knows her/his mothers. Although Western feminist theorists have long equated the labor of producing the text with that of the child, it was Emecheta who introduced the idea into the Nigerian equation, thereby emphasizing the woman writer's role as Big Mother in contemporary Nigeria.

The woman writer as Big Mother is altruistic. According to Chodorow, "On one psychological level, all people who have experienced primary love and primary identification have some aspect of self that wants to recreate these experiences, and most people try to do so. Freud talks about the turn to religion as an attempt to recreate the lost feeling of oneness" (1978, 79). The writer/ mother wants to replicate her own personal success at the individual and familial levels on a national scale, using her novel as a medium for palavering, as prophecy. The traditional recourse in crisis to the omniscient *Ifa/Afa,* for example, or propitiating one's *Ori/Chi,* and the current urban religious frenzy with its born-againism and speaking in tongues are manifestations of what W. R. D. Fairbairn referred to, in a different context, as "infantile dependence" (Chodorow 1978, 59). The hard times of economic depression lead to desperation—overt religiosity centers on the collective search for a public mother to make things right.

In a move ostensibly to improve the quality of life by controlling the population explosion, President Babangida proposed that each woman should have no more than four children. Significantly, he did not limit the number of children each man could father. Radical women were irate at the insidious attempt to institutionalize male irresponsibility, or increase the Muslim population, since each Muslim can marry up to four wives. By focusing on the woman, Babangida unwittingly recognized her as head of the nuclear unit that, in Nigerian terms, comprises a woman and her offspring. He was trying to limit its size to the number he felt a woman can conveniently fend for. In affirming mothering by indirectly freeing men from responsibility for their children, he was, in effect, providing the coffin for the family already in its death throes in many urban centers. Shortsighted men, seeing only the immediate benefits of legally hopping from one woman's bed to another, approved.

The sophisticated Yoruba woman has traditionally limited herself to the number of children she can care for. The Igbo woman is yet to follow, taken in by the rewards she receives in recognition of her role as a baby factory, particularly if there are many sons to show for her industry. Institutionalized polygyny in Islam and in society at large has taught the Yoruba woman a lesson that her Christian Igbo counterpart must learn.

The Igbo woman has also been "protected" from being trifled with by high bride prices.[21] The decadent, cosmopolitan centers might change all that, es-

21. The feminist finds the payment of bride price, particularly a high bride price, objectionable. According to this view, bride price turns woman into a commodity, making her her husband's property. However, the bride price is not mere monetary exchange in the marketplace, but a ritual that legitimizes a union. Ability to provide the bride price is a sign of maturity and readiness for marriage. The hardship of saving up for the bride price can prevent a man from frivolously abandoning his wife, as he can hardly afford the expense of marrying another woman, and it

pecially with the Western feminist insistence on abolishing the bride price, misread as a sign of the wife as commodity "bought" by the husband. Abolition of this important ritual gives men easy access to women, erasing a ceremony that seals the marriage contract between two extended families-in-law and therefore makes women more respected—not "picked off the streets," as some men now refer to the idea of "free" women in heated quarrels with their "wives." No African woman has questioned the money involved in the parallel, but more expensive, exchange with the Western man giving his woman a diamond engagement ring for her devotion; after all, "diamonds are a girl's best friend." The "girl" with her portable property never gives a thought to the Sierra Leonean or southern African woman who is deprived of her mate: his work in the mines partly enables her Western counterpart to romantically celebrate a ritual that ensures but glosses over financial security. Feminist insensitivity to these cultural differences and their fallout in economics and psychology when formulating an international women's agenda continues to be a cause for alarm.

Western political and literary influence on the writer is inevitable, in spite of these differences. Claire Kahane (1985) informs us that "dead or displaced mothers" are common in the "gothic" (335). Dead or absent mothers proliferate Nigerian texts, but they do not make them gothic. Rather, the mother's absence or death or displacement signifies the absence of Nigerian literary foremothers, while surrogate mothers occasionally stand for foreign influence. Orphaned by a switch from the oral-aural medium, with its immediate audience-teller reciprocity, to the scribal medium, with its delayed, critical response, the author mourns her mother's death, the rupture in her literary heritage; when ancestral connections are maintained, however, they aid the child, a magical phenomenon which contributes to the development of juju fiction.

This death or absence also represents the vacuum created in public life by the fact that not as many women as men are educated. Educational imbalance, with its misogynist implications, was once more thrust in our face when the composers of the latest national anthem demonstrated their total disregard for

---

seems to stabilize the Igbo marriage. With the Yoruba, the bride price has become a token in memory of *Iya Iwo*, the suffering endured by an ancestor in securing a wife among the Iwo people. A wife is now known as *Iyawo* (a contraction of *Iya Iwo*), retaining the mixed emotions involved in newness, suffering, and subjugation. As if in penance for that ancestral suffering, the *Iyawo*, that is the "small"/junior/new wife is totally disfranchised under the senior wife, the *Iyale*—the mother of the house. Addressing a woman as *Iyawo* can be used by the family to distance her and keep her alienated in her marital home, just as it can be used as a term of endearment.

women by masculinizing the verses.[22] Its subtext underscores the philosophy of the military-industrial complex. Without meaning to, it elicits negative vibrations that estrange pacifists and the majority of women. Since many Nigerians come from polygynous homes and consequently have more fond feelings for their mothers than their fathers, attempting to formulate a national consciousness with a call to support the fatherland appears to be a futile exercise. It is as incongruous as it was to expect the Nigerian Airways to fly efficiently with the elephant as its emblem. Perhaps, the anthem writers were unconsciously expressing the Nigerian dilemma, which closely resembles the tensions of a polygynous household.

Contemporary polygynous practice is one of Nigeria's intractable gender issues, breeding low self-esteem among some women. Steady (1981, 6) plays down its negative aspects, particularly the occasionally murderous rivalries among women, when she declares, "Polygamy . . . also facilitated the shared mothering of children and guaranteed women some autonomy, personal freedom, and greater mobility than would be possible in a monogamous, nuclear family. Women had more time to themselves, developed strong bonds with other women, and experienced a more limited, rather than absolute, form of patriarchy." This observation has become dated. Conscious of its inequities, the new Nigerian woman, especially the educated one, has begun to subvert

---

22. A verse of the national anthem will prove the point:

> Arise, O compatriots,
> Nigeria's call obey.
> To serve our *fatherland*
> With love and strength and faith.
> The labours of our *heroes* past
> Shall never be in vain;
> To serve with heart and might,
> One nation bound in freedom,
> Peace and unity.
> (emphasis added)

The fact that the countries in Africa were artificially created by European men scrambling for landed property and bequeathed to African men at independence is problematic. The situation becomes more complicated as men refer to each country as fatherland rather than motherland, while Africa is considered the motherland by writers and blacks in the diaspora. In a place with polygynous households, like Nigeria, the notion of a fatherland (bequeathed by the British Lord Lugard) creates emotional stress. It engenders disloyalty to the nation, even civil war (Nigeria and Liberia are both good examples), as the men tend to be more loyal and tender to their mothers than to their fathers, not to mention foreign ones. Since Africa belongs to all, the continent suffers from benign neglect, and unity is difficult to foster, because there is only a vague sense of belonging together—unlike the situation when giants like Kwame Nkrumah were still alive.

polygyny by becoming polygamous herself. She lives with her children, away from her husband, or rather, her children's father, who has access to them. With such an arrangement, she has her own space and the advantages of marriage, while escaping co-wifely rivalry and the tedium of keeping house for the man and his numerous relations. What this means for the structure of the Nigerian family is yet to be seen (see Wambui wa Karanja 1987). In many urban households, with their space shortage, polygyny no longer possesses its former resilience. Not only has it lost the spirit that previously made it work, women's growing discontent with its incongruities and male anxiety about controlling wives will ultimately destroy it.

The gap between men's veneration of their old mothers and the spite and distrust with which the same adoring men treat the younger women who are their wives and the mothers of their children causes rifts in gender and marital relationships. Misogyny has become so alarmingly pervasive that the contemporary woman has countered by becoming tough. She expects little fulfillment in marriage, which has become an enervating war front with the wife treated as an intimate outsider or the enemy within.

Economic austerity has compounded the condition of the Nigerian family, rendering it more dysfunctional. Chaos and decadence produced the need for an ethical revolution in the 1980s. Sponsored by people who were themselves unethical, the revolution failed to root out dishonor, greed, violence, and crime, all of which plague the nation and spill beyond its borders to create an embarrassing image of the country abroad. If unchecked, this country of about 100 million people will eventually be undone, and over half of that population—rural and urban women and their children—will become further endangered. Nigeria's demonic *ogbanje* spirit, ever changing with the rapidity of the newsreel, must be exorcised before it makes irrevocable inroads into the female consciousness. As women have to fend for their families, particularly their children, they bear the brunt of cruel governments, notorious for institutionalizing widespread corruption and mismanagement. With the economy in disarray, many husbands abandon their families physically and/or emotionally. This partly accounts for the predominance of women as patients to the *dibia/babalawo* and the *woli;* it also explains women's soaring membership of Evangelical and Pentecostal churches. Speaking in tongues, with or without interpretation, is commonplace, though it is more mystifying than unraveling traditional oracular conundrum. Time and hindsight invariably serve as interpreters and teachers. The harsh facts of vestigial colonialism, neocolonialism, mismanaged independence, failed democracy, the civil war, the oil boom, military misrule, acquisition of instant wealth without accountability, and the debt culture, with its inevitable economic depression, have taken their toll on women.[23] Each hardened face confirms the insecurities of a harried life.

Husbands are hard put to help out their wives. They refuse to buy into that Western import, romantic love, while they no longer accord their wives customary respect as the mothers of their children, who in turn will venerate their mothers. Men pass on to their growing sons a model of disrespect to wives as machismo, thereby perpetuating female oppression. The age gap between husband and wife, sometimes generational, partly accounts for the lack of respect for the wife in a culture where age usually goes with authority. In some cultures—the Yoruba and the Edo, for example—the fact that a wife kneels before her husband or his kinsmen, and dares not call them by name, already puts her in her place. Operating under a harsh patriarchal lore, she must construct a matricenter for recuperative purposes to insure self-esteem and lifelong intimacy with her children. The power in motherhood is truly vested in the old mother who, understandably, wields her influence in her son's household when it is her time. Young mothers, as wives, are bereft of any meaningful power at their prime when they most need it. The saving grace is that the abused wife might be some man's cherished mother, sister, aunt, or daughter.

Like the Igbo, the Yoruba father can refer to his daughter as *Mother* with aplomb. As Niara Sudarkasa noted, "Among the Yoruba [and the Igbo, too], a woman refers to her own spouse, and in certain contexts, to his lineage members, including her own children, as 'husband'" (1987, 31). Thus, woman deprecates herself as wife, unconsciously ingratiating herself in numerous relationships by holding up the male as husband. It is interesting that woman refers to her son not as *Father*, but as *oko mi*, "my husband," causing an American student of mine to remark, irreverently as I thought, that the Yoruba woman must be blamed for the Oedipus complex. This misreading of the Oedipal arises from a literal rather than a figurative reading, because if there is an incestuous element, it is then not limited to the son. The potential preciousness of a husband is rarely manifested in reality; the wife grapples with the bitter disappointment at this turn of events by using "husband" as a term of endearment, as something unattainable. Ironically, she rarely uses the term for the putative husband and his kin, except in flattery, to achieve some

23. Gita Sen, the Indian scholar, facetiously dealt with this problem from a woman's point of view in a talk given at the Women's Research and Documentation Center, University of Ibadan, Nigeria, in April 1988. According to her, third-world women keep hearing about debts and have no clue how they were accrued or what was done with the borrowed money, the sin for which women now have to pay a horribly drawn-out atonement.

goal. The woman can playfully control her son-husband in a way she cannot influence the kin-in-law. Mother and son collaborate to resist the brutal husband(s), for her son's presence in the household assures her of a place; hence the importance of sons as allies who never leave the homestead to marry, as most daughters invariably do. In-lawism implies that a mother goes to her daughter's house typically to serve (as when her daughter has a baby), but goes to her son's house to be served by her daughter-in-law.

The phenomenon of the departing-returning father is therefore troubling.[24] The hapless wife accepts the challenge to fend for herself and for her children as society demands. The sons who suffered with their mothers unconscionably replay the roles of their disreputable fathers. It is not surprising that national governments are like the fathers; they appear and disappear, neither caring for the people nor providing them with the wherewithal to make life viable. In the confusion, woman provides the subsistent living she can afford. The writer expresses this hardship as a form of anxiety by the mother, for example, Emecheta's Nnu Ego, lest her sons also abandon her or fail to appreciate her effort.

Part of the coping strategy of the new Nigerian woman is to deliberately rid herself of the husband. She would disagree with Key on the uses and misuses of men: "Key deplored the inclination of some women simply to use men as impregnators, both to have children without the patriarchal trappings and to avenge men's age-old sexual abuse of women" (Register 1982, 607). The modern, educated woman would part company with Key, because, at this point, she sounds quaintly Victorian. The breakdown of the polygynous system and the dichotomous male-female expectations in monogamous marriages have toughened the urban woman. The new Nigerian woman has learned a great deal from witnessing the harshness of men's treatment of her mothers. She has also learned from the customary court system that women are rebelling: for example, many Ibadan women recklessly mimic men by practicing serial monogamy, bigamy, or polyandry, with the offspring mortified by the claims and counterclaims of kinship among the vying fathers.

The fundamental revision of the Nigerian constitution asserting that no child is "illegitimate" has freed women from the stigma of having children without "fathers." The single or unmarried mother, with the usual extended family support system, has therefore become a feature of the urban setting,

---

24. Man disappears, not in the Western sense of going to work, but in the trickster's sense of flying away from seemingly insoluble child-raising problems. He invariably returns, with his extended family and friends, to claim kin with its numerous benefits, when the children are grown and responsibility for them is over.

catching the government off guard. Since the original impulse in liberating all children was for those in power to protect the children they recklessly father out of wedlock, little did they know that women also would take advantage of the opportunity to free themselves from sexist males. The new, single mother is merely actualizing, sophisticatedly, the situation of the rural wife in a polygynous household. This urban woman seizes the advantage of not having to attend to obnoxious or demanding relatives-in-law, for the wife a bewildering and benumbing feature of Nigerian marriage. The new development, besides breeding promiscuity, will further widen the existing gap between roving husbands and exploited wives whose "legitimate" children will now have to share their patrimony with their "outside" siblings.

In the past, women generally accepted polygyny, as it enhanced female bonding, sometimes to the detriment of the male, as Steady has noted. With Western impact and the change in economic productivity, women resent and increasingly undermine it for greater liberating goals, for the equation of one husband to two or more wives rankles, and, from the economic perspective, the husband can no longer easily play the role of the lord, distributing largesse to his obedient wives. The writers, especially Emecheta and Nwapa, depict the practice as retrogressive, something to be obliterated from all religions and societal spheres, if Nigeria is to advance with genuine female contentment and commitment.[25]

Marriage is regarded by the Igbo as *ije di,* "a journey to the husband," undertaken by each wife. The quest involves the inevitable departure from home; the painful existence in a vast, unknown world peopled by those to be served; overcoming (or failing to overcome) the difficulties in the new environment; and arriving at the end, which might turn sour or culminate in happiness, tolerance, death, or a deplorable return to the natal home. Thus, marriage is an adventure fraught with danger and rewarded with little pleasure. Marrying a foreigner, like living in exile, is considered *ibu,* "an onerous burden," borne without the relief of ever putting it down; hence the wariness in giving daughters in marriage to strangers or to people who live far away. Responsible families want to monitor their daughters' welfare, for a daughter married to a man who batters her can be defended by her male kin, who retaliate by beating the man up.

For woman, a gap exists in the glorification of the older woman as mother,

25. It is noteworthy that Muslims in Arabic states rarely practice polygyny, because of men's inability to provide equally for several wives or for husbands to keep Mohammed's injunction to love the women without showing any partiality.

exhausted from overwork and anxiety, and the hatred reserved for the younger woman as wife, destined to take her place. That inexplicable hostility toward the wife was once again demonstrated in 1988, in the case of the northern child bride, the late Hauwa. Seeking freedom from the shackles of patriarchal marriage, Hauwa unwittingly endangered her life by constantly running from her tyrannous husband to her uncaring father, who always promptly sent her back to her marital home. Fed up with her defiance of his authority, her incensed husband chopped off one errant foot to teach her a lesson. Since her father did not protect her, he was named an accomplice to her murderer. Interestingly, her mother did not feature in the drama, partially recorded on the pages of Nigerian newspapers with all the gory details. Many men could not decipher the new handwriting on the wall until Women in Nigeria (WIN), the group of radicals fighting for women's rights, took up her case in the courts. The wholesome tradition of battered women being rescued or avenged by their male relatives has been ineffectively replaced by the disrespected police who, conveniently, have no jurisdiction over marital disputes. Literate women must openly acknowledge their illiterate sisters on their crippled walk toward full independence.

Women find the marital discord so painfully baffling that it must be tackled for psychic health. Most of the writers register their resistance by retaining their maiden names, legitimizing themselves as daughters rather than wives—Nwapa, Emecheta, Ulasi, and Fakunle are examples.[26] Eno Obong goes further, in her rejection of a masculine surname, marital or paternal. She split her given name into two, as if to protest against disenchanting wifehood while resisting the all powerful father whose name also defines his daughter.

Childbirth, menstruation, adultery, or mourning, which entail *idi na nso,* "to be tabooed," are occasions when it is forbidden for a woman to have dealings with men, especially her husband, and sometimes her children. Society uses these occasions to keep women away from meaningful intercourse with men, particularly the elderly and *dibia,* in different religions (including some Christian sects) and rural cultures. For reintegration, a cleansing ritual, minor or major, depending on the gravity of the situation, usually follows. *I ju na omugo* (cleansing after childbirth), *i wu cha* (after menstruation or mourning), and *i sia ishi* (public confession by women after adultery) are necessary

26. It is curious that Nwapa, Emecheta, Ulasi, and Fakunle all use their maiden names in writing. It seems that their attitude is a self-defending phenomenon. The father, though patriarchal, now old or dead, provides a sense of belonging and is more tolerable than the more virile, pain-inflicting husband.

rituals in Igbo villages and towns, after which the woman can once again openly join the community. Man's innate fear of woman's blood, with its magical possibilities, and his perception of his wife as sexually threatening are partly responsible for such excommunication. No matter the circumstances surrounding a man's death, the young widow or the widow without sons is usually assumed to have "killed" her husband, particularly if he died young. Once presumed guilty, she is rarely proved innocent; she ends up in deep trouble with her relatives by marriage. She is confined, to punish her and to prevent her from wreaking further havoc.

The proximity of the woman's natal family is sometimes advantageous when the marriage ends with the untimely death of the husband or in the event that the woman has no sons for him. In many Nigerian cultures the most humiliating treatment is reserved for widows, and older women-in-law make sure that every demeaning feature is carried out. The least offensive is the insistence on shaving the widow's hair as part of the obsequies. Many cultures force the widow to drink the water used to wash the corpse; adverse reaction implies that she had a hand in his death. Confined in unhygienic surroundings, the old women monitor the food and water grudgingly provided for the widow. The period of mourning is turned into punishment for the widow, as if they are angry with her for daring to survive their son. They are gratified to see the widow, hair shorn and looking forlorn: they have got the young woman where they want her. Poverty necessitates levirate, since customary law deters the widow from inheriting her husband's property. Literate or illiterate, nobody considers a wife as her husband's next-of-kin; the legal ramifications stem from this dissociation.

As I mentioned earlier, a husband's death at an early age is a cause for constant censure of his widow. No matter the cause of death, she is invariably regarded as a malevolent force who killed off her spouse in order to be free. They might be right, if we examine marriage from the woman's viewpoint. Since marriage is the greatest hoax perpetrated on many women, it will not be surprising if woman's secret desire is for poetic justice: to end her harrowing experience with the archvillain dead. The few widows who manage to escape excessive trauma and retain some dignity to mourn the dear departed are usually educated, rich, or have grown sons in a position to protect their mother. Even then, the predicament of such women never can be as easy or as legally straightforward as that of their Western counterparts.

In spite of these limitations, custom still grants women some rights. Women can "war" on an obnoxious man by invading his house in a concerted effort to force him to change his ways. A sit-down strike in his home or "satirical singing and dancing" (Van Allen 1976, 68) effectively break a cruel sexist, putting him on notice that he is under close scrutiny. Elechi Amadi explores that power of rural women in his 1986 novel *Estrangement*. The reformative agenda of the women writers necessitates that they play down the exercise of women's power.

Female power ultimately lies in postmenopausal women, the salt of the earth. These are usually seasoned veterans, respected out of fear of their mystical power or the spiritual agency that enabled them to survive the hardships of life as a woman. And they should be feared, for mostly the tough do thrive with their children, amid the tribulations of daily existence. Despite this female potential, the missing factor for women's contemporary politics is the lack of solidarity among women. The older woman can act sadistically toward the younger woman grappling with perennial female hardships. Indeed, it is usually the old woman who polices other women, and complicates life for them, instead of using her power to fight for female liberty. To break the cycle, old women must be recruited and reeducated by radical women, to establish a new world order among women. Also, young women must participate in the process to prevent them from later venting their anger on other women.

The old woman reinforces her power by accessing spiritual forces: the *dibia/babalawo*, or herbalist, with his medicines and palliative rituals; the juju used to ward off evil or to attack the enemy; the prophecy, obtained from indigenous divination sources such as the *Afa* (Igbo) or *Ifa* (Yoruba) and now commonly extended to the Nigerianized services of the church "visioner," or the Muslim Imam with his divining board. These are as necessary and commonplace in our harsh world as the doctor or therapist in the Western. The basic philosophy is that every problem has some solution; the supplicant can interpret that premise as best s/he may. The aim is for the subject to obtain needed emotional support for stress management, to clarify or resolve her predicament. The woman writer, young or postmenopausal, is accessing an identical source of power. Her novel—which one can refer to as juju fiction because of its potential for transformations and instilling self-confidence in its owner, as juju is expected to effect—emanates from this context as a verbal agency for change. Reading and believing it make its tenets be. As men fear the force of women's education in bringing about change, so they fear the juju potential in the novel by women. The problem is how to convince them that change in all mothers is also for men's good and that the energy expended in wife-control is wasted and should be used for more constructive purposes.

However, men do have cause to fear women, because men continue to treat them unjustly. The text as juju is a verbal, talismanic force, crafted to fend off evil by naming and confronting it, as we saw above in many traditional cleansing rituals. Every single novel going to be considered names some evil that Nigerians, especially women, still face. The novel has become the contemporary woman's *ofo*. In a showdown, the *ofo* is the sign of conjuration that identifies the holder as protected and on the path of victory because the cause is just. This is akin to the traditional setting in which Igbo men display their *ikenga* (two hands, or horns), while Yoruba men refer to their contestation as *agbomeji* (two rams battering each other to the death for territory or the ram's horns filled with juju—protective or adversarial potions), symbols of their masculinity and authority. Juju is powerful as a sign, for, at its most potent, it can empower its owner or disempower the adversary; it plays a vital role in establishing justice.

The juju text is necessarily apocalyptic. For closure, writers occasionally endow their victimized characters with juju power as manifested in some mystical agency: Nwapa's Efuru, Ulasi's Olu Agege, Emecheta's Nnu Ego, and Eno Obong's Mayen are a few memorable examples. The efficacy of juju is rarely in doubt; it stands as a metaphor for metamorphosis. People depend on it for inner strength. Juju, as well as the text, are prayers that can be seen and held. Reliance on the metaphysical is psychologically sound, as generations of confused Nigerian women have found. If Nigerian women can explore such power for public good, the country could be a different place. Key had theorized on the potential of a different form of female power. According to Register, "Key's goal, then, was for women to have equal impact on public life without surrendering their special character: 'What private life has taught her, she must now in turn teach the public!'" (1982, 605). Key might have been speaking to the Nigerian situation, because her theory articulates Nigerian women's reaction in a crisis.

Yet some young, literate Nigerian women show no national salvational enthusiasm. Their vicarious enjoyment is derived from Mills and Boon novels, usually written by English women, who lure their female readers into dreaming of a virginal, romantic life, dependent on a handsome, monogamous man who provides financial and emotional security. This boring Eden jarringly contrasts with the stark reality of their Nigerian mothers' lives. In that tie between mothers and daughter, she realizes, as Dinnerstein so dramatically put it, "the prototype of the tie to life. The pain in it, and the fear of being cut off from it, are prototypes of the pain of life and the fear of death" (1976, 34). The young woman must be meaningfully empowered to endure and change her lot in life. As her predecessors, the writers help to ease the pain of her life by capturing it, far removed from the falseness of a Mills and Boon–

ordered existence. Simplistic though it may sound, it needs reiterating that the Nigerian woman's novel must first be made accessible to Nigerians in schools and libraries if it is to have any impact at all.

Nigerians have also benefited from the Senegalese novelist Mariama Ba. Writing and speaking in different tongues as she was, the Nigerian reader needed an interpreter to understand her. Modupe Bode-Thomas performed that function with dispatch, opening up an untapped realm in which a Muslim woman fearlessly critiques Islamic practice as it impacts the educated woman, whom one assumes is privileged. *Une si longue lettre*'s 1980 appearance and *So Long a Letter,* Bode-Thomas's 1981 English translation, were strategic in ushering in a decade in which the I and the self became boldly written into the Nigerian woman's text.

Ba's and Bode-Thomas's concerted effort concretized the vast difference between Nigerian women's writing of the 1960s and 1970s and their writing since the 1980s. The first two decades concentrated on the rural, not only as a geographical place, but also as a character type, whose configurations as illiterate doomed her. The latter decade has made the transformative jump to the urban. Here the writer has firmly established that there are identifiable problems linked with woman, no matter what her status. The new novel marks a shift to the self, and at the center is a new woman (or man) whose agenda corresponds with the writer's: mainly, to engage in controversy by exposing social inequities with the hope that they will be openly discussed for progress.

In the earlier decades, the writer clearly concentrated on the story of her rural parents. Ruralism has its constraints. By straightjacketing illiterate characters into texts that were inaccessible to rural people without the privilege to read or who, if read to, would not understand the foreign language in which the novel was written, the writer was self-defeating, displacing the oral storyteller without effectively replacing her. The writer had shifted storytelling from the intimacy of oral performance (in which the storyteller and her audience have an identical agenda and tell and listen to their very own stories) to the distortion implicated in writing (the advocative role in which the writer tells another's story to an unseen audience, national and international). The role of the writer as a powerful, voluntary advocate is in itself oppressive, for, unfortunately, the agenda of the writer is not always identical to that of the people depicted. Indeed, the writer sometimes indirectly benefits from the oppression of the rural people.

With the 1980s came the pressing need for the writer to tell her own story, the story of the elite women in Nigeria, and to tell it straight in the hope that change at this level will filter down to their rural mothers. (Emecheta had told hers in England, an interesting albeit not quite representative experience.) The timing of *Une si longue lettre* was, therefore, opportune. It helped to smooth the transition from dealing with the analphabetic parents who could not tell their story in book form to the self who could. Writers shifted to concentrate on their sophisticated, urban selves and needs instead of on their parents.

Efuru, speaking for all rural women, regrets her inability to fulfill her aspirations to go to England or to "learn book," as she put it; books which were not written for her or in her language. Ironically, she becomes a book, which could never have been spoken or written by her, nor could she have heard or read it, even if she wanted to. In other words, others can read her, but she can never read herself or acquire self-knowledge through this medium.

Reading as part of Western education is undoubtedly a decisive step in becoming liberated and urbanized. Efuru's fictional daughters and granddaughters are no longer as limited as Efuru. They have England brought to their homes, classrooms, and workplace, and they can make their choices as to what to take or to reject. These fictional daughters serve as alter egos to the writers of the 1980s and 1990s, writing themselves into the texts. Nigerian readers can identify with the product of such imagination with the writer finally writing what she herself would like to read. Where the earlier texts identify the palava, historicizing it, the problem has now become transformed by moving from objectification to characters who speak authoritatively for themselves in a national discourse—the palaver.

Chapter Two
(En)gender(ing) Discourse:
Palaver-Palava and African Womanism

Womanist is to feminist as purple to lavender.
　　　　　　　　Alice Walker, *In Search of Our Mothers' Gardens* (1984)

Male ridicule, aggression and backlash have resulted in making women apolo-
getic and have given the term "feminist" a bad name. Yet, nothing could be
more feminist than the writings of these women writers, in their concern for
and deep understanding of the experiences and fates of women in society.
　　　　　　　　'Molara Ogundipe-Leslie, "The Female Writer" (1987)

The Feminist novel in Africa is not only alive and well, it is, in general, more
radical, even more militant, than its Western counterpart.
　　　　　　　　Katherine Frank, "Women Without Men" (1987)

Just as all family members' resources were needed for the family to be well and
strong, so they were needed for a healthy community/family.
　　　　　　　　Elsa Barkley Brown, "Womanist Consciousness" (1989)

Palavering: Bones of Contention

Palaver, a word in use since 1735 when the fine, diplomatic art of talking
empty talk between Africans and Europeans became institutionalized, is derived from the Portuguese *palavra*. Webster's defines palaver as "a long parley
usually between persons of different levels of culture or sophistication." Even
if they did not let on out of self-pride or self-preservation, Africans learned that
the meaningless discussions were dangerous cat and rat games, used as a
prelude to dazzle and cow them with military, industrial, and, later, technological power. Whiskey and gin eased matters, as Europe palavered its way to
shaping African geopolitics, in order to benefit from the seemingly limitless
economic advantages of owning the continent.[1] Northern shenanigans, espe-

---

1. Vestiges of the brisk European trade in alcoholic drinks were still apparent in Nigeria in the
late 1950s and the 1960s. Brands such as Johnny Walker, other Scottish whiskeys, Gordon's Gin,
Irish stout (which is considered a cure-all for stomach ailments), Heineken, etc., were commonplace, while locally produced *akpeteshi* or *kaikai* became known as "illicit gin," since the British

cially as manifested in Swiss banking, have replaced them in contemporary negotiations, making Switzerland, and other northern countries accomplices to sons-of-the-soil in perpetrating heinous crimes currently crippling Nigeria.

Racism was a denominator in the tedious negotiations culminating in colonialism. The question of gender hardly featured in the deadly, masculine games that were played, and still continue to be played, with the North always emerging victorious, because almost all Nigerians in key positions unwittingly play for the North out of greed to advance their own private, monetary interests. To put it broadly, almost every Nigerian who has palavered with the North in some capacity has emerged from the confrontation browbeaten, a europhone, speaking in the master's voice, as phoney as they come. Nigeria, obviously, offers things the North cannot do without. The North, in turn, undoubtedly has something the Western-educated Nigerian wants, but which s/he has not yet put in place in Nigeria to prevent further aggravation. However, the interdependency remains unnoticed.

Dorothy Hammond and Alta Jablow (1970) sum up succinctly the long-standing relationship, from the limited British viewpoint. They write, "The British colonial official saw himself in a paternal role exerting a benevolent authority over dependent and inferior subject peoples. In the thesaurus of empire, African, child, and savage are synonymous terms, and so strongly entrenched is this equation in the writings of officials that it shows no signs of debility, even in the work of the most recent and sophisticated" (30–31). This background explains the creation of the country Nigeria. The invention of Nigeria, a black Athena popping out of the Zeus-like head of the imperialist Lord Lugard, without indigenous or female mediation, has psychosocial consequences. The resultant political instability and the embarrassing economic dependency stemming from Nigeria's proverbial mismanagement of her enormous wealth have taken, and are still taking, their toll. They create anxiety, cynicism, and alienation in the silent majority and violence, fanatical religiosity, and virulent ethnicity among those who still work against the amalgamation or are determined to be the divine rulers. It is the postcolonial phase of Osun's story being played out again.

---

declared them illegal in order to boost the sale of imported drinks. So institutionalized are some of these foreign brands that varieties of Dutch Schnapps regularly feature in traditional rituals for pouring libations, "washing" a car, that is, praying over a newly bought car, and even funeral, marriage, and naming ceremonies. One vernacular advertisement for Seaman's Schnapps is so incredibly Yoruba that one could believe it an indigenous product. Nigeria prides itself on its prize-winning Star Beer, which has ranked even above German beers in several international competitions, despite that country's expertise in beer production.

Colonialism silenced women and made them invisible, since the colonialist talked only with male leaders to keep the peace. Postcolonialism is beginning to restore women's voice, to some degree. The nation's history affected the female consciousness, sensitizing women to the complexities of our predicament, which is compounded by an ubiquitous and seemingly indomitable foe. Female destiny parallels the nation's history of subjugation in Emecheta's *The Slave Girl*. With colonization came Western education, which further drove a wedge between men and women, as men were more likely to be formally educated and put in positions of authority to help the colonial master control the country. Women finally gained a limited, westernized, public place with the country's independence, an event that intriguingly coincided with the advent of women journalists such as Theresa Ogunbiyi and Adaora Lily Ulasi and the novelist Flora Nwapa.

Since its colonial inception, the palaver was conducted by people unequally yoked, the skewed power dynamics enabling the superior to negate the seriousness of the talk. He denigrated the other, who appeared to him naively garrulous, and schemed to mislead or beguile him through the play with languages. To the Germans, palaver was talking trivialities. One can also read into the French "parlez vous?" some doubt as to whether the other can speak at all, especially French. However, if the more powerful person in the discourse needs something from the other, there might be a need to cajole to avoid violence. In use since 1645, when it was borrowed from the French, "to cajole" is "to deceive with soothing words or false promises." The French word *cajoler* implies "to chatter like a jay in a cage." A jay belongs to the crow family. This is significant, as the literature demonstrates that the African's talk has rarely been meaningful, as Joseph Conrad illustrates in *Heart of Darkness*. The words *palaver, parley,* and *cajole* are thus colonially and racially nuanced. Given the power dynamics and the implied inequality of the discussants, with one caged and the other acting as jailer, the jailed, frustrated, engages in a lot of empty talk, while the jailer attempts to soothe him, fully knowing that the cage is performing its function. These inequalities have for generations created friction between Africans and Europeans. By writing at all, women have entered the fray and have successfully established a counterdiscourse.

From the beginning, Africans in contact with Europeans realized that talk was hazardous, for they were literally and figuratively not speaking the same language. For the Africans, palaver soon became a metonym for calamity, and its homophone palava, as trouble or quarrel, was in place.[2] Gates' (1988)

2. The word *wahala* is widely used in Yoruba and Nigerian Pidgin English; it is derived from

comment about the relationship between African-American and mainstream English is cogent in this parallel development: "Ironically, rather than a proclamation of emancipation from the white person's standard English, the symbiotic relationship between the black and white, . . . between black vernacular discourse and standard English discourse, is underscored here" (50). *Palaver* and *palava* are thus as mutually dependent on each other for meaning and as differently nuanced as Gates found in theorizing *signification* and *Signification.*

The Babel of European tongues (English, French, German, Portuguese, Dutch, Spanish, Italian) was a problem in itself, necessitating interpretation, which incorporates translation spiced with analysis. The interpreter, as messenger, had to be wary not to appear as the source of an unpleasant message, hence the need for him to analyze and sift what to transmit for self-protection. Editorial mediation creates a gap between what is said and what is finally heard. The resulting interference prolongs discussions (in addition to having to go over materials twice because of the need to translate and explain), not to mention the disparity created by cultural differences. The difficulty in capturing indigenous concepts in European thought processes, and vice versa, plus the tedious faking of genuineness, deterred meaningful communication. Thus, a palaver ostensibly designed to iron out differences came to be used by each side to test the other and to widen the gap between the discussants. Meaningful communication had not really occurred; therein lay *one kin' palava.*

Interpretation, both as textual analysis and as translation from one language to another, is central in palaver management. Misinterpretation through misreading or misunderstanding generates palava or quarrel. The critic as interpreter attempts to set the record straight, to resolve disputes through illumination to make a text more easily understood, especially as most are written in the language of the colonizer.

The gap between users of European languages and indigenous people who do not speak them but have to negotiate in them is satirized in Nigeria, a point echoed in Remi Foster's stay in Germany in *Yoruba Girl Dancing* (Bedford 1992). The gap has given rise to numerous situation comedies about high courts, where the official language is English. As many litigants do not understand English, the weirdness of the translations and the strangeness of the proceedings—in stark contrast to customary case hearings in indigenous languages—would make court sessions meaningless and laughable, if lives were

---

Arabic and is synonymous with palava.

not so tragically affected by their outcome. As a journalist, Ulasi captures the tragicomic potential of language use in her novels as a marker of the insidious and contentious nature of colonialism with its built-in racism. The paradox lies in Nigeria's continued use of these vestiges of colonialism as a safety valve to avoid ethnic blowup.

Another palava for the illiterate discussant is the inaccessibility of the foreign language and its written form, a double jeopardy which the primary audience for the novel by women currently faces. Those from a writing culture can afford to be disingenuous during an oral discussion. Its ephemerality makes it less binding, hence the need for affirmation through minutes (which are not verbatim reports) and signatures. For the discussant from an oral culture, discourse is never that fixed. Its give-and-take ensures flexibility, affecting power dynamics; such a situation is indispensable for mutual consent. Real palava arises when the recorder arms himself with the authority of the written word (hence the Nigerian myth that written words do not lie), legitimized by the native's sign—the cross he must bear in a Christian sense and the trial at a bewitched crossroads he must face in a vernacular sense.

In international palaver, therefore, oral and written discourse can appear disconcertingly inflexible to the African. For the "conflation of the senses, of the oral and the visual" (Gates 1988, 137) is at odds with the aim in indigenous palavers to find out the truth of a case by meticulously examining all sides of a subject orally and aurally, to effect a resolution. The cultural desire for closure through unanimity instead of oppositionality, and the majority carrying the vote, as rooted in the democratic process, is partly at the heart of the Nigerian political debacle.

To pave the way for an uncontested resolution, at the beginning of a formal speech, the Igbo utilize the rallying word *kwenu,* a shrill, urgent call that must be heeded, to recognize and ratify the decision-making process; its intent is to silence needless protest or dissidence. *Ndi b'anyi, kwenu,* "My people, consent," is a gambit, inviting the audience to say yes to a joint decision. *Kwenu* is thus a cry for attention, for order, an invitation to modify the tenor of a debate, and, finally, a ratification of what has been determined. Reiterated during a palaver, it guarantees submission, integrity, total agreement with the common will, and unity in action. Its exhilarative and affirmative effect magically transforms dissonance, which a disintegrating community can ill afford. The ultimate aim is to establish a moral equilibrium and a feeling of belonging in each participant, rather than allow the creation of a restive minority, disruptively at odds with the majority.

Bakomba Katik Diong (1979, 79) defines this view of palaver as "a collective social act, for it concerns the community as a whole." The vast difference between the unwholesome nature of the international palaver and the communion implicit in the indigenous is telling. Among people of the same ethnic background, speaking the same language, though boundaries might be drawn on geriatric, gender, or other lines, the palaver is a genuinely affirmative action. The built-in expectation of "group solidarity in sentiment or belief" predominates; compromise through mutual concessions curbs alienation in the minority or the less powerful in the conflict; this is a fundamental feature of all successful indigenous palavers.

The preface to the publication, *Sociopolitical Aspects of the Palaver in Some African Countries* (UNESCO 1979), sums up these constructive and contrastive aspects: "[T]he term palaver has the positive meaning of organized and open debates on various issues in which everybody, regardless of age or sex, is encouraged to participate, with a view to reaching consensus and keeping the community closely linked. They also emphasize the importance of the traditional values in guiding the development of modern Africa." Significantly, the commentator glosses over controversial areas of gender and geriatrics, which are crucial in determining the outcome of the local palaver. In spite of this limitation, palaver emerges as critical discourse—serious as well as trifling, logical and rambling, orderly and haphazard, written and spoken, a celebration of the contradictions of life with the principled use of word power for communal good.

Such a painstaking attitude is hardly replicated in the type of palava emanating from gender discord. The brazen-faced Nigerian Pidgin English slogan inscribed on buses or used as bumper stickers, *Woman na palava,* "woman is trouble," is not just misogynistic; it blatantly displays the fierceness of the undeclared gender war in Nigeria, and is designed to give woman a bad name to confine her in her place.[3] The extent of the problem can be deduced from the

---

3. Hammond notes that to the colonial master, "Africa represents a dream of sexual satisfaction without attendant obligation or responsibility" (Hammond and Jablow 1970, 132). The master seems to have bequeathed this terrible psychological state to the Nigerian male, with dire consequences for the nation. The notion of being uncommitted has become entrenched in the family and the government. The Nigerian male's encounter with the British can be likened to the African-American male's with whites in the United States. Susan Willis traces negative black male reaction to black women in the African-American situation to this psychosexual origin. She comments on the metaphorical import of the devastating humiliation suffered by the black boy, Cholly, during his first sexual encounter with a black girl as white men gaze at them, and shine a torch at the couple, directing the very act in Toni Morrison's *The Bluest Eye:* "This incident suggests the foundation of black male misogyny, whose historical basis is white male domination. . . . In capitalist society, where race is the means by which the white bourgeoisie defines its domina-

sloganeer's reductive approach to the hard times by synonymizing woman with palava, thereby projecting Nigeria's problems onto woman. Interestingly, in writing, bitching woman disturbingly exhibits an unspoken but recognizable collective male anxiety.

That anxiety is also present in other connections. When a man has woman palava, that is marital problems or difficulty with women, he is down on his luck; he becomes an object of male empathy or the butt of scurrilous jokes. He invariably provides a rallying point for male solidarity. Equally off-putting for woman, especially the successful Nigerian woman, is for a man to address her as "Africa woman." The phrase consists of two contradictory impulses: admiration grudgingly bestowed, with an undertone of exasperation at the woman's perceived uppity behavior. As evidenced in these mixed signals, men and women interact with alarmingly hostile undercurrents.

To contain such truculence, I wish to restate the phrase "woman palava" ideologically to counter any cop-out. If we read it as "wo/man palava," that is, as a problem involving both men and women and needing both sexes for resolution, we will be showing signs of maturity by accepting responsibility for the Nigerian predicament. Discarding the unproductive blame model is crucial in our palavering, because when a situation has gone as wrong as it has in Nigeria, it cannot be only one group's doing: the majority is implicated for not resisting and for its wrongheaded movement toward a consensus by joining the wrongdoers for individual gain rather than the national good. In these trying times, when the country's wealth is still up for grabs, the indigenous palaver seems to be returning to its original meaning of idle talk, as in meaningless probes, constitutional conferences, or even more dangerous rumormongering and pernicious e-mail exchanges. This movement must be stemmed to make words still meaningful.

Africa wo/man palava, as I envisage it, and as the women novelists capture it, goes much beyond gender in its specificities: it encompasses different facets of the Nigerian dilemma and the bold, radical treatment by intelligent women midwifing the complicated labor to birth a country. Opposition to this admirable goal takes many forms within and outside the text. This book, for obvious reasons, concentrates on the female, literary contribution to that end.

---

tion, the hatred of the oppressed class is deflected away from the source of domination and channelled upon those in the most inferior position: black women" (Willis 1985, 230). *Onye nwa okuku lu ike ka ona tugbu,* as the Ogwashi say. Indeed, "the chicken has no option but to attack its most vulnerable enemy." Misogyny is palpable in the Nigerian air, and it is captured in the slogan, "Woman na palava." These words cryptically sum up the pain of the frustrated male. That frustration has generated increasing distrust between men and women; it needs mediation.

Writing it from outside Nigeria, in exile as it were, brings home the unacknowledged point that Africa wo/man palava is unsettling for many Nigerians, who escape for survival. This has been referred to as brain drain, and no military ruler is willing to repair the drainpipe and then get flushed out. To use a different metaphor, we are in the soup.

Palava as being in the soup imagistically captures the mother's role as nurturer. This culinary turn draws us to palava sauce. In Liberia and Sierra Leone, palava sauce is the stew served with *fufu*, "pounded starch," while palavering to ease the talks. Altered by elision as *plasas*, the name in Sierra Leonean Krio, it is known in Nigerian Pidgin English as soup, a generic term for different varieties of the West African dish. The sauce or stew or soup or callaloo is nutritious, prepared with essential ingredients such as palm oil, vegetables, condiments, various meats, and seafood.[4] The greater the variety of ingredients used, the more zestful and rich the sauce. Preparing them is painstaking and exhilarating, requiring experience to bring out the best of each of them. This magical interaction is comparable to that in a meaningful palaver, while the daily labor of cooking is similar to the energy and attention to detail that go into creating a novel. The resultant text is a palava sauce. The tediousness of the cooking is in itself the palava.

Palava sauce also appears to have a Yoruba connection. In distress, the Yoruba exclaim, *Mo k'eran*, "I collect meat." The rejoinder, sometimes dismissive, is, *Eran ko, a sa m' egun ni*, "It's not meat but the unsalvageable bones" (that you are dealing with), implying that the person is in deep trouble. The bone of contention as subject of dispute to be settled in a palaver takes us deeper into the culinary, even as it dramatizes the point that the palava sauce in itself can become a source of generating dispute. The analogy of palava sauce with textuality and the possible disputes arising from textual interpretation is instructive. Also, the conflation of cuisine and trouble is logical in cultures with seasonal famine and without modern gadgets to lessen the tedium in the kitchen.

Nevertheless, the Nigerian kitchen—whether fixed, moveable, or improvised—is a place of power, the woman's domain, where she practices her culinary arts without male interference. The wife's clout lies in what she prepares in this exclusive place and in the manner in which she distributes the end

---

4. *Plasas* is known as *ofe* in Igbo; thus we have *ofe okwulu* soup/sauce (made out of okro), *ofe egusi* (made out of *egusi*, a type of melon seed), *ofe agbono* (*agbono* is a seed), etc. In Yoruba, it is *obe*. ... Each of these soups can be served with any type of *fufu*—*nni ji* (pounded yam), *nni akpu* (pounded cassava), in Igbo; *eba (garri), amala* (from yam flour), *lafun* (from cassava flour), etc., in Yoruba—or rice.

product. To protect himself from such promethean, wifely authority and from being dominated by one woman, man resorts to polygyny to counter the idea that "she who has the soup owns the husband," as the Yoruba wryly put it. The appreciation of palava sauce as a delicacy rewards the mother/wife for the effort that goes into the elaborate dish. Her superb cooking secured a husband for Nwapa's Efuru, though losing him later problematizes the Nigerian woman's continued willingness to wield this domestic authority. The text as palava sauce has to be sampled, if women are to begin to win men over.

Further, the text/palava sauce can be construed as a sweet compromise enjoyed by and nourishing for the entire body politic. Many communities traditionally settle disputes by levying a fine on the guilty party. Rather than being monetary, such fines often take the form of a rooster, a goat, or, in a very grave case, a cow, sacrificed and cooked as a reconciliatory gesture, to cleanse people of sin and to connect the living with ancestral spirits who partake of the largesse to guarantee peace and prosperity.

Hunters share their game with others in the community, whose goodwill envelopes them in an aura of fortune. Fishermen share their catch. Throughout the year, people exchange gifts of raw and cooked food, gather spontaneously or formally during festivals to cook and eat as a sign of togetherness. Weddings, funerals, naming ceremonies, chieftaincy celebrations, and birthdays provide formal occasions when huge quantities of food are prepared and consumed. The division of labor is gendered: men butcher the animals, women do the cooking, while children of both sexes run errands. On such occasions, the host family's reputation is at stake about how palatable the food is and whether sufficient quantities are provided. It is the women of the family who create fresh palava or finally settle old scores by the quantity and quality of the palava sauce they produce for the huge mounds of *fufu* and rice consumed and washed down with alcoholic beverages. Both sexes are thus indispensable in any harmonious long-term settlement of any form of palava. Even in those difficult cases where the *dibia/babalawo* intercedes, it is customarily a woman who escorts the patient or devotee to the medicine man. When *saara* is prescribed, women prepare the food and share it out to humans and spirits to restore health and well-being.

Palava sauce as text therefore forms part of a revisionary tradition. What is palaver, that is, idle talk, for the British degenerates into palava, quarrel and trouble, for Nigerians. What is palaver to Nigerian men, intent on establishing a moral equilibrium, becomes for women counterdiscourse, as they factor themselves into the talks by writing novels. Palava in the Nigerian literary context is therefore woman's counteridentification with a master's voice; it is a quarrel about how the Nigerian situation is perceived by the dominant forces and how things are run as seen from a woman's more inclusive perspective. For women, palava sauce, as a site for (comm)union, of eating together, epitomizes complaint and reconciliation. Palava sauce becomes the woman writer's text, the pièce de résistance, served as a gesture of conciliation in resolving national problems. However, in performing this textual function, it opens up as discourse a great deal of controversy. Thus, it provides food for thought: to gather together, to quarrel, to reconcile. It is gratifying that women play an important role by providing needed closure. The novel by women is part of this healing process, necessarily preceded by an unpleasant diagnosis. The main textual ingredient is the maternal input, the inclusion of a strong mothering/daughtering ideology.

Unfortunately, there is a catch to this scenario. Who does the woman writer write for, since some of her prime subjects, especially rural women, can neither read nor understand the foreign tongue in which the text is presented? The writer almost acts as a voyeur, peeping into women's lives and thereby creating a gap between her and them. As Femi Ojo-Ade (1991, 10) puts this dilemma in a comment on writers and writing, "Such is the pain and pleasure of writing: you claim to be the voice of the voiceless, only to hear the shrill cries of the voiceless telling you to shut up, to lead the way to the den of the winners." Since the voiceless rarely read, the problem is compounded. It becomes increasingly clear that the writer writes about them, not necessarily for them. With the present liberal policy on female education, more girls will become literate. They might relish reading about characters with whose experiences they can identify. One hopes that enlightenment will lead to more ways for more women to escape the drudgery of poverty.

There is also the difficulty of not communicating meaningfully with male readers. According to Annette Kolodny (1985, 2), "Since women and men learn to read different worlds, different groups of texts are available to their reading and writing strategies." This statement needs rephrasing to suit the Nigerian context where women and men read the same worlds differently; what is more, men refuse to read women's texts, though women are forced in schools to read men's. Concerned with male misreading, Kolodny insists "that, however inadvertently, he is a different kind of reader, and that, where women are concerned, he is often an inadequate reader. . . . Symbolic representations . . . depend on a fund of shared recognitions and potential inference. For their intended impact to take hold in the reader's imagination, the author simply must . . . be able to call upon a shared context with her audience. When she cannot, or dare not, she may revert to silence, to the imitation of male forms, or, to total withdrawal and isolation in madness" (256–57). More often than not, the Nigerian male does not even bother to read the female text in or out of school. The writer laments the lack of meaningful communication between the sexes, a situation that leaves women emotionally brutalized, insane, or even dead, as in the polygynous households of Emecheta's *The Joys of Motherhood.*

Besides depicting various, local manifestations of hardship, the writers occasionally trace the international ramifications. Writing in English puts them in a women's network currently hung up on gender issues. However, like other women in the South, Nigerian women novelists realize that their problems are complex, as they include and go beyond gender matters. How can the writer balance the issues of gender with those of the nation of which they are a part? How can men be emancipated from the careless, self-serving ideologies of masterhood? How can women be reinstated so their voices can once again be heard and respected as they obviously were, even in eleventh-century Ife, as the sculpture from that period indicates? How can women and men resolve the socioeconomic crisis to advance together into the twenty-first century? These are elements of the palava.

In the confusion, girls and women need women's writings as guides. Female camaraderie and betrayal, and positive and negative characters and situations all have their functions. Though restrained and tentative, women's texts have political contexts, criticizing failure in the domestic and public domains. They serve as the public conscience. By writing at all, the writers attack a machismo mentality that kills dissidence, puts woman in her place, and appropriates creativity. As legitimate daughters claiming a place in the discourse, they preface their works with the driving force of refining and complementing what has gone before. Nwapa's gesture of taking her *Efuru* manuscript to Achebe was not adversarial. She prefaced that symbolic dialogue with the male world with the traditional *kwee,* "consent." Achebe responded, encouraging publication, thereby launching the women with his paternal or fraternal approval. The Achebean resounding "Yes" is his answer for the women to carry on. He has been listening ever since; other men would do well to listen as he does. This is so because Nwapa's *Efuru* not only speaks to Achebe's *Things Fall Apart;* also, her Uhamiri is a career-long reply to Soyinka's Ogun. Her oeuvre, like that of the other women writers, speaks to Soyinka and other male writers, as they establish women, literate and illiterate, as a vital group of "interpreters" of our common Nigerian destiny.

To reiterate, Nigerian women writers do not view the twenty-first-century problem simplistically as "woman na palava." Rather, their constituency is all oppressed people, including men. In their texts, women feature more often, though not exclusively, because the majority of the oppressed are women, limited by too many children or disturbed by not having any. The texts are studies and etchings of a harsh landscape that we must examine closely for understanding.

As Nigerian women, as writers, negotiate this unfamiliar terrain, they need to tread carefully. Emulating the legendary tortoise, well-known for his tortuous maneuvering in the hostile animal world, these women have had to present their material in subversive ways to ensure a hearing in the palaver. In a 1987 interview in India, Gayatri Chakravorty Spivak explored a similar terrain:

> We are not talking about discursive negotiations, or negotiations between equals, not even a collective bargaining. It seems to me that if you are in a position where you are . . . being constituted by Western liberalism, you have to negotiate to see what positive role you can play from within the constraints of Western liberalism, . . . breaking it open. . . . In order to keep one's effectiveness, one must also preserve those structures [of which one is a part]—not cut them down completely. (Spivak 1990, 72)

After nearly a decade, we have moved somewhat; this book, like the women's novels it discusses, situates itself in the intersection of national and international negotiations. It is addressed to insiders primarily as a suggestion; to those sons-of-the-soil and outsiders who continue to exploit Nigerian life for selfish ends, to see the harm they are causing; and to those whose international mediations can contribute to reshaping the course of this third-world country, to realize the cultural, sociopolitical, and economic complexities impacting our lives.

Diong pinpoints the constructive gesture in collectivism as opposed to individualism in the palaver, a point that overlaps with Nigerian women writers' ideology: "On the social plane an important characteristic of the palaver is the absence of a guilty party. . . . It is not the interests of the individual that are at stake, but those of the whole group of individuals. . . . Psychologically, the effect is that the 'culprit' does not feel alone" (1979, 85). Women's politics has emphasized the interdependence of the sexes as a womanist ideal, to counter isolating men from gender issues, which are critical in addressing the multifaceted Nigerian predicament.

The sociopolitical interconnections embedded in the palaver and palava affect women's writing. Palaver, as we saw, has international acceptance with built-in hierarchies, which Africans, two hundred years later, have managed to dismantle politically during countless protracted independence and constitutional talks with Europe. The punitive socioeconomic consequences of resisting through those talks can be seen in every country in postcolonial Africa. Retaining that original signal of distress about talks, the West African palava can still be regarded in Gates' words in a parallel situation, "As a double-voiced word, that is, a word or utterance in this context, decolonized for the black's purposes" (1988, 50). The decolonization becomes complete with palava sauce, an additional pidginization that incorporates a ritualistic component as a socioreligious means of coping with exacerbating conditions. If palaver typifies (post)colonial discourse with race and economics at the site of the struggle, palava exemplifies national discourse with gender, ethnicity, religion, elitism, graft, and inefficiency, juggling as denominators in the exchange, while palava sauce accentuates the implicit desire to bring about closure by enacting an apparent consensus. Women operate on these levels, moving from the international (race, economics, environment, imperialism) to the national (ethnic, military, religion, gender, etc.), with a maternal grace remarkable for its open-endedness and nurturance.

If black men's discourse is double voiced, and white women's is double voiced and clitoral (Showalter 1982, 34; Bennett 1993), black women's can be described as double voiced and vaginal (see Schor 1981, 213–15), once we factor in their more complicated position and sociopsychological clitoridectomies (compare Spivak's "symbolic clitoridectomies," 1981, 181; 1991, 10). Their counterdiscourse is expansive. Grounded in the vernacular, it speaks to black men's and white women's discourses from a view down below. Its counteridentification and revisionary stance define their creative product and determine our satisfactory reading of it. The mulatto metaphor might explain the conundrum: though the African, the English, and the feminists' worlds might claim them for their own, the Nigerian women writers have shaped an authentic sphere, made viable by its interlingual and intercultural celebration.

By presenting a more comprehensive picture of the issue, they respond to their male predecessors while refining their own text, thereby producing a postcolonial counterdiscourse; this is the palaver. The core of the woman's text addresses problems (as they affect the oppressed or as perceived by women); this is the palava. As cautionary tales, their text is offered as an olive branch, a labor of love; this is the palava sauce. By addressing such controversial issues as motherhood, childlessness, polygyny, oppression (gender, religious, colonial, military), corruption, madness, poverty, and the role of women in society, these writers mimic Osun's metafiction, expose Odu's secret text, imbuing them with a rural, urban, and/or contemporary twist.

Their palaver is never cheap talk. As counterdiscourse it serves as a crucial prelude to, and an agency for, change in communal behavior. Robert Armstrong's comment on the "palaver" in West African societies throws some light on the writers' concerted mission. He observes,

> West African societies are consensus societies. They assume that discussion will produce consensus if it is continued long enough— perhaps with adjournments. Similarly, the basic assumption of European and American courts is that the litigants need never see each other again after the trial, *but West African traditional courts operate on the assumption that the litigants and their families are neighbours and will remain so after the trial.* It is true of most West African public meetings that they are open-sided and that everybody may express his or her opinion. (1979, 14–15; my emphasis)

The Nigerian novel by women is part of this palaver tradition. Ensconced in it is a conciliatory spirit, in spite of the controversies, the palava. Women have to buttress the cause of peace and progress in Nigeria, because, when all is said and done, we still have to live with our fathers, uncles, husbands, sons, friends, lovers, and other male relations. This spirit of complementarity is central to Nigerian womanism, which I will now explore, bearing in mind that woman, etymologically, is the wife of man, prefaced by her daughterhood, which prepares her for motherhood, a grand finale.

African Womanist Ideology

First I wish to grapple with some sentences in French feminisms that I find puzzling. This venture entails rethinking Soyinka's negative response to Leopold Senghor's accent on négritude, which was engendered by Senghor's long exile in France. For if the tiger is no longer recognized as a tiger out of misprision, or, if nontigers playfully or figuratively claim to be tigers to the detriment of the tiger, an occasional rumble by the tiger to assert its tigritude is commonsensible. Writing novels in English, Achebe found it ritually necessary to reexamine Joseph Conrad's *Heart of Darkness*, placing this fiction by a nonnative user of English in proper perspective, so as to move on, unshackled, to the important task of telling the complex stories of his fatherland and motherland. His principle is exemplary and salutary.

In *The Second Sex*, Simone de Beauvoir writes, quite curiously: "If man is to be a demigod, he must first of all be a human being, and to the colonial officer's daughter the native is not a man" (1972, 643). Who is this mythical colonial officer's daughter? Is she the white daughter who accompanied her father on imperial duty in Asia and Africa, or is she the dark-light daughter the colonial officer fathered during his civilizing and pacifying mission? If it is the white daughter, does she represent French women or all white women? Is she Simone de Beauvoir? If the native is not a man, who or what is he? Going down hierarchically to the native woman, who is unmentioned in this context, who or what is she? If natives are the unknown, X-factor, it follows that they can have no substantial business with the putative, white daughter, linking us once more to the European subtext of the palaver as idling. However, my talk is not idle talk. If we review the constant attempt by Western feminists to run African women's lives in conferences without hearing or heeding what we have to say, the other side of our burden becomes clear—Western women are as much of a problem to us as black men, yet it might be worthwhile to work or walk with them, at least some of the way. Now I shall continue to clear away some impediments.

In her widely read 1976 *Signs* article "The Laugh of the Medusa," once again reprinted as recently as 1991 in *Feminisms: An Anthology of Literary Theory and Criticisms,* Helene Cixous writes, also quite curiously:

> Here they are, returning, arriving over and again, because the unconscious is impregnable. They have wandered around in circles, confined to the narrow room in which they've been given a deadly brainwashing. You can incarcerate them, slow them down, get away with the old Apartheid routine, but for a time only. As soon as they begin to speak, at the same time as they're taught their name, they can be taught that their territory is black: because you are Africa, you are black. Your continent is dark. Dark is dangerous. You can't see anything in the dark, you're afraid. Don't move, you might fall. Most of all, don't go into the forest. And so we have internalized this horror of the dark. (Cixous 1976, 877–78)

Cixous upgrades the native in Beauvoir's text by equating the condition of white women to that of the colonized. But first, he has to be "taught" his name possibly after he has learned to "parlez vous?" I hope I am not misreading her, because her pronouns are mystifying: who, really, are "they," "you," another "you," and "we"? At one point, I thought that she was addressing me, a black African woman. On rereading the paragraph, I realized that I was unwittingly eavesdropping, listening in to snatches of an ongoing quarrel between French men and French women, white men and white women. How is a Motswana or Zimbabwean or South African woman languishing under the old/new Apartheid routine to read this? Are white women who equate their fate with the condition of the third/fourth world, the slave, the colonized, the prisoner, the man of color, really serious or just insensitive? I fear both; they are serious and will sacrifice me, the outsider in this context, to settle their domestic politics, because feminism inevitably has a local face in spite of its global, cosmetic make-over.

Catharine Stimpson addressed this problem as far back as 1971 and concluded:

> I believe that women's liberation would be much stronger, much more honest, and ultimately more secure if it stopped comparing white women to blacks so freely. The analogy exploits the passion, ambition, and vigor of the black movement. It perpetuates the depressing habit white people have of first defining the black experience and then of making it their own. Intellectually sloppy, it implies that both blacks and white women can be seriously discussed as amorphous, classless, blobby masses. . . . Perhaps more dangerous, the analogy evades, in the rhetorical haze, the harsh fact of white women's racism. (1971, 473–74)

I believed that the 1982 publication of the collection of African-American essays, *All the Women Are White, All the Blacks Are Men, But Some of Us Are Brave: Black Women's Studies,* edited by Gloria T. Hull, Patricia Bell Scott, and Barbara Smith, which affirms some of Stimpson's stand, would finally put a stop to writing or reprinting such facile analogies.

As a Nigerian woman, how do I decode Cixous' brand of feminist theorizing? When the most sparsely populated continent and the richest in diamonds, gold, and cocoa, with a little oil and copper thrown in for good measure, is the poorest economically; when my familiar continent with its blazing sunshine is referred to as dark (Cixous acknowledges that the continent is not dark [884], though, inexplicably, she continues to write as if it is, a fact that makes it, for her, still explorable by whites[?]); how do I react to the paradox in the claustrophobia of academia? What is meant by black women's "resistance to theory"? How does such theorizing explain black women's reality or fiction? Naomi Schor had raised similar issues by asking, "can females theorize? . . . This may strike some readers as a rhetorical question, since the very writing and publication of this theoretical article attests to my belief in women's ability to theorize" (1981, 206–7). The fact that we return to this problem with regard to black women, fourteen years after Schor's article, demonstrates, indeed, that in feminism, all the women are white or passing.

Barbara Johnson's "Metaphor, Metonymy and Voice in *Their Eyes Were*

Watching God" (1984) prioritizes similar political concerns. The complication lies in the French con/fusion of their metaphor and metonymy, which intersect my geography and history. What are metaphor for them through analogy and metonymy through contiguity are my reality. Since they are not playing the dozens, it is difficult to know how to deal with such insouciance and the unwitting(?) travesty of my painful history. It is clear that, by including me metaphorically, they exclude me from their feminist agenda. As Johnson puts it in a comparable situation, "the question of the separability of similarity from contiguity may have considerable political implications" (207). She continues, "From Aristotle to George Lakoff, metaphor has always, in the Western tradition, had the privilege of revealing unexpected truth" (208). That truth, in the feminist discourse, is that I, a black African woman, viewed metaphorically as an aberrant without hope, will always be an afterthought in such feminisms because the mode of metaphor here is to juxtapose dissimilar things jarringly, to draw attention to the tiny area of their similarity, thereby attempting, unsuccessfully, to play down the major differences.

My instinct is, therefore, to flee from like-minded theorists and scholars juggling for power, such as Maggie Berg, who, in "Luce Irigaray's 'Contradictions': Poststructuralism and Feminism" (1991), exhibits the harem mentality or co-wifely rivalry in fighting other women to flaunt her superior understanding of Lacan, the male, the master, the ultimate authority, whom she wants to cut down to size. Yet, in the obsession to do so, to poison him, as it were, or to possess the husband with her palava sauce, to reiterate the culinary analogy, Lacan somehow becomes central, charmed, and apotheosized. The practice to privilege white male authority figures in feminist discourse while deflating works by women, in order to appeal to male readers in academia perceived as phallocrats, is part of a chain that I recognize. Its shackles make me uneasy, fleeing as I am from anything that reminds me of the negative side of Nigerian polygyny. These feminisms are revealing and cautionary for the would-be African feminist. Trinh warns us: "Thus, to simply denounce Third World women's oppression with notions and terms made to reflect or fit into Euro-American women's criteria of equality is to abide by ethnographic ideology . . . which depends on the representation of a coherent cultural subject as source of scientific knowledge to explain a native culture and reduces every gendered activity to a sex-role stereotype. Feminism in such a context may well mean 'westernization'" (1989, 106).

African converts to feminism will do well to heed her and Fela. Both pinpoint the futility of an assimilationism, which rides roughshod over our particularities. In one of his political lyrics, for example, playing with words interlingually in Standard English and Nigerian Pidgin English, Fela deconstructs democracy, presenting it as a debacle in Africa:

Democracy!
Dem all crazy
Crazy demo;
Demonstration of craze
Crazy demonstration.

He continues with a very pertinent question that should jolt any Western-style ideologist:

If e no be craze,
Why for Africa
As time dey go
Tings just dey bad?

Why has democracy failed in country after country in consensus-prone cultures of Africa?[5] Why is any democratically elected African government not approved of by the United States doomed to a short *abiku* life? What will be the aftermath of feminism in Africa if we do not modify it to reflect our realities and set our priorities?

Our harping on the embarrassing situation of privileging English over any Nigerian language to avoid a language civil war exacerbates the psychosocial questions raised by the centrality of liberty, equality, and sisterhood(?) in feminist discourse. Feminism's 1789 roots in the French Revolution, tribal with the exclusions implicit in colonialism, endanger our own ideological foundations. Since, historically, we have served as the butt of a very bad European joke, should we not be wary of this bicentennial sloganeering with its theorizing?[6]

---

5. This puzzle speaks to Lani Guinier's theory on modifying democratic practices so that the majority does not rule all of the time but that the minority should participate in ruling some of the time to avert complete alienation in the so-called democratic process. This theory takes care of the interests of minorities of color in the United States and the white minority in South Africa, to avert institutionalizing racism or ethnicism. (See Lani Guinier, "Who's Afraid of Lani Guinier," *The New York Times Magazine,* February 27, 1994, 38–44, 54–55, 66.) Even then, radical though Guinier might be, from the gender perspective, women are not genuinely represented, since they do not run for elections proportionately to their numbers in the population everywhere. Therefore, women are not fully participating in the democratic process; voting should not be one's only right.

6. I write this because I do not know what role, if any, French feminists have played to remove the South African Sara Bartmann's, the so-called Hottentot Venus, preserved genitalia still being displayed in a Parisian museum for public viewing. Perhaps they will do something when they

Barbara Christian's article "The Race for Theory" (1989) and Michael Awkward's response to it entitled "Appropriative Gestures: Theory and Afro-American Literary Criticism" (1989), as well as Houston A. Baker's working paper "There Is No More Beautiful Way: Theory and the Poetics of Afro-American Women's Writing" (n.d.), initially strike the reader as polar positions in their placement of theory in the production of the black text. On further consideration, they appear to reach a consensus that theorizing is important as long as it is Afrocentric, that is, vernacular or culturally grounded. I agree with them.

Ironically, Christian, like Schor, cannot help but theorize as she examines the question of whether to theorize or not. She perceives the abstract form of recent theorizing as a deliberate Eurocentric move to make the writer of color invisible at this magically charmed moment in literary history, when black men and women writers have been recognized and are becoming central in international literary consciousness. Awkward does not see theorizing as such a ploy, but advocates the production of an Afrocentered theoretical frame that will help illuminate black writers in praxis.

Christian's words help to clarify the constituency and responsibility of the "radical critic":

> For people of color have always theorized—but in forms quite different from the Western form of abstract logic. And I am inclined to say that our theorizing . . . is often in narrative forms, in the stories we create, in riddles and proverbs, in the play with language, since dynamic rather than fixed ideas seem more to our liking. . . . And women, at least the women I grew up around, continuously speculated about the nature of life through pithy language that unmasked the power relations of their world. . . . My folk, in other words, have always been a race of theory—though more in the form of the hieroglyph, a written figure which is both sensual and abstract, both beautiful and communicative. (1989, 226)

The deeper implication of these words in praxis is an epistemological thrust for illuminating the black text, its beauties and functionalities, which all link us once again with Osun. Christian would therefore agree with Awkward that there exists the "possibility that these critics [of black texts] *choose* to employ theory because they believe it offers provocative means of discussing the texts

---

celebrate the bicentennial of Bartmann's live exhibition of her private parts to French families who killed her.

of non-hegemonic groups, that theory is indeed viewed by them as useful in the critical analysis of the literary products of 'the other'" (Awkward 1989, 240).

However, in the Nigerian context, when the "other" is the self, this model must be modified. The incidence of indifferent governments raises ethical questions about the quality of Nigerian life: women, men, and children are victims of oppression in a very complex dynamic. Beside gender, ethnicity, education, state of origin, religion, buying power, and geographical location (the rural-urban axis) are crucial in distinguishing the insiders from the outsiders. Traditional gerontocracy has all but died out, leaving in its wake a great deal of disorder. Corruption, greed, and power mongering proliferate in Nigerian life. The source of the decadence can be traced to colonialism, the imposition of foreign religions that fail to touch the society's ethical core, the civil war, and a militarily aggressive consciousness that appropriates a majority of the budget for the military at the expense of needful areas that should have priority. These aspects should be central to any Nigerian theorizing. Mediation through compassion is necessary for fairness in sharing out the country's depleted resources. At the root of present anomie is the absence of the feminine principle in the public sector; it lies quiescent in women's texts, waiting to be instated to assist in sociopolitical fairness.

Yet, for making visible that which was invisible, for expressing the pain that was swallowed by silence, for imbuing with pride that which is female and therefore considered contemptible, for rising from the anonymity of women's oral storytelling to the individuality of authorship, the masculinist critic dismisses the Nigerian woman novelist's critique of society as "woman palava." This image of the novelist as trouble maker, subversive, and, at the worst, feminist, at least acknowledges and grudgingly gives recognition to a female perspective. Is she indeed feminist? This is a distractive point involving the complex politics of naming.

If, as Jane Marcus (1982, 223) insists, white women writers also show "pacifism in a terrible war." then perhaps this is not a peculiarly African position, although the word *war* fills one with trepidation in the Nigerian context of the palaver, as it implies that there will be bloodshed, casualties, victors, and vanquished, canceling the more generous spirit of traditional consensus politics.

Marcus reminds us that "The feminist critic is always at odds with the headmaster" (ibid.), the guardian of patriarchal culture (221). This is partially true in the Nigerian context. However, since the Nigerian headmaster reports to some bodies outside the country, we cannot *always* be at odds with one another, bound together as we inevitably are by national solidarity in the face of international inequities. For good measure, Myra Jehlen comments: "Feminist thinking is really *re*thinking, an examination of the way certain assumptions about women and the female character enter into the fundamental assumptions that organize all our thinking" (1981, 575). If these observations about feminism are valid—observations applicable to certain aspects of the writing of African women novelists who are *re*thinking, *re*examining, and *re*working male assumptions and, in the process, provoking the numerous headmasters in Africa—are the novelists therefore feminists? Does feminism mean the same thing to either side? Are there overlapping areas between the feminisms? Should they keep their feminism and I start looking for mine?

For example, what Susan Suleiman (1985) refers to as the "child-text" in her scintillating chapter "Writing and Motherhood" is different as used by Emecheta in her *Second-class Citizen*. In spite of the obsession for children, Nigerian women writers usually make children invisible in texts, as they are in real life, and because mothering is collaborative not totally individualized as in Western cultures. The text is the child in their analogy. To Suleiman, however, "[I]n the "child-text" it is a mother who writes of her experiences: childbirth, playing with her infant, watching over the sick child for the first time, feeling separated from and at the same time united with the child, memories of her own mother (the "other woman"), her relationship to language, to the Law" (369). Commenting on Julia Kristeva's theory of motherhood and writing, Suleiman notes that Kristeva "seeks to analyze and show the limitations of Western culture's traditional discourse about motherhood; she offers a theory, however incomplete and tentative, about the relation between motherhood and feminine creation; finally, she writes her own maternal text as an example of what such creation might be" (ibid.). Not having Kristeva's facility with a sensuous language nor the luxury of experimenting, the Nigerian woman writer, as mother, uses her text more functionally as she zeroes in on the problems that face her constituency—the oppressed women, men, and children who must somehow survive under her care.

Nigerian novelists experience no closeness with English, because they manipulate this rigid language that is not their own, and one that has been the master's instrument for control. They fail to see any milk of human kindness in it, causing Emecheta to lament the lack of an "emotional" language for writing. Handicapped in the battle of the races and the battle of the sexes, using English has entailed engaging in a war of words. The master never learned the language of the enslaved; instead, he made English, the medium of communication, insipid, a language of deceit. As Emecheta openly expressed

in her February 1990 talk at Sarah Lawrence College, it has needed a generation of nonnative writers like her and Salman Rushdie, prize winners in literature in English in the Commonwealth, to rescue the English language. They
have turned it to fresh, clean use by making it lean, as they divest it of those
fatty words that are hazardous to genuine communication. They speak and
write for the oppressed, using a language that alienates as it frees.

In her recently published book *What Does a Woman Want?* (1991),
Shoshana Felman comments: "Like [Juliet] Mitchell, I believe that feminism—the struggle toward a new awareness fighting sex discrimination and
redefining male and female roles—cannot afford to disregard psychoanalysis"
(69). She goes on to posit that psychoanalysis "teaches us that every human
knowledge has its own unconscious, and that every human search is blinded
by some systematic oversights of which it is not aware" (71), or, if I might add,
which it decides to ignore. Felman is writing about the phenomenon Baker referred to as "remainders." Since feminism and African-American womanism
overlook African peculiarities, there is a need to define African womanism.
This is necessitated by African women's inclusive, mother-centered ideology,
with its focus on caring—familial, communal, national, and international.
Not only is sexism a problem, other oppressive sites include totalitarianism,
militarism, ethnicism, (post)colonialism, poverty, racism, and religious fun-
damentalism. They prevent us from having a space of our own, in which to recuperate in order to join the international discourse from a position of
strength. As such, these issues must be addressed, and ignoring them is problematic. They are issues that must be thrashed out in the palaver, to offset future palava.

Locating her reading of African novels in a narrow feminist frame,
Katherine Frank, in her article "Women Without Men: The Feminist Novel in
Africa" (1987) asserts that the writers are feminists, since their novels
"embrace the solution of a world without men: Man is the enemy, the exploiter
and oppressor. Given the historically established and culturally sanctioned
sexism of African society, there is no possibility of a compromise, or even truce
with the enemy" (15). Frank's sweeping conclusion ignores imperialism, and
is premised on an adversarial feminism that ignores African sociopolitical
complexities and is at odds with the ideology of complementarity, of coexisting
while the palaver is still on or when it is over. The novels depict cultures in
which women still love their sons, brothers, and fathers even if they are not
romantically involved with their husbands, the "enemy." In cultures that put
a premium on marriage—indeed, where it is mandatory—a few women
might be without husbands (not to say men), but women rarely perceive men

as implacable enemies to be fought to the death. Even Nwapa's husbandless Efuru tells her story to a sympathetic male friend, since she wants men (as well as women) to hear about women's anguish in marriage to precipitate a change in the patriarchal marriage institution. The novelists reach open-ended conclusions that leave room for dialogue no matter how angry the female might be. The need for coexistence in countries made up of heterogeneous ethnic groups militates against uncompromising attitudes, particularly with the gender crisis subsumed under continental turmoil. The Ghanaian writer Ama Ata Aidoo's Sissie must write a letter with mixed feelings to her men in *Our Sister Killjoy* (1977). The maternal spirit of compromise and inclusiveness extends to and goes beyond a gendered perspective. Textual inconsistencies therefore abound when many of the novels are read under the general rubric *feminist.*

Aidoo (1981, 33) tackles the question of the black woman and feminism when she insists that she is not a feminist merely because she writes about women: "Unless," she remarks rather sarcastically, "indeed, as one suspects, women are not supposed to be proper subjects for tragedy or a celebration." More recently, in a keynote address at the 1992 WAAD—"Women in Africa and the African Diaspora: Bridges Across Activism and the Academy"—conference in Nigeria, Aidoo sounded more direct:

> When people ask me rather bluntly every now and then whether I am a feminist, I not only answer yes, but I go on to insist that every woman and every man should be a feminist—especially if they believe that Africans should take charge of our land, its wealth, our lives, and the burden of our own development. Because it is not possible to advocate independence for our continent without also believing that African women must have the best that the environment can offer. For some of us, this is the crucial element of our feminism. (Aidoo 1992, 5)

Aidoo's definition needs a qualifier and can be referred to as African Feminism; even this naming is problematic, since her goals of independence in development obviously do not tally with the feminist global agenda for Africa.

Other African women novelists feel the same way as Aidoo. For example, Nwapa and Emecheta consistently deny a feminist ideological bent, yet Nwapa supported Aidoo in the heated debate about feminism at the WAAD conference, implying that she too is a feminist, though once she had declared herself a womanist. In their novels, Nwapa and Emecheta explore, though not exclusively, female characters with national concerns sometimes foregrounded on a gender platform. However, all the writers never limit themselves to matters of gender.

Molara Ogundipe-Leslie, exasperated by women writers' constant about-face and the seemingly political drawback stemming from their inconsistencies, has lashed out at them (1987, 11). Their denial and affirmation of feminism stems from many reasons and a combination of motives: the fact that they are not consciously committed to a restricted female agenda; the fear of male reprisal if they openly ally with feminists; the need for independent thinking away from Western feminism; the necessity for evolving a black female literary theory; and the desire to tackle pressing issues about the hazards of Nigerian life, including gender. Although they might not formally be feminists, their successful, independent lives and their criticism of sexism as a deterrent to national progress belie this, and appear to be feminist statements. The contradictions are fascinating, as women writers try to establish a strong voice in the (inter)national discourse.

It needs to be reiterated that Nigerian women have traditionally disagreed with men without being called feminists. Male critics castigate women for fighting against the mentality of total subordination and commitment to patriarchy, the stronghold that supposedly will get us out of our mess. They consider it self-defeating, anti-African, and feminist to criticize the society openly, which they do, too. Feminism therefore continues to be offensive, though some respectable writers are daring to flirt with the ideology by Africanizing it. Let me point out once more that women have never been silent in communities when situations got out of hand. If this is considered feminism, then perhaps Nigerian women have always been feminists.

At any rate, to avoid the distractions attendant with this name, it is salutary to name ourselves in a bid, not merely to cover gender issues, but to confront the multifarious, third-world challenges, some of which are caused by the West, including feminists, who therefore are part of the problem. Western feminists exert an insidious pressure by insisting on teaching us how to fight very old wars with their own weapons. To use an Igbo Ogwashi-Uku saying, *I du hem akwa, kwa na shim,* "You accompanied me to cry, then cried more than me, the owner of the crying," or, in African-American speech, "Your blues ain't like mine." Naming ourselves meaningfully as we have always done in our cultures historicizes our circumstances and focalizes our politics.

The most fundamental question that needs to be addressed is: How can one be a feminist in military regimes where men are not even free to criticize the lowliest soldier for fear of a physical whipping or where civilian governments are perpetually in fear of a military take-over? If feminists have had a difficult time being heard in Western "democratic" countries, to palaver here on behalf of the oppressed, especially women, even indirectly, is an act of tremendous courage. In regimes where the constitution is suspended, civil rights are put aside, people live wretched lives, and the "free" press muzzles itself in order not to be silenced through governmental censorship or the manipulation of prolonged shortage of newsprint, women need to tread cautiously. It is no surprise that such extreme conditions would produce carefully thought-out critical novels, war fiction, and autobiographies by women.

No doubt "feminist" traits filter into the novels, perhaps because Nigerian women have never been passive, nor do they relish the role of victim, of working through guilt. The contradiction between the declared intent and actual praxis causes a clash. We must steer clear of the age-old intentional fallacy, since the problem lies in the politics of naming: our reluctance to give a highly charged English name, with an intricate international history, to a mode of behavior that is steeped in Nigerian cultural history. To appease the men—for we must involve them to prevent the palaver from degenerating into a monologue or an unproductive shouting match and to avoid a stalemate over naming and renaming with their postcolonial implications, perhaps the term *womanism,* as distinct from the more amorphous feminism, might be preferable.[7] In the cultures examined by these writers, parallel, if not consistently equal rights for women exist in the economic, political, and social spheres, an indigenous practice which Nigerians have hitherto not given a name to or consciously explored in developing modern political theory and praxis to suit our needs. The ideology is centered on collaboration and complementarity.

Although they might not be consciously and concertedly advocating equal rights, because "all fingers are not created equal," as we say, the writers criticize grossly unfair gender arrangements. Part of their progam thus coincides with the feminist agenda, though they do not, as of now, possess the know-how essential to bring about major political change. Certainly, this is not necessarily the writers' duty, though it might be an objective, since they have become spokespersons for women. As Aidoo put it, "It is high time African women moved onto center stage, with or without anyone's encouragement. Because in our hands lies, perhaps, the last possible hope for ourselves, and for everyone else on the continent" (1992, 6). The fingers of women's hands must cooperate and reach out to the men to achieve this revolutionary goal.

7. See also my attempt to grapple with the international implications of conceptualizing womanism: Chikwenye Okonjo Ogunyemi, "Womanism: The Dynamics of Black Female Writing in English" (1985).

I might add to this chapter's epigraph by Ogundipe-Leslie, that the African women writers are concerned with more than merely the "fates of women in society"; they also examine the effects of different forms of oppression on the fates of men, children, communities, and nations in a continent that has been raped and remains disoriented from continued sacking and pillaging by rapacious people and their local underlings. Since feminism is inevitably rooted in the democratic and economic systems of the West, which affect Africans adversely, the African woman has no viable position in such an affiliation, except perhaps to change its global orientation to achieve international equity through the women's movement. In Emecheta's oeuvre, for instance, Nigeria's subjugation is as cogent in her colonial and postcolonial discourse as the black man's and black woman's second-class citizenship. The same ideas reverberate in Aidoo's works. It goes without saying that, under these conditions, woman is the pariah, beating the dissonant drums that announce our continued enslavement. The writers are clearly interested not only in gender and class inequalities, but also in those stemming from race, ethnicity, militarism, religion, education, health, and bureaucratic and international control. Illiteracy is as debilitating for man as it is for woman. Enslavement afflicts both sexes, even if there are gender differences in its manifestations. Sad to say, women frequently oppress others, too, as many of the novels illustrate.

In presenting the palava, the woman writer tries to diminish the distastefulness by spicing it up to turn it into something palatable—a palava sauce at once delectable but peppery, food that is thought-provoking to nourish the mind in preparation for the rigors of twenty-first century existence. The anxiety in the texts is to achieve this barely stated goal. Each novel fits in as part of the palaver's hidden agenda. Since governmental mismanagement is deeply entrenched and even accepted by its victims, the ultimate goal is not to destabilize but to effect, gradually, a progressive attitude about human relationships and to drill it into the oppressed and oppressor that oppression in any form is offensive, counterproductive, and must be transformed. Thus, womanism, Nigerian style, is a weaving of three different strands in the ideology: contributing to the national discourse by writing (that is, *palaver*); the controversy generated in stating the challenges, especially from a female viewpoint (that is, the *palava*); and the attempt to make the issues accessible textually (metaphorically represented as palava sauce). The controversies generated from women's writing reflecting these aspects constitute an acknowledgment of a state of crisis.

Given this complicated background, the novel by African women is palava sauce, with numerous ingredients thrown in from the African and Western worlds. The novels and their grounding in mothering are meant to prepare people for growth and change. They bring up controversial issues in the palaver with men. Occasionally, therefore, the women appear pacifist and cunning, while at other times they can be firm and truculent, strategies necessary in such debate. For convenience, I have been referring to the women's ideology, which is comparable to Osun's, as "womanist."[8]

Alice Walker's (1984) definition of a womanist, though located in the African-American context, can help to sharpen my focus here. She sees the womanist as precocious, courageous, and serious. Within this context, she also includes the "sassy" young girl who questions her position vis-à-vis the adult and/or female world, aspects that are implicit in these writers' criticism of sexism and other manifestations of oppression. Feminism appears more rhetorical, polemical, and individualistic in its thrust, paling before womanism, which is communal in its orientation and is ideologically like a palaver in which the destiny of distressed peoples can be urgently discussed in a meaningful context to avert disaster, not just to talk abstractly. This is the essence of Osun's example. Flexibility, maturity, a maternal disposition, a steadfastness of purpose, and all-inclusiveness are hallmarks of writings by womanists, whom Walker describes as whole, "Or as 'round' women— women who love other women . . . who also have concern, in a culture that oppresses all black people . . . for their fathers, brothers, and sons, no matter how they feel about them as males," especially as husbands (xi–xii, 81). I have added *husbands* because they oppress women most. Consequently, quite often in Nigerian texts, they play the disquieting role of the misogynist to highlight the fact that marriage is a problematic space. Such a thrust criticizes Clenora Hudson-Weems' utopian Africana womanism, which tends to romanticize black male-female relationships, ignoring its myriad dangers for women. However, her insistence (1992, 4) that the black woman has the right to and must name and define herself rather than fit into molds of feminism defined by others is compelling.

The atmosphere has never been conducive for the woman writer. Emecheta and now Mabel Imokhuede Jolaoso Segun (see Fayemi 1991, 37) claim that their husbands burned their manuscripts to prevent their being published.[9]

8. For more details see the following: Alice Walker, *In Search of Our Mother's Gardens: Womanist Prose* (1984); and Elsa Barkley Brown, "Womanist Consciousness: Maggie Lena Walker and the Independent Order of Saint Luke" (1989).

9. Reluctance or refusal to publish is one way men cope with subversive texts. The banning of Miriam Tlali's *Muriel at Metropolitan* (1979) by the racist South African government and the burning of Buchi Emecheta's first manuscript by her husband are different ways of achieving

When women pick up the gauntlet and get published, hostile criticism and limited circulation are ways of containing them.

Without literary foremothers to call her own in the genre of the novel, the novelist knows she is descended from generations of raconteuses, who told their children folk tales, and professional folklorists, whose voices were heard not too far from their own moonlit compounds.[10] The oral quality of her work stems from this memorable, scattered beginning. Women tried to bear whatever they experienced in their fathers' houses and later in their husbands', because it was impolitic, sometimes forbidden, to mention unspeakable experiences, though women have always tried to share such experiences, if only with limited audiences. This female heritage of occasional defiance, complicity, grumbling, secrecy, silence, conformity, suffering, and unwitting collusion with the male has perpetuated gross misbehavior by men. The novelist's dilemma in the fast, more open society of the 1980s and 1990s is how far to go in her revelations in the palaver, while still hoping for conciliation. She has moved from the camouflage of the folk tale to tell, directly, the fictional and autobiographical stories her predecessors did not dare to voice to an unknown audience. The authorial voice is gradually becoming a cultural determinant in palavering, for the movement toward Nigerian, not just female, liberation to be achieved. In guardedly breaking her mother's silence to delineate some of the horrors that were tolerated, she has broken the boundaries of so-called decency, transforming herself into a spokeswoman, to the chagrin and consternation of Nigerian conservatives. People react by seeking a scapegoat, blaming the phenomenon on too much Western exposure. They are partly right about the ripple effects of Western education. However, many women who did not go to school were already poised for change. What is saddening is the fact that it has taken a few women so long to tackle the palava from a domestic front.

Commenting on gender matters, Sudarkasa (1987, 36) observes: "I have always been intrigued by what appear to be linguistic clues into the 'neutral-

---

control over the oppressed from racial and gender perspectives, respectively. The exclusion of the woman's text from school curriculums on the pretext that it is trivial carries the struggle to another level. Women's outcry against the policy is beginning to bring about a change of attitude.

10. It is quite significant that women told these stories only at night, which was when they had time after the work and chores for the day were done. The night, even when moonlit, veils issues. It also can serve as a cover for subversive renderings and interpretations sometimes muted in the stories narrated to women, girls, and very young boys. With the coming of electricity, the bright lights have destroyed the romantic setting of the moonlit compound, emphasizing instead the harshness of rural life.

ity' of gender in many African societies. The absence of gender in the pronouns of many African languages and the interchangeability of first names among females and males strike me as possibly related to a societal deemphasis on gender as a designation for behavior." We can infer from this statement that Nigerian societies have always benefitted from collaborative efforts among the sexes. Crowder (1983) reminds us that "Writing overcomes oppression not by serving as a catharsis for individual rage and impotence, but by inspiring political action through the evocation of a cultural heritage of strength and autonomy" (125–26); such is the premise of Nigerian womanism.

The 1991 African Literature Association Conference advanced the womanist ideal. Its focal point, Nwanyibuife, sums up cryptically the womanist tenet. In turning to Achebe's novel, *Anthills of the Savannah* (1988) to obtain this very feminine name, Nwanyibuife, to use as a rallying point, the organizers were making a gesture of goodwill to the men, to ensure that men would participate significantly in the ensuing palaver. Nwanyibuife affirms the powers of woman who is *also* worthy to be praised. The tonal word play in the name additionally stresses woman's responsibility, her burden-bearing role, which Hurston imagistically categorized ambivalently as muledom in *Mules and Men* and *Their Eyes Were Watching God.* Since the women novelists have chosen to speak for a constituency that did not give them a mandate, they, like the conference organizers, have to watch against political extremism. Acting as spokespersons for women and men who are not in a position to speak for themselves in the medium that we are concerned with, their duty, like *Chi*'s, is sacred and maternal.

To the womanist, therefore, the vital unity of a people evolving a philosophy of life acceptable to both men and women is a better approach to the wo/man palava than a debilitating and devastating political struggle for women's liberation, independence, and equality against men, to prove a feminist point. This inclusionary and very African stance demands strategies in reading the novels and sometimes necessitates probing on several levels to reach the subtexts.

Elaine Showalter (1982, 34) has identified a unique element in women's fiction that might help in our understanding of the nature, sensitivity, and maneuvering in the Nigerian novel by women. According to her, women's fiction "can be read as a double-voiced discourse, containing a 'dominant' and a 'muted' story . . . in which we must keep two alternative oscillating texts simultaneously in view." A similar reading is imperative when people resist extremely oppressive milieus, such as Nigerian civilian and labor unions operating under a military regime.[11] In the palaver of Nigerian women writers as a group, writing under the aegis of the post/colonial and military rulers who entrenched themselves in government and have occupied the country, they have had to be more adroit, moving beyond Showalter's frame of reference. In their text, the dominant is national in outlook, the muted gendered. A third dimension is international, concerning Nigeria's place in the globe, as the country with the highest concentration of black people anywhere in the world. With roughly every fourth black person a Nigerian, her political and cultural importance for black people is evident.

Women's reluctance to embrace feminism openly while making the women's issue and other forms of oppression crucial aspects of the national agenda has been a sound strategy. Out of the maneuvering has emerged, especially, Emecheta's international "Been-to novel," which concentrates on the destiny of characters who have traveled away from their natal homes and, like the *ogbanje/abiku,* consequently broadened their vision. By not narrowing the "woman palava" down to women's affairs, the writers have adroitly managed to diffuse a clash between the sexes, while giving a female slant to Nigerian concerns. If the awards to women writers are signs of how things are, then one can claim that there is an ongoing palaver and that some men are listening and responding to the women. The writers have thus served the womanist end of encouraging a healing process, which, willy-nilly, incorporates change, including gender relationships. Here healing is not synonymous with a soppy sensibility; it can often be surgical, aggressively dissecting to make whole.

In this literary development, the preponderance of Igbo vis-à-vis Yoruba

11. The need for circumspection in dealing with military regimes became obvious when the intellectually threatening Association of University Teachers struck in 1981. At the union meetings, the officials took special care to put the real desire of university teachers for higher pay to match the soldiers' (military officers are paid excessively, not to mention their "fringe" benefits) as the fifth or sixth point in a series of valid demands, so that the teachers would not appear self-centered and unpatriotic. This was necessary if we were to gain popular support. However, we were humiliated when the government took a hard line, and we were rendered homeless by a decree ordering us to vacate university housing, an important fringe benefit. We had the temerity to ignore the decree. The doctors' strike some years later employed a similar strategy. The doctors put issues emanating from patients' interests before the crucial demand for better pay, shorter working hours, and the opportunity for private practice. The strategy in the women's writing and the women's movement puts national interests before the women's, even though women's liberation is the issue at stake as it affects the broader subject. Thus, the war front might be national but the home front is the nucleus of the women's struggle and is cogent. The women's movement might be for power and so feminist, but no sensitive Nigerian strategist, desirous of gaining individual and collective power for women, will openly associate herself with the offensive term. Also, the anarchical state of the country deters one from taking a feminist offensive.

women using the novel as a political medium is disquieting. The relatively unknown Yoruba writers Funmilayo Fakunle and Simi Bedford appear to be exceptional. Why have Yoruba women, who were the first to receive formal Western education in Nigeria (see, for example, Michael Echeruo's *Victorian Lagos* [1977]), not yet produced a distinguished woman novelist? Why has the sophisticated Yoruba culture, strongly entrenched in the Americas, not found a woman to pass on its tale in English? Why does the first African Nobel laureate in literature not have a sister writer? Do cultural differences between the Igbo and the Yoruba account for the conundrum? Can the gap be ascribed to the fact that the Yoruba are more conservative or less egalitarian than the Igbo? Or is it because the Igbo are more competitive in spirit? Since there are higher bride prices and, therefore, a lower incidence of polygyny among the Igbo, a circumstance which could earn women more respect and a higher self-esteem, could the psychological boost have facilitated new ways for Igbo women to express themselves in a reformative medium such as the novel?

Yoruba women, on the other hand, excel in the art of public nurturing, hosting great, even grandiose, parties, weddings, and funerals. Such displays are signs of a different type of artistic genius. In addition, Abiodun suggests that the battle of the sexes has been long and especially wearying among the Yoruba, giving credence to the cultural theory that Osun's story has a tremendous impact on women. The advent of colonialism further divested traditional and mystical powers from women, driving what was left underground. According to this theory, the struggle has enervated women to such a degree that they have lost the will to tell the story of their humiliation, particularly in English, the tongue of one of their conquerors. For self-expression, they have chosen less controversial, though visible, forms, such as fashion, architecture, and the intricate arts of amassing wealth and educating their children. These are solid achievements of a different sort, to be read as statements of their independence in the womanist palaver.

Womanism, with its myriad manifestations, is therefore a renaissance that aims to establish healthy relationships among people, despite ethnic, geographical, educational, gender, ethical, class, religious, military, and political differences. The oppression emanating from these differences has to be addressed to counter further divisions and hardships. For a postmilitaristic reconstruction, womanism asks relevant questions: What is wrong with the relationship between men and women? What are the strengths of men and women, and how can they be optimally utilized for their own and the national good? What can be done to stem the current nihilistic trends in the country? The womanist addresses such issues in the palaver with the understanding

123

that political and economic stability and social consolidation can be established through meaningful dialogue. A consensus must be reached as to the implementation of those ideas that will work to prevent a devastating Nigerian blow-up and to put in place the foundation for genuine national prosperity.

Womanism, with its inclusiveness, or a closely related ideology is crucial for rehabilitating Nigeria. Womanism's community orientation rather than the individual, corrupt amassing of wealth is centered in the Igbo concept of *Odozi ani,* the "rehabilitator": the person who wants to make amends to ensure that the country supports its people from an environmental, ethical, and judicial viewpoint. The central concern of womanism is the harnessing of talents and opposing oppression, especially (though not exclusively) its manifestation as wo/man wahala or palava. Manipulating the palaver on behalf of the oppressed is the palava woman, who shakes people out of their complacency with her fresh mandate. The woman writer is part palava woman and part sweet mother, for the successful mother knows when to be affectionate and when to act the disciplinarian. As bell hooks (1992) put it for African-Americans in a situation similar to the Nigerian, "We believe in solidarity and are working to make spaces where black women and men can dialogue about everything, spaces where we can engage in critical dissent without violating one another. We are concerned with black culture and black identity" (19). This palaver must be meaningfully sustained or else we will be headed for worse disaster than we already face.

Public acknowledgment of woman's place in myth and history by modifying the official patriarchal view is crucial in reinstating her. For example, many universities and state governments have named important landmarks after women: Amina Way, Idia Hall, Moremi Hall, Emotan House, Efunseitan House, Lady Jibowu School, Lady Manuwa House, and Tinubu Square celebrate this trend. In *Ake,* Soyinka (1989) began to pay his dues to his mothers by grudgingly acknowledging his foremothers, whose exemplary radicalism in their 1947 Egba rebellion imbued him with the courage he needed in a career that has increasingly become controversial. In this autobiography of his childhood, the conflation of female and male principles as female nascent nationalism, though made to depend on covert male guidance, sets the pace for Nigerian irredentism. This issue and the current rereading of the southeastern women's struggle as a widespread confrontation with the British colonial master by women (see Nina Mba's [1982] interpretation, for example) are cogent statements about women's place in the national palaver. They have broad ramifications as sustained efforts by women to dislodge aliens and their local supporters. It is significant that, when the men were at their wit's end, the women stepped in on these two important occasions and earlier on, in 1919, to attempt to salvage the situation. As in the Osun story, the country is once more at a crossroads, waiting for women who have been politically exiled to become meaningfully reintegrated within the community. The novelists are heeding the call. As a scholar, I am, too.

In the process, it is not surprising that positive and negative approaches to the themes of pregnancy, childlessness, and childbirth are prevalent in the novels. Occasionally pregnancy is represented as a trap, imprisonment, something overpriced or deadly, as in Emecheta's *The Bride Price* and *The Joys of Motherhood*, Fakunle's *Chance or Destiny?* and Eno Obong's *Garden House.* Though Nwapa uses it metaphorically as labyrinth in her portrait of Idu, she later deconstructs this position, presenting it and childlessness in *One Is Enough* as woman's trump card in the games that contemporary women play with men. A similar trend is apparent in Ulasi, Okoye, and Alkali. The writers thus echo and refine one another in the establishment of a tradition. Pregnancy, childbirth or childlessness, and different aspects of mothering help to establish significant resemblances in their writing. Signifying is therefore a system of family traits indicating a Nigerian women's fictional tradition.

The choice of subject matter for novels is undoubtedly deliberate. According to Farwell (1988, 100), "Women writers have chosen images and metaphors that have ranged from demon and sickness—images that evince the conflict and turmoil surrounding the woman's effort to create—to mother and androgyne—images designed to affirm and empower the creative woman." Emecheta's striking metaphor of woman as the goose that lays the golden eggs coalesces the Nigerian woman's indispensable reproductive and economic functions, moving issues of motherhood to the artistic center of the palaver. Sunday Anozie's comment on Senghorian aesthetics is pertinent here: "all arts in Africa are social, that is, functional in the sense that they are both collective and committed" (1984, 113). It is interesting that Emecheta transforms the valueless goose eggs to the invaluable golden eggs. As a ripple effect of the Osun myth, the laying of golden eggs expresses a form of creativity and beauty, involving labor and economic commitment to the collective. The outcome, the egg-text, is for communal good. Success in female literary creativity is similar to goosehood: carrying on because the family—that is, the nation—can only benefit from this example of Nigerians establishing a tradition of hard work and self-renewal through a tedious creative process.

The bird image generates a subtext pregnant with meaning. It encodes the flight of the gander from the productive process, a female complaint that men must address. If with the golden eggs Emecheta openly acknowledges woman's economic importance, other animals in other writers' novels remind us of women's complex fate. For example, one associates the tortoise, the archetypal strategist, with Nwapa; the parrot, the archetypal parodist or ventriloquist without a vocabulary of its own, with Ulasi; bloody animal sacrifices to ensure a new beginning in the tradition of ritualistic cleansing, with Fakunle, Okoye, and Eno Obong.

The self-searching soul journey undertaken by a character occasionally benefits the public, especially the sisterhood formed as an outgrowth of individual development. Recounting the experience clues in listeners to the process. The example of the Nigerian women writers belongs to a global trend for renewal. Josephine Donovan's (1987) vision concretizes the new female endeavor: "Gynocriticism is part of the process, of the praxis, through which the voices of the silenced are becoming heard. Not only is gynocriticism naming and identifying what has never been named or even seen before, it is also providing a validating social witness that will enable women today and in the future to see, to express, to name, their own truths" (107). Though women might be the women writers' primary audience, men also have to hear the conversations that take place among women, to better understand the whole world. Such collaboration unleashes tremendous power for good.

The question of power therefore looms large in womanist writing, as with women elsewhere. The need for women to support other women in the national journey toward healing is crucial. In that womanist venture, four principles, call them the four C's—conciliation, collaboration, consensus, and complementarity between women and men—predominate. They are customary principles in Nigeria; they are fair. Once this mutual endeavor cancels out obnoxious machismo by factoring in respect to include men and women, across ethnic, religious, educational, geographical, and military barriers, the womanist ideal can be realized, and we can tackle outside oppression together. We all have to learn that there are advantages in the large number of ethnicities in Nigeria with their myriad expertise; that the Nigerian peoples, who include the gender categories men and women, among others, are mutually dependent. Our present tendency to harp on and work in the divisional mode has to be replaced by our taking advantage of our multiple perspective for consolidation, for we can only survive as a whole when we internalize this simple but profound knowledge and seriously apply the rule. The federal government's simple battle cry throughout the duration of the civil war was heeded then, and it led to a victory of sorts. It can still work now to rehabilitate us in spite of our differences:

"To keep Nigeria one
Is a task that must be done."
As one, yes, with no cannon!

That is my womanist addendum.
Ndi b'anyi, KWENU, for the women will now speak through their texts.

PART TWO

Aso Ebi: Textile-Textual Patterns

Chapter Three
Flora Nwapa: Genesis and Matrix

For Ine, my husband's mother who believes that all women married or single [childless or with children] must be economically independent.

Flora Nwapa, *One Is Enough* (1981)

Each person has his [/her] god though it requires a certain level of maturity before a person can set up a shrine to the god. In special circumstances, however, the shrine may be set up earlier.

Donatus Nwoga, *The Supreme God* (1984)

The woman who belongs to herself.

Eskimo phrase, cited by Adrienne Rich (1980)

Strategies in the Palaver

Flora Nwanzuruahu Nwapa, Mrs. Nwakuche (1931–1993), was the first African woman to publish a novel in English in London, with the appearance of *Efuru* in 1966. With the international publicity, she has subsequently been referred to as the mother of African women's literature (see Andrade 1990, 100; and Nasta 1992). Stratton (1994, 58) has cautioned us about this claim by reminding us that Grace Ogot published short stories before 1966, and her novel, *The Promised Land,* also appeared in Nairobi in 1966. No doubt, the twin texts, *Efuru* and *The Promised Land,* as pathfinders, have fortunately had a prolific following. Specifically, Nwapa, as Igbo Onyeisi, "leader," or Yoruba Taiwo, that is, "first" (of twins), generated a supportive ambience particularly for her sisters Ulasi and Emecheta. She opened international publishing doors for these and other women because of her feat in keeping up her writing with the production of two more novels, *Idu* and *Never Again,* within the next nine years when Ogot produced only *Land without Thunder* (1968), again in Nairobi. Thus Nwapa has been fertile as Onyeisi in leadership, and primal mother, consistently using the water deity as a model.

In her role as public mother, or *omunwa,* this personable woman graciously encouraged other men and women with a support system grounded in her publishing business and her attitude. It is not by chance that Nwapa started off her writing career by initially securing male approval when she took the manuscript of *Efuru*, to her good friend Achebe in Nigeria; she ended that illustrious career by entrusting her last manuscript, *The Lake Goddess*, to yet another man, the Jamaican Chester Mills, to type in the United States.[1] Although Nwapa died before she saw the typed manuscript, Mills, like a dutiful son, typed it, and a version of the work is still lodged in his computer. The Ethiopian Kassahun Checole of Africa World Press is enthusiastic about publishing it posthumously. Her faith in black men, nationally and internationally, is demonstrated by this fruitful, circular journey, which defines her womanist politics. Its defiant spirit is tempered by conciliatory moves and the need for a compromise to work together in the production process.

Nwapa is as mysterious and self-effacing as Odu herself. Like Odu's calabash, *Efuru*, as a matrix, with its ingenuous and encyclopedic outreach, serves as the original on which other Nigerian women's works keep signifying. The implosion of themes has made it possible to talk about the Nigerian women's novel. With its textural patterns, *Efuru* is the fabric whose replication turns the entire Nigerian women's corpus into an *aso ebi*.

To shift from a textile to an equally cogent culinary image, by embroiling herself in the national palaver, Nwapa, as the materfamilias of Nigerian women's fiction, has launched a comprehensive wo/man palava, and has figured out the essential ingredients in the palava sauce.[2] Her text is enriched with the inclusion of juju metaphysics, illness, the been-to element and rural-urban dynamics, slavery and war, fathers and daughters, mothers and daughters, polygyny, misogyny, (post)colonialism, education, childlessness, mothering, women's role in the community, the marketplace, women's careers, the critique and circumventing of tradition, and spirituality in the Mammywata tradition. She is undoubtedly the tastemaker who has produced an appetizer or savory dish. The spices in her palava sauce have been transformed into the flesh of other women's narrative. Emecheta's *The Joys of Motherhood* (its title is derived from *Efuru*), Okoye's *Behind the Clouds*, and Eno Obong's *Garden House*, whose thematic echoes speak for themselves, are three significant examples out of many. As storytellers, the women retain the profundity of the griotte with the precision of the proverb, for ingrained in their works are the simplicity of plot and the orality of sentences (see Wilentz

1. The arrangement was partially completed at a 1992 party arranged by Nwapa's cousin, Angela Lucas, in Scarsdale, New York.

2. During a heated debate at the African Literature Association Conference in Claremont, California, April 1981, it was interesting to see Emecheta call on Nwapa to settle a dispute, as if she were our mother. In a sense she was, or rather a Big Sister, away as we all were from home.

1992, 7–8), sustained by memorable characters who problematize the community's moral equilibrium.

Most importantly, Nwapa has bequeathed a rich, literary legacy to us by prominently featuring characters drawn from the collective psyche, especially the Osun-like Uhamiri, her fictionalized version of Mammywata (see Nwapa's children's book *Mammywater*), or Ogbuide, the Ugwuta Woman of the Lake, who invariably presides over her texts. Efuru, another enigmatic figure, raises issues associated with the colonial Mammywata: female independence and wealth, self-perceived inner and outer beauty, the inventiveness of fertility, nurturing/mothering and woman's career and role in the community, and the nature of marriage and gender relationships. Nwapa tries to maintain the delicate political balance between the sexes, an important feature of the original myths.

In 1984, at the London Book Fair, Nwapa, more reactionary than avant-garde, not surprisingly bristled at labels, refusing to be called a feminist. If one were necessary, she preferred, reluctantly, the African-American tag of womanist (Perry 1984, 1262). In a talk given at Sarah Lawrence College on April 23, 1991, she affirmed that position, insisting that she did not want to be "branded" a feminist. She confirmed my suspicion that she could not be a womanist in the Walkerian sense when she said she did not know what the full implications of being a womanist were. Distancing herself from lesbianism by being politely silent on the matter and deftly, or perhaps not so deftly, changing the subject when students questioned her about it clarified matters. According to her, she wrote primarily because she loved telling and listening to stories. It is clear that her political agenda was not vociferously articulated; she arrived at it through indirection in the text, like any griotte.

It is necessary to reiterate that the womanist praxis in Africa has never totally identified with all the original Walkerian precepts. An important point of departure is the African obsession to have children as well as the silence on or intolerance of lesbianism.[3] To buttress the female position in the palaver, Nwapa's womanism attempts to rid itself of the innuendos attached to feminism. In the face of continuous gender divisions, it constantly seeks conso-

---

3. This is exemplified in Rebeka Njau's *Ripples in the Pool* (1975), Aidoo's *Our Sister Killjoy* (1977), and Nawal El Saadawi's *Woman at Point Zero* (1975). Nwapa does not deal with lesbianism in her oeuvre as it is not part of the vast wo/man palava in the Nigerian context. Note also the sentiments against South African homosexuality in Bessie Head's *A Question of Power* (1974). The African position contrasts with the advocacy of lesbianism in Walker's *The Color Purple* (1986), Ann Shockley's *Loving Her* (1974), and Audre Lorde's *Zami: A New Spelling of My Name* (1982), to mention a few African-American works.

nance, sometimes at a price. In a difficult situation, it prefers to maintain the status quo at the expense of female victory while it bides its time for the inevitable compromise in the relationship between men and women. To borrow Brown's phrase in an epigraph to chapter 2, to which Nwapa would readily acquiesce, men and women are "family members" whose resources must be pooled together for survival. However, such a compromise does not preclude an occasional confrontation between men and women. After all, family members are liable to fall out only to become reconciled. What counts is the nature of the palava and the spirit of the ensuing palaver for conciliation.

Viewed thus, the "dominant" perspective in Nwapa's novels is communal/national rehabilitation; this encompasses the liberation of all the people from attitudes and practices that retard progress and the use of released energies for social and spiritual development. The "muted" operates on the personal level, and is gender-oriented in its specificity. Its thrust is women's role in the familial. It concentrates on disabling gender arrangements that prevent women from performing optimally in the private as well as the public spheres. Both strains are interwoven as the personal merges with the public in communally oriented cultures where the boundaries are not always sharply defined. The personal must therefore be liberated to enhance development in the public arena. The third level of Nwapa's discourse has international implications, with particular regard to colonialism and its disorienting aftermath.

The feminist critic is apt to consider the thrust of her works feminist. However, such would be a misreading or a partial reading, as it would ignore the dominant strain, the writer's concern for the larger community whose interest is superimposed upon her female politics. This multiple concern necessitates prevarication, as Nwapa wobbles between the individual and the community, with the latter triumphing over women (and men) who had dared to be different in her first two rural novels, *Efuru* and *Idu*. The ensuing disequilibrium culminates in the civil war in *Never Again*. The open-ended closure of the last two international novels, *One Is Enough* and *Women Are Different*, affirms women's independence within an evolving, heterogeneous context. Following her mythical models, Nwapa usually leaves room for dialogue between the sexes, for ancestral connections have to be maintained together by men and women for collective stability.

Unlike most firebrand feminists, Nwapa remained married in the traditional manner until her death in October 1993 (although she appended her maiden name to her works), tolerating co-wives because of her children.[4]

---

4. Nwapa never bore the name Nzeribe, though her first daughter was born to Gogo Nzeribe;

Children make her desire an integration with, rather than a separation from, the male world. Her womanist ideology causes her to gravitate toward female characters, who, like her, are economically independent, to make the point that women should also have important managerial roles to play. Her male typically needs female support because both sexes suffer under excessively oppressive cultures. Men and women are in a cultural bind and, therefore, are mutually dependent.

In keeping with this Ugwuta spirit, which entails replacing patriarchy with the precolonial dyarchy including women (see Okonjo), Nwapa metaphorically blasts the canons of literature when the last cannons are fired at the death of Efuru's father. The explosion marks the passing of an era and unwittingly announces the beginning of a new one that includes women. Lillian Robinson's "Treason Our Text" triggers, for me, this theoretical explanation of Nwapa's seemingly innocuous yet incendiary presentation of the final rites of a funeral. In a mop-up operation, Nwapa fires the canon of British literature, imposed on the Nigerian school system, and the canon of African male literature, replacing it. With *Efuru,* more revolutionary than critics care to think, she conceives the inchoative stages of Nigerian literary canon formation, embodying a national discourse by men and women writers.

The theme of childlessness—which Nwapa has obsessively woven into, worried over, and reworked in her novels—reveals to the embarrassed feminist that, perhaps unconsciously for Nwapa, anatomy is indeed destiny; she consciously fights the dilemma by depicting the tragic reality of Nigerian women who fail to arrive at the given destination.[5] For Nwapa, the issue is not Simone de Beauvoir's European concept of the "painful burden of pregnancy" (1972, 455), but the Nigerian horror of the gnawing emptiness of barrenness. Nwapa would readily agree with James Olney (1973, 173) that "the aim of Ibo life is invariable, the same for men as for women: to produce as many legitimate children as possible," hence the anguish and despair in novel after novel about childlessness. There is clearly a need for a material symbol, specifically, a

---

neither did she use the name Nwakuche in her career, though she married Gogo Nwakuche and had a son and daughter with him. People did refer to her as Mrs. Nwakuche in the social circles of Eastern Nigeria, an expression of the Nigerian obsession for every woman to be perceived as married. The use of her maiden name appears to be a feminist statement, or one can take it that she was really being an Ugwuta woman, remaining the *ada,* the first daughter of her father, with all of the rights attached to the status.

5. In the twenty-year span of her career from *Efuru* (1966) to *Idu* (1970) to *One Is Enough* (1980) to *Women Are Different* (1986), Nwapa has concentrated on the theme of childlessness with such intensity that the critic must reconsider what is going on in these texts.

child, for the woman to cling to, regardless of whether a marriage is meaningful or not. Osun is the arch exemplar. Like Nwapa, Ulasi, Emecheta, Okoye, and Eno Obong have developed a similar idea, since they all draw from a common cultural pool.

Childlessness is important as a spiritual issue in indigenous religions. It creates a gap in the antenatal-living-postmortem cycles that must be maintained for consonancy. Traditionally, there were hardly any men without children, since the infertile man could remarry, and/or it could be arranged for the wife to become impregnated by somebody whose identity was kept a secret.[6] This arrangement to ease man's anxiety through a sperm donor exacerbates the spiritual anguish of the barren woman, who has to resort to surrogate motherhood, with people knowing that she did not actually give birth to her child. This emptiness is agonizing for the Nigerian woman, as, once in the other world, she has no living child to "feed" and propitiate her.

On the metaphorical level, childlessness represents the Nigerian angst. Specifically, it is partly Nwapa's lamentation over women's anomic existence and the lack of female productivity in the world of the lettered. Her preoccupation also encompasses men, who, according to Susan Stanford Friedman (1991, 381), can also aspire to "'a male motherhood of authorship,' an archetypal fantasy of great power and persistence determined by largely unconscious fear and envy of woman's sexual and reproductive powers." Nwapa subscribes to this theory, for in her vision it is not only women who are victims of patriarchal society. Men can be too, especially childless ones. Many writers have been unproductive, silenced by sudden death, threats, imprisonment, fear, or lack of inspiration or appreciation.

Nwapa creates a womanist ambience, at once conservative and evocative, through seemingly "directionless" conversations[7] that establish the importance of wifehood, motherhood, sisterhood, and daughterhood for individual, familial, and, by extension, national health. She embraces what Betty Friedan (1965) refers to as the "feminine mystique," in which the woman considers

6. Witness Amarajeme, Ojiugo's sterile husband in *Idu;* he commits suicide for not having children, because he is unable to bear his peers' contempt and pity for his impotence. Nwapa characterizes him as a woman's man because of his considerate nature, and, to criticize offensive mores, she emasculates him for his inability to procreate. So with Ojiugo, we, as fellow victims, mourn his demise even if patriarchal society wills otherwise. Children represent a cementing of the relationship between man and woman, which is the ultimate womanist goal.

7. See O. R. Dathorne's (1975, 206–7) phallic criticism of Nwapa in *African Writers in the Twentieth Century.* It contrasts sharply with Lloyd W. Brown's (1981) positive interpretation of the oral quality in Nwapa's writing, in his *Women Writers in Black Africa.* See also the chapter on *Efuru* in Wilentz 1992.

herself "as her children's mother, her husband's wife" (55), only to decon-struct the notion by dealing with woman's public role and career. For Nwapa's characters, the issue is not the problem without a name, the wish for some-thing larger than woman's anatomical and domestic horizons. For the Ug-wuta woman whom Nwapa typically portrays, trading, farming, fishing, or other professions in the contemporary period are accepted as extensions of the domestic sphere without a fuss. In fact, most healthy Nigerian women are ex-pected to pursue a career or else they will be deemed lazy. Women and men do not consider childcare, eldercare, and housework sufficient preoccupation to prevent the woman from working to supplement the family income, to be eco-nomically independent of her husband, or, as is increasingly the case, to fend for her children, given the current economic depression and the breakdown of traditional support systems. For Nwapa's Mammywata character, that di-vinely gorgeous figure, the art of "catching" a husband is relatively simple, and the job of holding one is mostly completed as soon as children have been produced.[8] Then, the duty of maintaining the children begins, with or without their father.

Nwapa incorporates traces of Western culture in her novels that, though muted, seem quite subversive. Olney observes that the African community begins to disintegrate with the incursion of foreign ideas. He identifies love and the romantic culture around it as one such "dangerous idea" (1973, 175), a concept Nwapa explores as part of her womanist discourse in *Efuru* and *Idu*. Colonialism and traditional obligations create a wedge between husbands and wives who are "in love." In Nwapa's novels, children can be produced without love, for Western-style love, according to Olney, is reserved only for one man and one woman. In indigenous circles, such love would be considered exclu-sive and destructive, with its focus on the couple rather than the community, separating them from the extended family. Yet Nwapa, following Western tradition, which she adopts in *writing* the novels, would have us sympathize with those in love at the expense of the community, parts of which she cher-ishes. These are mixed messages. Perhaps Nwapa sees the ideological advan-tage in having patriarchal society disintegrate to give way to a new womanist society where women and men could be romantically involved, then survive to glory in the telling of their happy story, if there is any such thing.

Like many women writers, Nwapa presents a woman's point of view as she

8. See Beauvoir: "To 'catch' a husband is an art; to hold him is a job—and one in which great competence is called for" (1972, 486). This hardly applies to the rural Nigerian woman, who is sought after by men, but, if she is barren, easily loses her husband to a younger woman.

criticizes many received customs considered anachronistic by the modern woman. Where childlessness "denies" that she is a woman and she accepts the fact, leviratic practice "diminishes" her womanness and she rejects it. So the widowed Idu, with her self-destructive mechanism, escapes the ignominy of remarriage to her irresponsible brother-in-law. Woman's choice of a male partner is to be determined by her, in true Western fashion, and not by the patriarchal community. However, Nwapa kills off Idu in a move that Maryse Conde (1972, 143) sees as a failure of the feminist vision. The inconsistency or pluralism in feminist interpretation becomes obvious in contrasting analyses. Commenting on Jean Rhys' heroines, who are comparable with Nwapa's, Judith Gardiner (1982) does not see them as "failures of imagination"; rather, she regards them as a clever manipulation of the reader's feelings. She concludes quite discerningly that the "author who creates these characters never voices her own anger, yet we become enraged at the patriarchy and sympathetic to its victims" (188). This approach is an excellent strategy in the palaver to win favor for the cause of the oppressed.

When Nwapa glosses over clitoridectomy and refers to it as a "bath," by translating the Ugwuta word for the ritual, the feminist is at her wit's end what to make of her. She touches on sensitive feminist issues, uses them as thought teasers, only to retreat, escaping from the battle zone where feminism has taken a stand against patriarchy. Her intentions are altruistic and womanist. Her Nigerian culture, at this stage, cannot tolerate a cataclysm, so she hints at dissonant elements, ironically and metaphorically juxtaposing the pain and needlessness of clitoridectomy to the pleasure and desirability of a long bath. In her depiction, with clitoridectomy institutionalized as part of the marriage ritual (see *Efuru* and also the forthcoming novel *The Lake Goddess*), Nwapa profoundly states that marriage is the rape of every young woman, insidiously legitimized by older women. She will not scream and dwell on a custom that is so patently senseless and offers no real solution to barrenness and the perceived "horror" of female promiscuity. The participants in a palaver are sensitive to hints.

For Nwapa, clitoridectomy represents, metaphorically, a cutting down to size, a reduction of individual female power at the crucial point when woman, at the peak of her strength, moves into the marital sphere. The community of women who perform the ritual realize this loss and so pamper the young woman, for the last time, as she is central in the rites. Just as clitoridectomy transfers woman's sexual pleasure to other sites, what Gayatri Spivak refers to as "symbolic clitoridectomies" (1990, 10) are metonymically important, as women's pleasure and their agenda become displaced in relationships with men, especially husbands. However, the problem is not penis envy. Nwapa attacks psychological clitoridectomy implicit in woman's self-denial for the sake of husband and children. Characteristically, her heroine is the prototype of woman who fights psychic abuse, restoring her lost parts as she moves toward control through spiritual power, as most older women do, and all women should.

"A man may have both paternity and power, but a woman must too often choose between maternity and comparative powerlessness," declares Stimpson (1982, 253). Efuru has childlessness thrust on her, but in finally embracing her alter ego, Uhamiri, Nwapa performs an about-face, giving Efuru all the power she wants through surrogate motherhood. She controls and nurtures both men and women, since having a child or a male husband is no longer a distraction when Uhamiri becomes her "female husband" in the Amadiumean sense. At a 1991 conference, "Queens, Queen Mothers, Priestesses and Power: Case Studies in African Gender," held at the Schomburg Center for Research in Black Culture, Nwapa revealed her desire to write a sequel to *Efuru* to be titled *Efuru in Her Glory.* It was to explore woman's spiritual power in the community.[9] Nwapa was an indefatigable womanist with subversive traits; she realized that the birth throes of a womanist Nigeria can only follow the death throes of Nigerian patriarchy, so in her writing she presents her case carefully through an undisclosed agenda. Hers is a womanist dialogue with men and women engaged in the palaver, not a monologue haranguing men and totally alienating them and some women. She needed men and sought them out, and she usually found treasures. This serendipity contrasts with what Stratton (1994, 87ff.) perceives as Nwapa's "negative relations" with Nigerian male writers, relations which I view as complementarity, because it was Nwapa's nature to dazzle with her smile and try to cultivate good relations while quietly maintaining her own truths.

Uhamiri and the Secrets of the Ugwuta Homestead

In Flora Nwapa's five published novels—*Efuru* (1966), *Idu* (1970), *Never Again* (1975), *One Is Enough* (1981), and *Women Are Different* (1986)—Uhamiri, the Ugwuta Woman of the Lake, the woman-who-is-not-a-mother-but-is-the-mother-of-all, the superwoman of Nigerian literature, takes center stage to control her children's affairs. She is Nwapa's persona, her alter ego, her mother, her daughter. Beautiful, wealthy, mysterious, indepen-

---

9. Before her death, she did complete—but did not publish—the novel, called instead *The Lake Goddess,* soon to be published by Africa World Press.

dent, Uhamiri, as a "feminist" deity, locks horns with arrogant gods and men in Nigerian literature.[10] However, she extends her largesse to her children (female and male) in Ugwuta, which functions as a microcosm of Nigeria. Her energizing aura is a place of anchor, for as the *Chi* in Nwapa's turbulent Igbo world, she stabilizes her children. The heroines are meant to be human extensions of this powerful deity.[11]

With her favorable disposition toward aesthetics, Uhamiri has the makings of an artist, whose political strategy wields immense spiritual power.[12] Though her attributes are diametrically opposed to those of motherhood, with its clutter, gregariousness, busyness, and harassment, they are exemplary for efficient handling of the role. She is celebrated as a revolutionary archetype doubling as Nwapa's muse.

She presents Uhamiri as a model of a successful woman. Strong, ageless, rich, and powerful, the Woman of the Lake married the Great River Okita, and their marriage symbolizes the eternal conflict implicit in that institution as patriarchal societies practice it. It is pertinent that most of the marriages in Nwapa's novels are unsuccessful. Nwapa is advocating a different type of marriage: the reintegration and rehabilitation into society of industrious women through the womanist ideals of tolerance and mutual understanding of each individual's worth.

Nwapa has done a great literary service to Nigeria, by fictionalizing the Ugwuta goddess, Ogbuide, as Uhamiri.[13] Coming from Ugwuta society, which worships Ogbuide as Big Mama, it is only natural that Nwapa should use her to spotlight people's liberation struggle from stultifying aspects of traditional life. Reputed to be the land of independent, prosperous women, Ugwuta is ideal as a traditional location for her works. Lagos serves as its urban

10. See Pauline Nalova Lyonga (1985), who deals with Uhamiri's feminist disposition in her dissertation. This interpretation seems somewhat anachronistic, though one might use it for convenience.

11. Ugwuta folk belief tends to heroize women, because they are held to be under the purview of their powerful water deity, Ogbuide. Nwapa extends this conviction to her fiction.

12. Uhamiri has the trappings of an artist and a revolutionary; she can also be regarded as a mere aesthete, an image that is fraught with ambiguity. Although she does not achieve these goals herself, she is able to do so indirectly through her complex relationship with her favorites (including Nwapa), who, consequently, are successful in their own spheres of influence, if we judge them by nontraditional norms, as we must.

13. The goddess is known locally as Ogbuide, occasionally referred to as Uhamiri, and Nwapa fictionalizes her as Uhamiri. It is not fortuitous that Nwapa's first novel came out in 1966, six years after Nigeria gained her independence from Britain. At this time, Negroes were fighting for their rights, as Malcolm X informed us during a memorable visit to Ibadan, Nigeria, in 1964.

extension. By infusing the spirit of Ogbuide/Uhamiri throughout all her works, Nwapa, who is Ugwuta to the core, produces some thought-provoking situations, for she portrays Uhamiri as the prototype of all independent women and a shining example of what women, particularly childless ones, should aspire to.[14] Uhamiri is therefore drawn as the protector of women, occasionally as the husband of some chosen ones; Nwapa is also deeply concerned about men who are either childless or ordinary, who are worse off when they marry successful women.

Using Uhamiri as counterpoint, Nwapa examines the subjugation of women and the subsequent societal loss. Without being iconoclastic, she contextualizes issues by exploring traditional mores subsumed under a (post)-colonial, superficially Western ambience. Employing the revolutionary as subtext, she grapples with different manifestations of patriarchal marriage, the primary site of woman's oppression. Sexism, levirate, excessive dowry or bride-wealth, polygyny, rivalry among co-wives, clitoridectomy, misogyny, and childlessness retard the advancement of women, who are all destined and are apparently willing to be married. The ripple effects inhibit society's progress.

Nwapa's women are usually types that find it hard to become pregnant, though they easily conceive ideas beneficial to society. Like their spiritual mother Uhamiri, they are resourceful and economically self-sufficient, sharing their wealth unstintingly with less fortunate members of the community. For emotional well-being, they engage in numerous activities, establishing female bonding. Their sense of belonging to a special inner community encourages women to face marital problems in a society with practices injurious to its members.

Uhamiri combing her thick long hair, a sign of marine prolificity, Uhamiri draping her hair "loose on her shoulders" (like a white woman or a westernized Nigerian woman with a permanent wave), a sign of her post-colonial status; the self-loving Uhamiri looking into the mirror to reflect on her beautiful, inner self; Uhamiri preoccupied with wealth, which is synony-

---

14. A childless woman in traditional Igbo society is considered a nobody. Nwapa's panegyric on the childless Uhamiri is radical and threatening to the sexist world that uses childlessness to humiliate and subjugate the barren. Nwapa's intention is to liberate men and women from irre-mediable situations. Such liberation can extend to weaning people from retrogressive practices and beliefs, with particular reference to health care delivery systems, education, marital practices, etc. Efuru's community-directed goals are good examples of progress. They show a selflessness of purpose, as she aids others while she grows and gains a voice, liberating herself from her stifling marriages.

mous with children; Uhamiri "married" and childless and living separately from her husband; Uhamiri worshipped in white, with white sacred objects, unfolds as an archetype of the new black woman. Womanist, she is interested in selfhood in the context of society, and is a sign of possibilities. Different from the archetypal black matriarch, Uhamiri is never a fixed idea; she serves as an ideal proffered by Nwapa as an alternative to the Nigerian obsession with childbearing and carelessness with childcare.

By firmly establishing in her fiction that patriarchal marriage and children are not essential to woman's success, Nwapa has shifted the national discourse with profound implications in the ongoing palaver. It would appear to make her the foremost "feminist" on the Nigerian literary scene. However, her subtlety undercuts a feminist ambience, as she lacks the energy and directness that we have come to associate with contemporary feminism. Her indirectness makes her open to a womanist compromise in the palaver, for she knows that, without the support of men, not necessarily husbands, there will be little progress for women.

To maintain a healthy balance between male and female principles, Nwapa presents Uhamiri as an answer to Soyinka's Ogun (see Stratton's interesting interpretation identifying Simi as Mammywata [1994, 91]). In Nwapa's subversive fashion, Uhamiri contrasts with the macho Ogun, that artist manqué, who recklessly roams the roads, using his skill in metallurgy to destroy and create. He is a schizophrenic bundle of contradictions, Nigerian to the core. Soyinka internationalized his spirit as Nwapa has attempted to do with Uhamiri. Restricted to a submarine existence, Uhamiri swims noiselessly, quietly spreading her revolutionary message. She has caught the female imagination in literature and, it appears, represents urban Nigeria. Through her ideology, Nwapa connects Uhamiri with the movement for the freeing of the oppressed, embarrassing the participants in the palaver by internationalizing the agenda.

If the aquatic Osun is the "Yoruba Venus" (Awe 1985, 17), Uhamiri, as Mammywata, is her westernized Igbo counterpart. Uhamiri appears even more revolutionary than Osun, usually represented among the committee of gods by her son. The childless Uhamiri, enigmatically the mother of all, knows that there is indeed no total joy in motherhood or marriage, as society would make women believe, though the power lurking in the institutions can be used for good. As a social mother, this is her most liberating and inspiriting message for women and men.

Ugwuta practices Uhamiriology—the study, worship, and emulation of Uhamiri—yet puts a premium on children, a contradiction that generates spiritual disorientation, creating a gap between the worshippers and the object of their adoration because they seem to forget the Igbo name Nwabuego, "Child is wealth"; but wealth is no child, or is it? Nwapa traces this phenomenon in *Efuru* and *Idu.* She records its psychological repercussions in *Never Again,* finally resolving the issues in *One Is Enough* and *Women Are Different.* Nwapa's message, that breeding children and/or marrying are not necessarily the greatest achievements in life for women and men, becomes increasingly insistent from novel to novel. Other fulfilling goals, aesthetic and/or career oriented, improve the quality of life as exemplified by Uhamiri and her progeny. Those who wait on her, worship her patiently, and try to emulate her ways, are comfortable and become spiritually fulfilled.

Unlike distant, unfeeling governments, Uhamiri is clearly interested in the welfare of her people. She is not interested in bare survival, for she is hedonistic, and she is committed to justice and fair play. These positive aspects are critiques of governmental insensitivity to people's welfare. Nwapa sometimes finds her revolutionary zeal disquieting. Consequently, she plays it down by making her women characters flounder between tentative "feminist" gestures and womanist affirmation in the first two novels. Though Uhamiri is not a character in *One Is Enough* and *Women Are Different,* her ideology permeates the entire Lagosian milieu of these novels. The female protagonists grow more assertive in the last three, a hint that women are being driven into a more militant stance in the contemporary era.

However, Nwapa's womanism leads her to grapple with the female dilemma, to establish ways in which contemporary women can thrive while changing societal attitudes. Psychologically, the community voice is a decisive factor in individual lives. It serves as the background against which the reader perceives the protagonist: as she suffers, so does the community of which she is a member. For its misogyny, Nwapa makes many disasters befall the community rather than specific individuals. In the plots of her novels, the community experiences fire disasters, floods, eclipse of the sun, armed robbery, corruption, war, and destabilized families, all signs of a general malaise—the absence of an Uhamirian principle in public affairs.

Her two memorable heroines, Efuru and Idu, are, like Nwapa herself in the literary field, motherless daughters seeking mothers. Those heroines who have mothers, such as Kate *(Never Again)* and Amaka *(One Is Enough),* do not seem to receive satisfactory emotional support from them, exhibiting ambivalent mother-daughter relationships. In *Women Are Different,* she experiments with the concept of the collective protagonist in the trio Rose-Dora-Agnes who mother each other. In the end, they remain virginal in spite of marriage (such as it is) and childbirth. Upheld by effective female networking, they are extensions of Uhamiri. The female protagonists are typically mothered by Uhamiri, older women, friends, sisters, servants, mothers-in-law, aunts, and/or midwives; they form with them a closely knit sorority, though there are many women captured in positions pitted against other women. The women's community contrasts with the male world chaotic with war, unpredictable with mendacity, and undependable with its abandonment of women through desertion, emotional disloyalty, (post)colonial stress syndrome, or death.

If motherhood keeps Western women powerless in that they merely control small children (Lilienfield 1981, 159), perhaps Nigerian motherhood differs, as it empowers women to control people privately and publicly. Uhamiri exercises this authority vested in social motherhood. With her womanist endings, Nwapa makes her women escape obnoxious traditions to establish their independence. Efuru, Uhamirian to the core, ends as an ex, a single woman who tells her story to a man, who happens to be a doctor; her story is meant to heal. Idu, through death by anorexia, rejects the Igbo idea of woman as moveable property in the extended family. Kate, as a therapeutic agent, rehabilitates the society by narrating their experience in *Never Again*. Amaka functions effectively as a single parent to *twin sons* in *One Is Enough*. Rose-Dora-Agnes, as the three musketeers, take potshots at the educated elite in *Women Are Different*. These women grapple with the status quo.

They are the fictional versions of Madam Tinubu, the southeastern women warriors, Funmilayo Ransome-Kuti and her band of Egba women rebels, Margaret Ekpo, Biafran women, fighters who refused to look on as spectators while Nigerian history was being made.[15] Yet these women have been erased from the annals of Nigerian history, which are written by men. If and when they are remembered, their revolutionary spirit hardly comes across to the reader, except when the writer is a Western feminist scholar, a growing phenomenon since the 1970s. Those distorted pages in Nigerian history have restricted Nwapa from being a strident radical. They make her cautiously contain her anger, depicting her characters matter-of-factly. Thus, they rebel without seeming to, proffering a gradual but inexorable womanist reconstruction of society.

Nwapa, the woman author lacking the authority of the men or of the white

15. These are women heroes in Nigerian history remembered for their fights against female subjugation by colonial masters and local male leaders. Judith Van Allen (1976a, 34) comments that "Dissatisfaction with European control of market prices was, in fact, one of the factors in the 1929 rebellion in Nigeria that the British call the 'Aba Riots' and the Igbo the 'Women's War.'" See also V. C. Onwuteaka (1965), "The Aba Riot of 1929 and Its Relation to the System of 'Indirect Rule.'"

woman writers, courageously plays with the English language as a vehicle for conveying Igbo speech and culture on the domestic or private level (for greater details, see Wilentz's [1992] chapter on *Efuru*). She uses as subtexts the days of the Igbo week, rituals that mark politeness, untranslatable Igbo folk tale refrains, and innocuous female conversations. Such traditional linguistic forms mark her characters' rootedness. She differs from Achebe, who expressed in English the public aspect of Igbo speech as realized in Igbo rhetoric, especially the formal speech patterns that resonate with proverbs. Moving away from the oratorical, she has feminized the language, steeping it in women's culture which male critics (for example, O. R. Dathorne) find aimless and frivolous. In fact, the conversations are conservative, therapeutic, and essential in generating an immanent psychic aura, which invariably shapes the lives of those engaged in the chitchat. Their choric slant speaks to a complex and interconnected society.

Nwapa captures the evolution of Nigeria through the status of women. The political awakening in the 1930s following the southeastern Women's Struggle is manifested through the spirited Efuru; Nigeria's misguided participation in World War II, resulting in the brooding rebelliousness of the 1940s and 1950s, is dramatized in the uncertainties Idu faced; the turbulent 1960s are represented in Kate's civil-war destiny; the roaring and corrupting 1970s and 1980s are depicted through the economically independent women, Amaka and Rose-Dora-Agnes. Nwapa returns once more to her spiritual origins in her unpublished novel, *The Lake Goddess.* Having been a commissioner in East Central State, Nwapa was conscious that women have little political clout in spite of their numbers and their individual power as mothers. To make a political point in the palaver, she deliberately grounds women in the society, merging their destiny with the community's. Women's fate then becomes an excellent barometer to measure Nigeria's international status.

Efuru: In Search of the Mother

It would ha[ve] been dreadful if I had been denied the joy of motherhood.
Flora Nwapa, *Efuru* (1966)

Efuru's quest for mothers and for motherhood turns Nwapa's novel of that name into an allegory of origins—Nigeria's political history and women's written literature. One's mothers are invariably linked with one's father(s). That the motherless Efuru is lovingly nurtured by her father is an example to the modern absent father that his parental duties go beyond siring a child. It reminds us that Lord Lugard fathered Nigeria, which now needs attention and

145

love for stability. It also reminds us of Nwapa's successful move in consulting Achebe about her *Efuru* manuscript, thus making him the father of Nigerian women's literature in English.

Rich and beautiful, Efuru, like Nigeria, is ill used, then abandoned and picked up by corrupt and worthless men, her life jeopardized in this prophetic tale. Twice ex-aisled, Efuru's unfortunate marriages represent her destiny: her haste and giddiness in making these alliances replicate Nigeria's haphazard association with other nations, particularly Great Britain. Efuru's husbands, Adizua and Eneberi, are charlatans—criminal types who can be likened to Nigeria's careless, ever-changing leaders. Solid citizens such as the dedicated doctor and the reputable *dibia* exist, though the latter, quite regrettably, is part of a dying breed. Her one great gift is her resilience. Like the childless Efuru, Nigerian women had no novel to boast of before *Efuru* appeared. It has since had a strong following. Though women's writing has received a severe battering from masculinist critics, it moves on. Empowerment comes to the writers, as it did to Efuru, through an intricate female support system that resists oppression.

Nigerian citizens' ambivalence toward their country parallels the inconsistencies in people's attitudes toward Efuru. She mothers the community at large, but people repudiate her for not being a biological mother. A community bereft of love, honor, and appreciation of the hand that feeds it is headed for destruction. In 1966, when the novel came out, the implications of the plot were quite clear, with the headlong plunge of the country toward the civil war. Yet, Nwapa does not leave us hopeless. When the doctor and Efuru part after she tells him her harrowing story, they wish each other well: *ka chi fo o*—"Let day break" (1966, 221). *Chi a di k'ofo*, "The day is never like the dawn," the Igbo say, and rightly so, for the events of the day can hardly be predicted from the nature of the dawn, which is always a new beginning. *Efuru*'s open-endedness holds the seeds of many beginnings in the *ogbanje* operations system.

To women, Efuru's story is not unique, for it is as old as the folk tale in *Efuru* (106). The female protagonist, casting caution to the wind and disobeying parental instruction, marries a man unworthy of her. To Efuru's chagrin, her choices are mismatches that force her to return to her father's homestead husbandless and childless, a double tragedy in Igbo eyes. That is the first half of the story. The second half is corrective and instructive. In traditional terms, Efuru's second marriage is as disastrous as the first, viewed from a sexual-political angle, but Efuru needed to repeat the experience before grasping the true nature of patriarchal marriage. She ends up marrying Uhamiri, a more peaceful, codependent relationship.

As a *Bindungsroman, Efuru,* in separate, ambivalent, blundering moves, traces the ideological confusion, political awakening, maternal maturing, and spiritual development of Efuru. She journeys from preoccupation with mundane desires, such as wanting children and male husbands, to a growing sensitivity to the inconsistencies of a colonial existence as a native and, most particularly, as a patriarchal wife. Reluctantly, she develops her selfhood within the larger society, fatherless, husbandless, and childless, but wealthy and humane, with Uhamiri acting as her mother and mentor and, later, as her matriarchal husband. She changes from the Angel in the House, and, in her transcendence of the female predicament, she metamorphoses into a sweet woman, her own authentic self, no longer any man's appendage. Having successfully resisted oppression and told the story to a man, she is a model of the Nigerian woman par excellence.

As "sweet mother," Efuru loves men, but she maintains a pride in herself as she strives to be financially independent by pursuing her business career. She seems to be politically aware, like a feminist, of the proprietary implications of a man paying the bride-price for a woman. Perhaps this is why she elopes with Adizua without the mandatory payment and why she provided him with the money with which he finally paid it. In other words, she was never "bought" by any man, a point that gives her a psychological advantage. Is this revolutionary act the reason why the marriage never lasted?

When Efuru, as prime mover, with token help from husband number one, produces the money to pay her own bride-price and arranges the ceremony, the implications are far-reaching.[16] She appears narcissistic, marrying herself as it were. In another sense her action is self-defensive, as she subverts male authority—her two husbands and kinsmen—by providing the money herself. Indeed, one can go so far to say that, legally, her paying the original bride-price invalidates the marriages. This coup de grace to the male establishment is known only to Adizua and Efuru. Is this a womanist joke to deal sexism a secret blow while seeming to uphold it? Efuru temporarily becomes a prisoner in her absent husband Adizua's house. Nwapa uses the situation to criticize patriarchal marriage, which subjugates a bright, successful woman, placing her under a lackluster husband who misreads her or is not intelligent enough to read her at all. Or, perhaps he reads her clearly and fights back through silence.

Nwapa stresses Efuru's maternal qualities as she pursues her trading ca-

---

16. Combining the incomes of husband and wife is a Western, not an African, practice. As Callaway (1987, 198) observes, it does not necessarily make for a strong marriage.

reer, cooks, cleans, cares for people around her by mothering her servant Ogea, and patiently sees to Nwosu's hernia and Nnona's ulcerous leg. For her pains, Nnona's daughter "compliments" her: "You have done what only men are capable of doing and so you have done like a man" (132), typically masculinizing female tenacity while playing down the caring. To confirm the gravity of the self-effacement and self-disparagement in women's internalized thought processes some female gossips remark disparagingly, "Efuru was a man since she could not reproduce" (24). In another sense, this choric voice (or Nwapa) indirectly deals men a blow by reiterating male incapacity to reproduce children in the special way women can. Yet, there is no doubt that the successful materfamilias, *omunwa*, is stereotypically ambiguous: part man, part woman, tough and tender, postmenopausal. For the Igbo, the distinguished woman is genderless or an honorary man. Clearly, Efuru is unequally yoked to the shiftless Adizua, who abandons his farming to join their unequal hands together in her trading profession. "Trading," Judith Van Allen insists, "enables women to continue their traditional independent social life with other women" (1976a, 40). Adizua becomes feminized and dependent by changing careers.

In this transitional stage, Efuru endures the pain of tradition by becoming circumcised. Through the episode, Nwapa stresses the point that woman is her own worst enemy: older women oppress younger women and resort to subterfuges to explain away their position as the police for patriarchy, a situation Nwapa reverses in *The Lake Goddess*. In *Efuru*, Nwapa refers to clitoridectomy euphemistically as a "bath," echoing the older women. Circumcision, its pain and confinement, insist these misguided women, "is what every woman undergoes" (15). Adrienne Rich (1980, 189) feels that "clitoridectomies [are] for 'lustful' nuns or for 'difficult' wives. It has been difficult, too, to know the lies of our complicity from the lies we believed." Efuru is indeed "lustful" for eloping and "difficult" for not conceiving a baby quickly, a process the circumcision is supposed to facilitate.

Chodorow (1978, 156) confirms Rich's position when she quotes Charles Sarlin that "the pubertal rite of clitoridectomy represents a crude physical attempt to accomplish in a primitive and direct fashion the very same objective which Freud established as the necessary precondition on a psychological level for the establishment of a feminine identity." The determined Efuru resists female opposition to transcending her victimhood. She changes as "things are changing" in these colonial times, even if "these white people have imposed so much strain on our people" (Nwapa 1966, 11–12). A few pages later, she surreptitiously provides the wherewithal for the "dowry" ceremony with its drinking, money exchange, and male camaraderie. The lone female, Efuru looks on, perhaps bemused (for Nwapa is silent on this) at foolish, absurd, egotistic males. For the 1960s this is *bolekaja* criticism of the society, as Nwapa wants men to come down from their pedestal to palaver with women on women's silences about the economic aspect of marital arrangements.

Efuru is different because she does not do things as they should be done (169), a point against her in the society. In the secret conflict between the sexes, she exchanges weak, albeit loving, paternal authority for an absent marital authority, all the while striving for autonomy. Poor Adizua, following his shiftless father's footsteps, walks away from the relationship because patriarchal Igbo marriage insists on male superiority, not equality of the spouses and certainly not the wife's superiority. To borrow a Yoruba praise-name recorded by Ulli Beier, Efuru is the "Mother who kills without striking / . . . My mother kills quickly without a cry / Mother who kills her husband and yet pities him" (Abiodun 1989, 12). The Guadeloupean writer Maryse Conde takes exception to Nwapa's portrait of weak males, as it "conveys a very poor impression of her society" (1972, 136). However, Nwapa is interested in the fate of the strong female yoked to a weak male as a hypothetical situation from which to criticize patriarchal marriage and Nigeria for not maximizing female potential.

More militant than the stereotypical victim, Ossai, her abandoned mother-in-law now "married" to her absent son, Efuru returns to her paternal homestead after Adizua's desertion, refusing to be immolated like Ossai. The cleanliness of Efuru's room—that is, her political acuity—contrasts with the mess of Ossai's room, which is symptomatic of her unbalanced emotional state, marked by anorexia, vomiting, and the victim's contemptible cry: "I have lost the willingness to live" (157). Later Ossai moans: "But Adizua hated me. He hated me just as his father hated me. . . . I cannot live a purposeless life" (157). Efuru proves that not having a husband or a son does not result in a purposeless life. She thereby breaks with the tradition that subjugates her to a mother-in-law (Van Allen 1976b, 33) and an irresponsible, unproductive, absent husband.

Through her actions, Efuru mirrors several people. Commenting on the pre-oedipal struggle between the daughter and her mother, which is relevant in Efuru's case, Claire Kahane (1985) writes: "This ongoing battle with a mirror image who is both self and other is what I find at the center of the Gothic structure, which allows me to confront the confusion between mother and daughter and the intricate web of psychic relations that constitute their bond" (337). Though *Efuru* is by no means a gothic novel, Efuru does mirror her dead, biological mother as she begins to define herself spiritually. In terms of her marital experience, she also battles with her mother-in-law's example, shattering her reflections in her life in the process. In the political sphere, her other mirror image is Ajanupu, Ossai's aggressive sister. She is superimposed on Uhamiri on the spiritual plain. Efuru learns from these four radically different women how to be a strong surrogate mother.

Significantly, on her return to her natal home, Efuru turns her father's house into a shrine by her cleansing rituals. As she decorates the house, she leaves her handwriting on the walls in *uli*, thereby making an aesthetic and political statement. Unfortunately she will marry again, this time with parental approval after the traditional courtship, for she has not quite mastered her mothers' teachings. She will be enslaved again in yet another marriage, as if to atone for the sins of her fathers, who enriched themselves by participating in the international slave trade.

Debts feature in another way in the novel. With our third-world debt culture, this is prophetically a jab at our dependency status. These debts are the financial and, by extension, the societal obligations that people owe each other, yet are unwilling to pay. They breed amnesia in black relations as a way to cope. The debt culture is a fundamental problem that pervades society; it is a sign of extreme poverty as well as a mismanagement of one's resources. Neighbors turn against Efuru, cursing and ostracizing her. The *dibia*'s refusal to treat her because she is menstruating demonstrates the enormity of traditional male chauvinism that turns a biological process into a taboo. From different spheres she remains an exile, the outsider within.

Efuru unwittingly gravitates toward westernization, epitomized by her marriage to Eneberi. His pride in his newly acquired English name, Gilbert, indicates that he aspires to Europeanhood, which, as he will soon discover, has its shortcomings. Susan Z. Andrade, in her otherwise stimulating analysis, "Rewriting History, Motherhood, Rebellion: Naming an African Women's Literary Tradition," concludes, partly erroneously, "that Efuru's life appears to have no contact with Europe, certainly none with European-style feminism, means that the narrative's prototype of female power is Igbo" (1990, 98). Though her female power is Igbo based, Europe does come to Efuru in tangible ways even if Efuru does not go to Europe. Her "superiority" over the other women partly stems from this fact. She uses her Western-trained doctor friend and a hospital to carry on her charity work and her maternal duties in the community. Like her father, her trading career is based on an international/colonial economic system. Most importantly, Gilbert's partial education and incarceration deal a deadly blow to their marriage. The prison, a crucial factor in upholding British imperialism, is an obnoxious symbol of white supremacy over black men. Prison emasculates the individual as much as colonialism does the nation. Nwapa backgrounds the text with the masters' other prisoners—idle, invisible, passive white women whose boredom rouses idle curiosity in Efuru. She does not embrace Europeanism giddily, hence her inability and refusal to use her husband's alien name, Gilbert, which to her is a sign of his loss of identity.

Nwapa writes that "Efuru was growing logical in her reasoning. She thought it unusual for women to be logical. Usually their intuition did their reasoning for them" (1966, 165). This implies that Efuru is developing intellectually beyond the limits placed on women by Nigerian society. Efuru's ancestors had dealings with white slavers, as the shooting of the cannons indicates at her father's death (201). Perhaps this link with a dreadful heritage necessitates retribution and the spiritual atonement that form the closure, an essential religious gesture to counter the amnesia about Nigerian participation in the slave trade and contemporary nefarious links that connect an avaricious black elite with unscrupulous foreign partners.

European intrusion into her life opens Efuru's eyes to spiritual possibilities, such as moving toward Uhamiri. When Efuru starts dreaming of Uhamiri, who is perpetually at loggerheads with her husband, Nwapa foreshadows the end of Efuru's second marriage. Fortunately for her, she replaces her adoration of her husband with the worship of Uhamiri, a jealous female force that demands celibacy for at least one quarter of the time, moving her into what Rich would consider a lesbian continuum. "What is called lesbian," observes Marilyn Farwell (1988, 110), "does not depend on women loving women genitally but, rather, on the presence and attention of women to other women that is analogous to the act of loving sexually another like oneself. In fact, words like presence, attention, and sight are used most often to describe this metaphoric lesbian." Efuru yearns for what Uhamiri stands for: a lucrative career with its attendant comforts, freedom, leisure; in short, the good things of a Western woman's life, which, Efuru now realizes, can include not having children, and/or a male husband. Efuru lacks the ability to read, a road to genuine liberation that provides access to other ways of knowing and doing. In a telling conversation, she and Ajanupu lament the fact that they are not been-tos, since they cannot go to the "country of the white people" because they "do not know book" (Nwapa 1966, 164). To compensate, Efuru, triply an outcast because she is a woman, single, and childless, dreams of Uhamiri the goddess, especially devoted to the underdog in society.

Efuru drops out of her second marriage, doubly galled by Gilbert's wrongful accusation of adultery despite his own adultery, his imprisonment for an undisclosed crime, and his sexist irresponsibility in not thinking it proper that he should account for his movements to his wife. Ajanupu, as her surrogate mother, had defended her honor like a man by physically attacking Gilbert, having him hospitalized, limiting his freedom. "I stood by my husband" (219), laments the loyal Efuru about Gilbert's imprisonment, but Gilbert fails to reciprocate during her illness. It is significant that, even at this late stage, Efuru, unconsciously, still succumbs to patriarchy as she lies sick and passive, after Gilbert's false accusation of adultery, unable to strike a blow in self-defense. Being replaced by a ne'er-do-well in the first marriage and by somebody younger and fruitful in the second are harrowing for Efuru as an older woman. She finally realizes that the husband can become the implacable enemy within. By leaving her marital home, she escapes the humiliating public confession that is mandatory for an "adulteress."[17] Importantly, she is cleared during another ritual in her father's house, now free from male domination. Having renounced the oppressive male world, she clings to Uhamiri. Her world is still heterogeneous, as it includes her male friend, the doctor, but he is supportive and a good listener.

In spite of securing men through her culinary skills, Efuru finally learns the hard lesson that a woman cannot own a man, which drives her to react accordingly. She too will not be owned by a man. In spite of her pain, the ending to the work brings some relief. Rewriting Achebe, whose Ekwefi in *Things Fall Apart* was so dumbfounded that she could not tell her story, Nwapa turns Efuru into a raconteuse, recounting her story because woman's voice must be heard also. In being able to tell her tale of woe, Efuru therapeutically faces her stressful situation, and, by becoming mistress of it, she is healed of her unnamed ailment. That psychosomatic illness shows the extent Efuru had been deflected from her cause and her true self because of men. Revising the work of an African-American writer, Zora Neale Hurston's *Their Eyes Were Watching God,* Nwapa has Efuru tell her tragic, marital story to a male doctor instead of to another woman.[18] Nwapa's choice of a male audience is deliberate. Nige-

17. This tradition coerces a woman into naming men (real and, in moments of psychological stress, imagined) who have touched her physically or made passes at her. The purpose is, supposedly, to placate the gods and ancestors by the public confession so that the victim, her children, and/or her husband can escape ill luck. This ritual is usually performed when a woman is particularly vulnerable—when she is anxious and spent, because of a traumatic situation, and is willing to lie to ameliorate her condition.

18. This difference in the primary audience is indicative of Nwapa's womanist vision, which includes black men. It parallels Efuru's. With the scribal tradition of the village letter writer, the question of point of view and who the writer is are interesting. The relationship between the illiterate villager, whose story is being told, and the writer is not always clear, with the personality of the

rian women already know Efuru's story, having lived it or known somebody who has gone through similar pain. Men need to hear/read the story in a womanist praxis that seeks male involvement, enlightenment, and change. This story narrated by a woman who "knows no book" to a doctor who has studied so many books introduces a fresh phase in human relationships—the illiterate has something valid to say to the literate. In trying to resolve wo/man palava, men must listen to women. The doctor will help to bring about a healing for the casualties (if any) in the palavering.

Nwapa ends *Efuru* with a puzzle: Uhamiri "had never experienced the joy of motherhood. Why then did the women worship her?" (221). Andrade has problematized these enigmatic sentences (1990, 100). I must add that, in the text, men also revere Uhamiri as Mother. The women worship Uhamiri in order to conceive—children and/or "logical reasoning"; they worship her to be wealthy—with people and/or material possessions. Thus, the subversive rhetorical question is calculatingly limited to women and connected to Uhamiri's mythical world to spiritually energize women to imbibe her oracular secret, then personalize its interpretation. Accessing this imaginary meaningfully unleashes the secrets of the joys of a creative motherhood, a creative life. Emecheta confirms this reading in *The Joys of Motherhood*, when she answers Nwapa's question in her positive portrait of the wealthy Adaku, who experiences the joys of motherhood with daughters and material wealth sans husband. In contrast, her rival, Nnu Ego, accesses the secret vista belatedly in death, having conceived only children in her lifetime. Eno Obong signifies on all of them with her highly evolved Mayen. Not only will Mayen have healthy children after her Mammywata worship, she reasons logically, and surrounds herself with people with whom she gains access to material wealth. She is the new woman, par excellence.

Efuru as primal character is not as fortunate as Mayen. In personalizing her relationship with Uhamiri, Efuru dreams of a supreme female principle that is emotionally and spiritually healing. The dream is obviously utopian. Not wanting to be accused of being an incurable romantic, Nwapa introduces

---

writer oftentimes intruding in the text. It is unlike the relationship between the boss, dictating a letter, and his secretary, who writes the words down almost verbatim, leaving little or no room for her own creativity. The illiterate villager, whose voice is spontaneous, without the structuring needed in the scribal medium, comes between the literate writer and the text that has to be orga - nized. The writer is forced by Western traditions to rearrange words, phrases, and thought patterns, then present the material in paragraphs for another literate person to read and perhaps translate to the addressee, unless the addressee is as literate as the writer who took down the ideas in the first place.

the conundrum. This ending reminds us of the mundane world where child-lessness still remains problematic but where each afflicted woman can begin to come to terms with a condition that cannot be changed while changing those that can be, as Efuru did.

Nwapa herself acts like Uhamiri by enabling Efuru to maximize her potential, thereby serving as a model, for the power of *Efuru* lies in Efuru, that she is worthy of being gossiped about, written about, and read. In this context, Efuru's growth as she accesses male authority is important. As she serves her guests "illicit" gin and gains illicit powers, through the kola nuts she obtains ancestral intervention, and with her delicious palava sauces she owns men, even if temporarily, through control of their stomachs. This otherworldly woman constantly travels as a trader, almost living a nomadic existence as she wanders from one abode to another, in her search for a suitable place. After these journeys—which are spiritual and political, domestic and public—Efuru emerges free of husband and children, to become a mother completely committed to herself and the community. Suffused by an Uhamirian ethos, she is a metaphor for the new Nigerian woman and the dawning of a new era where women can be fulfilled without children. The deity whose worship involves a narcissistic gaze into her own waters for union and identification serves as a model of maturation for the womanist in caring for one's self to enable one to show responsibility toward others.

This self-centeredness is also rooted in the *ogbanje* phenomenon. Efuru's palava is essentially *ogbanje*-like, with her success in reversing power positions or sharing power. These are played out in *Efuru*, the textual *ogbanje*, or in Efuru, the *ogbanje* as text. To succeed as an *ogbanje*, the character can explore two choices. S/he can seek and play out the powerlessness already at the site of power to appropriate some power or s/he can locate the power embedded somewhere in the site of her/his powerlessness to access some power. Consequently, the wife can take precedence over the husband, the childless woman over the mother, as Efuru gains agency. Efuru becomes Uhamiri incarnate, beloved and also hated throughout the text for her power. This is because Efuru is worshipped, as people appeal to her as if she were a divine agent, and she is mocked, as humans fear, revere, and mock their gods.

Thus, the center of each powerful entity is a weak nucleus containing the possibilities for its dismantling. Nwapa conflates her gender and colonial statements, for in the phenomenon of the power-in-power(lessness) and its reverse lie the agency for change—the collapse of imperialism, enslavement, colonialism, and sexism as new formations of nations, leadership, women, and gods and goddesses emerge to replace the old arrangements. Throughout the text, Nwapa implies that the power scheme can be dismantled by identifying the weak spot: the rich man whose family were slavers is, tellingly, replaced by his childless daughter (this implies the end of a patriarchal line and/or the beginning of a new era); the mighty *dibia* fails to heal himself and dies; the powerful mother-in-law is rendered helpless by anorexia; husbands are exiled, imprisoned, or knocked down in this rendition of a praisesong for Efuru, the childless grass widow. This is a world where change is assured, where nobody or group has it all. Nwapa portrays a changing community "where women were worshipped and despised," to borrow Jane Marcus' observation of Virginia Woolf's society (1981, xix). The community in *Efuru* worships Uhamiri yet treats women as outcasts, just as Nigerians worship their mothers and despise the wives. Nwapa is concerned about the contradictory impulse in the society.

Nwapa has humanized the marital dilemma by mythicizing it. She produces a conflation of myth, geography, and sociology with her dramatization of Uhamiri's turbulent marriage to Okita. Uhamiri, the goddess of the beautiful blue lake, placid and steeped in domesticity, contrasts sharply with Okita, the brown, murky river that flows into her in a Freudian symbology. As a highway, Okita poses danger to its users as it serves as a warning against the dangerous road that a substantial number of men have decided to take in marital relationships and other gender matters in Nigeria.

Taiwo (1984, 52) observes that Nwapa "has used Uhamiri to symbolize the freedom of women generally and to vindicate their ability to free themselves from the shackles imposed by society in favor of men." This conclusion is rather misleading, as women are not generally free in the novel or elsewhere, and only exceptional women can liberate themselves. That is why Nwapa resorts to myth to convey her concern. Uhamiri is presented as a model for the freedom loving woman in a sexist society. She is Efuru's guardian, "an extension of her sense of self" (Banyiwa-Horne 1986, 127). As the human exemplar, Efuru has a hard time of it, in spite of spiritual support. The Nigerian critic, Virginia Ola, complains that the novelist does not handle the character adroitly enough as "the anger of Uhamiri [is] hardly manifested" (1981, 101). By this comment Ola pinpoints the difficulty faced in reading Nwapa as a feminist. If we believe, and indeed we must, that Uhamiri controls the destiny of the Ugwuta people, we have to read closely. The arch villains do not go unscathed: Adizua is lost in exile and suffers in his mesalliance; and Gilbert goes to jail and cannot have his "outside" child live with him, as his "small" wife is an embittered woman. Uhamiri is angry, inasmuch as her self-controlled creator can be said to be angry. By holding her fire, Uhamiri has generated (m)other texts such as Okoye's *Behind the Clouds,* Emecheta's *The Joys of Motherhood,* and Eno Obong's *Garden House.* They disabuse our minds of the romanticization of marriage and motherhood.

We can compare Efuru's tale to that of Virginia Woolf's *Night and Day,* which, according to Shirley Garner (1985, 319), "reflects the desire for union with an idealized and nurturing mother and at the same time the fear of engulfment by her." Efuru's can be read as a passionate love story between a daughter and her mothers. Her search to be a mother—that is, a search for the lost self—becomes one with her quest for a mother, for wholeness. The joy of motherhood (and fatherhood as experienced by Efuru's father) intersects with the joy of daughterhood. Efuru becomes one with the goddess as she gazes into the pot of Uhamiri's water, inside which Efuru is reflected any time she consciously looks into it. Uhamiri, as the mother dwelling within, frees Efuru from sexism and colonialism. Efuru's power becomes metaphorically located within that pot of water, which holds a secret: every peep into it, a new Efuru is born/reflected. This indeterminacy confirms her power. As in *ogbanje*hood, the bound text generates boundless significations and interpretations. In the labyrinths of the community, Efuru finally finds a place where she can dwell comfortably, where she can unite with the mother within and the mother without. This return to the spiritual after all the worldly distractions leads to a moral equilibrium, unleashing her potential. The most important message is a truly Nigerian one: motherhood is not limited to the biological but extends to the social where it better serves woman, gender/politics, and community/nation.

To become a mother-artist for the first time can be a formidable venture, as Efuru/Nwapa finally realize. When Efuru's only child dies and her absent husband remains silent, Nwapa unconsciously records her fear of male indifference to the fate of *Efuru*. Efuru's seeming childlessness and motherlessness parallel Nwapa's heritage as she gazed into the empty spaces before and beyond her in the barren literary desert. The oasis will appear later. *Efuru* is Efuru's and Nwapa's child-gift, a "manual," to borrow Taiwo's word, on how women can cope with the single state and childlessness. Nwapa as mother is also interested in men. Through her synecdochic use of the tortoise as "our father" in the market scene in *Idu* (1970, 180ff.), she underscores the folkloric origins of African literature, reminding us that women also have a literary patrimony. In other words, women novelists have literary brothers/fathers. The tortoise, the archetypal trickster that provides a substantial portion of our folk tale repertoire, fathers Efuru and Idu as also Achebe and his novels precede Nwapa and *Efuru*. *Efuru* is the *Chi* or light that comes after a courageous woman's labor in the dark. *Idu* ensures that she will be enshrined in living memory.

Twice-Told Tales: *Idu* Revisited

There was something wrong in the town and the elders would have to do something about it.

Flora Nwapa, *Idu* (1970)

Idu, the eponymous heroine of Nwapa's second novel, is steeped in oral literature and history, for she is named after the legendary Idu n'Oba, the old Bini kingdom. This never-never land in the Igbo folk tale repertoire is a place where something is bound to go wrong and where people are expected to right it. The certainty of a moral equilibrium at the end of each plot makes the tales popular and reassuring, especially with the young. Nwapa's decision to make a woman the protagonist is not fortuitous, since both sexes feature commonly in the tales. Also, the choice of the name is deliberate, for Bini is remarkable for the Queen Mother, who "is represented as a senior chief and equated with a male" (Kaplan 1974, 386). She is the invisible power behind the throne, which she helps to control from the outskirts of the city, in Uselu, where tradition exiles her.

Nwapa's plot involving Idu the woman signifies less upon those folk tales with their predictable endings than upon the tortuous story of Idu n'Oba—the moribund motherland, whose glories and tragic end historians are grappling with to construct a narrative about the formation and collapse of indigenous power. *Idu*, like palava sauce, is an amalgam—the vernacular and the foreign, orature and history enhance each other even as they supply food for thought during the complicated palavering in the 1970s postwar era.

As such, the stories of woman and Bini overlap; they are ancient, historical, and political. The narrative of Idu, the illustrious woman whose destiny leads her to a tragic descent into second-class citizenship and death, intersects with Bini's traumatic colonization, only to emerge from her vernacular chaos to be downsized, as Benin Province, and currently remembered only as Benin City. The silence in the folk tales about the silencing of Idu-Bini creates a rupture that has far-reaching psychological implications for the Nigerian collective memory. The repressed knowledge that the kingdom which dared to challenge European authority was destroyed prepares the reader for Idu's death by starvation—for food and for affection—for rebelling against patriarchy. The stories also alert us that elders and those in authority are not resolving contemporary palava in gerontocratic communities, as indicated in the epigraph to this section.

Echoes of *Efuru* can be heard in *Idu*. Efuru and Idu can be read as sisters or as a mother-daughter dyad; their beauty, long hair, kindness, and childbearing problems identify them as descending from one maternal line—Uhamiri. Yet, *Idu* is not simply *Efuru* retold, as many complain. It certainly signifies upon *Efuru*, refining it in many ways: Idu is to Efuru as Anamadi, Idu's uncontrollable sister, is to Idu. The gaps are generational, and the unjust and difficult society, left untackled, exacerbates the people's condition (especially women's). With gerontocracy displaced, law and order have broken down. The subversiveness in the worship of the goddess Uhamiri in *Efuru* turns into an open rebellion in *Idu* with women's growing political acuity. Named to assess indigenous power, Idu is Nwapa's belief that the status of woman indicates societal progress. Idu is the strong, but confused, rural woman of the 1940s, when skirmishes against the British were in place. Naming her first two novels after rural women, Nwapa, in these epochal texts, contributes to the verbal conflict by thrusting into the Nigerian consciousness the necessity for the radicalization of culture from the grass roots.

The themes of *Idu* are enunciated within the first three crucial pages: Idu's childbearing problems, indicative of the barrenness of the society and women's literature; her husband Adiewere's sickness, a sign of the sick society; and the stream as the meeting point, an unexploited spiritual palliative for a society in disarray. Water, as Abiodun tells us, is *ero*, placatory, "able to effect harmony, peace and to eliminate tension and reduce heat through magic powers" (1989, 11). Uhamiri, as intercessor and part of the traditional religion involving water deities, possesses these magic powers lost to her children.

Consequently, confusion exists at different levels: the individual, the marital, the familial, the societal, and the cosmic. The numerous deaths and suicides in the novel are signs of rupture in the community. Onyemuru, the cantankerous "witch," is its voice. To buttress the point that the society has gone awry and in addition treats its womenfolk disrespectfully, Nwapa employs animal images throughout *Idu*. The tortoise is "our father," "the soul of the clan" (Nwapa 1970, 181) in Ugwuta, yet, like sexism, colonialism, and militarism are strongly entrenched, he is brazenly imprisoned by a stranger in the open market. The jailer is eventually forced by people's protests to release the tortoise into the water. This significant episode occurs in the marketplace to demonstrate the spiritual malaise. The wisdom, wiliness, tenacity, and triumph against all odds associated with the tortoise in folklore have been erased from the souls of the people he represents, and he is as endangered as they are. As a result, the clan/nation has no soul, no sense of purpose, but palavering with its *kwenu* spirit can effectively achieve a desirable goal.

Children get beaten in school because "sometimes the children do behave like goats" (184). For committing suicide, Amarajeme "would be thrown away, as a dog is thrown away when it is dead" (146), "thrown away, as you throw away a dead goat" (149). Degeneration into bestiality extends to people barking because they have been bitten by rabid dogs. Although *Idu* is set in the colonial period, the fact that Nwapa wrote it in the 1960s affects her imagery. This turbulent epoch in Nigerian history needed mediation, as the country was heading for the disastrous civil war; Nwapa suggests that the malaise is rooted in colonialism and our denial of its consequences.

Moving from the political perspective, Nwapa revisits the issue of childlessness and love in a polygynous context. How does polygyny affect a close-knit but childless couple who are forced into polygyny as a remedy? What is the fate of the intruding younger wife? Although the young wife typically displaces her senior in their husband's affection, if not in the domestic power play, this is not the case in *Idu*, where she is treated as a mere expedient. Considered an outsider in Adiewere's polygynous household, she is even denied her conjugal rights. She is the prototype of the embittered, neglected or abandoned wife. To get back at her victimizers, she speaks out and spreads rumors that Adiewere is impotent and Idu adulterous. "I have never heard things like this before," declares the incensed Ojiugo, Idu's best friend (56). Ironically, Ojiugo does not just hear such things, but, in the changing pace of the community, she boldly commits adultery with her husband's friend, to have the child her impotent husband cannot father.

Appalled by the polygynous marriages around her, Idu resents the intrusion of the other woman in her home much more than Efuru did hers, and she connives with Adiewere to get rid of her co-wife. Hers is the Western marital ideology of love involving one man and one woman to the exclusion of all others, even children. Adiewere's death, which turns her into a lonely widow, underscores how alien her attitude is. Lovelorn, she starves herself to death. Idu is indeed different. Within her power as a beloved wife lies her undoing. Her deviant behavior following her husband's death is no surprise, as Nwapa moves from the ills of polygyny, for women, to those of widowhood to portray woman as victim in the larger sexist society. Now unprotected by her doting husband from the community's cruel demands, she turns openly rebellious. She refuses to cut her beautiful hair and wear black to make herself unattractive, as is demanded of a widow. Society's leviratic practice demands that she be acquired by her shiftless brother-in-law, whose wife "is hatching children like a hen, yet Idu who supports them has got only one son" (88). Tortured by a sense of loss, envy, pride, and regret and repelled by the idea of levirate, particularly remarrying beneath her, the pregnant Idu is exposed to the loneliness of widowhood, the loneliness of motherhood without a husband to help, the loneliness of the rebel, and the "loneliness of the pregnant woman," to borrow Rich's words in another context (1980, 84).

To free herself, Idu, like an *ogbanje,* decides to go on a lonely journey to the other world, abandoning her children and all responsibility, to join her late husband and playmate. Her own emotional needs come first. Anorexic and mentally unbalanced, she refuses to be subjugated by the claims of motherhood, thus ignoring the living son and the unborn child. In her illuminating study of anorexics, Noelle Caskey concludes:

> That anorexia is a libertarian gesture, a demand for freedom, is also suggested by an interesting relationship between anorexic eating patterns and primitive eating patterns. When anorexics eat what they *do* eat, they eat in small odd amounts and at irregular intervals throughout the day (and the night as well . . . anorexia is apt to induce insomnia). . . . Bruch suggests that anorexics are in part rejecting the modern patriarchal structure when they "revert" to patterns of an earlier, less power-structured organization. (1986, 180–81)

Since Idu "took in" to please society, she refuses to "take in" food to be in control of her body, "punishing" society by not nurturing the fetus. The last meal that she "takes in" is a self-administered extreme unction, as she sets off on her journey to the other world.

Nwapa leaves the nature of Idu's death vague as she drifts into it through a deep sleep. It is unclear whether it is suicide, a sharp contrast to the violence of Ojiugo's husband Amarajeme's self-inflicted death.[19] Margaret Higgonnet (1986) observes that to "embrace death is at the same time to read one's own life. . . . In their deaths, many are obsessed with projecting an image, whether to permit aesthetic contemplation or to provoke *a revolution in thought*" (69; my emphasis). Our puzzle about Idu is solved when Higgonnet continues: "Eighteenth-century heroines like Clarissa accommodated the official condemnation of suicide by a form of anorexia, in which they lingered pallidly, relishing in anticipation the reception of their message" (71).

---

19. Ojiugo's departure from Amarajeme is like a death sentence. His reactions are as schizoid as Idu's at Adiewere's death: the anorexia, the psychological imbalance, the suicidal impulse, the intractability, and the last sumptuous meal preceding the departure to the ancestors are obvious signs. Not willing to change sexual partners, they remain virginal to the end. They are meant to remain on society's conscience.

Undoubtedly, Idu's rebellious acts are politically motivated. Her "unwillingness" to live on after her husband's death is meant to provoke the community. However, Higgonnet states that "Love itself can, of course, be taken as a form of suicide for a woman" (73). When a woman dies for love, she has killed herself twice over, if that is possible. Should Idu's suicide then be read as a revolutionary act (the heroine escaping victimization) or a suttee-like waste? The blurb of the novel declares that "children are not the only thing she [Idu] wants from life"; if the only other thing she wants is to be loved by a man, then she is a loser, because she spurned the love showered on her by women at the end. That the plot ends with such a suicide is as problematic as an ending with a patriarchal marriage, a metaphor for the death of a heroine (74). Signifying on the typical Victorian "heroine" who dies or marries (Driver 1982, 207), Nwapa creates an *ogbanje* textual situation with her repetition and refinement, making Idu go the unenviable way of her predecessors. It is telling that Nwapa should protest so vehemently against patriarchy using female and male suicides and a stillbirth to make her point. The palava is that the heinous system takes a toll on the unborn, relentlessly pursues those who opt out of it through suicide, and gives no quarter to the living—children, women, and men who fail the macho test.

In both *Efuru* and *Idu*, Nwapa is metaphorically crying out about the position of writers, especially women. As Efuru had produced a daughter and Idu a son, so Nwapa had given birth to her daughter Ejine (born 1959) and her son Uzoma (born 1969) and produced another child—the book *Efuru*. The death of Efuru's daughter is indicative of Nwapa's fear of *Efuru's* reception, while Idu's second pregnancy represents her terror that continued hostility or indifference will stultify her potential as a writer. What, indeed, would have happened to Nwapa, if *Idu*, like Idu and her pregnancy, was a dead end? According to Higgonnet, "The ambiguity with which the woman author represents female suicide may betray what Freud described as the universal denial of our own death: our unconscious 'does not believe in its own death; it behaves as if it were immortal.' Although she must deny her own death, the author can, nonetheless, experience death through her work. . . . The woman author is, as it were, reading her own death in that of her protagonist" (1986, 80–81). Nwapa is so deeply terrified about her writing career that she expresses her trepidation in not one but two suicides. In the final analysis, *Idu* can be read as a 218-page suicide note by a writer who failed to take her own life, as many threats of suicide by females fail to materialize. Writing for woman is in a sense suicidal, but Nwapa manages to survive her ordeal. The note expresses the writer's desire for attention; Idu dies for Nwapa to obtain that attention. Her fears for the fate of the second text are as palpable as that of Idu for her second child. Idu dies, and, phoenixlike or *ogbanje*like, gives life to *Idu* while reminding us of the fates of Idu-Bini and Nwapa herself. As character and text, she serves as a warning to those interested in a wholesome Nigeria to examine the nature of human alienation in the country.

Idu's suicide for an ideal is also comparable to Biafra's failed attempt to obtain justice through the civil war. This analogy is not too far-fetched, because *Idu* was written during the turbulent years preceding the outbreak of hostilities and was published in 1970, after the Nigerian civil war. Idu can therefore be considered a sacrifice proffered for communal good, while *Idu* can be read as a propitiatory text by an erstwhile Biafran woman to the Nigerian public. Idu is also a pun on the pidgin sentence, *E do*, "It is enough," or, when uttered in exasperation, "Enough is enough." The pacific Nwapa is saying *E do*, "That will do," to the belligerent parties to cease the war that engulfed Idu (modern Benin and its environs). The cosmic dimensions involving the eclipse causing darkness at noon clearly indicates that all is not well in the community. She is saying *E do* to the cruelty inflicted on women, children, and other helpless people in the society.

As indicated previously, *Idu* critiques the tyrannical hold of the society not only over women but also over a few men and children. An examination of the subplot involving Ojiugo and Amarajeme will illuminate this context. For the second time in one text, Amarajeme and Ojiugo's tragic love story with its theme of childlessness reminds us of Nigerian social reality. This childless couple contrasts with Adiewere and Idu, who also experienced some anxiety before they had their son. Importantly, Ojiugo and Amarajeme's story signifies on J. P. Clark's 1961 play *Song of a Goat*, linking us again with the midwestern part of Nigeria, specifically with Bendel state (Benin-Delta state) in the subplot. This yearning for and journeying to a mythical place beyond Ugwuta demonstrates Nwapa's national concern.

Nwapa's Amarajeme, like Clark's Zifa before him, hangs himself when his wife humiliatingly exposes his impotence by becoming impregnated by another man. Although Ojiugo is inconsolable, devastated by guilt for Amarajeme's suicide, it is instructive that Nwapa as a woman author lets her live and keep her child, whereas Clark, the male dramatist, permits all the characters to die in a cataclysm, implying that, without the paterfamilias, the rest of the family must not exist. In rewriting Clark's story, Nwapa boldly touches a sensitive point in the Nigerian consciousness. She has dared to put the unthinkable into words: that man, and not always woman, can be infertile. Through the portrait of Ojiugo, she has liberated many women (and mature men). She is saying that woman cannot continue waiting indefinitely for man, neither will she continue to protect a man who is not ready to face reality. She is saying *E do* to all the lies, pain, and subterfuges that healthy but childless women endure in a society that demands they bear children. Her point is that, to save the family, couples have to work together, not separately; if the man is unwilling to cooperate, as most are, woman must extricate herself from the mess and strike out for her own self. This was heterodoxy in 1970s Nigeria, yet Nwapa, as always, manages to make these powerful statements without being offensive.

In keeping with this negotiatory spirit in the palaver, Nwapa does not treat Amarajeme dismissively. Tactfully, she presents him also as her child, albeit a son who finds it impossible to cast off centuries of conditioning in masculinism. On the metaphoric level, she uses his sterility to typify the inadequacies in Nigerian and specifically Igbo culture and literature. According to the Nigerian scholar, Ernest Emenyonu (1988, 36), "After *Omenuko* [1933], Igbo literature suffered another period of barrenness which lasted for thirty years." On the political level, Amarajeme's infertility is also Nwapa's outcry against the unproductiveness of the men in power in Nigeria; complementarily, she wants the women, like Ojiugo, to deliver the community from the lack, no matter how painful the duty is. At this moment in literary history, Amarajeme's isolation from the community is billed to fault the societal lack of appreciation for his unique contribution; it also critiques the failure of the literary world to acknowledge African literature, an international problem that men and women writers have had to face together.

When Amarajeme hangs himself, we remember Achebe's Okonkwo in *Things Fall Apart* and how unbridled masculinity takes its toll on men. Because suicide turns one into an outcast, little better than an animal, the writers are commenting on the unfeeling and unsupportive nature of a society that would drive a man to such a dishonorable end. Society uncannily self-destructs. This is far from a *kwenu* operative system and is indicative of the flaw in the power structure that leads to a breakdown in the palaver and the collapse of a way of life. For Nwapa, societal insistence on child-bearing without provision for those who cannot (or even do not want to) and without appreciation of other forms of productivity is ultimately suicidal.

"What we are all praying for is children. What else do we want if we have children?" (Nwapa 1970, 150), Nwapa sarcastically interjects in *Idu. Idu* shows that society pays lip service to caring for children. Pride and joy seem to come from the emotional power that owning children confers, not in their nurturing. Nwapa attacks the obsession for producing children. In *Idu,* she traces its

163

insidious effects on the Nigerian collective unconscious by focusing on the folk tale about the king with his ten, wretched wives, whom he adroitly controls by exploiting their co-wifely rivalry. Their value is reduced to their ability to produce an heir. The most hated and despised of the ten women graduates to become the Queen, after the King sifts through the women's lies to identify his heir's true mother. It is significant that a young girl named Efuru tells this story of intrigue and barrenness in the royal household—that is, in the national leadership. She reminds us of the earlier Efuru, intimating us that the blame for barrenness is internalized by women from girlhood. Interestingly, nobody, including the ten women embroiled in their roles as victims, questions the fertility of a King with ten barren wives (ibid., 151–53). This cautionary tale reveals the essence of the problems that beset the family and governments in Nigeria.

The vignette criminalizing Oguagara, the *dibia* with fifteen wives, is equally revealing. Man degenerates into a stud, irresponsibly overpopulating the community. Something is psychologically wrong with a people that puts a premium on children yet fails to care for them. Simply put, Nigeria pursues interests inimical to herself. Uncared for children develop into apathetic or criminal adults. The irresponsible couple Ishiodu and Ogbeyanu, Idu's brother- and sister-in-law, fail to care for their children; Idu abandons her children to pursue her dead husband; Ojiugo, guilt-ridden about Amarajeme's suicide, is inconsolable in spite of her child. In *Idu,* Nwapa elaborates on the proverb that articulates the inherent tragedy in having children and childlessness to make her point: something is wrong with a nation that prevaricates and does not seriously grapple with the profundity in a proverb of their own creation or incisively deal with human problems before they get out of hand. The entire population must become increasingly sensitized, to prevent the type of collapse we witness in the war-engulfed society of *Never Again.*

Never Again: The War to End All Wars

The Woman of the Lake . . . had never allowed the conquest of Ugwuta by water or by land or by air.

Flora Nwapa, *Never Again*

Nwapa's novella *Never Again* (1975) is another landmark in Nigerian women's writing. Based on her personal experience in war-torn Biafra, it is the first war narrative written by an African woman. Emecheta signifies on this work in *Destination Biafra,* which is a more detailed account about the civilian, especially women's role in the civil war to establish the abortive dream of a safe, liberated state. Since a woman authored the war novella, it is not surprising that Nwapa is hardly ever mentioned when critics deal with Nigerian war fiction (Umeh 1987, 194).

The breakdown in the national palaver, which had kept the country as one polygynous household, brought about the worst palava we have ever experienced: the Nigerian-Biafran civil war. From the Biafran, secessionist perspective, Nwapa regales us with the politics of lies, deception, terrorism, and propaganda that are part and parcel of modern warfare. Verbal war replaces the negotiatory spirit of the palaver, as speeches in numerous, pointless community meetings are mere Gatling guns.

The novella moves with great speed, recapturing the confusion that predominated in Biafra during the Nigerian civil war. This is a mad world where war is fought with "impotent words" and where, strangely and absurdly enough, the youths are "going to face automatic weapons with sticks" (Nwapa 1975, 52). Women are pivotal in this war: some cross borders, daring to go where their men cannot, shrewdly and aggressively maintaining contact with the enemy through the "attack trade" (13); the remaining women are to arm themselves with "mortar pistols," (mortars and pestles) (12), a double entendre which underscores women's truculence and their vital role in feeding the civilian population and, most critically, the soldiers, a ragtag, hungry bunch who obviously need palava sauce. Thus, the central issue is the role of women as mothers in a society devastated by war, a patriarchal preoccupation. Nwapa cannily chooses a war situation to demonstrate the mutual dependency of the sexes because, in Judith Steihm's words, "War is another situation in which survival takes precedence over custom. Men and women easily become partners when it aids their survival" (1976, 230). Kate, the protagonist, and Chudi, her husband, are codependent, as are most of the couples. Most compellingly, the Ugwuta population need Uhamiri, the Woman of the Lake and their mother, to protect them from the invading Nigerian forces. In her turn, Uhamiri needs them to recognize her strategic importance as a defensive body of water, and she wants her middle-aged daughters to talk with her trustingly and, despite the hard times, feed her with numerous sacrifices of choice animals. The women's public ceremonies help to end the deadly *ogbanje* cycles of Ugwuta and, by extension, of Nigeria.

For the first time in her writing, Nwapa's protagonist tells her story directly, writing the self into the text with the unforgettable "I." Kate's purpose in telling the story, which coincides with Nwapa's, is maternal—to teach the pernicious nature of war in order to save rather than destroy lives. The opening gambit is revealing: "After fleeing from Enugu, Onitsha, Port Harcourt and Elele, I was thoroughly tired of life." This *ogbanje* wanderer, seeking a safe,

165

clean, "other place," continues, "I meant to see the end of the war. Dying was terrible. I wanted to live so that I could tell my friends on the other side what it meant to be at war—a civil war at that, a war that was to end all wars. I wanted to tell them that reading it in books was nothing at all; they just would not understand it. I understood it" (1975, 1). Nwapa is obviously speaking through Kate, her alter ego; for the first time in her writing career, the writer is dealing with firsthand experiences rather than retelling communal rememories.

Several wars are going on simultaneously in the novella, showing the utter breakdown of law and order in the Ugwuta/Biafran/Nigerian society. Kate experiences psychological disorientation as part of the chaos around her. The reader's uncertainty about her sanity spices the response to the narrative. Since Kate is the narrator yet thinks differently from every other person, the reader wonders whether her sanity will ever return and whether she is a dependendable narrator. The war of nerves among the Ugwuta people themselves—between mother and child, between members of the same family, between friends, between the leaders and the followers, between the soldiers and the civilians—is a sign of the times. So also is the spiritual war between the Ugwuta people and their mother Uhamiri. The civil war raging between the Nigerians and the Biafrans encapsulates all the warring tensions in the nation.

Kate's English name marks her double-consciousness, alienation, and outsiderness, since Nwapa usually gives characters foreign names for a symbolic purpose. In her despair, Kate questions her own sanity, while, in typical *ogbanje* fashion, she is disgruntled with everything, most especially criticizing Biafran propaganda. The frequency of community palavers is in itself alarming, particularly because the *kwenu* spirit is nullified as words cease to convey any meaning, complicating the palava. She dissociates herself from her spiritual mother Uhamiri. Her sanity will be restored when she reunites with Uhamiri, whom she distrusts because she, Kate, is a Christian. In the religious war that serves as subtext, Kate, horrified at her mother's defection from Christianity to "heathenism" declares: "You are no longer a Christian? You could go with the heathens to the shrine of the Woman of the Lake to sacrifice to her!" (39) Kate is yet to learn contemporary liberation theology. She fails to see the Christian God as the patriarchal father, insensitive to people's plight. Uhamiri, on the other hand, is female, the mother through whom salvation finally comes. As the Igbo say, Nneka; mother is indeed supreme in this novel.

By narrating the event, Kate unwittingly starts off on a quest for the

mother and for order. In her role as daughter, she resurrects the deity, enervated by evil in the warring patriarchal society of Ugwuta, Biafra, and Nigeria.
Her narrative is both therapeutic and womanist, restoring order through
woman. Her panegyric on God the Mother palliates the anger of the Woman
of the Lake, arousing her maternal instincts to protect her children. As Kate
becomes mother identified with her tribute, she becomes gradually healed. For
Nwapa, who has projected herself onto Kate, *Never Again* affirms her perception of woman's role in society as central and maternal, not in the narrow
sense but in a universal role to ensure order, because those were women's children dying in what turned out to be an unnecessary war. I use the word
unnecessary because, writing from hindsight, Biafra was as mendacious as
Nigeria, an *ogbanje* replica.

The theme of the mother confronted with her warring children is important. Initially, Kate is highly suspicious of the role of her mother in the dis-
tressing situation: "If my own mother handed me over to the Army, then the
world had come to an end. I'll make a painful exit. But I must talk to my
mother" (28). The use of mother here has a double meaning. It could refer to
her biological mother or her spiritual mother Uhamiri, whom she refuses to
acknowledge consciously. Later, she evolves into a split personality, as she acts
as Uhamiri's mouthpiece while not believing in her. She projects her suspi-
cions of her natural mother onto Uhamiri, the mother of all. She fears that
these mothers will not or cannot perform their maternal functions—to protect, guide, and guard their people.

The credibility gap between the leaders and the followers is yet another
source of tension. The novella is replete with ironic twists depicting the leading
men and women as willfully perverting the truth of their terrible situation.
The vignette about the madman Ezekoro, heading back to the besieged Ugwuta
instead of running away like the other citizens, aptly symbolizes the chaos and
lack of purposeful direction in the society.

The absurdity of war and the terror it generates finally prompt the limited
narrator to address Uhamiri, the knower of all things: "The Woman of the
Lake, the thunderer, the hairy woman. The most beautiful woman in the
world. The ageless woman. Why, why have you done this to your children? . . .
Why have you brought this death on us?" (54). At the core of the novella, Kate
identifies the spiritual gap between Uhamiri and her Ugwuta children,
brought about by the latter's sins of omission and commission. In the topsy-
turvy world of the exodus from Ugwuta, an exhausted woman on the road,
wracked with labor pains, cries out to her dead mother, trying to connect. Her
dead ancestress is deaf to her pleas, and she, like Idu in her birth/death throes,

also turns deaf ears to the cries of her children around her. The failure of communication between mothers and children is symptomatic of the people's spiritual death, but in death lies the possibility of an *ogbanje* birth—that is, a new beginning—as they journey haphazardly toward safety.

The fundamental sin of unbelief in the mother, in Uhamiri, particularly on the part of the Ugwuta Christians, is matricidal and, therefore, disorienting. With people suffering from paramnesia, the magical use of words in the distortional Biafran propaganda is homicidal, as the patriarchs controlling the war send off to the fighting zone boys armed with sticks. Only men would perpetrate such a crime on women's sons. Those who escape the slaughter turn picaros, like Obinna in Tony Ubesie's Igbo novel, *Juo Obinna* (1977); Obinna sets out on a quixotic quest, feigning madness to circumvent the madness of the war zone. Indeed, "Nigerians have robbed us of everything including our common-sense" (Nwapa 1975, 31), as Nwapa's mad Ezekoro, a case of déjà vu, exemplifies the communal tragedy.

Moved by their numerous sacrifices, both animal and human, Uhamiri finally relents. Her children forgiven, she uses her mystical powers tò defend her people. The work calmly ends on a positive note: "The only thing that stood undisturbed, unmolested, dignified and solid was the Lake. It defied war. It was calm, pure, peaceful and ageless. It sparkled in the sunlight, turning now blue, now green as the sun shone on it" (80). The Lake is a symbol of the possibilities of Ugwuta. It reaffirms the strength of the Woman of the Lake. It affirms the peace that followed the cessation of war. The last scene is significant, as women worshippers go to perform sacrifices to her in appreciation of her deliverance and to cleanse the pollution caused by numerous deaths. The maternal principle finally becomes reestablished in this wholesome environment. As war creates a barrier between children and their mother, the movement toward peace wears down that boundary, reuniting those at peace with their mother/motherland. Ugwuta's original incorruptibility is symbolized in Kate's uncle's almost neonatal dependence on the Lake: "If I open my eyes and don't see water I'll die. . . . He was a very clean man. His clothes were never dirty" (44). His cleanliness and need for water to keep clean—that is, his closeness to maternal discipline and purity—is an outward manifestation of a state of grace, which the Ugwutans/Biafrans/Nigerians had lost through filthy corruption. The flight from the land and god the mother is their final undoing, because they run unprotected into hostile territory, where they are scorned for not defending their land and for losing contact with their deity.

The cessation of war restores sanity. This enables the unbalanced Kate to view the situation with equanimity and, very importantly, tell her story; this is the voice of woman. Her solidity, like the lake's, shows the firmness, strength, order, and mystical power in a world controlled by a female deity in contrast to the disorder of a patriarchal society that thrives on the subjugation of people and controlled by the impotent, male, Christian God. The defeat of God the father is total in the war of the deities on the periphery of the novella. As the resurrected female deity is reinstated in the minds of her people by Kate-Nwapa, the female power for good becomes openly acknowledged by men and women. This womanist vision is also seen in action in *One Is Enough*.

One Is Enough: Bitter Wife, Sweet Mother

As a wife, I am never free. I am a shadow of myself. As a wife, I am almost impotent. I am in prison, unable to advance in body and soul. Something gets hold of me as a wife and destroys me. When I rid myself of [my husband], things started working for me.

Flora Nwapa, *One Is Enough*

If the war against God the Christian father is peripheral in *Never Again*, it becomes central in Nwapa's *One Is Enough* (1981) with her condemnation of the patriarchal Roman Catholic Church. The attack is necessitated by the oppressive role the Church plays in the Igbo world, exacerbating woman's pain in a society already dysfunctional because of its sexist traditions. At this point in the evolution of sexual politics, Amaka, the protagonist of *One Is Enough*, has gone beyond the consciousness-raising positions of her predecessors, Efuru, Idu, and Kate. Her role is one of reconstruction, to establish a womanist sphere after opting out of a childless and intolerable patriarchal marriage. Amaka uses erotic power ("bottom power," in Nigerian parlance), hitting the man below his belt, in a manner of speaking, to achieve her political ends. Yemi Mojola finds such power, harnessed by women for "financial gains through debauchery and corruption," as she put it (1989, 25), objectionable.

In a gutsy move in which Nwapa daringly explores the sexuality of women and Roman Catholic priests, Nwapa revises this traditional, sexist opinion against women's use of eroticism to gain power. She rewrites the Nigerian novelist Cyprian Ekwensi's negative treatment of bottom power in *Jagua Nana* and *Jagua Nana's Daughter*. She would agree with Audre Lorde (1978, 1) that "We have been taught to suspect this resource [erotic power], vilified, abused, and devalued within Western society. On one hand, the superficially erotic has been encouraged as a sign of female inferiority—on the other hand women have been made to suffer and to feel both contemptible and suspect by virtue of its existence." Nwapa discards the Ekwensian, sexist premise in *Jagua Nana*

169

and *Jagua Nana's Daughter,* two offending novels where Ekwensi sentimental-izes, trivializes, judges, and devalues two prostitutes, a picara and her brilliant daughter who is a lawyer. Nwapa exploits the weapons that some women have used to access power, to show that there is nothing shameful about them ex-cept that men have made us believe that they are reprehensible, even when used to serve men. If brute force is acceptable in men in sports, for example, why should female eroticism not be equally amoral; or, put in another way, why are only women blamed for their sexuality when it only becomes a reality when men exploit it? Thus, she criticizes the narrow-minded socialization that invariably binds women in a double-standard morality that is silent on their male partners. Her handling of this aspect of the palaver is intended to be con-troversial: not only does she open up the issue of male adultery, she also breaks the embarrassing silence on the licentiousness of Roman Catholic priests, es-pecially their problematic siring of children in the face of their vows of chastity. Surely, one such exposure is enough to open a dialogue on the sexual and religious aspects of the palava. The community and the church need to re-but such insinuations or confess the sins of the fathers, rather than continue to cover up or ignore the problems about the promiscuity of Nigerian males in positions of authority.

Remarkably, Amaka's troubles start off in the eastern part of Nigeria. Suf-fering from the aftermath of the civil war, the East is parochial and extremely antiwoman. Nwapa zeroes in on her theme with the loaded question, "Was a woman nothing because she was unmarried or barren?" (1981, 25). With this rhetorical question, it seems as if we are back to *Efuru.* However, she presents a different dynamic, with Catholic nuns and priests in an atmosphere as con-fining as the traditional Igbo world. Amaka must leave her Igbo cage to estab-lish her true self in a more progressive world. Ambiguity creeps in when we realize that this different world is the West, in decadent Lagos.

Before then, Amaka and Obiora's marital hostilities erupt in an open war. As if Ajanupu in *Efuru* were her mother/tutor, Amaka rejects the role of the victimized wife by battering her husband in a self-defensive attack. She is a "he-woman" for winning the argument with her husband (30). Her husband, identified as the enemy within, is significantly named Obiora—that is, ev-eryman, or, rather, the mind of *everybody* (including women). He stands for the steamrolling *kwenu* mentality ingrained in the Igbo community and, by extension, the Roman Catholic Church. So, Amaka's struggle is colossal: fighting her own socialization (which is suicidal to women) and the whole patriarchal establishment as represented by Obiora-Everyone and the church.

There follows a criticism of the sexist husband from this viewpoint of the

combative woman: "Your rightful place is not in the kitchen as we erroneously think, but right under his thumb. He would like to control your every
movement, and it is worse if you depend on him financially" (30–31). Amaka
is her aggressive mother's daughter. Her mother had retreated from her husband's polygynous battle zone to lick her numerous marital wounds in the
safety of a trading career. Amaka advances westwards to the safety of cosmopolitan Lagos, where women enjoy unbounded freedom, like men. Somewhat like Efuru, she buys her freedom formally and legally by returning
Obiora's dowry with her own hard-earned money. One husband is enough.

Thus the East, from a political viewpoint, is dominated by sexists like
Obiora. In the darkness of this harsh, male world, barren women are nothing,
and "herstory" chronicles the cruelty perpetrated against mothers whose twin
children were considered an aberration, and, consequently, killed. Amaka's
barrenness marks female alienation and futility in a masculinist world torn
apart by war. Lagos, on the other hand, enjoys a peaceful, postwar oil boom. In
contrast to Onitsha/Biafra, Lagos/Nigeria is an enlightened world where freedom and opportunities exist for women. In Lagos, female solidarity thrives in
the all-women Cash Madam Club. The Club has cast off male authority and
uses eroticism to access power. Like their nineteenth-century predecessors,
these Lagos women flaunt their wealth. Theirs is what Adrienne Rich would
call a "lesbian continuum," with its female "bonding against male tyranny"
(1980, 23). The fear and/or contempt of men for women without men, commonly expressed toward lesbians, is extended to the Club members. Nonetheless, they represent female autonomy.

From the feeling of inadequacy and hurt in the East, Amaka's "eyes were
opened in Lagos and she began to see what she could do as a woman, using her
bottom power as they say in Nigeria" (Nwapa 1981, 126). Like Efuru, she had
tried to conciliate her husband by sharing her income with him and by presenting him with gifts, but she had failed to resurrect the dead marriage. As a
declaration of her liberation from men, Amaka joins the Cash Madam Club,
gaining economic independence with the added bonus of female bonding.
These women realize that behind every unsuccessful woman is a man, a
tyrant. Amaka's sister Ayo, "Joy," has a Yoruba name, to demonstrate how far
this Igbo family of Amazons have come in their enlightenment as they embrace Yoruba, female libertarian ideology. To the Lagosian Ayo, man is
merely an extension of woman, part of her outfit: "A woman needed a nice
man to be by her side when she was properly dressed for an outing, and for
procreation" (141), she declares matter-of-factly. Her world is far from Ellen
Key's Sweden. Nwapa's palava against male polygamy takes a decidedly new

turn, with her women becoming polygamous as they follow Ojiugo's footsteps in *Idu*.

Ayo's philosophy is an outgrowth of their mother's, who, like other successful women of her age, married "small wives" to do the "soul destroying chores for their husbands while they themselves concentrated on their trade" (123). Now the new, liberated woman just had the children without bothering about the man, leaving such mundane issues to his hapless wife. "Hail mistressdom, down wifedom!" Ayo seems to say. The men had brought this situation on themselves with their tyrannous hold on women, which the modern women whom Nwapa depicts are determined to break. These women have left behind them men's deceiving silences, which we see in the instance of Obiora (and Efuru's Eneberi before him), fathering children out of wedlock, a typical sign of Nigerian machismo. Rich feels that "To discover that one has been lied to in a personal relationship . . . leads one to feel a little crazy" (1980, 186). Amaka becomes a little crazy and makes up a story about miscarriage. But trust a woman (Obiora's mother) to detect another woman's lies. For sanity, Amaka moves out of their home after laying Obiora prostrate, to mark the collapse of their marriage.

In Lagos, Amaka turns out to be Ayo's quick student. She goes beyond Efuru and Ayo, to show how a single woman can lead a fulfilling life. Politically shrewd, she takes on the Roman Catholic Church, with its insistence on priestly poverty and chastity. Wielding the indomitable erotic weapon, Amaka uses the Catholic priest McLaid, who is also connected with the government. McLaid unwittingly becomes her sperm donor, and, through him, Amaka accesses wealth. She refuses to marry McLaid, the father of her children, for one sexist husband is indeed enough in one lifetime.

Amaka attacks the church where it is most vulnerable—its denial of sexuality and its exclusion of women from its hierarchy. In a role reversal that redefines the missionary position, Amaka plays the "he" woman, and McLaid is laid by her. Her victim is an Igbo mother's Catholic son, adopted by and named after an Irish priest who acts as the surrogate father. By contrast, Amaka makes the Nigerian priest a natural father. This Irish connection internationalizes the political ramifications of the novel. The reference to Ireland and its priest-ridden mentality indirectly connects the work with Irish feminism. McLaid is touched by it all in Dublin. Not surprisingly, he starts working on the horrors of female circumcision, as "He was interested in the obnoxious customs and traditions that chained his people to ignorance and disease . . . that kept the females in bondage . . . that enslaved some people in different societies to perpetual second-class citizenship" (Nwapa 1981, 110).

Amaka has infected him with her libertarian zeal. "His people" refers to his original Igbo society and, most importantly, his adoptive Roman Catholic group, which incorporates the Irish.

Another victim won over by Amaka is the initially hostile, Roman Catholic woman Adaobi. Horrified at Amaka's daring sexual escapades with McLaid, Adaobi refers to her as the calculating seductress of an innocent man, which McLaid is not. Nwapa establishes the fact that McLaid was socialized in the hypocritical Catholic tradition (witness how easily the straying McLaid is forgiven by the Bishop), and comes from a cruel, Igbo, social background. His intemperance is dramatized in his constant demand for fish and beer at Amaka's, fishing for trouble in alcoholic waters. Furthermore, he is polygamous. Adaobi succumbs to the sin of envy and uses the proceeds from associating with the so-called seductress to build the house she and her husband retire to. Amaka has thus indirectly shaken the patriarchal basis of Adaobi's marriage, reversing its gender-defined roles when the woman becomes the provider at the humiliating termination of the husband's appointment.

Amaka has come a long way, from both a historical and a geographical perspective. As a mother of twins, her world is far from McLaid's mother's, whose traumatic experience over a twin birth serves as background. Though Amaka rejects husbands, her womanist sphere includes her twin sons who will thrive unmolested. She realizes that "recognising the power of the erotic within our lives can give us the energy to pursue genuine change within our world rather than merely settling for a shift of characters in the same weary drama" (Lorde 1978, 8). Amaka's sphere of revolutionary action is not limited to Lagos but extends to the East, since she has homes both in the East and in Lagos. Her journey westward in space entails psychological, material, and political growth. From the parochially closed-in Onitsha, she moves to the cosmopolitan Lagos; from Evean innocence she graduates to Salomean experience; from being the Angel in the House, she becomes the womanist in the public eye.

Amaka's character updates us on Nwapa's political development. In contrast to Efuru's *sleeping* off her troubles at the end of the first novel, Amaka is presented as an activist. On a triumphal note, Amaka rejects all the subordinate positions of women—"wife," "mistress," and "kept woman"—and gains independence from men (Nwapa 1981, 105). She has grown from and beyond Efuru, who finally realized that men can be Draculan, vampiric, sappers of women's energy. She has grown from and beyond Idu, who did not will herself to live to fight a cruel sexist society. In an about-face that indicates Nwapa still wants to palaver with men, to simplify the palava, she deliberately makes the twins boys. They serve as the pièces de résistance in this palava sauce proffered to the Igbo world that rejected twins and to the church that calls its priests fathers though they are not permitted to sire children. Though one husband might be enough, ironically, one man is not necessarily enough for the female protagonist in this womanist novel.

Why did Nwapa make an Irish nun, curiously named Sister Maria Angela, announce McLaid's return to the Catholic fold now in disarray? "Catholic women's orders have provided women employment and opportunities for professional training and practice. Though it obliges them to forego marriage and motherhood, the religious life has been the means through which the talents and energies of many women might be utilized with Church approval," write Mary Porter and Corey Venning (1976, 89). Sister Maria Angela represents what the church can do for womanhood. Virginal, this Maria is angelic to boot. She is similar to her sister, the early Amaka, whose name denotes physical and spiritual beauty. The sharp contrast with the later Amaka shows how far the latter has traveled in her journey toward female transcendence. The next target for total liberation is, apparently, Maria Angela. As a go-between, she takes to McLaid the message expressing Amaka's gratitude for his "proving to the world that I [Amaka] am a mother as well as a woman" (Nwapa 1981, 160). Maria Angela can never aspire to be a full woman the way that the church is presently constituted. Amaka's collaborators will hopefully continue their transformative mission in the Catholic fold as elsewhere because women are differently constituted.

Women Are Different: Stasis

Her generation was telling the men that there are different ways of living one's life fully and fruitfully. They are saying that women have options. Their lives cannot be ruined because of a bad marriage. . . . Marriage is not THE only way.

Flora Nwapa, *Women Are Different*

Nwapa's fifth novel is *Women Are Different* (1986). It is the Nigerian version of Shirley Conran's *Lace* (1982), which was shown on Nigerian television, as it chronicles the secondary school and tumultuous adult lives of four protagonists. Three of the close friends, Dora, Rose, and Agnes, are popularly called the "three musketeers," after Alexandre Dumas père's *Les Trois Mousquetaires* (1844). Nwapa signifies on these two Western novels as she brings in elements of scheming and battling for women's genuine freedom, which she parallels with Nigeria's struggles against colonialism.

Women Are Different is also a fictive representation of Nwapa's sentimental journey back to her missionary adolescence, which informs her political ideology. The novel unfolds from the pristine, provincial, Christian, Igbo milieu of Elelenwa, moves on to the deviant, urban, pagan, Yoruba culture of Lagos, and ends with the amoral, godforsaken, international, cosmopolitan scene of the women, their daughters, and their men. The nicknames for the collective protagonists, Rose-Dora-Agnes—the three musketeers—is appropriate because of their checkered careers with men, since modern Nigerian male-female associations are, invariably, battlefields. However, by associating these contemporary women with a nineteenth-century weapon such as the musket, Nwapa ensures in this womanist move that the gender struggle will be carried on under friendly fire; it will not be a battle to the death.

The story covers about forty years (1945–85) of the protagonists' lives, and spans three generations of women. They are Uhamiri's daughters, because marriage is a turbulent affair for these wealthy women. Dora's daughter, Chinwe, and Agnes's, known as Zizi, have also imbibed Uhamiri's spirit: marriage is not considered seriously by this generation. Through the novel, women become increasingly enabled intellectually, economically, and emotionally to attack the patriarchal bases of marriage.

Being schooled at Elelenwa, near Port Harcourt, the Archdeacon Crowther Memorial Girls' School, renowned for its excellent training of women in the colonial period, is the beginning of the girls' journey toward emancipation from British colonial and Nigerian sexist constraints. Ironically, the Nigerian men who are the women's allies in the colonial struggle will become the enemy later.

The Christian colonial teachers, Miss Hill and Miss Backhouse, unwittingly provide a utopian matriarchy for the upbringing of these new girls. Males are unwelcome intruders. The school prepares the girls intellectually to be hostile to men, though the outer society requires them to marry. This basic contradiction forms a stumbling block for them later in life. Since their British mentors did not marry, these surrogate mothers are not suitable models for the Nigerian women destined to become wives and mothers. It is interesting that Uhamiri's attitude toward marriage intersects with that of the British missionaries, reinforcing their *ogbanje* heritage with its boundary crossings and uneasy mingling.

The protagonists arrive at the school by train, a symbol of their journey toward modernity and freedom, away from the examples of their biological mothers. Later in their lives, they own powerful cars, travel light like their colonial mistresses, and try to become part of the international jet set. The stories of the three or four (Nwapa deals with Comfort cursorily) women are interwoven. Historically, they represent Igbo migration to Lagos in search of the ease of a Western lifestyle, the fairy-tale transformation from rags to riches. Geographically and spiritually, it is a move from the east to the west, from innocence to decadence. The pidgin adage, "To go Lagos no hard, na return" (Nwapa 1986, 5), expresses it all, for once they set out on their road to freedom and the good life, there is no turning back to the narrow *kwenu* mentality.

In the secondary school, the girls reside in Clock House (7), indicating that they are birds of passage. Like the clock, they are perpetually on the move, always changing in spite of their sameness. They debate with the boys in the neighboring school whether "the education of girls is a waste of money" (12), an idea that some brainwashed girls, like Comfort, unfortunately support. The disconcerting aspects of the arrangement for the debate—the broken-down vehicle and the consequent long walk in the dark—are signs of the dislocation and the bitter-sweet nature of male-female relationships. The women survive because of their intricate network that stretches across generations and nationalities.

Nwapa devotes the rest of the book to showing that there is a need for the education of girls to ensure female independence, which will enable women to keep up with their male counterparts at school, at work, and at home. For Miss Hill "had not graduated in Oxford and come to Nigeria to train Nigerian girls to be good wives. She was not a wife. She was a missionary who had shunned all worldly attractions to do the will of God" (23). Her lesson goes down very well because there isn't a single happy marriage recorded for her protégées or their children. Their careless world, stereotypically Lagosian, fascinates as it nauseates. The entire book is, therefore, paradoxical: Nwapa seems to blame colonialism, which broadened the vision of Nigerian women, for the tragic breakup of the family. Hers is a revised version of the story of Eve and the fruit of the tree of knowledge. Knowledge, stemming from the fruits of colonialism, frees the individual woman from many oppressive institutions. The colonial web becomes even more intricate as the girls admire Nigerian freedom fighters and defiantly read banned newspaper articles demanding Nigerian independence from Britain. By educating Nigerian men and women in Western ways, Britain had unintentionally opened a Pandora's box.

Nwapa uses Rose as her alter ego, as she is conceived with a few autobiographical touches.[20] Of the three girls, Rose is the most ardent student of Miss Hill and Miss Backhouse, for she, like them, remains single and childless at

20. Like Nwapa, Rose had an aunt in Achimota College and an uncle overseas, went to Archdeacon Crowther Memorial Girls' School, Elelenwa, in 1945 and to Queen's College for her postsecondary education, completing her higher education at the University College, Ibadan. There are thus some autobiographical overlaps between Rose and Nwapa.

the end of the novel. The most sensitive of the girls, we see the others through her critical but understanding eyes. Miss Hill would have been proud of her, for "she felt Nigeria needed well brought up Christian girls who would take their places when they eventually handed over power to the people. Miss Hill could see the handwriting on the wall since the advent of [Dr.] Nnamdi Azikiwe" (23), one of the foremost Nigerian leaders. Rose turns out to be one such girl through the chance occurrence that each of the four men in her life proved to be unsuitable as husband material.

The English names of the women reveal their British heritage, which is superimposed on the Nigerian. This dual heritage creates an *ogbanje* identity in their split personality, their been-toism. The same goes for their male friends: Ernest (for Rose); Chris (for Dora); and Sam (for Agnes). Each of the men, saddled with a double-consciousness as a result of colonialism, turns out unfulfilled, even criminally inclined. The more sophisticated Yoruba men— Olu, Tunde, and Ayodele—replace them in the women's lives. The women then become polygamous through their adulterous relationships, casting off their earlier Christian socialization to become what Wambui wa Karanja (1987) refers to as "outside wives."

From all the unstable marriages depicted, it seems that the new man and the new woman are up in arms against the institution, for each drifts easily to other relationships. Individually, the women achieve the good life through their education and wealth; afterwards, it is too late for them to return to the emotional security of their roots in the communal *kwenu* spirit. Unscrupulous men, like the bribe-taking Chris and the male gold-digger Mark, exploit them as outside wives. Karanja explains such deviant male behavior thus: "Also as a rebellion against their colonial past, many elite men argue with passion that it is 'incumbent' upon them to go back to ways African. The institution of 'outside wives' or private polygyny, then, is seen by some as one articulation of such a sentiment, since it is said to be intrinsically bound up in African traditional cultures" (258). All the male characters, with the exception of Tunde, are polygynously inclined in an emerging culture mimicking Western ways when it is convenient.

The marital crisis has turned the Nigerian marriage into an *ogbanje* institution, with couples floundering across indigenous, Western, and Muslim boundaries, with dire consequences. Agnes's arranged child marriage fails; the traditional view of marriage with children as an integral part "of a full and complete marriage and of womanhood" (ibid., 249) leaves the new Agnes cold. She exercises female power by refusing to cook, when her husband does not permit her to go to night school; to further emasculate the old man, she cuckolds him. The women have become so "detribalised" that Agnes's stepmother can shamelessly take over her stepdaughter's husband without considering it incestuous and taboo (Nwapa 1986, 59). It appears that when women refuse to compromise by practicing indigenous principles, for example, the four C's—conciliation, collaboration, consensus, complementarity—and obtain sexual equality with men, chaos ensues. Janet's madness, like Ezekoro's and Kate's in *Never Again*, becomes a sign of societal discord. The mothers (and fathers) have gone crazy; long live the children.

When Chris deserts Dora and their children for a German woman and Ernest drifts into drug trafficking with women collaborators, forgetting Rose, Nwapa dramatizes what Esther Smith (1986, 40) refers to as the "legacy of colonialism in post-independence Africa." We readily agree that "there must be something in Europe that makes our men behave in that strange way" (Nwapa 1986, 107). Exile, as always, is harsh and disorients. The marriages of the next generation—Chinwe and Zizi—in the 1970s are a far cry from those of the 1940s because Nigeria has become a "cultural melting pot" (101). Because of a lack of female solidarity, women manipulate their kinsmen against their wives. In this "rotten" society, Christian education is inappropriate because it tries to make women thus socialized "angel[s] among devils" (115). Miss Hill was right to have been agitated about the girls' preoccupation with boys, a warning they should have heeded, considering that their virginal lives at school prove to be more peaceful and fulfilling than their turbulent marital lives. Illogically, Chinwe marries a married man, though she had left her home in a pique when her husband married another woman. The haven of school changes into the hell of adult life.

Perhaps Miss Hill had foresight to recognize that independence had come to the country (and educated women?) too fast and too soon. She knew that the psychological repercussions of colonialism, which creates an ethos of adult dependency, would affect male-female relationships and also create unstable governments. Her fears become justified, as Nwapa indicates: "The young parliamentarians and the secretaries thought that taking over from the British meant having license to corrupt young schoolgirls and their mothers. . . . To them, independence meant living in the GRA . . . taking over the positions of the British, driving cars like their colonial masters, but ignoring the grave responsibilities attached to their new positions. . . . *The civil service was still regarded as the white man's service, and therefore one could cheat the government, and boast about it, because it was a foreign government*" (63; my emphasis). Here, Nwapa boldly pinpoints the Africa wo/man palava: the feeling of unbelonging that perpetuates irresponsibility in a majority of Nigerian citizens. It stems from our polygynous beginnings as a nation. The crisis is embedded in our chophouse mentality: to consume, as indiscriminately and as openly as possible, the palava sauce Nigeria miraculously keeps providing—tragically now through loans that will keep the country perpetually indebted if nothing is done about it.

Nwapa agonizes over the fact that the original Nigerian freedom fighters, Nwafor Orizu and Mbonu Ojike, with their ideology for Nigerian cultural hegemony, remain unheeded. Predictably, the colonialist in Miss Hill does not like them, nor the nationalist zeal of the newspaper, *The West African Pilot*, which she bans from her school. The lack of a Nigerian identity for the girls and the mixture of the local and foreign end in disaster. Nwapa's stance toward the relevance of female education is finally ambivalent: education ensures the eradication of abject poverty through the rise of the nouveaux riches, but it brings about female restlessness, hence the marital muddle. Education makes the new Nigerian woman feminist, mimicking her European counterpart's bid for equality. This is stereotypically linked with sexual promiscuity. Obviously, Nwapa does not encourage this version of "feminism," which is far removed from Uhamiri's ideology of female independence and chastity; Nwapa depicts its evolution in Lagos as a cautionary move in the palaver.

In *Women Are Different*, the recklessness in every phase of life is a sign that "Nigeria needed a time to learn that when they were independent, it did not just mean taking over from the colonial masters. It meant taking over responsibility from the colonial masters. It meant being patriotic, taking decisions that would benefit the country just as the colonial masters took decisions that benefitted the mother country" (90). Nigeria's misogyny, evidenced by the ill-treatment of women and the indifference to the spirit of nationhood as conceptualized in the notion of the "mother country," becomes Nigeria's undoing. Since the "men were chickens" (113), as Nwapa portrays the male characters, the repercussions are serious as the chickens come home to roost. "Practically all public and civil servants have divided loyalty. He is either loyal to his tribe, his state or his religion or his friends but rarely his country," observes Tunde. "You think this is due to our colonial heritage?" Rose asks rhetorically (136).

Thus, the colonial heritage has not only turned men into chickens, but it has twisted their thinking leaving Nigeria in shambles. Consequently, families become alarmingly dysfunctional because they are headed by self-centered women. In a curious move, Nwapa kills off Tunde's close-knit family, which could have served as a model since the wife teaches Tunde how to cook. Tunde becomes catatonic from guilt at having been responsible for his family's death. Mourning keeps him from loving anyone else. Consequently, he misses an opportunity for future growth with Rose, who might have saved him. In all this chaos, love, in the form of female bonding, keeps the women going. The love of mothers for their daughters, even wayward and criminal ones, and the love of younger women for older ones like Rose's for Ernest's mother, forms a formidable force for good.

The psychological impact of colonialism, aggravated by the trauma of the civil war and the corruptibility of international culture, with its easy wealth, have devastated the Nigerian soul, as captured in *Women Are Different.* In this novel, Uhamiri's daughters, educated by questionable British surrogate mothers like Misses Hill and Backhouse, have an uphill task moving from the female backhouse to the forefront to participate meaningfully in running home and country. The collapse of the Nigerian marriage—arranged, child marriage, polygyny, polygamy, monogamy and the phenomenon of the outside wife—marks the imminent collapse of the Nigerian urban family and, perhaps, the nation. Survival is possible in this topsy-turvy world through female love and magnanimity, which Tunde, the lone male toward the end of the novel, recognizes: "Very few women will do what she [Dora] has done," that is, pass her lover Tunde on to Rose. "Many will, Tunde," rejoins Rose. "We women are different from men in many ways" (137). The predominantly negative images in the novel represent Nwapa's despair; they serve as a warning that something concrete must be done to salvage the mother country, Nigeria, through saving the women *and* men.

Nwapa's Political Acuity: "A Woman Protects a Man"—Silently

In the tradition of *"awon iya wa,"* those inscrutable mothers who unobtrusively oversee the well-being of the community, Nwapa's inspiriting contribution to the palaver with these five novels leaves us finally with a semblance of peace, or perhaps a truce, for the work of the fighting woman, engaged in the war for decent survival in the anarchic Nigerian world, is never done. Tedious and thankless, like housework, it must continue to be done, or else the living conditions will become too hazardous for women, men, and their children. In his war novel *Survive the Peace* (1976), Ekwensi uncannily recognized that life in peacetime can be more arduous than the struggle to survive in a civil war. Echoing him, Nwapa, through her novels, reiterates the point that women and men can survive only through collaborative effort in the tortuous journey Nigeria must undertake for rehabilitation.

Nwapa's typical protagonist is a dynamic personality who can protect people, though she might be somewhat limited. In spite of a successful career and her care-giving commitment, Efuru's anxiety about her standing without a husband or children is telling. Her doubts are finally resolved when she accepts the female principle, Uhamiri, giving up conventional thoughts of wifehood or motherhood to serve her community in a differently productive capacity. Idu's rebellious nature, which causes her to abandon her children for union with her husband, demonstrates compellingly that a new breed of women is emerging. Kate's narrative reordering of a world gone mad in war, Amaka's remapping the family through her single parenting, and Rose-Dora-Agnes' experimental matriarchy are powerful statements about the journey toward transcendence in the Nigerian household. The protagonist of each novel serves as a foremother and pathfinder to the next, while each character carries the state of the ideological struggle a step further than she found it. Thus, there could have been no three musketeers in *Women Are Different* without their predecessors. Behind the surface banter of the novels, beneath the calmness, is a psychological prop derived from an indigenous female tradition which Nwapa has tried to pass on in novel after novel. The talismanic, maternal presence of Uhamiri, especially in the first three novels, parallels Nwapa's conciliatory, womanist gestures. However, if society is reluctant to compromise or to reach a consensus in the palaver, her vision, in the last two novels, is disquietingly apocalyptic: the proliferation of a new breed of tough, educated women, whose newfangled ideologies and radicalism will reproduce an unrecognizable Nigeria.[21] Her strategy is cautionary: to will men to engage in a meaningful palaver instead of having such "feminism" thrust upon them.

A true womanist, Nwapa, through her Ugwuta ideological experience, knows that a powerful Nigeria needs tenacious women. Therefore, she privileges women with clout (with all its nuances), contrasting them with passive women wallowing in their rhetoric of silence. In different ways, however, most attempt to change their community by action or manipulation. Inexorably subversive, Nwapa arms her strong women with the traditional pestle and the Western hammer (physically and symbolically knocking macho men down to silence them, since they cannot discuss their discomfiture), and muskets, for she will not spare the rod and spoil the man. In the marital guerrilla war of her novels, she counters polygyny with polyandry; her interpretation of polygamy is not the average Nigerian's—to Nwapa, the spouse, male *or female,* can have more than one mate at the same time. Canceling the woman-the-victim stereotype, she also presents us with men whom one feels sorry for.

---

21. Emecheta's Nnu Ego in *The Joys of Motherhood* is Uhamirian in this sense after her death, refusing to grant prayers for children.

By using biological motherhood as an agent to effect a matriarchal shift, Nwapa has shaken the very foundation of patriarchy, thereby reinstating complementarity as a vital aspect of postcolonial discourse.

Incredible as it may seem, in Nigeria, Nwapa has insidiously influenced hitherto masculinist authors, such as Achebe and Soyinka and many up-and-coming novelists (for example, Isidore Okpewho and Ben Okri) who now write with sensitivity on gender issues and other sociopolitical matters.[22] They are all held accountable to an international readership increasingly respectful of women. This about-face is, ideologically, so much the better for the Nigerian palaver; as critical, urban women, *ogbanje* to the hilt, follow Nwapa's example, they negotiate from a position of maternal strength in an attempt to erase the colonial and patriarchal margins to install women in their rightful, postcolonial place in the midst of things.[23]

22. Achebe's *Anthills of the Savannah* and Soyinka's *Ake* show increasing signs of sensitivity.

23. It is fascinating to note that the last issue of *West Africa* in 1993, for example, reported the following: "About 300 women from Ohana Village [Cross River State, southeastern Nigeria] recently stormed the Obubra offices of the National Agricultural Land Development Authority (NALDA) in a traditional protest. Work stopped temporarily and thousands of palm seedlings were destroyed by the women who ranged from teenagers to the aged. The women alleged non-compensation for their land on which the NALDA project is located. Efforts are on to resolve the crisis" ("Dateline," *West Africa*, 27 December 1993–9 January 1994: 2355).

Chapter Four
Adaora Lily Ulasi: Juju Fiction

[W]e must understand that magic and witchcraft . . . are ritual terms of a short-hand which authors adopt to describe a system of beliefs and practices not entirely accessible to us now. In other words, [the novelist] is pointing toward a larger spiritual and religious context through these notations, so that ordinary diurnal events in the novel are invested with extraordinary meaning.

Hortense J. Spillers, "A Hateful Passion" (1987)

[The Gothic novel's] confusions—its misleading clues, postponements of discovery, excessive digressions—are inscribed in the narrative structure itself.

Claire Kahane, "The Gothic Mirror" (1985)

The term "magic realism" is an oxymoron, one that suggests a binary opposition between the representational code of realism and that, roughly, of fantasy. In the language of narration in a magic realist text, a battle between two oppositional systems takes place, each working toward the creation of a different kind of fictional world from the other. Since the ground rules of these two worlds are incompatible, neither one can fully come into being, and each remains suspended, locked in a continuous dialectic with the "other," a situation which creates disjunction within each of the separate discursive systems, rending them with gaps, absences, and silences.

Stephen Slemon, "Magic Realism as Post-colonial Discourse" (1988)

The Magic of Confusion: A Long (Overdue) Introduction

Dibia, babalawo, magus, or charlatan? These are the masculine words that intrude when one attempts to resolve the paradox posed by the most misunderstood writer from Nigeria—the Igbo woman, Adaora Lily Ulasi. Like *awon iya wa,* those mysterious mothers who work clandestinely for the good of the community, she frustrates the curious for she does not appear interested to throw a little light on her life or her works. My reading of her, therefore, might turn out to be a misreading, seeing things where they do not exist because she has fixed me with juju, or, it might out turn out to be illuminating, relieving her unwarranted eclipse.

In several ways, Ulasi's life uncannily mimics the Yoruba water deity's, the primary mother Osun, her adoptive *orisa.* Sent off by her father to the United States for higher education, this ex-ile was the first West African

183

woman to obtain a degree in journalism. As pathfinder and journalist, she had to work in a predominantly male world at the *Times* complex in Lagos, where, doubly exiled on ethnic and gender grounds, she lived in constant terror of being silenced with juju by her Yoruba colleagues. Writing the male-centered juju novel came to her naturally as she seemed displaced, like Osun. It secretly empowered her, as Osetura/Esu did Osun, extending her domain as she harnessed the hostile male world. There are elements of déjà vu, as Ulasi attempts to control her terrifying colonial environment, particularly in her most instructive novel *The Man from Sagamu* (1978a) where she consciously explores a fictionalized version of Osun and Osetura's spheres of influence; she dares to gaze at and chastise white imperialists and their Nigerian male underlings, who are punished for usurping Osun's divine office.

Ulasi's nationalistic impulse makes it imperative that she subsume gender under colonial politics, presenting us with unresolved issues in womanism that are part of the ongoing palaver. How does the native woman view the colonial officer? How does a Nigerian woman perceive other whites? How does a Nigerian woman consider her male counterpart? How should a Western-trained journalist and novelist deal with the pervasive juju atmosphere in Nigeria? Going back to the cultural imaginary for illumination, how did Osun regard the male *orisa*? Can the binary opposition "us" and "them" be dismantled to create a wholesome state? Ulasi grappled with such thought teasers, even attempting to resolve them, it would seem, when she married a white man, only to be divorced three children later.

Treating juju as mystery, which is what it really is and should remain, she has experimented with form, creating a new genre which I refer to as juju fiction. As practiced by Ulasi, juju fiction can be described as an *ogbanje* form. It can be envisioned as a bewitched crossroads, where many literary aspects intersect: juju, the mystery novel, fantasy, the ghost story, the tall tale, the gothic, etc., are grounded on a cultural imaginary that thrives on such inventiveness. This creative mixture is palava sauce par excellence.

Hitherto, Ulasi's writing has baffled critics straining to classify her. The conflation of mystery and juju, which she foregrounds, dramatizes an *ogbanje* imaginary. Genuine Nigerian that she is, she sees the centrality and psychological importance of juju in African culture; yet she is unwilling to let go her Western heritage, such as it is. In fact, she has successfully Nigerianized the mystery genre, paralleling the development that resulted in Nigerian juju music, an amalgam of diverse strains of traditional, jazz, popular, and foreign dance tunes.

With such preoccupations, Ulasi poses a problem for someone probing for feminisms in Nigerian women's writing. Moreover, she belongs to a group of intriguing black women writers who employ male protagonists to speak for women in the palaver. This strategy serves womanist ends, encoding the heterosexual pull in the Nigerian family. African-American women writers have explored this territory in an open manner by revising some English examples—Emily Brontë's oppressed but macho Heathcliff in *Wuthering Heights* and George Eliot's ostracized and feminized Silas Marner. Toni Morrison's Milkman, overprotected by doting women and endangered by those he had treated carelessly, in *Song of Solomon,* and Alice Walker's Grange Copeland, the grandfather doubling as mother in *The Third Life of Grange Copeland,* are cases in point. In Nigeria, besides Ulasi, Ifeoma Okoye's feminized and marginalized Chigo in *Men Without Ears* belongs to the same category. To these optimistic womanists who move away from the "narrowness" of the female world, men's vision, coterminous with women's, is "normative." The belief in male corrigibility is crucial in the palaver and makes the centrality of male heroes in female texts politically expedient.

A substantial proportion of Ulasi's characters are white, an interest that might stem from her interracial marriage. E. P. Abanime's (1986) comment on a similar phenomenon among African Francophone novelists is relevant in comprehending Ulasi: "One of the possible explanations for this preoccupation with whites in the African Francophone novel is the fact that practically all the present novelists grew up under European colonial domination. . . . Whites would therefore appear in the transportation into fiction of the experiences of the black writers' childhood and adolescent years" (126). Ulasi exposes us to the foibles of the white world and of the male, so we may understand them. Such knowledge can help to wear down neocolonialism, militarism, and sexism.

Ulasi, the didact, represents the dissatisfaction and resistance inherent in colonialism as a reminder that Nigeria should be a wholesome nation, sans intimidation and oppression; ideally, her wretched of the earth, including women and lowly men, should have a place ensured through overseeing societal power play, and the country must have a place under the sun through monitoring power politics. Hers is not strictly a woman's world, though women are in her world.

"Be it mimicry or bravery," writes Catharine Stimpson, "the woman who would be man reaches for status and for freedom" (1982, 247). If this statement were to be applied to Ulasi, the problem generated by her corpus in Nigerian literature might be further resolved. As the first woman among men creating a harsh, new political enclave through journalism, her role was difficult. Not surprisingly, her diffidence appears in her early fiction, which mimics some men's novels dealing almost exclusively with the intricacies of colonial politics. Furthermore, Ulasi writes from somewhere outside her female body, to borrow Adrienne Rich's expression in a different context. How else would a woman write four novels—*Many Thing You No Understand, Many Thing Begin for Change, Who Is Jonah?* and *The Man from Sagamu*—without a single memorable female character? She unconsciously wants to be one of the men, an ambition that did her no good, ignored as she is by men and women readers. Viewed from another angle, Ulasi appears to be delivering a clear message: If Nigerian men are so oppressed, as these novels indicate, and if white women are so controlled, as her novel *The Night Harry Died* (1974) dramatizes, what hope is there for Nigerian women who are inarticulate and invisible in society and literature?

V. Y. Mudimbe, in "Letters of Reference," (1991) also bemoans the long silence in women's literature. However, he assumes that silence means vacuity and that the "void" in literature in European languages is "frightening" (64). In his fright and europhonic despair, he discountenances extant oratures. Once oral literature—that is, literature in the vernacular—is thus silenced or remains unheard by those who do not know the language/s in which the stories are narrated, it is superseded by the noise of the few women's novels written in the masters' European languages. This is part of the African palava: the problem of not being able to use one's emotional language to tell one's very own story. Ulasi recognizes how involved the situation is, and she demonstrates its complexity by exploiting the politics of silence. Her marginal women characters remain silent when men speak, then respond apropos—more often than not, out of the man's hearing, particularly as the reader might be reading the woman's thoughts on an event. However, there is power inherent in some forms of silence, since the other is never acquainted with the subversive thoughts, and s/he remains a mystery. Like Osun, women have long used such silence as a form of resistance, particularly following violent incidents. I refer to such resistance as *siddon look* tactics when one sits down to recuperate only to take a fresh look at an intractable situation. Ulasi was born in 1931 in Aba, in the aftermath of the 1929 southeastern or Aba Women's guerrilla struggle, the defeat from which necessitated silence. She learned the meanings of such silence and, consequently, how to code her language. This silence, which is far from being a void, encourages a cross-pollination of ideas that precede other revisionary positions, even those in book form.

The women's struggle silently produced the Aba woman writer Ulasi, who grew up in the wake of that colonial insubordination and its restive aftermath, four decades later to have her worst fears realized in the Igbo debacle in the Nigerian Civil War. She has clandestinely carried on her own version of the struggle against oppressive forces in her novels. The ripples have helped to reproduce other women's novels as new sites of resistance, especially against the military, as well as alert organizations such as Women in Nigeria (WIN) to the extent of the struggle.

Ulasi's novels proffer several models of resistance in the culture. The most memorable features of her works are the colonial officer with his wife, court, police, church, school, and newspaper; these institutions contrast with the common people's marketplace, compounds, and male leaders, whose wives hover in the background. When these divergent worlds collide, as they often do, *palava* ensues. In Igbo this is *ise okwu*. *Ise okwu* is to quarrel, literally, "to pull the word apart." The court's jurisdiction is to bring about a settlement among warring parties, though the emergence of the colonial magistrate is of itself an act of aggression, since he has usurped powers traditionally exercised by the gerontocracy or peers, through the palaver system.

To Ulasi, the police ensure that the colonial officer's word is law and that what he perceives as order is maintained. *Okwu*, "word," is closely connected with another word, *uka*, as in *okwu n'uka*. *Uka* indicates doubt, debate, or tedious dispute, all aspects of the palava. The foreign church is *uno uka*, the "house for haranguing," where the white preacher, with his alien intonation, bullies his defenseless and silent congregation to submit to Western ethics. In the school Ulasi depicts, the children are indoctrinated early into imperialist word power, endlessly reciting what is meaningful in the colonialist's culture, which is meaningless jargon to the people and yet another sign of oppression. For the literate, the newspaper, even though run by Nigerians at this stage of the colonial experience, is not used to attack the status quo, as it is influential in consolidating the colonialist power structure. The true nationalist is the rebel who opposes the magistrate, the police, and the newspaper or disrespects any of the paraphernalia that keep the oppressors in power.

Using her novels to air the national problems of the misuse of word and power, Ulasi joins in an old palaver whose thrust is to dislodge those unlawfully entrenched in authority. Since she was writing during the military regime of Yakubu Gowon, she wisely chose to use the British colonial era as a safe place to attack postcolonial and neocolonial hegemonies established, ironically, by the colonizing Nigerian army. The root of these colonizations is economic: the insatiable yen to access and keep Nigeria's great wealth in private bank accounts. The dominant aspect of her writing is, therefore, nationalistic: her quarrel with the excessive power used by colonizing forces, foreign or indigenous, to control the magical possibilities of the spoken and the written word. As an occasional radio broadcaster, a journalist, and a novelist, she must use the word for critical reportage, yet, in a military regime, she must present her material slantwise, if she is not to be discredited or silenced.

Ulasi reads colonial Nigeria as an *ogbanje,* a distortion mimicked in her writing through jarring juxtaposing of the inexplicable. For example, she balances the Nigerian male capability to use juju to vanish or become invisible to escape from a moment of danger with the magical British male capacity to trespass, with impunity, a territory not his own. In her texts, the disquieting absence of the one and the ominous presence of the other function tropically to suggest the mystery or lack of leadership in the embattled Nigerian situation. Juju can, therefore, be nothing and yet be pervasive; a hoax, yet a saving grace. Though the Nigerian juju might leave the British skeptical and baffled, the magic of a colonizing presence and authority leaves the Nigerian disoriented and desperate. As I indicated in Chapter 2, the colonizer can be construed as an *ogbanje* figure because of his dual interests in his country of origin (the other place) and his country of abode. Inevitably, his intrusion is an albatross to the colonized—that is, the *ogbanje* parent, to complete the analogy. However, as the Yoruba assert, the child who says its parent won't sleep, s/he too won't sleep. The Ogwashi-Uku people couch the mutual suffering in culinary terms: *oo fu ose, o fu nkpilite,* "as it hurts the pepper, so it hurts the flat mortar used to grind it." The colonizer and the colonized are jinxed.

Ulasi locates her experimental juju fiction, in which she deconstructs the detective novel, on the site of the intersection of these two malevolent forces. In her construction of the magic realistic plot, she prioritizes juju's agency in precipitating agitation, which unsettles authority. Through this code, she uses the example of the national struggle for independence from Britain to speak to the civilian population currently colonized by its treacherous army. Besides this preoccupation with the different phases of national subjugation, with the sharpened sensibilities of a woman thriving among men, Ulasi grapples with the undercurrent of sexism and misogyny in the rank and file. In this subtext, she reviews women's complicit and complementary role, hampered by debilitating tyrannies that represent, in minuscule fashion, colonization's inroads into the Nigerian psyche.

Ulasi's portraits of black and white males are generally considered inauthentic. Is this criticism justifiable in the context of juju fiction? In portraying the colonizers as ordinary—going behind the impenetrable, official face, to caricature them as ineffectual and dependent on black women and men—Ulasi strips them of their "divine right" to rule. Indirectly, she comments on the Nigerian failure to dislodge such second-rate rulers expeditiously. By portraying colonized men as mindlessly violent, treacherous, lacking machismo, she proffers a psychological explanation for their sexism and misogyny. How are these portraits effected?

Elaine Showalter's general observation about language is useful at this juncture: "From a political perspective, there are interesting parallels between the feminist problem of a women's language and the recurring 'language issue' in the general history of decolonization" (1982, 22). As a woman and a "native," Ulasi is conscious of the limitations of the English language for the Nigerian, especially the difficulty in using it to conduct a meaningful palaver between the colonizer and the colonized. English and Igbo languages and customs are, consequently, mutually unintelligible in her texts. One of her characters, Chukwuka, criticizes the reading material used for Nigerian schoolchildren: in the 1930s and 1940s, colonial Nigeria was being hastily exposed to the mysteries of nineteenth-century, Victorian England through the "Queen Primer 1," for Queen Elizabeth II was not yet on the scene.[1]

Experimenting with language, Ulasi employs what she refers to as pidgin (in her works, it appears as an awkward mixture of broken and pidgin English) in conversations between British and Igbo men, for example Mason, a colonial administrator, and his colleague's servant, the Nigerian Ezekiel:

> "How the thing go, Ezekiel?" Mason asked.
> "All right, sir."
> "Good. When it ready, make you bring it come for your master him bedroom, O.K.?" . . . "Not too much, Ezekiel. I no think say Mr MacIntosh go fit eat plenty." . . .
> "Ezekiel," Mason called. The houseboy looked in. "We kill bad snake for nighttime yesterday."
> Ezekiel's face did not register surprise. He merely asked: "For which place you kill him, sir?"
> "For the door here. You see bad snake here before?"
> "No, sir. Only green snake for front house, sir."
> "I see. All right. That be all." (1973, 124–25)[2]

---

1. Chukwuka and his friend Okafor ponder at the content of the *Queen Primer,* with the incongruity of children reading about the cat that sat on the mat in a culture where domestic animals are treated as animals, and not as children.

2. With her "bad" pidgin, Ulasi may not have intended to indicate a breakdown in communication through broken English. However, her Nigerian characters sound the way villainous Germans speak English in American World War II movies. For a feel of how her dialogue could read in Nigerian Pidgin English (see Elugbe and Omamor's *Nigerian Pidgin: Background and*

Jane Bryce (1988, 135) clarifies the language situation in her interview with Ulasi. She informs us that Ulasi admits that she *anglicized* her pidgin to make the dialogue accessible to her European audience. This has created aesthetic problems that I try to grapple with by referring to parts of her dialogue as broken English, which is what it ends up being. Its links with Amos Tutuola's novel, *The Palm-wine Drinkard,* are clear, though Ulasi limits her use to dialogue unlike her celebrated predecessor.

However, when she also uses pidgin to stand for Igbo in a dialogue between Igbo speakers, her strategy no longer appears to make sense. That nonsense underscores the absurd situation of the colonized: the gradual loss of his own indigenous language and his inexpert command of the language of the colonizer. These are indicators of a loss of identity that marks the extent of his deracination. Nancy Vogely (1987, 785) also tackles the question of identity: "The situation of the colonial reader presents psychoanalytic critics with the problem of explaining how identity may be realized in literature if the language is inherited, if it is regarded as imposed or borrowed." Viewed metaphorically, this crisis is *ogbanje*hood, a state of perpetual estrangement from societal values with the inevitable bellyaching.

Yet, Tutuola has been praised for his "quaint" English, a Nigerian teacher's nightmare in the use of English as an nth language, as this quotation from his *The Palm-wine Drinkard* illustrates:

> I could not blame the lady for following the skull as a complete gentleman to his house atal. Because if I were a lady, no doubt I would follow him to where-ever he wouldgo, and still, as I was a man I would jealous him more than that, because if this gentleman go to the battle field, surely, enemy would not kill him or capture him and if bombers see him in a town which was to be bombed, they would not throw bombs on his presence, and if they

---

Prospects), the conversation could go thus:

"Ezekieli, how dey go dey go?"

"E dey go well, sah."

"Good. When e ready, make you bring am come for bedroom for master, you hear?" . . . "Ezekieli, no make am boku o. I no think say Mr MacIntosh go fit chop pelenty." . . .

"Ezekieli," Mason called. The houseboy looked in. "We kill bad snake las' night." Ezekiel's face did not register surprise. He merely asked: "Sah, na for where you kill am?"

"For door here. You don see bad snake for here before before?"

"No, sah. Na only green snake we been dey kill for fron' house."

"Na wah o. Bo ya, make you dey go."

throw it, the bomb itself would not explode until this gentleman would leave that town, because of his beauty." (24; this excerpt from the author's handwritten manuscript is replicated in the novel to show that the editors of Tutuola's text did little editing)

In contrast, those who deign to read Ulasi's novels complain about "her terrible pidgin." Let us pause for a moment. Was Igbo pidgin in the 1930s, the time when these novels were set, not "terrible" as it was just beginning to evolve? Is Igbo pidgin even at the present time acceptable? Are Igbo pidgin and Yoruba pidgin (if we might call it that; Ulasi uses this in *The Man From Sagamu*) not stilted? Perhaps a sample from *The Man From Sagamu* will suffice to illustrate the problem. Baba Kekere, the *babalawo,* is perturbed by his inability to make sense of the protagonist Agege's mysterious disappearance, and his wife, Bunmi, tries to calm him down:

> "Make you no worry," she advised him. "That be how life be. Sometimes it go up, up, up, and sometimes it come down, down, down. When it go up, you get many friends. But when it come down, your friends run away."
> "It be bad thing, Bunmi." . . .
> "This be first time for my life when I no fit put my finger inside a matter. I be fifty-two year old now, maybe my eye no fit focus clear now as when I be young man." (1978a, 61)

This dialogue is as stilted but not quite as terrible as what goes for pidgin in Soyinka's *Ake* (1989). Take the following as a sample:

> "No, I can like to take changey-changey. . . . Look 'am master, a no be lie. Look, genuine morocco leather. 'E fit you, big man like you must have leather brief-case for carry file. 'E be genuine. Put 'am one more shirt. Or torosa." . . .
>
> "If na headmaster of Ake be in father, I sabbe the place. But what 'im doing here?" (47–48)

I do not know whether these should be classified simply as bad writing or as a representation of a pidgin dialect different from the more mellifluous and acceptable pidgin of the coastal areas of Nigeria. For the purposes of authenticity, should a writer not reflect the language as it is spoken in the region s/he is concerned with?[3] How does a Nigerian woman writer write without a lan-

3. Dan Izevbaye will not exonerate her so easily. In a conversation, he blames her for failing to realize that Igbo pidgin is not poetic enough for artistic ends. Maybe so.

guage of her own, when even the men have no language? When Showalter sees parallels in the feminist and decolonizing language problems, even though white women, as mothers, are the primary cultural transmitters, isn't this part of the feminist insensitivity that I referred to in Chapter 2? That post-colonial crying need for an emotional language for writing appears in Ulasi's novels as it had in Tutuola, who wanted his works edited, realizing that his version of English is not the King's, nor is it aesthetically acceptable in Nigerian academic circles.

With such global concerns, it is not fortuitous that gender issues are marginal in Ulasi's corpus to indicate women's invisibility in colonial (and postcolonial) Nigeria. Wife-battering and male contempt for women are obvious indicators of male insecurity and the psychological desire of oppressed men to be seen in control. The minor white female characters do not fare better than their black counterparts; all resort to duplicity: "It was as if she [Mrs. Hughes, the white District Commissioner's wife] was enjoying his [Mr. Hughes'] dilemma, but at the same time trying to cover up by being solicitous" (1971, 51). Ulasi explores this double-voiced nature of female discourse, which women sometimes employ in palavers when they do not want to bother about thrashing out an obvious point with men. The misreading of or the failure to decipher such subtexts is problematic in dealing sensitively with real life situations and interpreting the female text.

Taiwo (1984, 95) fails to detect such a subtext, so he erroneously refers to Ulasi's *The Man from Sagamu* as a "detective" novel, a point I will elaborate on later. The mode in the novel, as in the others, is mythical realism. Ulasi employs superficial elements of the mystery novel, superimposing them on a magical/mythical world to produce what I have referred to as the juju novel. Through this genre, Ulasi plumbs the mystical depths to uncover the Nigerian collective dreamscape. She introduces us to the fears, uncertainties, and mystifying claims that are part and parcel of Nigerian daily life, just as she had done in *Many Thing You No Understand* and *Who Is Jonah?* Indeed, her American-based novel, *The Night Harry Died*, is cast in an identical mold. She makes use of efficacious juju and the supernatural to represent the undercurrents of a tumultuous existence, the marks of Nigerian angst.

Obviously, her novels are based on her own intricate experiences as an Igbo girl growing up in colonial Nigeria, an undergraduate student in the United States, a journalist in the Nigerian *Times* complex, and a wife and mother in an interracial marriage. Divorced, she lives in exile in Britain, like Emecheta, though in quiet retirement.

Curiously, or perhaps not so curiously, as I have indicated, she has never

received the critical attention she deserves, hence my long introductory remarks. Male critics have preconceived notions about her works, because she is
a woman and a journalist. Critics who have never read her novels (and might
never read them, since they are now hard to come by) wax eloquent on the de-
merits of her writing. What is clear is that she has produced five mysteries.
The novels are indeed mysteries (not in the popular sense of the word), set in
what Hortense Spillers, in another context, refers to as the "terrain of witchcraft" (1987, 189). In Ulasi, seeing is not always believing; seeing can be
blinding or deceptive. Her intriguing genre, the juju novel, appears to be
Nigeria's answer to the gothic and magic realism.

Ulasi's career as a journalist enhanced her writing by sharpening her eye
for detail; it helped ground her work in Nigerian realism. The discipline of investigative journalism broadened her vision, extending it to the seamy side of
life, the sensational, the fantastic, the mystifying, the journalist in her always
ready to tell tales that are newsworthy, if sometimes melodramatic. In doing
so, she captures the essence of Nigerian life.

The Nigerian writer who wants to delve into the collective memory is faced
with the problem of how to depict misfortunes, since they appear to the Nigerian psyche as inexplicable and mysterious, the handiwork of an enemy versed
in juju.[4] Ulasi's terrain covers the occult, dark, impenetrable tropical forests;
in short, vestiges of the supernatural world, which proliferate the Nigerian
imagination. Besides the existential dilemma, the tragedy of fratricidal skirmishes and European domination in its ever-evolving forms make living a
Herculean task. Many Nigerian writers tend to ignore this aspect by relegating
it to the realm of superstition, which is inappropriate material in decolonizing
the novel. Not so with Ulasi. She has modified Tutuola's imagination as a
fabulist. She explores the "inappropriate" because it is part of Nigerian life
and, therefore, a legitimate aspect to present. She depicts it metaphorically as
crime or violence.[5]

---

4. Wole Soyinka has given us a feel of tragedy in the concept of *abiku* in his poem "Abiku" and
in his childhood autobiography, *Ake,* with the portrait of Bukola. See above, Chapter 1.

5. Toni Morrison, the African-American writer, whose *Song of Solomon* won the 1988 Pulitzer
Prize, explores an identical terrain. She has accomplished, in a sophisticated fashion, what Ulasi
has tried to do—reifying the invisible soul of black life to produce a hybrid form, the magic realis-
tic juju fiction. For example, Morrison's Pilate, portentously without a navel, working roots in
Song of Solomon, seems to be a female descendant of Ulasi's Olu Agege, the Man from Sagamu.
Octavia Butler's equally intriguing fiction, her so-called science fiction, belongs to this genre.

Soyinka and Clark have written about the *abiku/ogbanje* syndrome signified on in Butler's
Wild Seed, Paule Marshall's *Praise Song for the Widow* (where the mandatory ritual dance is performed before physical and psychic health is restored), and Morrison's *Beloved* (where, also, the

Ulasi's unknown world appears feminine, in spite of her peopling it with men while women hover in the background and serve as the supportive mystical center. Alice Jardine (1985, 171) writes about such femininity: "Women may 'pull toward' this femininity which is unrepresentable, dark, outside of the symbolic economy, destructive of interpretation, and close to madness." Ulasi represents the profuse confusion in Nigeria as the womb, labyrinthine and tortuously mystifying. Her female characters are indispensable, silent midwives or cooks of the palava sauce, kept outside the pale from where they try to protect their disintegrating families.

The historical background for three of her novels, namely, *Many Thing You No Understand,* its sequel, *Many Thing Begin for Change,* and *Who Is Jonah?* is the resistance against British intrusion into the Igbo heartland in the first decade of the twentieth century, which culminated in the women's struggle in 1929.[6] What disappoints the feminist reader is that Ulasi never focuses on the struggle, though as a child she must have had firsthand information about the skirmishes. Although this insurrection and the Nigerian civil war are on her mind, like Jane Austen, who skirted the Napoleonic wars, Ulasi fails to mention them. As always, it is difficult to pigeonhole her. In the national palaver, her journalism and creative writing serve as her own skirmishes and separate peace, offshoots of her dissident mothers' and fathers' concerted resistance against oppression.

Critics have associated Ulasi with the popular form, the detective story.[7] They have faulted her for not following the genre consistently and for leaving the reader cheated and dissatisfied. The following reaction is typical: "Adaora Ulasi occupies the unique position of being the only Nigerian female novelist who, up till now, has written detective novels . . . although there are reservations as to the detective quality of her novels" (Mojola 1988, 178). From my

---

community's exorcism rids a family of their troubling beloved). Ulasi is fascinated by this phe-nomenon of dead people coming back with a mission, only to lead troubled lives, unsettling the community. Her white American character Harry and the Nigerian Olu Agege are clear examples of her attempt to explore the phenomenon, which is obviously not restricted to Nigeria. As a Nigerian, she accepts this unknown world intuitively. However, her journalistic training, with its need to present facts, Western style, makes it problematic. She resolves the paradox by fusing real-ism and magic, just as many Western-trained Nigerians do. The lack of closure in her so-called detective novels, the mystery that sometimes remains unresolved, recreates the lack of definitive answers.

6. The resistance had involved isolated killings of white administrators. They were invariably followed by swift British reprisals to prevent future intransigence.

7. Oladele Taiwo (1984) and Yemi Mojola (1988) make the subject of the detective perspective central in their analyses and find faults with her for disappointing readers' expectations.

prefatory remarks, such a reading of Ulasi's work is limiting. It has driven her into the limbo of forgotten writers, whose books are rarely read, not to mention using them as set texts in literature courses. Nwapa has been more fortunate than Ulasi in this political sense, since her *Efuru* finally made the West African Examinations Council reading list. The indefatigable Bernth Lindfors did not mention Ulasi's name among the authors in his infamous presentation at Bayreuth, "Famous Authors Reputation Test" (1985), so there was no question of examining her reputation as a writer, famous or minor, or as FART, as the acronym of Lindfors' title infers. The blurbs and covers of her novels have contributed by cheapening the works, relegating them to the category of detective fiction.

The detective story is distinguished by many features: the crime; the detective, be it a law enforcement officer, a private eye, or other interested party; the criminal; the evidence- gathering and -unravelling process; the capture of the criminal to uphold justice and maintain morality. Gates (1988) refers to aspects of the genre as

> the whodunit, . . . the thriller, . . . and the suspense novel, which combines the narrative features of the first two. . . . The whodunit comprises two stories: the story of the crime and the story of the investigation. The first story has ended by the time the second story begins. . . . Whereas the whodunit proceeds from effect to cause, the thriller proceeds from cause to effect: the novel reveals at its outset the causes of the crime, the *donnees*, . . . and the narration sustains itself through sheer suspense, through the reader's expectation of what will happen next. (227–28)

Viewed from these dimensions, are Ulasi's works run-of-the-mill detective stories? In novel after novel, she omits some vital element, leaving the reader nonplussed with her deviation from the norm.[8] This deliberate omission has led me to believe that perhaps Ulasi is dealing with something touching on, but larger than, the detective story; she is not quite Nigeria's answer to Agatha Christie.[9]

---

8. In *Many Thing You No Understand*, the "killers" are known to the reader but not to the "detective(s)." They go scot free. In *Many Thing Begin for Change*, the unravelling process is con-fused and there are too many "detectives." In *The Night Harry Died*, the alleged murder never took place. *The Man From Sagamu* has nothing that can really be referred to as a crime, except we call Agege's action an insurrection. *Who Is Jonah?* would have satisfied every aspect but for the impor-tant fact that the criminals escape from the investigators with the magical use of juju!

9. Nwapa acknowledges being a voracious reader of Agatha Christie's works. Ulasi must have read many of Christie's books, because they have been available in Nigeria since the 1950s.

Ulasi's pattern is clear. She deconstructs the detective story by criminalizing Britain's colonialism and, by extension, Nigerian military rule. Though Nigeria continues to suffer from its repercussions, Britain remains uninvestigated and goes unpunished. She expresses the results of colonialism as alienation and anomie among the indigenes. Ulasi creates a hybrid form by fusing the detective story, steeped in the material world, with the magical, the tall tale, the supernatural. What Dinnerstein (1976, 125) observes about Simone de Beauvoir, Margaret Mead, and H. R. Hays can be applied to Ulasi: "What all three of these have pointed out is their feelings of awe and fear, sometimes disgust (also, Hays adds, destructive rage), toward all things that are mysterious, powerful, and not himself, and that woman's fertile body is the quintessential incarnation of this realm of things." In Ulasi, it emerges startlingly as juju fiction, in which the British are also enthralled, though the women remain out of sight, working their potions for change, like the chief's mother in *Many Thing Begin for Change*.

Furthermore, Ulasi follows the footsteps of previous writers such as Casely Hayford, whose *Ethiopia Unbound: Studies in Race Emancipation* (1911) was "of considerable historical interest as black Africa's first novel and first satire" (Viera 1982, 22). The novel has an anticolonial strain also evident in Ulasi. Echoes of British colonial and popular literatures resound in her works, even as she deconstructs the British writers who "use every opportunity to curdle the blood; juju, cannibalism, ordeals, sacrifice, mutilations, and torture—all the possible horrors are conjured up" (Hammond 1970, 49). Soyinka (1989, 16) reminds us, that *abiku*, that is *ogbanje*, is an echo which connotes mimicry. Ulasi's is a refined, Nigerian version of this type of writing, with her characteristic omissions/silences, juxtapositions, and contrasts, to make the British gentleman appear ineffectual. Her works mimic "a relatively small yet significant body of popular literature which satirizes the nineteenth-century stereotype of the Empire" (Viera 1982, 3). She deconstructs the detective novel whose ethical subtext fails to touch its amoral audience.

Ulasi's forte has been to revise the southern, Nigerian colonial story to establish that vast territory as a dystopia. (In *The Night Harry Died*, she tells the story of a comparable rural community in the American South.) Where Achebe perceived the colonial history of southern Nigeria in epic terms, depicting a macho Igbo world, Ulasi, like Nwapa in *Idu*, responds from a woman's viewpoint by portraying the same world in shambles, the unmitigated aftermath of a bitter conquest. Indeed, she saw, with Beverly Lindsay (1980, 25), that "colonialism provided transformations in African society that depressed the status of women" as much as it did men, particularly the illiterate.

She includes anti-British sentiment, mocking the concept prevalent in British colonial literature, that servants love their British masters. Typically, her servants pretend to be loyal to their masters, just as Nigerian subordinates in the colonial service invariably mask their resentment of their British superiors. Women, sensing the prevalent misogyny, surreptitiously pitch themselves against men. Thus, her works dramatize Beauvoir's discerning statement: "All oppression creates a state of war" (1972, 726).

Gail Pheterson (1986, 159) has also warned us that "it is important to note that internalized oppression and internalized domination are experienced as a mutually reinforcing web of insecurities and rigidities." The Nigerian male's superiority complex, for example, is juxtaposed to the demoralizing effect of (post)colonial or militaristic oppression. In a mistaken bid to survive psychologically in this embattled situation, he oppresses women, thereby reproducing chains in which he is further entangled. To break the chain, Ulasi subverts patriarchy by dramatizing the helplessness of the male, white and black. In every novel, the male is helpless before his wife, without whose private support he would collapse in the public arena. The need for compromise and complementarity become patently clear.

Angela Davis (1983, 66), pinpoints the interconnectedness of different forms of oppression with reference to the American political situation when she states that "the leaders of the women's rights movement did not suspect that the enslavement of Black people in the South, the economic exploitation of Northern workers and the social oppression of women might be systematically related." Ulasi's American exposure and her close ties with the white world sensitized her to note the connection in the Nigerian experience: the domination of her country by another, one race by another, one sex by another, one group by another, one individual by another. As she states quite succinctly in her first novel, the basic problem in our unfathomable universe is a lack of mutual understanding, which exacerbates our existential dilemma.

Many Thing You No Understand: The Curse of Ignorance

Ulasi's imprecatory titling of her first novel, *Many Thing You No Understand* (1973; first published in 1970), has ripple effects with its indeterminacy. Whenever uttered, the title boomerangs in the implied shift of responsibility through the callow repeating of the word "You" (rather than I). The lack of mutual understanding and the implied lack of profundity in reading the self are the bane in human relationships, invalidating the palaver. As one of *awon iya wa* (our mothers), Ulasi's "noiseless and concealed power," to borrow Abiodun's words, are used for "constructive or destructive" goals (1987a, 72), to institute discipline. Thus, the title doubles as a statement of fact and as a maternal curse, designed to effect some change, for, obviously, men do not understand many things about women, just as colonizers are ignorant of the colonized, and the untutored cannot grapple with the mystical, nor *you* understand *me*. This inadequacy in apprehension and appreciation is unsettling. Unfortunately, the continued misreading of Ulasi's text is predicated on the curse, enabling the reader also to accuse Ulasi of ignorance.

Many Thing You No Understand is situated in Igbo territory. It spotlights the impudent colonial administrator John MacIntosh, unwisely determined to prosecute the head hunters responsible for a ritual killing. As his name indicates, he is impermeable. His superior, Maurice Mason, the prototypic empire builder, tries to discourage him. The men involved in the killings, Okafor, Chukwuka, and, implicated by his position, the new chief Obieze III use juju to confound their British and Nigerian opponents. The novel opens with the following statement: "You take the train from the coast and in four days you're at Ukana, a former village which now enjoys the rank and style of a township" (Ulasi 1973, 5). This indicates that Ulasi is taking us into the interior on a psychological journey into the past to illuminate the present.

The first scene is, ironically, in a court where the young and callow MacIntosh tries to administer justice to litigants older than himself in a society where gerontocracy is strongly entrenched. Thus, Ulasi demonstrates how low the Nigerian men have fallen. MacIntosh relies on an interpreter because, as he points out, "I don't speak the language." Mason quickly adds, "And neither do they speak ours. We can't attempt to understand their customs" (32). This gap in communication and understanding warrants Ulasi's title *Many Thing You No Understand,* which can be read as addressing the colonizer, the "You," the outsider. By writing the title in broken English, she distances herself from him. With characteristic panache, Beauvoir (1972, 732) observed that "justice can never be done in the midst of injustice. A colonial administrator has no possibility of acting rightly towards the natives nor a general towards his soldiers; the only solution is to be neither colonist nor military chief; but a man could not prevent himself from being a man." In Ulasi's oeuvre, colonialism is a jinx to be countered with Nigerian juju, with courts occasionally providing a symbolic backdrop.

These court scenes also represent popular television programs in different parts of Nigeria. Specifically in the novel, they symbolize a people's disunity, British divide-and-rule tactics, with the outsider and enemy expected to establish peace between indigenous litigants whose mores he despises. Significantly, the first case is a land dispute, which speaks symbolically to the nature of colonialism. In spite of the tediousness in communication, MacIntosh returns the land to its original owner. Ulasi's message is clear: justice demands that Britain, like the upstart who took the land because of the original owner's misfortune, be forced to give up Nigeria. The British can never find the land useful, "For the red earth in Ukana, though it looked promising enough, was not productive. Not for him [MacIntosh/Britain], at least" (Ulasi 1973, 17). MacIntosh's judgment is thus self-defeating and foreshadows the later historical event of Nigerian independence spearheaded by southern belligerents. Writing with the advantage of hindsight enables Ulasi to be quite cunning.

Native hostility against the administrators is hardly veiled. One of the major characters, Chukwuka, speaks the Nigerian mind on colonialism when he says, "The thing I know be say since he come everything as we know it before stop. He change boundary. He say we pay head tax. You hear anyone before pay tax for live for him own village?" (13) Chukwuka's is a question that touches on the central issue that precipitated the women's struggle and that still rankles under military dictatorships: taxation without representation.

British insensitivity and difference are countered by open hostility and nationalist aspirations, creating an adversarial ethos against Western-style government. Chukwuka's grumbling registers the discontent. The repercussion of British rule breeds irresponsibility and unstable governments in postcolonial Nigeria, the time when Ulasi was writing her novels. Initially, Nigerian patriarchy smarted under colonialism: "Small boy and foreigner threaten me, Obieze III!" (98). Obieze's wife characteristically advises him to be patient. Patience is the solace of the helpless, be it the threatened man or the wife he insults in his frustration. The Nigerian divisions are not only gender based. MacIntosh's servant, the literate Ezekiel, as a member of the new elite, further upsets the imbalance of native power.

When Chukwuka and Okafor lie, pretending to be dead to avoid facing MacIntosh, they have sounded their own knell, unwittingly erasing the vestiges of Nigerian male authority. In their self-incarceration, they are reduced to what they perceive as the humiliating status of women. Mason grasps the dilemma of the Nigerian male, but MacIntosh, who, as a Scot, should empathize with the pains of a subject people, is totally insensitive to the Nigerian predicament. Instead, he bedevils the situation by carrying on a homosexual liaison with his *servant*. Ezekiel feels no loyalty toward him, because of the *forced* intimacy that exacerbates their numerous differences. This household, if it can be called that, epitomizes the untenable relationship between the colonizer and the colonized. With the battle lines thus drawn, Mason's facetious remark, "I think one of us must keep his head in the process!" (33), becomes almost laughable but for the grim implications of his assassination later. The double meaning of being calm and of seeing that one is not decapitated becomes serious when, through juju, MacIntosh goes off his head while Mason's head is chopped off in *Many Thing Begin for Change.* Making MacIntosh mad mocks the British idea of the urbane, self-controlled gentleman.

As the battle goes underground, the weapons become mysterious. Obieze, like the embattled Moses in the let-my-people-go stalemate, uses juju (again like Moses with magic) to conjure up a snake, spiders, ants, headache, and fever, which finally makes MacIntosh hallucinate. This necessitates his return to Britain. In this episode, Ulasi dramatizes the fulfillment of the dream that the powers ascribed to juju are indeed potent enough to deliver black people from white domination.

On another level, Ulasi deals with gender issues, which she subordinates to the more pressing colonial problem. As she is very conscious of her oppression as a woman, she revises the male colonial novel by introducing misogyny and women's inferior position as leavening agents. Chukwuka complains about his restricted movements when he *chooses* to go underground: "This be woman life!" (85). He also notes that contemporary life differs from life in his father's time when there were no whites and thus no restrictions. Logically, colonial life with its loss of freedom "be woman life!"

Misogyny and contempt for women are so widespread that men do not bother to hide their feelings or watch their language. Intolerance for the widow, independent or not, is articulated, for "as widows they were as nothing" (16). Ulasi also mentions leviratic practice as viewed by men who perceive it as wholesome, in spite of the anguish felt by some widows for becoming objects to be chosen or rejected. This coincides with Nwapa's stand on widowhood in *Idu,* which, it is interesting to note, appeared in 1970 with *Many Thing You No Understand.* The late chief's wife, that is, Obieze III's mother, with her hairy chest (an obnoxious sign of her masculinist disposition), is rumored to have killed her husband through the "medicine of witchcraft" (36). Ulasi recalls here the wicked-have-done-their-worst syndrome that dogs every woman who can cope in widowhood in Nigeria. Quite tellingly, eight pages later, the men who accuse Obieze's mother use juju on their enemy, Sylvester Ndu, turning him into a madman.

In several scenes involving British or Nigerian couples, Ulasi depicts women as psychological props for their husbands, who never reciprocate. The polygynous Chukwuka, though infatuated with his latest wife Amanna, declares, "I no be woman or children to hide in fortress. . . . I no like to be prisoner for my own town and for my house" (69). In spite of his "love" for

Amanna, he can never see himself in her position for she is other, to be grouped with children. Womanhood implies incarceration, eliminating freedoms taken for granted by men. Chukwuka makes the beloved Amanna (literally, "she who does not know her father," here represented by her husband) taste the wine and eat the kola nuts to determine whether or not they are poisoned, to protect the men. The import of Ulasi's depiction is that every woman is expendable. Ulasi deftly comments on the fruitlessness of male-female relationships, even romantic ones, by making Amanna childless. To strike back further at the men, not only does she feminize them, through Chukwuka's words they emerge as prisoners, bestialized and infantilized in their underground existence. In the palaver, Ulasi's sexual politics involves making the men feel what life is like for women.

The first female character to appear in the novel is Comfort Ndu, to reiterate the role of woman as her husband's comforter. Woman is treated as chattel; once paid for, her husband is free to batter her, and, if he is still dissatisfied, he can return her for a refund, as one court episode reveals satirically. In another court scene, a father is alleged to have raped his daughter; since he owns her, he can do what he likes with her. Emecheta later develops this introduction of incest into Nigerian literature in *The Family*. Ulasi also deals with the sexual side of marital life. Chukwuka arouses jealousy in his household by favoring Amanna while ignoring the sexual and emotional needs of the other wives. In discussing his absent wife Lettie with MacIntosh, Mason is quite blunt: "Lettie's past all that bedroom drama. Except when I'm curled up in a warm comfortable position—and then she wants something. I smack her bottom to stop that nonsense. Poor girl, she deserves a lot better than me" (25). That statement sums it all up for women—they deserve a lot better than the men they end up with.

The frequency of madness as a theme in the novel indicates a world gone awry. Chika, the *dibia* attending the madman Sylvester Ndu, ascribes his madness to a cultural disorientation manifested by the use of English names and the consequent loss of identity. The deracination is exacerbated by Christianity, which severs the link with the ancestral past, reason enough for insanity. With her portrait of Sylvester, Ulasi is signifying on Nwapa's unreliable Gilbert in *Efuru*.

As I indicated earlier, the question of language is important, as Ulasi's references to it show her sensitivity to the problem. Ezekiel, who had completed Standard Six, that is, approximately eight years of schooling, inexplicably fails to speak grammatical English. Sylvester Ndu, equally formally educated, can hardly express himself coherently in English. His "My brother crrr!" is worse than Joseph Conrad's infamous "Mistah Kurtz—he dead." Ulasi follows Conrad, Joyce Cary, Rider Haggard, and many others in the British tradition, to show the native without a language of his own. She tries to mellow it with a touch of humor by dealing with the problem of interpreting (or rather misinterpreting) languages, which has given rise to many hilarious TV programs. She also represents the laughable attempts of the British administrator to speak Igbo, a tonal language. As Mason humorously put it, "Mispronouncing the words of their language during an ordinary conversation is one thing. But doing it from the pulpit and reading from the Bible is another!" (29). Ulasi has a fine ear for capturing the English language as spoken by the English. She deliberately makes her Nigerian characters speak awkwardly. They sound more like villainous Germans trying to speak English in American World War II movies. The emphasis on villainy as survival tactics is an aspect that she develops in another novel, *The Night Harry Died.* Her main concern is not the simple morality of the shallow detective novel but the more absurd and complex nature of criminality and strategies for political survival in a resistant, colonized community.

This objective explains why Ulasi concentrates on symbolic colonial institutions. Scenes take place in the court, with its adversarial ambience; the hospital and native clinic, with their atmosphere of sickness; and British and Nigerian households at times of stress. References are made to indoctrination through the church, with its built-in controversies, the prison, taxation, and interracial sexual liaisons, with particular hints to homosexuality, which is taboo. Such deliberate choices adequately convey the notion that there are many things people do not understand; the result is anarchy. Ulasi further explores this abysmal situation in the sequel *Many Thing Begin for Change.*

Many Thing Begin for Change: For Better, for Worse

Many Thing Begin for Change (1971) opens symbolically with the gruesome beheading of Mason by Obieze and his men. Mason's absence triggers a search by the District Commissioner, George Hughes, and other white colonial administrators. Another murder, that of a Nigerian miner Ephraim Obi, complicates the plot, bringing in a journalist-investigator who tries to expose the secret society involved in the killings. With no explanation to the reader, Hughes incriminates Obieze and dupes him into expecting a knighthood. On the way to receive this, Obieze commits suicide when he realizes that he is heading for imminent disgrace. Thus, Ulasi peppers the novel with killings: it opens with the assassination of a white man trying to destroy Obieze's chiefdom, becomes complicated with the murder of the miner, and ends with the chief's death.

Indeed, many things have started to change as colonialism takes a bloody toll. The title of this novel echoes Chukwuka's speech to his wife Amanna in *Many Thing You No Understand:* "Everything now begin to change before my eye. In my father time, nothing change. Everything stand still. Even the harmattan come sometime late now" (Ulasi 1973, 85). Most Nigerians, especially their leaders, found the environmental and political upheaval intolerable, and they reacted accordingly. Like Achebe's Okonkwo, in his futile bid to restore the status quo ante in *Things Fall Apart,* Obieze is pushed to the limits of indiscretion, heinously killing Mason. Is assassination fair in war? The response to this conundrum determines whether *Many Thing Begin for Change* is read as a detective novel or as a Nigerian response to colonial repression.

In *Many Thing Begin for Change,* the colonial theme is once again linked with gender issues. One character comments: "Govment job be like woman job, it no finish. You work like jackass!" (Ulasi 1971, 105). Where Hurston presents the black woman as the mule of the world in *Their Eyes Were Watching God,* Ulasi goes further. In the (inter)national scene, Ulasi conceptualizes, albeit for the moment, the black man and woman as jackasses, mindlessly and arduously performing endless tasks with no tangible reward. The lack of a stake in governance devolves into minuscule acts of sabotage against whatever government is in power. This heritage of resistance against totalitarianism is a tragic change institutionalized during colonialism by those supposedly sharing power with the rulers and passed down to the body politic. That self-defeating model remains in place, with continuous modification to suit post-colonial times.

Ulasi also tackles the politics of work from a cultural perspective. Traditionally, Nigerians do not consider white-collar duties and housekeeping as work, since they are not always physically tasking. Both, interestingly, help to reproduce the enemy. Thus, Nigerian aversion to desk jobs or *olu oyibo* (white men's job), which benefit anonymous oppressors, is inherent in the work ethic. It accounts for continued inefficiency in the public sector.

Problems in professional ethics extend to the British administrators, who are not as efficient as they would have been in their country. At one point, Hughes expresses his own helplessness about the nature of his work in the colonial administration, controlling subject peoples. "'The open I can fight,' he said out loud. 'The secretive I don't know how to tackle, but I'll try, even if I die in the attempt! And on top of all this I'm having my hands full with Millicent [his spouse] as well'" (122). Despite several moves, he fails to unravel the mystery surrounding Mason's disappearance, which is soon linked with the murder of the miner Ephraim Obi. Later, we find that one Josiah Agba killed Obi, then hanged himself. Credit for the successful detective work and exposing the machinations of the secret society goes to Nigerian newspapermen, supported by a few policemen, rather than to Hughes, the primary detective. Ulasi seems to imply that power is shifting from the British to literate Nigerians, an anticolonial end to the story. Also, indigenous power has moved from the traditional rulers to the educated elite represented here by journalists, who played a historical role in Nigeria's independence struggle. Ulasi's narcissism is hardly veiled in her display of investigative journalism and expertise in newspaper production.

Hughes' power diminishes in yet another direction. His craving for pornographic material is no secret to his wife Millicent. Her silence about his prurient behavior is a sign of strength, which helps to calm her confused husband at a time of stress. She realizes that the danger posed by her husband's ineffectuality as the chief administrator is greater than that of fantasizing in their marriage, so she props him up in private. For Millicent "was a capable woman with an attractive personality, but unfortunately her husband never allowed her head to rise above water" (51). Her head had risen above water, no doubt without her husband's help, as Emecheta's had, as recorded in her aptly titled autobiography *Head Above Water* (1986a), which signifies on this section of *Many Thing Begin for Change*. Stronger than her husband, their secret striving ends as Millicent emerges victorious with "a look of secret enjoyment on her face. It was as if she was enjoying his dilemma, but at the time trying to cover up by being solicitous. He chose to ignore it. . . . He decided that, laugh at him or not, he needed her support now more than he had ever imagined he would" (Ulasi 1971, 51). Her strategy of silence or making noncommittal remarks works on the long run.[10] Three pages later, Hughes openly acknowledges defeat: "In the most important things in life she's always had it over me despite my outward show of strength. Real strength lies within" (54). The marital power struggle has to be resolved if he is to function satisfactorily in public, for, in that outer world, real strength lies with the Nigerian population, if only for their sheer numbers.

Killing Mason boosts Obieze's morale, temporarily giving him a new lease on power. The resultant change in him is reminiscent of Bigger Thomas' psychological transformation after smothering and decapitating the white girl,

10. See McConeghy (1987) for a stimulating illustration of such strategies used by women in their marital power tussles.

Mary Dalton, in Richard Wright's *Native Son*. Emboldened, this native son fights Hughes openly in the ensuing diplomatic struggle. Hughes' offer to knight Obieze is a sleight of hand: he plays on the chief's fragile ego with characteristic British panache. The naive Obieze thinks Hughes is trying to make amends for an earlier insult to his father, who had been denied the knighthood for resisting the colonial administrator determined to build a road to pass through his farm land.[11] The contradictory impulse in Obieze, perhaps stemming from insecurities traceable to colonialism, exemplifies a tragic national disposition. As earlier indicated, it dates back to the inequities in palavering between the natives and Europeans, in which the chief, ignorant of the complexity of the issues at stake, concedes much more than he realizes. In a self-denigrating move, Obieze, a ruler in his own right, is delighted at being offered a British knighthood. As the schoolchildren try to decode the English alphabet to understand the power tussle in the cat-and-rat game depicted in the dead Queen Victoria's *Primer*, Obieze, an ensnared rat, unable to read the writing on the wall, foolishly goes to his death.

Ulasi presents colonialism and sexism quite dispassionately, from the perspective of an oppressed insider. Her description of the architectural intricacies of the chief's compound, with its complex social dynamics, shows that women are relegated to the back of the main house, literally and figuratively.[12] However, her detailed description of newspaper production simulates the spirit with which colonialism was opposed. Ulasi feels at home in both arenas, writing from her personal experience as a chief's daughter in the early part of the

11. Historically, this was a railroad, constructed to move coal from Enugu and Udi, in Eastern Nigeria, to the coast. Chief Nwakpuda, whose name has become immortalized in a proverb for foolishness, died needlessly while physically trying to stop a train, to show his anger about the railroad running through his land (see Nwachukwu-Agbada 1988, 15). In this illuminating analysis of recent Igbo proverbs, Nwachukwu-Agbada illustrates a self-deprecating tendency in Igbo people following their defeat by the British. Consequently, on recovering, the Igbo mimicked those British tactics that had won them the empire. This partly enabled them to move toward independence and energized them for the Nigerian civil war.

12. The details about the architecture of a chief's abode, with its backhouses, are politically instructive. The architecture sharply contrasts with contemporary architecture, which is quite intriguing in its formidably prison-like appearance and its ineffectiveness under attack from burglars. While it imprisons the house owner in its arrogant display of mortar and metal, it rarely prevents the intruder from storming and penetrating the bastion. The Nigerian architect has yet to produce an effective design to aid the house owner against burglary. Perhaps it isn't his duty to do that, since the government, that nebulous force out there, should make concrete moves to lessen the incidence of burglary and armed robbery that endanger life and property. When there are more women politicians, activists, architects, and engineers, they might arrive at a Nigerian solution, since women are the most traumatized victims with the added risk of rape.

century and as a journalist and a woman in the postcolonial era. In spite of internal schisms, she ultimately ascribes the dislodging of the British to Nigeria's magical power with the written word. In contrast, she portrays the British colonialists and couples as enervated with their rivalries, bickering, gossip, lechery, and eating and drinking binges. Their increasingly hedonic attitude contributed to the collapse of the British Empire. If she settles the colonial question thus, she leaves the unsettling gender question up in the air only to tackle it again in her next novel.

The Night Harry Died: Resurrection and the Arts of Divination

Curiously, Ulasi's third novel, *The Night Harry Died* (1974), is set in rural Alligator Creek, Mississippi, in the American South. Quite remarkably, all the characters in this turn-of-the-century tale are white. This unique turn in the Nigerian/African novel by women can be read as a daring attempt, characteristically Osunian as a pathfinding enterprise to globalize the wo/man palava. What can provincial American women teach Nigerian women? It is necessary to summarize the plot of this book, because few are acquainted with it.

The story opens with a couple, Edna Collier and her lover Sam Goodwin, in the act of smothering her invalid husband. He is the miserly Harry Collier; almost thirty years older than Edna, he coerced her into living with him. His body mysteriously disappears from the undertaker's premises. Harry's "ghost," in the company of another, flits in and out, throwing the community into a panic. Meanwhile, Edna and Sam are detained. The terrified sheriff finally arrests the situation, and we learn that Harry had not actually died. Duke Lane, Harry's identical half-brother, surfacing from nowhere, had played ghosts with Harry, terrorizing Edna and the town. In court, the judge upholds justice by giving Edna a share of Harry's money. However, he jails her and her lover (he is also wanted elsewhere for murder) for attempting to kill Harry.

The African-American Zora Neale Hurston had written an unpopular novel, *Seraph on the Suwanee,* with an all-white cast, and so had her compatriot, James Baldwin, with *Giovanni's Room.* The latter attracted interpretations describing David and Giovanni, the two main homosexual characters in the novel, as blacks in white face, a useful cue in approaching Ulasi. These writers may have influenced her choice. Her stay in the United States has helped her to create an authentic setting, and her ear for the southern dialect is satisfactory, if not accurate.

The story and the central characters, Edna and Harry, are imbued with Nigerian qualities. Edna ponders over the strange hold her old husband has over her. "Sometimes she wondered whether he tied her to him with *witchcraft* but she never told him that to his face as she was scared of him" (Ulasi 1974, 14; my emphasis). The distrust is mutual: "Each time he [Harry] made up his mind to tell her, *unseen hands* seemed to cover his mouth and on such occasions he was always left with the most curious thought that he'd die in her hands on account of the money" (25; my emphasis). Ulasi further creates a Nigerian or gothic ambience with the ghosts that appear and disappear magically. She employs a similar technique, with characters using juju, in her last two novels set in southern Nigeria.

A juju imaginary suffuses *The Night Harry Died*: the ubiquitous ghosts; the noonday darkness that lifts at 3 P.M. when Sam pounces on the traitorous Edna; Harry's dark, isolated shack, ideal for mysterious occurrences; the horrifying scene at the undertaker's, with open and closed coffins, representing the horror and secrets of maternal spaces. Suspense and terror pervade the entire novel, turning it into the thriller (Gates 1988, 228). Yet, these also have the makings of a gothic novel.

The couple's shack, the prison, the dark woods, and Edna's fear are elements of an "imprisoning structure" (see similar examples in Kahane 1985, 334). Young Edna is transformed into a helpless, middle-aged woman, under constant threat from an intrusive, masculinist world that keeps narrowing her space. The labyrinthine settings and the witching nighttimes darkly mirror Edna's tortured mind. The living-dead Harry, with his split personality, mystifies the reader as he flits about in his wizardly fashion. He has the powers of the *ogbanje/abiku*, except that his victim is a wife who has cared for him as a nurse and a parent. Edna is everywoman as she copes with the perennial problems woman faces in a patriarchal marriage. Through the juju mode, Ulasi captures both an African interiority and woman's political reality.

Superimposed on these are elements of the tall tale and the suspense novel: the identical nature of brothers Duke and Harry (every woman's Tom, Dick, and Harry); their agility in spite of their old age and ill health; the fact that the smothered man did not die but held his breath for so long that he deceived Edna, Sam, the doctor, the pastor, and the undertaker and his assistant. It is important to note that Edna (alias Stella Slade) and Harry did not really know each other, since each was wearing a disguise, as couples act out expected roles in most marriages. Edna is a fugitive from justice, though she did not commit the crime she thought she had committed, while Harry is a rich man living a wretched existence so as not to share his money with his wife. Marriage is the ideal arena for this sordid battle of the sexes. Turning the Nigerian man's worst fear of being killed by his wife into the fiction that it is and isn't serves as

Ulasi's warning in the palaver about what a desperate wife can do.

When Edna stuffs Harry's money into her "bloomers" and other strategic female places on her body, she symbolically "impregnates" herself, transforming her sterile marriage. When she is forced to "give birth" to the money during the exposure scene, which resembles an Igbo woman's open confession of adultery, the judge permits her to keep part of the money-child as payment for the services she rendered to indifferent men who never acknowledged them throughout her checkered life. She proves that when a woman chooses marriage or friendship with a man, she is headed for disaster, destined to live unhappily ever after. The story ends in her imprisonment, an extension of her marital life, since her union with Harry had been one long nightmarish incarceration.

At the core of the work is the female quest for freedom from obnoxious masculinisms, which Ulasi shrewdly attacks in another culture to avert a Nigerian quarrel. Edna is the typical trapped wife, reduced to nursing a seemingly ailing, querulous husband, who represents unacknowledged male dependency on the housewife, an unenviable role that he refuses to reward. Edna temporarily finds freedom in adultery, thereby eliminating her husband's tyrannical hold now unwarily replaced by her dependence on her lover. Edna's attempt to (s)mother her husband is, metaphorically, a retaliatory act against Harry's unlawfully imprisoning her in their barren twenty-year marriage. The unhealthy conditions of their shack are pathological symptoms of a debilitating relationship, aggravated by a sadomasochistic masculinist outer society.

This society is, for all intents and purposes, Nigerian. The country has smothered Ulasi, who, like her alter ego, Edna, uses indirection to deal with Nigerian sexism or misogyny. Significantly, Harry does not die, because rarely can a wife smother a husband; rather, she mothers him, unwittingly reducing him to infantile dependency. In her dilemma, Edna acts like a terrified Nigerian wife, foolishly seeking help from a man to resolve her marital problems. Like Bessie Head's Dikeledi, who inflicts a mortal injury on her obnoxious husband by genital mutilation in the short story "The Collector of Treasures," and Nawal El Saadawi's Firdaus, who fatally stabs her insufferable pimp in *Woman at Point Zero*, Edna gains our sympathy as a wronged woman. Telling the stories from the women's perspective ensures understanding for the victims' actions.

There are other Ednas in the novel, playing the role of the wife as mother and comforter. For example, Mrs. Evans, the banker's wife, demonstrates the supportive role the wife often plays in private. She takes care of her husband as she does her grandchildren holidaying with them: "Seeing the shivering and stuttering spectacle that was now emerging from a once self-confident husband, Mrs. Evans, like a spider emerging for the first time out of its cocoon, exhibited a hitherto unsuspected strength" (Ulasi 1974, 56). The image of woman as the wily Ananse is instructive, with its womanist touch.

Each character in the novel has a skeleton in the closet. The judge had fled from an unrevealed past to settle in Alligator Creek with just the clothes on his back; the doctor is careless; the undertaker is dubious and so is the banker. Deconstructing the form of the thriller, Ulasi replaces the image of the macho law-enforcement agent with a sheriff paralyzed with fear of the "ghost," while his inept assistant is overly ambitious. Furthermore, with this scum of the earth serving as the "good guys" in the novel, the reader self-consciously heeds the biblical injunction—judge not. Ulasi's message seems to be that men and women are guilty for their irresponsible sexual politics; both sexes have to change their attitude to settle the palava.

In the final analysis, *The Night Harry Died* is a hoax, since there was no such night, as Harry did not really die. On second thought, perhaps he did die, metaphorically speaking, for he and his widow enter a new phase of life. Ulasi teases the reader with a lot of hocus-pocus, superimposing juju on the thriller. The mirror images of Edna, who (s)mothers Harry as his mother had done before her, and Harry, with his identical half-brother, reflect cycles in history and, particularly, the lack of progress in woman's battle against the unfair sex.

It is not surprising that *The Night Harry Died* was published by Educational Research Institute Nigeria in 1974. This was the period of reconstruction after the civil war, when people saw the historical similarities between Nigeria and the United States as prognostic for a Nigeria that will emerge healed and, ultimately, a world power rather than a pariah. The colonial subjugation under Britain, the struggle for independence, the state creation and the federal character, the civil war, the Reconstruction, the evolving constitution, the multiple ethnicities, etc., are uncanny, *ogbanje*like resemblances between the two countries. This tentative Nigerian hope for a better future is further explored in the next novel.

Who Is Jonah?: From the Belly of the Fish

Michele Barrett's definition of feminism as "an alignment of political interests and not a shared female experience" (1986, 160) is instructive. If, as Beauvoir puts it, the imperialist's daughter or wife fails to see the native as a man (1972, 654) but the Nigerian woman does and takes him seriously, a conflict of interest arises, jeopardizing female solidarity. To the colonizing woman, the native woman is a nonbeing, hence her mortification when the white character Frobisher is linked sexually with a Nigerian woman in *Who is Jonah?* (1978b). The situation is reminiscent of sexual arrangements in southern plantations in America, with the white wife's psychological trauma or denial of her husband's raping and sexually harassing his unremunerated, black female workers. Ulasi explores the underpinnings in interracial sexual relationship in Nigeria, an unexplored area in Nigerian political discourse; Emecheta will signify on it in *The Family*. The special contributions of black women involved in interracial relationships open up a crucial aspect of the palaver—the question of collaboration or disruption.

Mojola (1988) describes the racially disruptive *Who Is Jonah?* as the "best" of Ulasi's novels. For those who care for straightforward "detective" fiction, this may be so. The novel is an investigation into the murders of the British Frobisher and his pregnant Nigerian woman. MacIntyre, the British police officer, tries to track down the killers with his men. After some false leads, they finally arrest two Nigerian suspects—Jonah Isu and his son Joseph, a nurse in the hospital. Using juju, however, they vanish mysteriously from their British and Nigerian captors. Ulasi uses juju subversively, pitting its unknown possibilities against imperialism's formidable guns and administrative clout.

Satirizing the concept of the indomitable empire, Ulasi traces the beginnings of its breakdown when Frobisher and his native woman were lynched. This strong political message is necessary, for Frobisher embodies the empire's cannibalistic spirit. He lived off the people by showing them silent movies, thrusting their zombiehood in their face, and selling them trinkets as his white forebears had sold trash to their black forefathers. Since Frobisher seduced and impregnated Joseph's fiancée, this sociopolitical ramification makes the reader ambivalent about the murdered couple and their unborn, biracial child, whose mediatory roles are preempted by Ulasi. In fact, the reader does not really know them, as they are already dead when the novel opens. Yet, their absence is felt, since its presence controls the actions in the work.

MacIntyre's portrait as an aggressive bully has political overtones to complement the implied rape of the country conveyed through Frobisher. From the Nigerian perspective, MacIntyre is the stuff of which the empire is built. His journey through Ubibi division with his assistant Greaves reveals the vastness of the territory, a vastness that conceals its secrets from these insatiable people. Though MacIntyre unravels the murder mystery, he remains mystified by black magic, which enables two criminals to disappear from his custody. By allowing the criminals to escape justice, Ulasi once again questions the moral core of the detective story, which insists that the lawbreaker be punished and pretends that every criminal is apprehended and brought to justice in real life. Unquestionably, MacIntyre himself is a criminal type let loose on the colonized. Indeed, he has little moral standing to effect justice for the interests he represents—the British imperialists who had murdered some of the people and then annexed their stolen land to make it part of the British Empire.

Ulasi presents two contrasting communities. The British world is disenchanted, while the Nigerian is replete with mysterious, implacable forces, controlled by a few shamans such as Hezekiah, alias Jonah, and his son Joseph. Conflating trying phases of Jewish history with Nigeria's turbulent record through her naming, Ulasi's choice is politically honed. Hezekiah-Jonah and Joseph are charmed, like their biblical namesakes: the father is named after Hezekiah, the repentant king, whose territory was destroyed but whose life was prolonged for his penitence, and Jonah, the reluctant prophet who had to spread God's strictures after emerging from the belly of the fish. Joseph is the dreamer and archpolitician rolled into one. Both stand for spiritual transformation and being reborn, and represent types of leadership among a beleaguered people. Lynching seems to be fair in war—Frobisher, for crossing sexual and racial boundaries, and the unnamed woman, for what can be read as her complicity. It is noteworthy that the Nigerian woman is an anonymous figure, considered expendable because she has allied with the enemy.

Ulasi revises U.S. sexual/racial history, as manifested in the lynching of southern blacks, by having Jonah and Joseph cut off Frobisher's penis in a ritual charged with political rage at white access to black women and black possessions. "'I wish someone would talk, said Greaves quietly. . . .' 'They will, when they learn that a woman was involved. The men here are very jealous of their womenfolk'" (Ulasi 1974, 23). The silence marks the people's resentment, hostility, and refusal to waste their time palavering with the trespasser. Nigerian policemen, somewhat like the journalists in *Many Thing Begin for Change,* are in league with the colonialists; they represent the new class of oppressors fast replacing the more beneficent traditional rulers. They, too, fail to receive cooperation from the people, since they are considered part of the enemy.

As MacIntyre travels through the division, he rides roughshod over the Nigerian psyche. We know we are in the psychological realm with Ulasi's switch from realism to the fantasy of a juju world. Clear pointers in the text are the commonplaceness of the supernatural, ghosts, and the spooky search

211

through the eerie woods for Frobisher's missing body. Even the hardened police intruders associate the unnerving forest, thickly populated by cobras, shrilling monkeys, owls, and laughing jackals, with the occult. Though it is noon, the forest is dark and hardly penetrable, as the underbrush is thick and littered with the unburied bodies of evil people. This colonial jungle is a psychological representation of the Nigerian mind, terrified, alienated, and trapped by evil forces.

The hustle and bustle of life in the town is in sharp contrast. It represents the surface reality. "As they drove through this large town with a large urban population of forty thousand, it seemed to them that half the population were out in the streets. Lining the streets on either side were hawkers; fruit sellers; palm wine merchants; soothsayers; dealers in cotton fabric manufactured and imported from Manchester . . . bicycle repairers and street criers" (118). The chaos is symptomatic of Nigerian life, which contradicts the idea of order in the empire. Through this market scene, Ulasi criticizes the British economic manipulation of Nigeria by representing this town/nation as one huge market ready to buy trash from British factories. The *omu/iyalode* as market mothers have been displaced and have disappeared from this colonial urban jungle.

People's ability to appear or disappear at will, which recurs in Ulasi's last three novels, is a fictional realization of a folk conviction in Nigeria that those versed in juju can fly from danger. Ulasi deliberately makes Jonah disappear in the presence of white men, well known as doubting Thomases as far as juju's efficacy is concerned, to authenticate the fact. "I think he made juju on himself and disappeared," explains the Nigerian policeman Agu to his amazed British superiors (28). We have to suspend disbelief, like the average Nigerian listener, and accept flying as literal or metaphoric.

Moving from colonial to sexual politics, the reader notes that the victimized Nigerian man in his turn dominates the Nigerian woman without seeing the links in this intricate chain of power and oppression. The dispenser Ofulu, confused because MacIntyre wrongly accused him of stealing the drugs in his care, discusses the matter with his wife Rosa. MacIntyre's offensive treatment leaves him without an appetite. So, "As her husband still sat undecided, she got up, went nearer, and stood over him as suppressed African wives do when they get the chance" (56). That "women should be cautious or silent" (McConeghy 1987, 773) Rosa knows and demonstrates. The image of the hovering woman, protective of her emotionally battered husband, is quite graphic. That role is taught, and Rosa is a good learner. She helps her husband recover by plying him with food and nurturing him. In this womanist aside, Ulasi clearly states that no matter how unequal their relationship, the Nigerian man and woman have to fight the colonial monstrosity together.

Father and son confront white oppression, with violence and black magic. Ulasi reminds her audience, black and white, that Jonah, as well as the novel, is God's message to an erring people. The *object* of a search, the so-called criminal, becomes the *subject* fleeting through the discourse. Intriguingly, Jonah is rarely encountered by the reader, though his aura suffuses the text. Through positioning Jonah as folk hero, pariah, and *other* (black, juju maker, criminal), Ulasi arouses our sympathy for him as the underdog. As this enigmatic figure moves from the periphery to the center, he personifies potential Nigerian manhood. Jonah's double name and protean nature are also marks of his possibilities. Ulasi scoffs at the anglicizing and christianizing of the Nigerian by presenting Hezekiah-Jonah and Joseph as *ogbanje/abiku* figures, fleeting between British and Nigerian spaces. This strike at imperialism through rumor and indeterminacy is also explored in *The Man from Sagamu,* which came out the same year as *Who Is Jonah?,* that is, *Who/What Is Nigeria?*—such an enigmatic riddle.

The Man from Sagamu: Divine Mediation

In *The Man from Sagamu* (1978a), the protagonist, Olu Agege, is alleged to be able to appear or remain invisible, powers that are potential agents for a general disorder. He appeals to the Nigerian imagination, which thrives on tall tales and rumors that become weirder as they travel from one mouth to the next—the fascinating side of the oral tradition. He is an *orisa*like figure who likes children. After one of his disappearing acts, he appears mysteriously to the Oba and the magistrate (both oppressors by the very nature of their careers), frightening this emergent black group into reconsidering their misuse of power, which helps to entrench the colonialists in office.

The novel's religious ambience, with its preparations for the worship of the water deity Osun, captures the motions of a confused people, roused spiritually in their vague search for a healing male-female principle. The androgynous Agege acts the role of divine mediator Osetura/Esu, Osun's offspring. After all the commotion, Agege is apotheosized: Osun has borne a son who restores Sagamu kingdom (read Nigeria) to its old glory when men knew the penalty of not heeding the female voice. On this prophetic note, with Osun and Son, Inc. (not Ltd.) in place, Ulasi teases the Nigerian reader to think through the spiritual uses of myth and juju and the political necessity to cooperate across gender lines to salve the country.

The Man from Sagamu is Ulasi's most touching and tender novel. It magically represents her career and her perception of the state of Nigeria, which continues to exclude women from public/political life. The extent of Ulasi's personal pain shows in her imaginative leap as she, an Igbo woman, manages to identify with the Yoruba *orisa* Osun, turning her into her muse and protector. In her thesis, Jane Bryce (1988, 141) recounts the terror in which Ulasi lived as an Igbo among the Yoruba and as a woman journalist in a predominantly male institution. She lived in constant fear of being mysteriously eliminated with Yoruba juju, because in important aspects of her life she remained an outsider. These strong personal feelings of unbelonging and the belief in juju account for her constant introduction of juju in her texts. She gradually becomes wizardly at its literary uses, thereby empowering and emboldening herself to continue to write and earn a living as a journalist and a novelist.

As a woman among men, Ulasi clearly identifies with Osun's plight among the male *orisa*, who, after their space explorations, failed to acknowledge her importance in managing the earth. Similarly, Ulasi's contribution to the palaver through her novels has been ignored by male critics, the opinion makers in the Nigerian literary world. *The Man from Sagamu* acts for her as mediator in the battle against hostile reception, as Osun sent her son to represent her in palavering with the sixteen male *orisa*. Ulasi produces male-centered texts with feminine attributes to make a tangible connection with the mythical origins. Olu Agege is realized specifically as Osetura/Esu, Osun's incarnation/son, in *The Man from Sagamu*. Olu Agege's disconcerting actions are reminiscent of Esu's mischievous disposition. However, imbued with the divine aura of Osetura/Esu and Osun herself, Agege has the community's well-being at heart.

As a deity, Osun is marginalized in the Yoruba pantheon. Bolanle Awe (1985, 3) explains: "The myths reflecting the female condition are those in which she [Osun] is identified as a woman, participating in the world of male divinities. . . . According to one tradition . . . she was the only female divinity out of the seventeen divinities sent from heaven by the supreme God, Olodumare. . . . [T]he male divinities neglected her and did not take her into their counsels," so everything went awry. She is the Yoruba Demeter with a son instead of a daughter. "Oshun's presence is crucial to the sustenance of life and order on earth," Abiodun (1989, 3) informs us. "She is the source of potency for most if not all male-dominated cults like the Egungun . . . 'ancestral masquerades,' Oro . . . 'the collective male dead, whose voice is the bull-roarer,' Gelede . . . 'to honour our mothers' and Ifa . . . the Yoruba divination deity.''

The gods, who were to blame for things falling apart, are finally enabled to establish universal well-being with her intercession. Agege mediates like Osun; he is also other.

As a journalist, Ulasi is used to the notion of one being a pariah. When she was working in the *Times* complex, there was a Yoruba bulletin *Aiyekoto* (parrot), powerful for its pungency, forthrightness, and fearlessness in criticizing Nigerian politics. Aiyekoto was also the pen name of a courageous *Times* columnist. Ulasi synthesizes these facts in her novel by making Olu Agege's pet a parrot. She conceives the parrot as Esu (for elaboration see Gates 1988), the master interpreter of Ifa divination and literature with the disruptive consequences. As a master mimic, the parrot, like the *babalawo,* recites the heard text, but, occasionally, again like the inscrutable *babalawo,* the parrot can speak in his/her own voice, to the discomfiture of the audience.

However, Olu Agege's parrot is female, curiously with no power of speech. The silencing of this bird, like Osun's, parallels the silencing of the (post)-colonial Nigerian woman. The parrot is flamboyant, like a brightly attired woman. With two toes pointing forward and two backward, she is a symbol of woman's ambivalence in the palaver; woman's prevaricating, treading crookedly because of her divided loyalties to national and gender issues, confounds issues in the palava, which can only be illuminated by clearly stating that women want it all: the good of women and country. The spiritual center of the text is therefore maternal in its specificity, yet it captures the masculinist ethos of *Aiyekoto.* This doublespeak attempts to harmonize as it invalidates gender and ethnic schisms. In myth, fiction, and reality, it is obvious that progress depends on female cooperation, the lack of which results in a dysfunctional society.

The Man from Sagamu is similar in plot to *The Night Harry Died* in the fact that a man's disappearance and reappearance throw an entire town into turmoil. The meat of the later story is the mystical vanishing of the pariah, Olu Agege. As the son or incarnation of the *orisa,* his exile a few days before the Osun festival in Sagamu, a town in western Nigeria, is disquieting. It causes anxiety in different strata of society: Roy Whitticar, the colonial Resident Officer, fears a breakdown of law and order in keeping with the myth of Osun as iconoclast; the oba is sleepless for fear he will be accused of having killed Agege for ritual purposes; the Nigerian magistrate suffers a nervous breakdown after Agege's magical, nocturnal visit. The story becomes a reenactment of the myth. Without the female principle, as represented by Olu Agege and his parrot, there can be no peace. For closure, Agege magically reappears during the festival, only to vanish after blessing the town.

"Black magic," as Ulasi refers to juju, is central to the book. According to her,

> There isn't a single country in the whole of the African continent where the inhabitants are free from black magic. Indeed, some will openly tell you that they need black magic to safeguard their lives, to enable them to hold down important or even ordinary jobs from which they will otherwise find themselves ejected, to acquire wealth, to prolong life, to bring about the death of a business rival. There are wives in polygamous homes who use black magic to aid their survival and to stay married. (1987a 24)

Ulasi uses black magic to engage the reader as she unfolds juju's oft-vaunted powers. Olu Agege is adept at manipulating black magic; even Baba Kekere, the diminutive but reputed seer and medicine man, is no equal to him. Most importantly, Olu Agege fazes white people and the educated usually considered impervious to juju.

Peter Jones, a white administrator and Whitticar's colleague and friend, seems to have been affected when he claims to have seen a strange beast on the road and to have been trapped in a mist (Ulasi 1978a, 43). This is ominous for the British: the rolling in of a new Nigerian dispensation. Embarrassed and unwilling to think deeply about the prognostication, he later lies to Whitticar, claiming that he was joking. If the reader naively takes it as a joke, then s/he concludes that Ulasi is telling us a tall tale. However, the tale is obviously more than a hoax, as it makes a clear political and existential statement.

The bird and flight motifs in the Nigerian folk repertoire are associated with independence and self-preservation, the need to escape quickly from danger. Ulasi modifies these motifs, through her use of the parrot's cage. To maintain a mystical aura, the reader catches only a few glimpses of Olu Agege, at meal times, leading a very simple, lonely life. He is the archetypal exile. Yet, where "Virginia Woolf's notion of androgyny masks colonisation" (Baines 1986, 175), Ulasi employs it, through Olu Agege, to expose and destabilize colonialism for womanist ends, thereby demonstrating the constraints on a women's global political alignment. Ulasi's choice to make a man embody the notion of oppression is calculated to appeal to a male audience. As oppressed Nigerian men paradoxically exploit their women, so Olu Agege holds his only friend, the female parrot, captive in their hut, located at a crossroads. Colonialism and sexism intersect at this Nigerian juncture controlled by the divine mediator Esu; s/he determines the auspicious moment and the road to be taken. After a ritual, Olu Agege finally frees the parrot, enabling her to talk and mate. Her freedom is conditional: she has a gag rule not to reveal his secrets. However, this injunction is unfeasible because it is the parrot's nature to repeat what she has heard. Ulasi hopes that the condition-alities imposed on Nigerian women will be lifted to enable them to speak out and come together; the men must help to make this possible.[13]

Thus, in the novel, Ulasi makes the ominous conditions following Olu Agege's disappearance correspond to the calamitous circumstances pursuant to Osun's strategic withdrawal from cooperating with the other *orisa*. This crime without a name speaks to the larger crimes of colonialism and sexism. As an undercover agent, he, operating as *awon iya wa* do, clandestinely intimidates and disorients each of the authoritarian figures distinguished by or named after their titles. He forces the Magistrate, the Oba, the *babalawo* Baba Kekere, the Resident Officer Mr. Whitticar, the administrator Peter Jones, and the policemen, to temporarily experience the devastating nature of tyranny. Ulasi enacts juju's triumph as a transformative agency as well as its tropical power. Following their figurative routing, each, in Ulasian fashion, seeks so-lace from his wife. Through grace, Olu Agege, as Osun incarnate, answers the unspoken prayer of the overwhelmed people, rejuvenating them to provide the needed closure that the town's religious celebration had opened up.

From the preceding discussion, it is clear that we can understand many things about Adaora Lily Ulasi. Unraveling *The Man from Sagamu*, with its messianism, is central to grasping the import of her writing. She craftily steeps the novel in Nigerian myth, infiltrating the Nigerian collective unconscious to actuate deep-seated changes that may not be visible to the cynic's eye.[14] From this vantage point, she captures Olu Agege, that is, the colonized and the different, in the crucial moment of actuating resistance. The parrot, Olu Agege (both also as wo/man palava), Sagamu, Nigeria, and the British Empire are linked in an absurd vertical arrangement in the process of being dismantled. At each level, she presents a gap between the democratic spirit touted by the free West and the British Empire's hegemonic negotiations with peoples on the fringes.

It is important to note Whitticar's embarrassment when Peter Jones teases

---

13. I use *conditionalities* deliberately, to echo the world organizations' magical word power used to control Nigerians in the current debt crisis. Its unspeakable effects on women and their children would make even the most fanatical racist in the world bodies speak out, if only to state how dehumanized people have become through the collaboration of transnational managers uninterested in the plight of the poor.

14. Mojola (1988) lists the flaws in the novels, particularly the pidgin, and Ulasi's nonadher-ence to the mode of the detective story.

him for being preoccupied with Olu Agege: Jones naively considers the circumstances of Olu Agege's birth as purely superstitious. However, Whitticar realizes intuitively that the birth of Agege at the crowing of the cock announced the dawn of Nigerian liberation politics and theology. Agege's closeness to children is critical in the Osunian context.

As a finale, *The Man from Sagamu* is profound. Ulasi makes exile, invisibility, absence, and silence dynamic forces in juju fiction. Like a woman cooking a delicious, aromatic pot of soup, she throws in several ingredients in a seemingly haphazard manner, mixing myth, the supernatural, the bizarre, and the commonplace to produce this unusual novel. *Callaloo*, blacks from parts of the Caribbean call such a mix; *ofe ntedo*, "soup to last a long time," as the Igbo say; *obe asepo*, "soup with numerous ingredients cooked together," according to the Yoruba; palava sauce or *plasas* for the Krio. Toni Morrison's *Song of Solomon* and *Beloved*, Erna Brodber's *Jane and Louisa Will Come Home*, Paule Marshall's *Praisesong for the Widow*, Alice Walker's *The Temple of My Familiar*, Gloria Naylor's *Mama Day*, Bessie Head's *A Question of Power*, Buchi Emecheta's *The Joys of Motherhood* and *Kehinde*, Rebeka Njau's *Ripples in the Pool*, and Flora Nwapa's *Efuru*, to name a few contemporary novels by black women, come from the same kitchen. *The Man from Sagamu* is Ulasi's offering, praisesong, and prayer to Osun to use her maternal resources to renew postcolonial Nigeria.

"*Ise,*" Say I—To That Prayer of Ulasi's

As the Zimbabwean Tsitsi Dangarembga has demonstrated in her juju novel *Nervous Conditions* (1988), oppression is a form of wizardry that can only be dislodged by like forces. She is certainly Ulasi's daughter in spirit. Ulasi's forte in her contribution to the palaver is typically the litigant text, with her acting the womanist advocate using black magic for defense. Through her texts, we realize that the oppressed have survived partly by the magical power of the word, thought, and juju, not only by physical resistance. She has used the popular and well-known form of the detective story to frame her juju novel, where juju is mystery par excellence. Serious and unpredictable, occult and melodramatic, the mode is typically Nigerian. Since the readerly expectation of the works as detective novels can never be emotionally satisfied, Ulasi's reception has become a classic case of misreading.

This misreading and its negative effect on her reputation partly account for *Ngambika*'s silence on Ulasi. It is also remarkable that Kirsten Holst Petersen (1985) fails to mention her in her article, "Unpopular Opinions: Some African Women Writers." Yet, what Petersen writes about African women writers is pertinent in considering Ulasi: "It is impossible to sum up neatly the ideas and developments of these woman writers. One of the points I have been trying to make is precisely that: their achievements lie not in the solutions they offer—they often seem confusing—but in the courage and determination they show in dealing with unpopular subjects and having unpopular opinions" (ibid., 120). Ulasi does proffer a solution, with her advocacy of myth and juju. Indeed, she is courageous, for going back to the past, taking up colonialism and sexism, and depicting British and Nigerian men with their foibles. It is also risky business to deal with the magical, which the educated Nigerian pretends no longer counts in spite of its pervasiveness. Ulasi can only bide her time and, like Osun, wait for a redress of life's numerous injustices. Her silence since 1978 and her exile in Britain call for an urgent comeback in the palaver. Moving from fear, anger, and violence in the early novels to round up her writing pacifically in hope and prayer, one's intuitive response to her gesture is *"Ise"* (Amen) in Igbo. *Ise* also means five. Where Nwapa's five novels despairingly move toward the apocalyptic, Ulasi's five novels affirm the spiritual need for blessing and mediation while playing out the womanist principles of complementarity and collaboration for a healthy Nigeria.

Chapter Five
Buchi Emecheta: The Been-To (Bintu) Novel

To think we [women] raise all these men who later suppress us!

"I felt so fulfilled when I finished it, just as if I had just made another baby," she had told Bill, and he had replied: "But that is how writers feel. Their work is their brainchild. . . . Books tell a great deal about the writers. It is like your own particular child."

Buchi Emecheta, *Second-Class Citizen* (1980b)

As a society seeks to transform itself from social and economic backwardness to some degree of self-sufficiency and decency, it cannot use a literature that presents madness, desolation, and nihilism as the predominant human emotions.

Selwyn R. Cudjoe, *R. V. S. Naipaul* (1988)

[T]he woman is made to feel without having to experience that thing first, whereas a man generally does not really understand what the situation is all about until he experiences it. And it appears that the woman has to be that way because it is through her that life gets nurtured, and so I feel that is the advantage . . . a woman is always creative anyway, so whatever she does, whether she is cooking in the kitchen, minding a baby, shopping or dressing, she is always constantly creating. And if that is employed, you find that you reach deeper than the man who might have some obstructions. I am not saying that a man does not feel, but his own texture is different, and if a woman is blunt, that is, her feeling is blunt, it is worse than a man whose feelings are blunt.

'Zulu Sofola, Interview by Onuora Ossie Enekwe (1988)

The work is more than the work; the subject who is writing is part of the work.

Michel Foucault, *Death and the Labyrinth* (1986)

The Been-To (Dis)Advantage

Buchi Emecheta's greatest achievement lies in internationalizing the Nigerian novel by women. Her been-to fiction straddles sharply contrasting worlds, which she departs from, arrives at, revisits, and longs for, yet criticizes, like a restless *ogbanje/abiku*. Her disenchantment centers on the urban and the rural, men and women, the literate and the illiterate, Britain and Nigeria, peace and war, the writer and the subject, the self and the other, etc. Her attempt to synthesize these polarities epitomizes her writerly *ogbanje/abiku* condition. In this dystopia, equivocating is the spice of writing.

Central to Emecheta's novels, therefore, is the motif of the journey, the intermittent quest for a better life. Like the *ogbanje/abiku,* her characters are high-strung, traveling across temporal, geographical, and social planes. When they return home—or revisit, as is more often the case—they are different from those who stayed behind, with their new been-to mentality, an attitude that says, "I know things you will never fathom with your limited exposure." Been-toism registers as sophistication engendered by contact with another world, with the traveler acquiring an improved lifestyle, to confirm the vast difference between the person who has been to the other place and the stay-at-home. That journey, however, invariably entails a penalty. In the hazardous venture for the material world, the character loses something valuable—the original self, innocence, and contentment—as s/he becomes gradually engrossed in the upheaval of a new existence, that spells displacement and unbelonging. The Igbo convey the notion of moving to better one's lot as *ije olu,* "going to work," ingrained in the idea of the upwardly mobile worker. Two different readings of work, especially *olu oyibo,* "white work," emerge: to the envious observer, the white man's work pays, providing access to currency, while to those immersed in it, work is a curse, because it is a permanent state of working. Paradoxically, it humiliatingly entails diminishment, apprenticeship, and second-classism; yet, it enables the worker to view the other world dispassionately and to see how far s/he has progressed.

It is necessary to contextualize Emecheta's fiction, because she is the most *ogbanje* of all the writers, journeying imaginatively and metaphorically in her texts. The spirit of the other world always beckons her, and she heeds the call. She consciously refers to a guiding spirit, *Chi* or *Presence,* in her works. If her *Chi* led her into voluntary exile, her *Ori* transformed its rigors into creative texts seasoned with remembrances of her beginnings. Though exile destroys the past, restricting it to memory, exile also creates a tradition of the new, following the archetypal pattern established by the colonizing *orisa.* Oboshi, Osun's Ibuza counterpart, serves as Emecheta's maternal guide.

Exiled from her hometown of Ibuza, Emecheta lived in Lagos during the most impressionable part of her life, married, then sailed to London, only to make London the home of her writing. She has optimized this richly endowed, triangular Igbo-Yoruba-British source to cook up an oeuvre of encyclopedic proportions. Her claim to three homes with three different languages and cultures makes her never really at home anywhere, though the happy confluence makes her work open and exciting.

However restless Emecheta might be as an exile, she has never severed the umbilical cord that links her with Oboshi in Ibuza, the primal mother who reigns over the Oboshi river and controls the ancestral mothers who inspire her. Not surprisingly, exile is her central concern, as it impacts men and women away from home and women ostracized from their men folk on gender grounds. The political thrust of her work is Osunlike: the reintegration of woman, with a voice, into the community where men and women belong together; and the necessity for the exile (wo/man) to return home or revisit, to avert physical danger and/or psychic trauma. Palava arises when home is no longer sweet.

Emecheta plunges into Oboshi's womanist, watery terrain, saying one thing one moment only to contradict it in the next through some speech, her way of life, or her writing. In the palaver, such unpredictability is a fascinating strategy that makes room for flexibility and compromise. Stressing the principle of collaboration in a 1982 autobiographical essay, she emphatically declares,

> I did not start as a feminist. I do not think I am one now. Most of my readers would take this to be the statement of a coward. But it is not. I thought before that I would like to be one but after my recent visit to the United States, when I talked to real "Feminists" with a capital "F," I think we women of African background still have a very very long way to go before we can really rub shoulders with such women. . . . So, my sisters in America, I am not shunning your advanced help, in fact I still think women of Africa need your contribution, and at the same time we need our men. (1982b 116–17)

Her irritation at being labeled surfaced once again while answering a question about her so-called feminist ideology at John Jay College of Criminal Justice on March 25, 1991. From what I gathered on that occasion, it appears Emecheta strikes an identical note with my ideas about womanism, its "dynamism of wholeness" and conciliatory spirit between the sexes. The ultimate vision is for blacks also to enjoy privileges in the world power structure. As Brown (1982) succinctly sums it up, "Womanism flows from a both/and worldview, a consciousness that allows for the resolution of seeming contradictions 'not through an either/or negation but through the interaction' and wholeness" (632). However, the desire to consolidate does not prevent Emecheta from harshly criticizing society, as is the privilege of a daughter-of-the-soil.

Consequently, womanism in praxis appears inherently muddled. That is the nature of the palaver. The muddle stems from the long-run, problem-solving strategy apparent in the profound Igbo saying, *Nwayo bu ije*, for "gently and slowly must be the undertaking of an auspicious journey." Tackling oppression from whatever source and even hinting at dismantling hegemonies, as Emecheta does, are palava of an unprecedented nature in an already destabilized country. Stating the problems that beset Nigerian societies at home and abroad in her forthright manner is an important prelude to the politics of change.

Change is inherent in her own politics. In a 1983 interview with Rolf Solberg, Emecheta expressed a strong belief in polygyny.[1] Since this statement comes after her diatribe against the institution in her 1979 novel, *The Joys of Motherhood*, Solberg concludes that she is still "struggling to clarify her attitudes" (1983, 260–61). As a sociologist, Emecheta cannot help but realize that polygyny has some good points that went unmentioned in the novel, even if, as a Nigerian woman living in feminist London, she personally finds husband-sharing offensive. Emecheta's unpredictability and apparent contradictions are excitingly Nigerian, constrained to juggle the pressures of multiculturalism.

By distancing her from the confusion and profusion of Nigerian life, Emecheta's exile has enabled her to create artistic order to become the most prolific Nigerian novelist, in spite of the fact that many male novelists had more than a decade's head start. Her novels reveal a paradox: a dual vision, one insistently feminist, the other consistently denying or punishing feminism. Her been-to exposure to European feminism engendered two early autobiographical novels—*Second-Class Citizen* and *In the Ditch*—while six of her titles speak directly to female oppression. Her gnawing desire not to be rejected at home in Nigeria because of a foreign, ideological import has necessitated her creation of a public image that denies feminist leanings. She attempts, unconsciously perhaps, to infuse this denial into her later corpus. So, in the eight important novels that come after the first two autobiographical works, she negotiates precariously the muddy ground between African and Western ideologies, and the hard-to-reconcile demands of conservative and progressive readers in her internationally mixed audience. This attempt at palaver control is characteristically Nigerian and womanist.

The subsequent tension in her works results in a mixed reception, particu-

---

1. Emecheta's response to polygyny has been conflicting, ranging from a feminist condemna-tion to a masculinist, African affirmation, if not in spirit, at least in theory.

larly in Nigeria, where, surprisingly, she is less popular than she is in Europe, where she has won prizes, and in America, where she is in demand on the lecture circuit, and where Fairleigh Dickinson University conferred an honorary doctorate on her in May 1992. Fortunately, the tension ensures that nobody remains indifferent to her, because Emecheta is versed in the intricacies of the palaver: "Every human emotion is expressed during a palaver—anger, indignation, joy, contempt, etc., and every skill is brought into play to sustain the architecture of this contest in eloquence" (Diong 1979, 87). Such a broad range of emotions and manipulative display distinguish Emecheta's corpus, establishing her negotiatory role in the national and women's agendas.

Like an outsider looking in with critical eyes, this been-to is the prototype of the palava woman; in an unprecedented fashion, she holds up for scrutiny different forms and loci of oppression: motherhood; child power and child abuse; rape, incest, and sexual harassment; militarism; sexism; slavery; imperialism; (post)colonialism; classism; elitism; ethnicism, and more. Her range is encyclopedic, yet this sociologist-storyteller does not appear spent. Her writing career shows courage and a doggedness of purpose to expose as many aspects of human interaction as possible to generate controversy, thereby fueling the debate. She addresses the issue of oppression metaphorically. Slavery, second-class citizenship, shallow graves, ditches, childlessness, madness, and motherhood typically approximate the victim's untenable position in society.[2] In this milieu, victims include women, men, children, peoples, and/or countries.

Emecheta has uncovered the cruel dynamics in gender relationships by looking into the sexual arrangements of the urban, underclass, polygynous bedroom. She displays the traumatized wife, who is forced into the role of the spectator or eavesdropper or voyeur, as her husband and co-wife engage in the sexual act. The silent nonparticipant is grossly violated, psychologically raped, increasingly maddened, and excruciatingly killed. Such an insufferable condition metaphorically represents the state of victimhood of Nigeria's hapless and feckless majority. Polygynous men who commit psychological violence against women are similar to uncaring and uncommitted military governments who play deadly games with the people they govern. Nigerian cultural

---

2. The following African Women's texts deal with the theme of madness in some form or the other: Emecheta's *The Joys of Motherhood* (1979), Head's *A Question of Power* (1974), Saadawi's *Woman at Point Zero* (1983), Ba's *So Long a Letter* (1981) and *Scarlet Song* (1986), Aidoo's *Anowa* (1970), Njau's *Ripples in the Pool* (1975), Ulasi's *The Night Harry Died* (1974), Nwapa's *Never Again* (1975), and Emecheta's *The Family* (1990), among others.

politics must address this aspect of life to avert fierce confrontations between the sexes and/or the peoples and to ensure stability of the Nigerian family and nation. As she demonstrates in *The Slave Girl* by nicknaming Okwuekwu (literally, "the word spoken") as Oda, pidgin for "order" and Igbo for "he fell," Emecheta desires Nigerian authorities to respond to the silent/spoken/written word and restore order in the family and the rank and file to avert the enslavement and fall of the nation.

One can question Emecheta's expectation of literature in a culture of illiteracy. V. Y. Mudimbe (1988) addresses an analogous situation: "Where does one place philosophy and the social sciences in Africa, if, as a body of knowledge and as the practice of essentially critical disciplines, they seem to be marginal in the power structure?" (186). I suspect that in Nigeria members of the military realize that the novel has a potential for effecting change, hence the inaccessibility of books through prohibitive pricing resulting from the high duties imposed even on educational materials by military governments.

From another cultural perspective, Emecheta has diligently explored the collective desire for children, especially the national obsession for sons, originating from the *orisas*' primal prayer. As Osun found, son-power represents vicarious authority, a female route to belonging. Reproducing the primordial urge toward security, Emecheta makes every important female character, no matter what her status, an *omunwa*, participating in motherhood for both political reasons and emotional fulfillment. This arrangement then mocks the woman who has only daughters. Like Nwapa, Emecheta speaks to the containment of the barren woman, deprived of any political clout through sexism. With her been-to eyes, Emecheta clearly sees the limitations inherent in the culture that made the colonial incursion possible. She continues to cite them to avert more cataclysm, but, predictably, she goes unheeded where her insights matter most.

Confining female achievement to mothering is the ultimate entrapment, for most women have become advocates of this downside of the *kwenu* mentality. Osun saw its drawbacks. She realized that a woman needs to be an achiever to access the wherewithal for effective mothering, since the male could not be relied upon to assist her wholeheartedly in the role. She remains a deity, the rights from which enable her to control an increasing sphere, as we saw in Ulasi's *The Man from Sagamu*. Her exemplary move has shown shrewd women that they can almost have it all: motherhood and the independent spirit to make it politically viable. Along the way, each successful woman pays her dues. From the myth, sociology, and personal experience in a difficult marriage, Emecheta lets her novels cook along with variations of this bitter-sweet recipe. Her contribution to the palaver is to play down the sweetness and complain most vociferously about the bitter experiences that limit women and their folks.

Emecheta was determined to make money out of writing to support her family, going beyond yet adroitly using the stew generated by her husband's attempt to control her. "If artistic creativity is likened to biological creativity," writes Susan Gubar,

> the terror of inspiration for women is experienced quite literally as the terror of being entered, deflowered, possessed, taken, had, broken, ravished—all words which describe the pain of the passive self whose boundaries are being violated. In fact, like their nineteenth-century foremothers, twentieth-century women often describe the emergence of their talent as an infusion from a male master rather than inspiration or sexual commerce with a female muse." (1985, 86)

Emecheta seems to agree with Gubar, for, if we were to accept her autobiographical account in the novel *Second-Class Citizen* (1974) and her autobiography, *Head Above Water* (1986a), her husband, Sylvester Nduka Onwordi, was that male master, who, unwittingly, infused her with the idea to write.[3] She cleverly used it as a means to spite him and become free of him. In the pertinent epigraph to this chapter, therefore, Emecheta can infer that her books are also her children. This possessive case or "maternal metaphor," as Gardiner (1982, 79) calls the phenomenon, can be as exclusive as it is smothering, since it implies a sometimes unhealthy attachment to the produced work. Even female critics are regarded as hostile outsiders rather than supportive mothers licensed to censor the child/text for the communal good, if and when necessary. Nwapa's Uhamiri without "the joy of motherhood" metamorphoses into a double source of joy, one procreative, the other creative, in Emecheta. But if children are not totally a source of joy, as Emecheta implies, the implications can be extended to her books. The idea of the child leading an independent life sometimes inimical to the mother is very troubling in her oeuvre. As a daughter herself, she too has traumatized her own mother, if not all her mothers, by speaking out for and against them, rarely letting them have their say. Her presence and sense of outrage against all wrongs dominate the texts, silencing other voices.

---

3. Emecheta affirmed this view of creativity in a talk at Sarah Lawrence College on February 19, 1990.

Since authorial promotion and public relations, taking the form of interviews, television appearances, book launchings, lectures, conferences, or ex-
hibitions, now are part of the book trade, the writer's self-projection in these
spheres enhances public understanding of the politics of the text. What finally
emerges in Emecheta as a been-to is the replacing of a parochial outlook with
a cosmopolitan vision that allows her to command an international space for
herself and Nigeria. Such visibility has its political responsibility, hence her
controversial stances and her paradoxical compromises arouse ire in the
palaver.

As a sociologist and a writer, Emecheta moves with a clear agenda from
theory to praxis. Her early novels, with their autobiographical thrust—*In the
Ditch* (1972) and *Second-Class Citizen* (1980b; first published in 1974)—give
way to jeremiads about oppression in Nigeria. Importantly, she has realized
her ambition reiterated in *Head Above Water:* "I said that I was going to write
a saga. That my books about Africa would take the form of a saga. . . . Every
five years or so, I would bring the saga up to date" (1986a, 203). She has more
than achieved this goal, particularly in 1982 when she produced three novels.
With *The Family* and *Kehinde,* she has brought her saga up to the 1980s, internationalizing its contextual frame to capture the African position in contemporary sociopolitical analysis. Whether in Africa or the diaspora, each African
operates under the shadow of the unrelenting African palava and under the
relentless gaze of the world.

With such a challenge, writing, for the energetic Emecheta, has been "therapeutic," oftentimes "contraceptive," as she puts it (1986a, 75). The spacing
and speed with which she produces her texts are comparable to those of a
woman anxious to produce all the children she can before it is too late.
Defending the rapidity, Emecheta cites as a model the British writer Barbara
Cartland, who has been known to produce twenty novels in one year, forgetting that it is not so much the quantity but the quality of the product that ultimately matters.

In the loneliness and comfort of exile, she laments and protests against oppression and powerlessness and the myriad ways in which they are manifested
in the lives of women, the poor, the black, and the analphabetic. In the later
novels, each artistic daughter takes center stage to represent herself and, allegorically, the country.[4] In them, she embarks on a return trip to Nigeria to

---

4. Efua Sutherland's *Foriwa* (1967), with the Queen Mother as an extension of the country,
and Flora Nwapa's *Efuru,* which can be read as an allegory of the Nigerian condition before and
after independence, are cases in point.

explore its political and psychological ramifications. On this hazardous journey home, she has appropriately adopted palaver tactics by demonstrating how vulnerable women, even strong ones, can be to the crushing effects of sexism.

In her texts, especially *The Bride Price* (1980a; first published in 1976), *The Slave Girl* (1977), *The Joys of Motherhood* (1979), *Double Yoke* (1982a), and *Destination Biafra* (1983a), the oppressed women represent the nation mismanaged or raped by colonialists, military leaders, and egotistic males; they also exemplify the family torn asunder by irresponsible men and overburdened women. The utopian goal in *Destination Biafra* is the moribund Biafra, that supposedly free, clear, cool place that a scattered band of progressive men and women yearned for, haltingly marched toward, only to lose their lives without realizing their goal.

As she enters the latest phase of her writing, her been-toism has embraced specifically Nigerian concerns and a stocktaking of the African diaspora as a carryover of the Nigerian muddle. Adultery, incest, and abortion are its controlling images: Jamaica and London feature in *The Family* (1990), originally published as *Gwendolen*, in England, in 1989, while *Kehinde* (1994) chronicles the abortive attempt of a been-to to resettle in Nigeria and her return to England. London, with its conflicting feelings of belonging and estrangement, has now inevitably become the black extended home. Staking a colonial claim to England is an appropriate coda for her been-to imaginary. The Emechetan vision, in its complex dynamics, is sometimes blind to gender differentiation among the oppressors and the oppressed, since victimizer quite often doubles as victim as the plot unfolds. The resulting intricate pattern exemplifies a we-are-together-in-this-palava/*wahala* philosophy.

Emecheta's vision of the black woman as an integrative rather than a disruptive force in society is ultimately womanist. In spite of her weakness, woman is the nucleus of a motley migratory group whose sheer numbers institute an unwritten, expansionary, and colonizing agenda in the cities or overseas; by default, she is the acme of resistance against different forms of oppression. Woman's progress marks the extent of national achievement; there is a need for cooperation across gender lines. Carol Boyce Davies and Anne Adams Graves (1986) refer to the ideal of male and female complementarity as *Ngambika*, "Help me to balance/carry this load." Women need male-female collaboration for the important goal of maintaining "the double allegiance to woman's emancipation and African liberation" (ibid., 12).

Accordingly, Emecheta's works have a cosmopolitan thrust. They have won her international repute, demonstrated by the fact that several of her novels have been translated into at least nine different languages.[5] Her prize-winning texts put her in the limelight. In 1975, she received the Daughter of Mark Twain Award for *Second-Class Citizen*. This was followed by two prizes for *The Slave Girl*, namely the Jock Campbell Prize in 1978, followed in 1979 by the Best Third World Writer for 1976–1979. 1980 added the Best Black Writer in Britain award for *The Joys of Motherhood* (Umeh, n.d., 3). Fortunately, she has not always sacrificed quality for numbers, as she looks forward to more prestigious prizes while she writes and rewrites her own story, her mothers' story, her father's story, her brother's story, her children's stories, and the stories of her friends and acquaintances in England.

Maneuvering between being a Nigerian and an Afro-English woman writing from a London base has its rewards. Since her subject matter centers on the oppression of blacks, particularly women's issues and the rampant sexism in Nigeria, she has shifted what was a strictly domestic agenda into the international sphere, thus situating the palava in the court of world opinion. Exposing what resident Nigerian women have been trying to address in a subtler fashion has injured the male ego now held up to world criticism and, perhaps, ridicule. This appeal to the world forum to pass judgment on the evils the black man has perpetrated on the black woman has created a great deal of *wahala* for Emecheta, but she is not one to back down. Indeed, she thrives on the attendant controversy, which keeps the palaver heated. Concentrating on the gender perspective is, however, a partial reading of Emecheta. Ultimately, she is courting world opinion about the place of black people everywhere in the world agenda, thereby judging the would-be judge.

As Cynthia Ward (1990, 85) has demonstrated in her article "What They Told Buchi Emecheta: Oral Subjectivity and the Joys of 'Otherhood,'" Emecheta's novels engender such disparate and desperate readings from critics that often the criticisms are pulled apart by tensions that fortunately leave the works intact, impervious to the arguments raging around them. Emecheta never leaves her reader cold; she is like a sister/brother to whom one reacts lovingly, and also irritably. Her texts are like the children she says they are, to be cuddled or smacked as the occasion arises. She, too, is one of her own worst critics; a reading of her autobiography, *Head Above Water*, easily establishes her forthrightness and her immense capacity to laugh at herself.[6]

---

5. Emecheta's novels have been translated into German, French, Finnish, Norwegian, Dutch, Swedish, Spanish, Italian, and Japanese. Some of the works have also been made into films with the author acting as a consultant. Bernth Lindfors (1985), in his "Famous Authors Reputation Test," confirms her popularity.

6. In a talk given at Sarah Lawrence College on February 9, 1990, it was edifying to hear her

She uses madness as a metaphor to convey the tyranny of the creative process.[7] It is noteworthy that madness, the *ogbanje* phenomenon, creativity, and been-toism coalesce, as each provides the exceptional person with the privilege to access more than one world. Emecheta also associates the madness of women with the tyrannical hold of children and with the stresses that women face as society becomes increasingly misogynistic. Woman's madness is an extension of the violated world around her, particularly in the urban centers.

Specifically, Emecheta deals with such epochs of Nigerian life as the post–World War I influenza, the internal slave trade and slavery, colonization, the Women's Struggle, urban migration, World War II, missionary and university education, emigration, independence and neocolonialism, and the civil war. This broad sweep puts her at the cutting edge of Nigerian fiction. Her multinational consciousness generates fascinating ideological contradictions in her life as well as in her texts. Thus, like a Western woman, she did not hesitate to walk out of her difficult marriage, penniless, with five children to fend for; yet the Nigerian in her still makes her feel a "nagging guilt" for not having a husband to slave for (Emecheta 1986a, 242). Since maneuvering is in consonance with the evolving nature of Nigerian womanism, as a sign of strength rather than weakness, it creates a space for negotiating the intricate terrain of the palaver as her ancestors had done before her.

Thus, though Emecheta had left Nigeria physically, she carried with her the Nigeria of the first half of the twentieth century, fixed in her memory. She writes about and criticizes the society she left behind, like an outsider looking in. This been-to strategy has earned her displeasure from male critics (see also

---

criticize the mawkish lovemaking scene in *The Joys of Motherhood* and wish she could rewrite it. Her autobiography is replete with similar criticisms, particularly the lack of thoroughness in the editing of the final productions of the earlier texts. In the same vein, Nnu Ego's self-reproach and Ibuza society's condemnation of her role in the imprisonment of her husband isolate her and drive her to loneliness and insanity in *The Joys of Motherhood*. The situation parallels Emecheta's feeling of unease at having abandoned her weak husband, the late Sylvester Onwordi, the now-revered father of her children.

7. In the same, February 9, 1990 discussion, Emecheta confesses that, during a writing spree, her heightened sensations and feelings can be likened to madness because of the speed and intensity with which she composes, laboring to produce a piece of work often precipitated by deep emotional anguish. An example is her temporary break with her first daughter, Chiedu, who, upon being told that she hadn't the aptitude to study Medicine, balked at Emecheta's apparent lack of support for female professionalism. In a pique, on December 22, 1978, she fled traitorously to the father who had long since abandoned them, "ruining" and yet not ruining the family's Christmas. Within six traumatic weeks, Emecheta had composed *The Joys of Motherhood*, which was ready for publication by the time Chiedu returned home, having broken up with her father. Writing is thus also an unburdening of pent-up emotions for Emecheta.

Stratton 1994, 5), especially Chinweizu and his *bolekaja* faction, engaging this loudmouthed, irrepressible woman in the palaver in a deadly fight to silence her and put her in her place. Her claim to a piece of Nigeria as a daughter is apparent in the vernacular thrust of her writing. Its simplicity and directness belie its complexity and urgency. The embattled Emecheta is Osun's daughter. She spills the old secrets stashed away in Odu's calabash, for she conceives creativity as strongly female. She would readily agree with Susan Gubar (1985, 308) that "The substitution of the female divinity for the male god, the womb for the penis, as the model of creativity was so pronounced by the turn of the century that it posed a real problem for such male modernists as T. S. Eliot, Lawrence, and Joyce," as it must have for Chinweizu, Jemie, and Madubuike. However, the good will in Jemie's eulogy about Nwapa's writing during her memorial in New York in 1993 might be an olive branch that could be extended to Emecheta. The men must realize that male-female cooperation cannot be left until it is too late; they also need their living female siblings to make Nigeria whole. In the less misogynistic contemporary international scene, Nigerian men must understand that it is passé to put a good woman down. Unfortunately for Emecheta's husband, the late Onwordi, it turned out to be too late for him to see the urgency for a compromise across gender lines.

In Emecheta's one-sided remembering of their marital crisis, Onwordi is an out-and-out scoundrel. He features fictionally as Francis in *Second-Class Citizen*, with Emecheta as Adah. Besides being second to Adah, Francis epitomizes nothingness, as he had neither the womb nor the brains to give birth to children and/or study and write books as Adah so effortlessly and prolifically could. He becomes, in deed, worth less than her. Though "Like men, women need time, space, financial security, education, support and validation from others, and stamina in order to write well" (Stimpson 1987, 2), for Emecheta, these necessities were luxuries that her husband could not or would not provide. Undeterred by such deprivations, even spurred by them, she went ahead to write and create new worlds to make exile from husband and country tolerable.

What Onwordi did provide by his boorish behavior was the raw material for an autobiographical novel, and Emecheta used it with a vengeance, uncovering the palava of marital relationships in her characteristically direct, un-Nigerian manner. Her exposé emboldens and empowers woman to move from wallowing in her victimhood to taking control of her life and her children's welfare in a familial matriarchy. Her interest in the prototype of woman, married or not, acting as femme sole, engages our attention in her subversive

231

world. It is important to Emecheta that woman should take that crucial first step in self-assertion, even if reaching her goal is hazardous. She must be fortified with the knowledge that there are predecessors.

However, the question of the foremother for the writer is problematic for the Nigerian woman. Emecheta traces her literary heritage from her Ibuza foremothers—her paternal aunt, Nwakwaluzo Ogbuenyi, and her mother, Alice Ogbanje Emecheta—rather than Nwapa, who preceded her in the scribal tradition by six years. Nwapa is perhaps too close to Emecheta in age to be a guide rather than a rival sibling. The tension between mothers and daughters in Emecheta's oeuvre stems from the strain in her own relationship with her mother and also that between her and her late daughter, Chiedu.[8] This has been a rich literary cache, to which she returns again and again. She exploits it in the relationship between Adah and Titi (presumably Emecheta and Chiedu) in her first novel *In the Ditch;* between Ma Blackie and Aku-nna in *The Bride Price;* as well as between Debbie and her mother in *Destination Biafra,* Sonia and Gwendolen in *The Family,* and Kehinde and Bimpe in *Kehinde.* Michele Wallace (1980) insists that "Black women have never listened to their mothers. No black woman ever pays much attention to any other black woman. And so each one starts out fresh, as if no black woman had ever tried to live before" (152). Though it might appear that Emecheta buys into this sweeping statement, her boldness did not come from a vacuum. Her authority is derived from her position as a legitimate daughter in the Nigerian household. Also, as mother, she in her turn leaves an unmistakable imprint on the fabric of Nigerian female society, even if it is based on rebellion against the preceding generation's tolerance of an intolerable black situation. After rebellion, then what?

Suffusing her texts with the magical ambience of a maternal presence, Nwapa concentrates on Uhamiri, and Ulasi on juju and Osun as reference points for people to survive despite their constrained circumstances. Emecheta uses as mystical background different water deities, such as those of the River Niger and, particularly, the Oboshi and Atakpo streams in Ibuza and the Ologodo in Agbor, to enhance woman's self-esteem. Maternal and fertile, bodies of water exemplify the woman writer's unique contribution to the Nigerian literary corpus. Fertility and the perpetuation of the race are of prime concern to Emecheta, so her sexual-political and social thrusts are, predictably, criticisms

8. Chiedu died in 1984. The death of one's daughter, particularly one's first child, is painful. The fact that she was at the point of getting married when it occurred made it even more poignant. Parting between two people who loved each other intensely and fought each other passionately, as Emecheta and Chiedu did, will remain indelible and will always make a compelling tale.

and protests on how people, especially women and children, live. As a daughter with high stakes, she returns again and again to the painful subject of a dysfunctional Nigeria; as a sociologist and a writer, she adroitly uses the material the maternal Nigeria unstintingly provides.

Where Emecheta is preoccupied with women as wives and mothers as indicators of the state of Nigeria and of black people elsewhere, Nwapa factors in childlessness, mediating by proffering alternatives for woman to pursue a contented life. In their different ways, both are radical. Nwapa, the stay-at-home, recognizes and is able to explore the built-in strengths of women amid the turmoil of a Nigerian existence. On the other hand, the been-to Emecheta, inevitably viewing Nigeria from a Western vantage point, remains disappointed. With her now-foreign *korokoro* eyes, she stares at the incredible oppressions and anarchy, then retreats into the haven of a foreign existence to prepare for the next round. Access to this foreign world tends to narrow the parameters of Nigerian women's fiction to critical despair. With the surfeit of criticism in the fiction, it might now be more stimulating to move beyond it to the crux of the palaver: how to deploy female potency and the arts of survival on a massive scale to counter the unpheaval in the country without giving up in despair. Since all Nigerians cannot become been-tos, the invaluable been-to perspective should not be restricted to the diagnostic but can be used as a recuperative resource to move the dialogue to another phase.

This is the implication of Cudjoe's comment in an epigraph to this chapter. For the body of her fiction, Emecheta skillfully uses reprehensible aspects of Nigerian life retarding societal transformation. Operating in the tradition of the expatriate writer, she provides exotic reading for her primary audience, the West, which eagerly awaits the next installment of her saga. For the Nigerian reader faced with her latest work, Kehinde's separate peace in abandoning Nigeria is understandable, and speaks painfully to our desperate situation: Nigeria is destroyed, and, to her loss, many are cynical or do not have the will and energy to undertake the tedious task of rebuilding, since it is easier to contribute to the progress of their other home abroad. This dismal conclusion raises issues on the place of the contemporary woman in a Nigeria in disarray even as it also speaks to Osun's example and Emecheta's praiseworthy, personal experience.

In the Ditch: But Conditions Are Looking Up

In the Ditch is "'Buchi's poverty book.' I had chosen to specialize in poverty and race."

Buchi Emecheta, *Head Above Water*

Sometimes it seemed that matrimony, apart from being a way of getting free sex when men felt like it, was also a legalised way of committing assault and getting away with it.

Buchi Emecheta, *In the Ditch*

The appearance of Emecheta's autobiographical *In the Ditch* (1972) as her first brainchild instead of the third—after *The Bride Price* (which she wrote first but which was burned by her husband), and *Second-Class Citizen* (which is chronologically before *In the Ditch*)—shows that she had compelling reasons to have it inaugurate her writing career. Appropriately titled, like the naming of an Igbo child, to capture and preserve the circumstances of the family at a point in their history, *In the Ditch* addresses Emecheta-Adah's abysmal conditions in society as a woman and the black head of a single-parent family. It also expresses the emotional straits both experienced bringing up five children in exile, without the traditional support systems that the Igbo woman normally expects and receives, having ditched, or having been ditched by, her husband.

In the Ditch weaves together the different strands of Emecheta's social-scientific international background. Playing with her life, she fictionalizes the teachings of Karl Marx's *Das Kapital,* Simone de Beauvoir's *The Second Sex,* Frantz Fannon's *The Wretched of the Earth,* and Richard Wright's *Native Son,* for class, gender, and race are her central concerns because of their impact on the individual black woman. She concentrates on the black woman as *femme sole.* She places the poor woman in the maze of bureaucracy and compounds her situation in a capitalist society by situating her black character, Adah, among white people in the dumps cynically referred to as "Pussy Cat Mansions." Then she demonstrates that, with the will to power, a black woman can escape the deadly claws of white bureaucracy. In Emecheta's reading of English society, poverty dogs the pariah: women who are single, separated from their husbands, divorced, widowed, old, single with children, and black and the single parent of a family with more than four children, in that descending order. Such women are the wretched of the earth, especially a black woman with five children, like Adah. It is not farfetched to trace Adah as Problem back to the ancestral ones of the original palaver: the unwillingness of white officialdom to hear blacks.

The binding force among these different categories of women is their poverty, marked by their living in Pussy Cat Mansions, a predacious place seemingly determined to destroy them. Its name also signifies their weakness and sexuality as women. Built on a cemetery, its tenants are the living dead, buried in the societal ditch. In its grim, fairy-tale atmosphere, they wait for a Prince Charming, in the form of the disinterested state, to wake them from the unwholesome tomb where they live in an almost vegetative state. Their passivity epitomizes their femininity. Here, humans and animals know no boundaries, as they defecate or urinate in the dark hallways; they exist in a pit latrine as the refuse of the world. The walls of the building ooze matter, and green moss grows easily in the damp rooms.

Adah's attempts to heat the flat to make it warm and livable are always frustrated by lack of money or ignorance as to how to ignite the coalite that would magically translate her from the ditch to a middle-class existence. As a reminder that she is still solidly at the bottom of the social heap, she can only afford (and knows how to operate) the paraffin heater whose odor marks the family long before they are seen with the holes and green moss on their clothes. When the children accidentally set the flat on fire, the occasion becomes an illuminating and purgatorial moment for the erstwhile ambivalent Adah. Moving out of Pussy Cat Mansions, with its pretentious name, is inevitable, for her children, the future generation, are determined to spring themselves from this jail by burning it down. The conflating of the religious and social dynamics is intriguing.

Adah's emotional attachment to Pussy Cat Mansions, with its "compound" rather than courtyard, is understandable; it reassures and reminds her of the traditional architecture of her home country, Nigeria. Its resemblance to village life with its communal and emotional support systems seems, for her, to outweigh its deadly, unsanitary conditions, physical discomfort, and ugliness. Her children's indifference to her alien origin makes her identify the bonds that prevent her from settling down in her exilic home. When she rejects the offer of a flat so high above the ground that it makes her dizzy, she affirms that her move from the ditch up must be gradual and practical. Her acceptance of the flat at Regent's Park moves her from the working class to the middle class, with the bonus of a green park. Exchanging the sickly green, hateful moss of the mansion for the vitality and freshness of the park, Adah remembers the luxuriant greenery of her rural beginnings. The park serves as grounds for a new life with old memories, far from the burying ground.

In the Ditch is thus a women's fight against officials who relish preserving them as statistical problems without solutions. As the war is between the haves and the have-nots, who are mostly women, the gender subtext is cogent. Adah's stint at the factory, with its Dickensian overtones, ends in her becoming sick, as did her predecessor; this Marxist reading of capitalist exploitation is superimposed on a racial axis.

The anonymity that surrounds blackness, in which all blacks are lumped together as "you people," demoralizes Adah. It prevents her from speaking out against the dog's droppings at her doorstep. The black mark of inferiority, internalized through persistent and seemingly innocuous racial remarks as well as colonialism, is a point that Adah must overcome as she gradually grows aware of her potential. Often "she wished she had been white and middle-class for then there would have been no need to worry—the doctor would have 'quite understood'" (Emecheta 1972, 83). This racial difference she has to battle with; in addition to her many other disadvantages, it shows that her own ditch is even deeper than those of her white friends.

What helps Adah survive the prison-camp atmosphere of Pussy Cat Mansions is female bonding, which unfortunately also binds and prevents her from moving on. From being an object for the bureaucrats to study, the other women, like Mrs. Cox with her matronly ways and Carol and Whoopey with their warmth and understanding, humanize her. With their support, she begins to speak out for her rights, as she demonstrates in the wash house. Trying her voice in public is indicative of her new independence, for "the position she was in reminded her of young nations seeking independence. When they got their independence, they found that it was a dangerous toy" (92). Adah, in a sense, is an extension of Nigeria. Her dependence on Carol and others, colonial in essence, has to cease if she must come out of the ditch of dependence, immaturity, poverty, and inferiority. "A week later she moved out of the Mansions, away from the ditch, to face the world alone, without the cushioning comfort of Mrs. Cox, without the master-minding of Carol. It was time she became an individual" (121). Individuation is the essence of been-toism.

Adah's persistence in writing, in spite of numerous rejection slips, eventually springs her from the ditch of worthless doles. Writing thrives on the type of individuality that the ditch tries to kill. The inventiveness unleashed by the landlord's juju threat at the beginning of the novel parallels Adah's innate creative genius. Like juju, her writing transforms the family's fortunes magically. "Out of the ditch and into print," as Emecheta puts it in an essay (1982b), her experience in the ditch enriches her text, thus ensuring publication, moving her from invisibility to the public gaze. Out of the ditch, she moves to Regent's Park and the middle class. In spite of the strong feminist drift in the novel, Emecheta's racial subtext leads her to a womanist closure that incorporates white people and black men. Adah renews her friendship with the white woman Whoopey, who is now pregnant by a black man. Adah warmly responds to the fraternal greetings of black men to boost their morale and to show that she still belongs in spirit to the black race, in spite of the exclusiveness of Regent's Park and its associations with the awe of royalty. In the fairy-tale ending, Adah is the new queen, candi(e)d closure that holds out hope for the embattled woman.

Second-Class Citizen: First-Rate Woman

She had written it, as if it were someone talking, talking fast, who would never stop.

Buchi Emecheta, Second-Class Citizen

Being constantly on the move and having access to several worlds are the essence of been-toism, which can therefore be read as a contemporary manifestation of the mystical *ogbanje/abiku* phenomenon. Where *In the Ditch* institutes been-toism through Adah's upward and geographical move and by her transforming Nigerian juju into the English magic of writing, its sequel, *Second-Class Citizen* (1980b), is a flashback treating us to the unprecedented move in the Nigerian novel by women—of a character, from Nigeria to England—that initiated the process.

Adah is the bold, adventurous, young woman sailing off from Nigeria to explore the unknown terrain of England. Discovering London opens up a strange new world. However, like the *ogbanje*, she never forgets the place of origin. As the first character in a Nigerian novel by a woman to think consciously of writing and to make writing a career, Adah's ability to conflate writing and talking moves the palaver to another plane. Transforming talk into the written mode introduces a been-to element that moves the palaver to the scribal level, whose advantages the colonialists had fully exploited. Now a daughter-of-the-soil was reversing the process and acting the colonialist. Representing the country by talking and putting down the words, through laboring by hand to write her manuscript, is awesome. Writing attempts to counter the monologic and narcissistic tendencies of Adah's loquacity, for talking, without the customary response, and continued talking are abnormal. The tragic price of exile is to talk to oneself or to talk and not be heard or to be heard by eavesdroppers and the unsympathetic. Discovering the secret of marrying talk to writing opens a productive world for Adah, in addition to her procreative advantage. Here are Osun and Odu incarnate, uncovered in all their glory. However, Adah's claims to writing have to be taken with a grain of salt,

237

because we never read anything she wrote: Emecheta writes for her and about her.

The frequency with which Emecheta had her children is comparable with the rapidity in producing her novels, or "brainchildren." Just as Francis continually broke their commandment "Touch not," consequently making his wife Adah pregnant, so Onwordi unwittingly provided the seed for Emecheta's second novel, *Second-Class Citizen.* In the novel, Francis is the second-class citizen, not Adah. She rejects the nomenclature, with its self-fulfilling prophetic overtones, particularly since Francis is the nomenclator. Rather, she writes herself into first-class citizenship, meanwhile abandoning the husband whose horizons were so limited and limiting.

In considering her works as her children, Emecheta disregards the husband's role in the production process, and understandably so. Subconsciously, she had sealed the fate of their marriage. In the fictional dimension, Adah is her alter ego. Adah's colleague, supporter, and mentor, Bill, becomes the surrogate father of her manuscript. When Francis later insists that their children be given up for adoption, he is merely stating what is already a symbolic fact. He forfeited his rights as a father by burning his wife's treasured manuscript, her child-text—the first version of *The Bride Price.* "Do you hate me so much that you could kill my child? Because that is what you have done," accuses Adah on discovering Francis's unforgivable crime to silence and thereby destroy her (1980b, 187).

Undoubtedly, Adah was treading on dangerous ground by writing. Since writing confers authority on the writer, she was asking for trouble from her insecure husband. In Pauline Lyonga's words, "Under the circumstances, the cliché, 'my brainchild,' that she uses to refer to *The Bride Price* constitutes an act of subversion, an invasion into an experience that seems to have been reserved for males" (1985, 167). Indeed, Bill's admiration of the work confirms symbolically the adulterous nature of the relationship. Francis sees such an implication; to punish and control Adah, he burns the offensive product, the manuscript whose publication would have moved her outside the pale of the marriage custom as he perceived it. In his Jehovah's Witness limited understanding, burning is purgatorial. It is meant to cleanse Adah of the sin of not being a virtuous woman, of not knowing her place. He did not reckon that out of the ashes of the manuscript would arise a new, militant Adah, determined to have her own niche as a writer and a mother and who is, from his viewpoint, a feminist.

Adah's name means literally daughter/woman, just as her daughter's name, Titi, means daughter/girl. Their tale is Bintu's, or every female's, story, passed on from one generation to the next.[9] Adah's marital saga recapitulates the harrowing but common experience of Nigerian women who marry "conservative" men, determined not to shoulder their traditional responsibilities in the family. What galls women is male refusal to discuss the matter. This vexatious situation, exacerbated since the civil war and military rule, compounds the Nigerian wo/man problem and makes one wonder who really is the first-class citizen.

Thus, Emecheta associates Francis primarily with the notion of second-class citizenship, while the reader, following the precepts of Beauvoir's *The Second Sex*, expects the phrase to refer to Adah. By thus highlighting the problem, Emecheta undercuts male power and scrutinizes gender relationships to capture the spirit of the women's movement in England. However, the question of the black woman's position in the scheme of things is ultimately left unanswered, for, if the black male is second-class, where does it leave the ordinary black female? This is a troublesome notion that Emecheta refuses to address, as she is writing an autobiographical novel and can therefore afford to be feminist in her sexual politics.

Francis is second-class by failing crucial examinations, siring babies without caring for them, while depending on his wife for sustenance. Succumbing to the insidious pressures of racism, he seals his fate. Emecheta finally silences Francis/Onwordi with the authority she has appropriated as she writes this master's piece, in spite of the burning of one manuscript. The telling of the story of the burning irreparably damages Francis's credibility. Thus, *Second-Class Citizen* is partially a vendetta against a man who represents Nigerian men's hostile reception of women's writing. When Francis refused to read Adah's manuscript, calling it "rubbish," Emecheta was not only recording a bitter personal experience but was also lamenting the nature of the reception of female work by African men in contrast to the more receptive English man, Bill. Not only are African men indifferent to women's writing and to their other accomplishments, she implies that they will do all in their power to destroy them, to maintain the status quo to man's advantage. Vexed by male intransigence, Emecheta characteristically vilifies man for his underhandedness in the palaver.

In *Second-Class Citizen*, Emecheta states quite compellingly that Nigeria turns her daughters into second-class citizens, in preference to her sons (for example, Adah's brother), who are given every opportunity for advancement.

---

9. Bintu is a common, female Muslim name. According to Webster's, *bint* is English for girl or woman; it is derived from the Arabic for girl or daughter.

The West, on the other hand, undiscriminatingly proffers opportunities to men and women bold and conscientious enough to seize them. Adah's library job in England makes her the *equal* of her *male* and *white* colleagues as she had also been privileged by dint of hard work in the American library in Nigeria. In other words, the West gives women access to the library or the labyrinths of the written word, which represents the opportunity to learn and express themselves denied them by their natal Nigeria.

Francis, a first-class citizen in Nigeria by privilege, degenerates into second-class status in England through choice and apathy. He tries to push Adah into a third-class position. She resists him by working and writing herself into first-class status, with her white colleague Bill as friend and supporter. Although Adah is a second-class citizen in the Nigerian half of the book, she consciously reverses the hierarchical structure in England by becoming the breadwinner and de facto head of the family, with Francis as one of her dependants. The crux of the matter is that, in Nigeria, though he was financially dependent on her, she was silent about it because he "owned" her. In the more egalitarian atmosphere of England, she finds her voice and makes him know that she "lays the golden eggs"; in England, gold, as in having access to money and producing manuscripts, means power.

For destroying the manuscript, whose true value eludes him, Emecheta makes a fool out of Francis. She depicts him as sadistic and senseless, juxtaposing his reaction at the burning with the manner in which he poisoned a pet monkey and whipped a goat for not coming up with the answer to two times two. Metaphorically, this whipping introduces wife battering as a subtext. If the goat in its goatishness did not know that two times two is four, Adah in her womanness knew; she also knew that the problems of four children were a simple question of multiplication. The use of the monkey image reminds us of the power tussle implicit in folk tales. To Gates, "The Signifying Monkey tales, in this sense, can be thought of as versions of daydreams, the Daydream of the Black Other, chiastic fantasies of reversal of power relationships" (1988, 59). *Second-Class Citizen* is a signifying-monkey tale in which the power tussle and the woman's dream become realized as Adah, tenacious like the goat, wins through writing. Emecheta reverses the power relationship by asserting that woman is a daughter, though men regard her like a domestic animal. With the legendary cunning of the monkey, Emecheta retaliates by exposing Francis for the brute he is. The ghost of the monkey in the book haunts and poisons Francis. With the stubbornness of a goat, Emecheta the accomplished arithmetician, records the story as incessant talk multiplying into a book: Adah-Emecheta finally transcends goathood and victimhood. The mature Adah-

Emecheta speaks/writes her perception of her marriage to a wide audience. Francis-Onwordi finds this mortifying, since he had only puerilely reported Adah to a limited audience—his parents—to complain peevishly about her obtaining contraceptives. Adah did not need to read *Teach Yourself to Write*, since she had the power of speech denied the goat and her writing to vindicate her. By writing, she becomes the mistress of her own destiny and the subject of her own manuscript that ridicules, and then marginalizes, Francis.

In dealing with autobiographical material, Emecheta was consciously concluding the battle against Onwordi that she lost in court.[10] According to Sidonie Smith, "An androcentric genre, autobiography demands the public story of the public life. . . . When woman chooses to leave behind cultural silence and to pursue autobiography, she chooses to enter the public arena" (1987, 52). She then becomes a man, for "she assumes the adventurous posture of man," Smith concludes (53). No longer the "good" woman, the virilized Adah triumphs over her husband (and the British judicial system) as she cries out against her oppression. She is more a soldier than a weak woman, and she ends up avenging women of male wrongs by using a male weapon, the pen, to put men in their place.

Adah's life is one long struggle against the limitations placed in her way by people who should encourage her. Her first enemy is her mother, who had limited Adah's horizons by insisting that she pursue a career as a wife and, quite tellingly, a seamstress. Guided by Presence, that is her *Chi*, who did not want to limit her to the seamy side of life, Adah defies her mother and goes to school, to another world. This early mother-daughter constraint we have found already manifesting itself with Adah and Titi in *In the Ditch*. Adah makes do with surrogate mothers in the form of *Chi*/Presence and her mother-in-law. Curiously, she refers to Presence as a masculine form because she preferred her father to her mother and so missed him after his death. Presence is her muse because s/he encourages her to write, reappears with the fourth pregnancy, and emboldens her to stop feeding Francis—that is, treating him as her child—a crucial step if she were to become free of him.

Adah's resiliency and refusal to take a backseat to anyone had earned her the nickname "Ibo tigress" in school, when she sank her teeth into the boy who was backing her to be flogged by a teacher. Adah's tigritude, her ferocious,

10. According to Emecheta, so incensed was she at the charade of the court proceedings after she left her husband that she lost self-control. Onwordi, acting the role of the gentle man, elicited sympathy for being tied to a madwoman for a wife. If she lost the understanding of the court, she has obtained the favorable judgment of a larger court—her international literary audience who have finally adjudicated the case and cleared her.

self-defensive attack against an aggressive male world, thus manifested itself early. Later, she counters Francis's battering, devising strategies in how to survive his violence. The text is also replete with mental abuse. As a Jehovah's Witness, Francis preaches about the virtuous woman, not linking virtue with man. His infidelity, which he takes as a right, and his animalistic sexuality mark him out for the hell fire of Armageddon. Thus, where Nwapa and *Efuru* received the paternal blessings of Achebe, Emecheta experienced a fiery, marital baptism that has embroiled her writing career in controversies with Nigerian men. She has remained feisty because that is the only way to thrive in the Nigerian milieu.

Emecheta's portrait of Francis-Onwordi can be classified under the literature of insult. Kofi Anyidoho (1982, 20) has specified its characteristics: "For our limited purposes we may identify three broad categories of insult used in *halo*: those dealing with physical appearance, those directed at deviant behavior, and the somewhat special class of 'obscenities.'" With his sex dangling in his pyjamas, Francis is ugly; he is also immoral, obscene, and irresponsible. Emecheta employs all these forms of insult, capping them with malediction, a form in orature, to end the marriage. She silences Francis-Onwordi permanently; one can almost declare that she kills him with her one-sided disclosures, because insults and curses are injurious to the spirit.

Adah and Francis's marriage starts off inauspiciously when they go to the wedding without the rings that should symbolically bind them together in a family circle. The wedding ceremony is a sham, foreshadowing the end of the loveless marriage. At Francis's departure for England from Nigeria, the plane door shuts him off as if enclosing him in a coffin. The Nigerian Francis dies, to be replaced by the second-class citizen that Adah meets later in England. Water-borne Adah, on the other hand, is in her maternal element as she sails, first-class, in the *Oriel* to England, refusing to be brought low to Francis's level. Their struggle is many sided: the battle of the sexes, the battle of the classes, and the battle between the writer and critic, rolled into one. Adah survives initially by playing the role of the trickster through lying, silence, withholding useful information, pretence, deception, and even bribery. Later, her forthrightness and confessional tone free her from these subterfuges, enabling her to portray the artist as a young wife and mother.

In depicting woman as the "goose that laid the golden eggs" (1980b, 42), Emecheta tackles the economic dimension of marriage. She affirms that power in marriage should be shared, or, in Adah's peculiar case, that it should lie with the person who provides the money, not necessarily with the man. Adah asserts her authority when she refuses to feed Francis. His socialization as an inferior person in England, grateful when he had the opportunity to sleep with a white woman, shows the extent of his degeneration. Changing religions from Muslim to Roman Catholic to Jehovah's Witness defines his lack of spiritual centeredness. When Adah forges his signature in order to obtain family-planning services, she temporarily descends to his level. However, Adah can never be Francis, so the contraceptives do not work. She becomes pregnant for the fourth time, but she is able to replace Francis with Presence as an inner fortification.

Adah's chance conceptions are reminders that her husband rapes her. Osun had been there before. The untold story is what happened to make Francis a changed creature in England. Why does Francis completely accept his second-class citizenship? What happens to a man who marries a woman superior to him intellectually and in earning and managerial powers? Here again, we come back to the problem posed by Efuru's marriages to inferior men. An intelligent woman cannot stay married if she displays her gifts. Adah's artistic gifts place her far above her husband and drive the final nail into the coffin of their marriage. Quite deliberately, Emecheta silences Francis by not letting him state his case, the way women are silenced by men. The novel is thus a literary landmark in domestic war. Through it, Emecheta demonstrates that women should be seen in the body of their writing and that their voices should be heard through their writing, as writing is a form of talking.

However, Adah-Emecheta, the mother of books, is in certain aspects a closed book. Appearing open, she is not completely decipherable as she tells her little lies and truths, all mixed together, leaving the reader to wonder whether she can be relied on as a storyteller. As the story culminates in the law court, where she does not fare well at all, we wonder about the limitations of listening to only one side of the palaver. Is Francis as terrible as we think, or is it Emecheta's plea that the court system is also against women? Whatever may be the case, we soon realize that we have been playing the voyeur and the eavesdropper in a marital battle that ends in a verbal exchange that Adah was ill-prepared for in court. Female unpreparedness in the court of life breeds injustice, as this *Bildungsroman* dramatizes. Emecheta remedies her mistake by writing about the events in full detail and seeking justice in the courts of world opinion. From this perspective, *Second-Class Citizen* resembles Okot p'Bitek's *Song of Lawino,* where we hear only the wife's lament but not the man's, a lapse that p'Bitek later remedies in *Song of Ocol* (1984). Emecheta will not do the same, holding man forever silent. Yet, this feminist novel moves surprisingly to a womanist closure when the abandoned Adah reaches out to a man and permits him to help her in her loneliness. Adah might be a been-to, however, she is unable to rid herself of that female Nigerian core, which reserves a place for some man, even just a sympathetic listener, as was the case in *Efuru*.

The Bride Price: What Price Freedom?

> A fatherless family is a family without a head, a family without shelter, a family without parents, in fact a non-existing family. (Buchi Emecheta, *The Bride Price*)

Written in Emecheta's characteristic tongue-in-cheek style, this quote is clearly ironic, coming after her success in raising a family alone. It is even more so in the decades of the *femme sole* as the head of state in the cases of Violetta Chamorro, Corazon Aquino, Benazir Bhutto (before she was hurriedly married, ousted, and reinstated), and, most intriguingly, the black woman who temporarily headed the state of Haiti, the widow Ertha Pascal-Trouillot. These harassed women of color, and such predecessors as Indira Ghandi and Mrs. Bandaranaike, contrast with their Western counterparts, the more successful Golda Meir and Margaret Thatcher. In spite of differences, it is important to note the entrance of women into what was presumably a male preserve. The prototype for these women is woman-as-head-of-family, an increasing phenomenon in modern life. One cannot help but read *The Bride Price* (1980a) anachronistically from this sociopolitical background to assess the leadership qualities of Ma Blackie as a widow and mother in contrast to her daughter Aku-nna, determined to find her way through a quiet rebellion.

In *Second-Class Citizen*, when Francis insists in the court scene that he did not marry Adah, he is right because he had not married her traditionally—he never performed the ceremony for the bride price. Since his impecunious state prevented him from completing the transaction, just as he had not bought the Western ring, he is irresponsible, certainly unprepared for marriage by traditional and Western standards. In the third novel, *The Bride Price*, Emecheta makes it clear that marrying a woman on credit does not legitimatize the relationship in traditional eyes; without the symbolic bride price, we are made to believe that trouble lies ahead for the defiant couple. Efuru experienced a comparable problem. Where *Second-Class Citizen* can be read as a jeremiad complaining about how a woman whose bride price was not paid was predictably mistreated, *The Bride Price* laments the tragedy that ensues for those willing but unable to pay, because they have strayed from the straight and narrow path of tradition through urbanization and westernization. The been-to pays a price.

The evolution of *The Bride Price* presents fascinating reading. One's initial curiosity is to ask why Francis-Onwordi burned the original manuscript. Was he motivated by hatred or envy or both? Did the tenderness and romance in the love story, which revealed an unknown dimension of his wife, make his joyless marriage to a woman he believed was "frigid" even more unbearable? Did it arouse feelings of guilt for his mistreatment of her? Or was he concerned by the manipulation of concepts from his vernacular to the English language? Did he read the manuscript?

Emecheta locates the core of the Nigerian marital problem as bartering/battering. She exploits the language of commodification implicit in the word *price* while maintaining an undertone of violence throughout the novel. She deliberately ignores the Igbo, cooperative spirit of *i bu ego,* "the carrying of money (and other requisite gifts)," as part of the elaborate, multiphased marriage rituals that connect the extended families of the bride and the groom. Just as the English term *in-law* frighteningly introduces a legalistic dimension not present in its lighthearted Igbo equivalent *ogo,* the translated phrase *bride price* turns woman into chattel, erasing the spirit of permanence indicated in the Igbo original. Of course, as is the case with broken marriages in most cultures, money oftentimes compounds the palava.

Emecheta's rewriting of the manuscript must have had a haunting effect on Onwordi. In reincarnating the book and the characters, she imbues the unique text with the *ogbanje* spirit. This is reinforced by the fact that Aku-nna, the protagonist, is herself an *ogbanje,* a living dead, that is, every oppressed woman. As Emecheta dedicates the work to her mother, Alice *Ogbanje* Emecheta, the thrust of this text, doubly dear because of its history, foregrounds the psychic tensions of the *ogbanje* strain. This in turn foreshadows the sad end of the rebellion and the love story, as we expect of most *ogbanje* stories.

As with the first two novels, there are also autobiographical strains in this work. Emecheta rewrites her history, spicing it with the romance that was missing from her grim life after her father's death to make the thought of that life more bearable. Aku-nna, her alter ego, is alienated from her people at Ibuza. Doubly an outsider because she is a girl and a cosmopolite, her situation parallels Emecheta's alienation in returning "home." It is natural that Aku-nna should empathize with her male teacher and mentor Chike Ofulue, also marginalized as a slave descendant and an outcast in traditional Ibuza society. In an ironic twist, Emecheta subverts the powers of patriarchy by making the insiders slaves to their tradition while the so-called slaves are free and control the progressive aspects in the backwoods society. The communal life that Aku-nna enjoys in urban centers like Lagos and Ughelli is more fulfilling than that of rural Ibuza, tinged with so many rules and regulations that make life almost prisonlike.

The question of levirate comes up in this novel when Ma Blackie, Akunna's mother, willingly marries her brother-in-law, to her children's dismay. Aku-nna feels that she has lost not only her father but also her mother, who now becomes embroiled in the vicious politics of the polygynous household. This creates a gap between mother and daughter, resulting in Aku-nna growing more introverted, secretive, and alienated. Aku-nna's aloneness, emphasized by her watching of two love birds building a nest together, shows her what is missing in her own life; it throws her into the waiting arms of Chike. These two second-class citizens (it is made clear that Aku-nna has no privileges, unlike her brother Nna-ndo) come together to watch some ants following one another. As outcasts who do not belong to Ibuza society, they will not act like ants, tediously following tradition, but they will pay dearly for their departure from the norm.

In keeping with the image of woman as a commodity, Emecheta names the protagonist Aku-nna, "father's wealth." However, Chike regards her in a Westernized manner as an "angel" (Emecheta 1980a, 85). This Angel in the House is in love with Chike, who wants to study sociology, making him Emecheta's mouthpiece in this critique of the unprogressive community. In this masculinist society, "An impotent man was very rare . . . and the few that existed were no more than living dead" (84); in other words, impotent men were problematic, like *ogbanjes*. The emotional upheaval, physical cramps, and secrecy that attend Aku-nna's menarche bring her closer to Chike, who helps her through the ordeal, instead of her mother. As an *ogbanje*, Aku-nna appears pliable, but she is not. Chike handles her with the customary tenderness and anxiety, acting the role of mother and mentor, thus displacing the preoccupied mother, Ma Blackie. This closeness between man and woman is idyllic. Where menstruation brings them together, it separates Aku-nna from traditional male society, turning her into an "unclean" person. This further ostracizes her from the society at large, as it prevents her from access to the stream where the unclean should at least have been allowed to try to be clean. The water goddess would have been tolerant. Her private menstruation propels her to the public gaze, as it announces her maturity as marketable property.

The *aja* dance that would integrate Aku-nna with her age mates to give her a sense of belonging becomes an occasion of further distress when she is abducted by a would-be husband. A prisoner of Okoboshi ("the son of the water deity Oboshi"), maimed as a sign of his degeneracy and unworthiness to bear his distinguished name, Aku-nna has to practice the art of storytelling, that is, lying, which she had learned from her Aunt Uzo, to prevent him from raping her. She becomes a snake in her wiles, disarming him like the snake that had crippled him previously. Battered physically and emotionally by "her new people" (141) because they believed her story that she was not a virgin, Aku-nna is rescued by Chike whistling their special tune, "Brown skin gal, stay home and min' baby" (135). The irony of this foreign tune will strike the reader on Aku-nna's death bed. Meanwhile, they walk away from the prison of this vicious society to the apparent freedom of an urban existence.

This second kidnapping, because that is what Chike's rescue is in essence (since it was not authorized by Aku-nna's family, and he is her teacher, and she is a minor), compounds the first, and earns Ma Blackie a quick divorce with a baring of the backside by the enraged Okonkwo, her new husband.[11] Making an image of Aku-nna, Okonkwo uses juju to call her back in the wind. Quite inexplicably, this free soul responds, to her death. "So it was that Chike and Aku-nna substantiated the traditional superstition they had unknowingly set out to eradicate. . . . If the bride price was not paid, she would never survive the birth of her first child. It was a psychological hold over every young girl that would continue to exist" (168). The hold was also over Emecheta, who personally faced the problem in her own nuclear family. It is the uneasy feeling of being not really married that Nigerian women experience if the bride-price aspect of the marriage ceremony, with its prayers, is not fully performed.

Aku-nna is held as a property—an object—by two men, her uncle Okonkwo and her would-be husband Okoboshi. Rescued by Chike, who treats her as a subject, the situation is comparable to that in Alfred Hitchcock's *Blackmail*. In a critique of the film, Tania Modleski (1987, 305) writes, "It might be argued that one of the main projects of the film is to wrest power from the woman, in particular the power of laughter, and to give the men the last laugh, thus defusing the threat of woman's infidelity, her refusal to treat

---

11. Islam and many indigenous religions treat women as nonpersons by the ease with which an angry husband can divorce his wife, leaving her without a share of their accumulated wealth. For example, a continent away in India, Zakia Pathak and Rajeswari Sunder Rajan (1989, 558) have written a scintillating account of the sullied victory of Shahbano, a peasant woman who fought against such injustice, all the way up to the Indian Supreme Court. The Court awarded her the unspeakable sum of "Rs 179.20 (approximately $14) per month from her husband, Mohammad Ahmed Khan." Under tremendous Islamic pressure, she renounced her symbolic victory after a ten-year struggle. The legal battle itself is noteworthy as a womanist triumph ending in a compromise, for Shahbano must be reintegrated within her community.

with proper seriousness patriarchal law and authority." Emecheta depicts Aku-nna as a hopeless victim. Interestingly, Emecheta returns to the plot in *Head Above Water:* "But I have had time to think and that, thanks be to God, has made me stronger both emotionally and spiritually than that girl in *The Bride Price* whose immaturity allowed her to be destroyed by such heavy guilt" (1986a, 4). However, Emecheta does not leave us utterly without hope with this upholding of patriarchy. Aku-nna leaves behind a daughter Joy, who, presumably, will be brought up by an enlightened father and uncle (Chike and Aku-nna's brother Nna-ndo), far from the grip of Ibuza traditions. In this tender romance, Emecheta unwittingly criticizes child marriages and the danger they pose for the brides, who are usually malnourished, anemic children. In keeping with the aesthetics of maternity, power is wrested from Aku-nna only temporarily, for the future lies joyous for those who survive her in an emergent womanist milieu of fathers and their daughter.

The Slave Girl: Slave Traffickers and Vernacular Ethics

Every woman, whether slave or free, must marry. All her life a woman always belonged to some male. At birth you were owned by your people, and when you were sold you belonged to a new master, when you grew up your new master who had paid something for you would control you.

Buchi Emecheta, *The Slave Girl*

The Slave Girl (1977), Emecheta's double-award-winning fourth novel, reassured the writer that she had something worthwhile to say, and her Western audience relished the way she was saying it. The story deals with a girl, Ogbanje Ojebeta, named after Emecheta's mother. Ojebeta's brother, Okolie, and her father, Okwuekwu, are named after Emecheta's maternal uncle Okolie Okwuekwu. This makes it a potential family saga, whose central thrust is an individual woman's, women's, a family's, and, ultimately, a nation's enslavement through male acquisitiveness, greed, and mismanagement. The theme of slavery underscores the freedom it earned the courageous storyteller.

In this momentous contribution to the palaver, Emecheta moves beyond Chike in *The Bride Price* to capitalize on the forceful metaphor of slavery and its domestic roots, to speak to Nigeria's political and economic dependency. A nation lost in the maze of slavery, with her men (and some women) tainted by illegal money exchange, treachery, and graft, is in itself enslaved. In this saga, Emecheta reminds us that our insidious actions often boomerang. She develops the metaphor of woman as commodity in a vast trading empire with its

ripple effects in Nigeria. Not only is woman an object for barter, her development is arrested, as the title of the book indicates, and she remains eternally a
minor. Emecheta's impassioned warning restates the oft-ignored truth that a
country's destiny inevitably parallels its women's. In an Osunian vein, she
demonstrates how intricately our political destiny is intertwined with the personal; exiling or marginalizing women, men inadvertently hurt themselves
and the country.

Though born at the center of town in Umuisiagba, right at the Eke marketplace, the hub of social and economic life in Ibuza, Ojebeta ends her life on
the periphery. As a girl, her brother sells her into slavery to a trader with European connections. Suggestively, the transaction takes place a few miles away,
across the River Niger, in Otu market—Onitsha, the biggest trading center in
West Africa. The marketplace as the site of human drama—a place for buying
and selling, an open theater for dances, funerals, rituals, fashion display, and
an international gathering of peoples—is the nerve center that touches everyone. Emecheta's interest in trade and its geographical and transnational
ramifications internationalizes this little girl's story. When she walks from
Ibuza, a rural town, to Onitsha, an international marketplace, and revisits
Ibuza before finally settling in the country's capital Lagos, Ojebeta, constantly
on the move, has the makings of a been-to in spite of her slave condition. For
this *ogbanje* girl, every journey takes her deeper into enslavement, putting her
at the nexus of global economics.

Further, Ojebeta is an *ogbanje* name cynically remarking that she did not
start journeying today; in other words, her condition is archetypal. Besides
identifying her as a restless spirit, destined for an uncertain future, the name
also marks her as everywoman, reenacting the ancient drama of enslavement
within the family through a betrayal of trust. The harshness and humiliation
of Ojebeta's life recall colonialism. On the personal level, besides representing
Emecheta's mother's destiny and Emecheta's unenviable heritage, as a jinx,
ogbanje speaks to the ups and downs in a writer's career in which the very act
of writing and its reception are always problematic and in need of mediation.

Emecheta's metaphor of enslavement aptly defines the female condition,
exacerbated in a colonized society where native women are nonentities. In his
heyday, Ojebeta's father, Okwuekwu Oda, had borne a sick white man from
Ibuza to recuperate in a more congenial environment. The notion of the black
man burdened by the white man bodes ill for the bearer, for westernization can
be catching and deadly. Okwuekwu Oda dies from influenza, spread abroad by
Europe's pollution of the environment during World War I. With a revision-

ary stroke, Emecheta replaces the violent, colonial images of Achebe's Okonkwo and Ulasi's Obieze with this amenable man whose kind act goes unrequited.

Ironically, Okwuekwu Oda, whose pidginized alias denotes his westernization, manages to bring order to the Babel of the colonial law court where he works, though his own house is in disarray.[12] Plagued by the *ogbanje* syndrome with the repeated deaths of his daughters, his family remains incomplete with two sons. This new man, who cherishes the female sex and understands its value, undertakes a dangerous journey to Idu to ensure that his newly born daughter, Ojebeta, remains alive. This is a folk tale. By making him travel to the mythical kingdom of Idu, Emecheta signifies on Nwapa's *Idu,* letting us know that her subject concerns the position of women historically and in the modern nation.

Besides, as an *ogbanje,* Ojebeta is enslaved by her controllers in the spirit world. Her father is determined to free her by following the *dibia*'s injunction to undertake the journey to end her frequent comings and goings. Okwuekwu's quest is a sign that society needs girls/women for their central role in holding the family/nation together. Tragically, he will not live to see his daughter perform this function because of her comings and goings in the physical world. The hazards of life in Nigeria are here likened to the fearsome *ogbanje* world.

Thus, *ogbanje* is a metaphor for women's insecurity and the feeling of being exiled as colonialism becomes strongly entrenched. Ojebeta remains in the physical world because her father demonstrated his love by risking his life to save hers. Her noisy charms speak out to ward off her companions in the other world, while the tattoos inscribed by her parents on her face are love letters, identifying her as belonging to them. Her face is the wordy document that shows how precious she is to those who authored it. Ojebeta's facial scarifications generate laughter at Otu market because the public has not yet grasped the significance of this writing on woman. However, it advertises to the reader the beginning of a new dispensation that must counter misogyny by treasuring woman.

If Ojebeta's body is the blank page on which her parents inscribed their love for her, the inscription on her mother's widowed body tells a different story of the cruel treatment custom metes out to widows. The unsanitary conditions in which the widow is confined invariably leads to her death. As an orphan, Ojebeta faces a hostile world without parental affection and, as a

12. It is pertinent to note that Emecheta is reinventing her mother's family in *The Slave Girl.*

pawn, she is promptly "sold" off into a benign form of slavery by her brother Okolie.

Just as the first phase of her life was marked by her father's dangerous journey, the second phase requires of Ojebeta an equally tedious journey in the company of her treacherous, self-serving brother. Where her father had traveled to free her from spiritland, her brother travels to enslave her in an alien world. He sells her to Ma Palagada, a relation who had two daughters for a white trader before she married a Nigerian referred to as a "foreigner." Interestingly, Ma Palagada is considered "lost" and "even sold into slavery" (33), in spite of her wealth. Since Ma Palagada, by dint of hard work and luck, attempts to reverse her own limitations as a female, perhaps Ojebeta, this slave of a slave, will also be able to take advantage of her new environment.

Enslavement in this text is ambiguous. Though it is a metaphor for woman's/nation's condition, it sends a conflicting message. Christianized and westernized, the slave girls have access to a better life as they learn to read and sew. In spite of their Western-style dresses, which they prefer to the *lappa* as a mark of their sophistication, they remain third- or fourth-class citizens, after the male slaves. As women, they are confined, buried alive in the shallow grave of existence, as Florence Stratton (1988) so aptly described it in her scintillating article, "The Shallow Grave: Archetypes of Female Experience in African Fiction."

Though not enslaved to the same degree, the colonized male, uprooted from traditional pursuits, is also limited. Okolie, for example, is portrayed as a thwarted artiste, who cannot live on his artistic gifts as a horn blower, singer, and accomplished dancer. Owezim, his older brother, leaves peremptorily to look for "the white man's job," becoming buried, in his turn, in the grave of metropolitan anonymity. The chain reaction is extensive. Okolie thought that he was not really enslaving his sister, but was *"marry*[ing] *her away to this woman relative"* (Emecheta 1977, 50). When a girl is sold to or marries a "slave" we have a conundrum. Women as slaves, who in turn enslave other women by marrying them, create a double bind, as Ifi Amadiume (1987) demonstrates in her fascinatingly titled book, *Male Daughters, Female Husbands.*

Emecheta appropriately backgrounds her novel with the southeastern Women's Struggle. She represents it as a political unrest with rumors of white people being assassinated and slaves killing their masters, thereby linking colonialism with personal freedom. The palpable fears in the Palagada household stem from class divisions, with the master and his son on one level, the mistress and her biracial daughters on another, followed by the male, then the female, slaves. However, all suffer under colonial rule. To emphasize this point, the emasculated master, Pa Palagada, is dependent on and named after his wife; in a role reversal reminiscent of the golden-egg image, Emecheta subverts whatever is left of indigenous patriarchy.

Nonetheless, Ma Palagada is a confusing character. She is to a certain degree Madam Tinubu's daughter. Her economic power, business acumen, and association with whites show that she is also a powerful Mammywata type; yet her husband inexplicably controls her. Not only does she tolerate his raping of the slave girls, she acts as if he alone can discipline the slaves, since he wields the rod. In spite of her Amazonian presence, Ma Palagada does not have ultimate power, because she needs some man to control her male slaves. This abdication of full power creates a dissonance.

Further, Ma Palagada does not appear as nationalist or feminist, as many critics have asserted. With the Women's Struggle raging in the background, she refuses to join the other women to fight against the colonial forces and their taxation of women. Rather, she undercuts her authority by insisting that the men should pay "for their heads, because they own us" (Emecheta 1977, 141). Her debilitating sickness prevents her from opposing the militant women or joining forces with them in their resistance against further enslavement of women and country. In death she is a casualty of some war: the headache of running a disorganized household and an extensive, capitalist empire jeopardized by radicals. Taxing women who were already overtaxed by a double-layered system of enslavement incurred revolt. However, Ma Palagada can hardly be loyal to her colleagues, with her blood and economic ties to white people. This Western connection is the headache that ultimately kills her. Not even Queen Victoria, whose picture dominates the living room, can help her, for she too looks overwhelmed in her widow's weeds, with Emecheta making intertextual links with Ama Ata Aidoo's *Anowa*.

Chiago, one of the slave girls, having observed an enslaved princess pushed into her mistress' grave and brutally clubbed, understands the limitations that are placed in woman's way. This is exacerbated for slaves in that their talents are not allowed to be fully developed. After the influenza, when only "ghosts of men" (82) were left, Nigeria's tragedy begins to haunt us as she buries her women's talents. The grim image of death is appalling.

The quiet slave without an identity is a robot that reminds Ojebeta of the "wooden dolls in front of her *chi* shrine at home in Ibuza" (89). When Ojebeta joins Amanna in mat-wetting, the psychological repercussions of enslaving women are clarified. In a portrait that recalls plantation conditions in the American South, the teenaged slave girl, Chiago, is raped by father and son in

Ma Palagada's household. Pa Palagada tortures the younger slaves by whipping them and making them fight each other. Without female solidarity, male violence and divisive tactics continue to hold women in bondage.

Ojebeta starts her new life as a slave by eating *agidi Akala,* symbolically entering the cosmopolitan and international phase of her life. By politely offering the food to Ma Palagada and the others as becomes a well-trained girl, she is initiated into the possible uses of food, of palava sauce, for diplomacy. She is embroiled with other nationalities, thereby broadening her horizons. She contrasts with Okolie, who eats pounded yam and "bushmeat" (venison), signs of his crudeness. His eating without offering others, as custom demands, marks his self-centeredness.

Ojebeta is presented metaphorically as the live thorn fish out of water being haggled over by the trader Ma Mee and a fisherman, just as Ma Palagada and Okolie had haggled over Ojebeta's monetary worth. When Ojebeta learns to read, she starts with the green Igbo book, *Azu-Ndu,* "live fish." Reading is not just a fishy business for those who are green, but one that will distinguish them from the rest of society. It is ironic that slaves are permitted to read, while the free daughters are protected from westernization. The literate thus have the potential to become fishers of women, freeing themselves from the Palagada household.

At Ma Palagada's death, Ojebeta prefers the "mushroom of freedom" to the "meat of slavery." But Emecheta's final statement is that a woman is never really free. In Ibuza, Ojebeta's period of being enslaved is equated with *olu oyibo,* that is, "working with the white people" (157). There is thus an ambivalence on Emecheta's part as to how she perceives Ojebeta's stay in the Palagada household, since *olu oyibo* is simultaneously westernization and enslavement, a case of mixed blessings. We cannot easily dismiss the benefits from this stay, as Ojebeta, the been-to, is admired for being more sophisticated than those left behind in the "freedom" of Ibuza. Ojebeta's exile, return, and departure follow the been-to/*ogbanje* pattern. On her return to Ibuza, where she is apparently free, Ojebeta receives another name, Alice, to mark the beginning of another nightmarish journey into Wonderland. She marries Jacob, nicknamed "the Whiteman because he behaves and acts mildly like a white man" (169). Both move to Lagos, the colonial headquarters. Here they eat the "mushroom of freedom," and the subsequent malnutrition takes its toll on Ojebeta.

Caskey (1986, 177) comments on the importance of nutrition in cultures: "The presence or absence of fat, then, and its perceived status in a given culture seem to vary in response to economic and social factors as well as biological ones. Beller and Bruch are both quick to point out that in subsistence level cultures, fat had high value as an indicator of prosperity and as a guarantee for the birth and survival of children." This is important in Clifford's perception of the aging and nervous Ojebeta, debilitated by malnutrition and the hardships of wifedom. Her failure to have more children is thus not only due to the spiritual and emotional effect of the soul-crippling debt owed Clifford, the *soldier* and new slave-master who inherited her from her husband Ma Palagada. It also stems from the crushing poverty that has taken its toll on her body, which was used to an easier life in slavery. Is slavery with meat preferable to slavery with the mushroom of freedom? Are the benefits of colonialism preferable to the chaos of an independent Nigeria? These are moot points in the palaver.

When Ojebeta changes her name again and becomes Mrs. Ogbanje Ojebeta Alice Okonji (the surname means "black man," and, by extension, "Nigeria"), she voluntarily enters the fourth phase of her enslavement. This moves her into the grinding poverty that leaves her worse off than the slaves who stayed behind in the Palagada household. It looks as if Emecheta punishes Ojebeta for her bid for freedom; also, we can read this as an indication that freedom has a price.

However, when she equates the fifth and final aspect of Ojebeta's enslavement with that of the nation in the last pages of the novel, Emecheta is stating categorically that the question of individual freedom under colonialism is a farce. In other words, no woman can be said to be free as long as her country or her people are in some way under foreign control or are exploited by military sons-of-the-soil. Through Ojebeta, she asserts, quite compellingly, that the female journey from cradle to grave, indeed from spiritland (for it appears that woman's *Chi* is conniving), is one insidious and invidious movement through different forms of enslavement, slightly alleviated by exposure to different worlds.

The Joys of Motherhood and the Throes of Fatherhood

> How could a situation rob a man of his manhood without him knowing it. . . .
> We women mind the home. Not our husbands. Their manhood has been taken
> away from them. The shame of it is that they don't know it. All they see is the
> money, shining white man's money.
>
> Buchi Emecheta, The Joys of Motherhood

Birth (and perhaps death) involves a product and a producer who reinvents the self from and after the experience. When the product is tangible, the relationship between the product and the producer can be well defined. Thus, where the experience of motherhood appears embracive, fatherhood tends to be adoptive, and a father often can afford to be absent. In emerging states, the extension of fatherhood to nationhood, as a product negotiated by men, oftentimes contains the seeds of chaos consequent to male absence or being out of touch with the people; Nigeria's Lord Lugard, the British man who fathered the nation, is a good example.

From a medical and a legalistic perspective, the case of the Ibuza woman Nnu Ego in Emecheta's *The Joys of Motherhood* (1979) can be read in this context. With reproduction as her main objective, she has joined her Ibuza husband Nnaife in the city of Lagos, the capital of the emerging nation of Nigeria. In spite of the been-to possibility that is put in place, Lagos conditions are fertile ground for tyranny. Not only are women oppressed, so also are men, children, and the nation in an intricate dynamic in which a victim easily transforms into a victimizer.

Nnu Ego and her husband Nnaife live in the "boys' quarters," behind the white master's and mistress's house in an arrangement reminiscent of American slave plantation architecture. The system, with its implications of immaturity, ironizes the position of Nnaife, who comes from a patriarchal background where wives live in segregated outhouses in the back yard. As the white couple's washerman, Nnaife is all washed out, with his pale skin and soft job. His duties include laundering his mistress's underwear, a bone of contention between him and the sensitive Nnu Ego, who finds it demeaning and intolerable with its sexual undertones. The first two sons best him, when they marry white women. Meanwhile, Nnaife is bestialized and feminized when the white man refers to him as a "baboon," while Nnu Ego sees him as a "pregnant cow" and a "woman-made man." How does this domesticated female animal father any children?

Nnu Ego herself is doubly a slave as her enslaved husband's wife. She is deeply entrenched in several hierarchies, because her *Chi*, who was originally a princess (cf. Chiago's story in *The Slave Girl*), is "a slave woman who had been forced to die with her mistress when the latter was being buried" (Emecheta 1979, 9). In her reincarnation, her *Chi* has bequeathed her with a head injury that manifests itself physically and emotionally. It culminates in her insanity (another metaphor for the chaos), which serves as the opening and closing scenes of the book.

Suffering the repercussions of the blow on her *Chi*'s head as she must under karmic law, Nnu Ego is disoriented and, like her *Chi*, constantly in the wrong place at the wrong time. Inevitably, she too has to endure indignities with people disrespecting her. They catch her in humiliating situations, as she does not know her rightful place or what befits her in the chaotic scheme of things. She is a fish out of water, a "Mammy Water" (43) outside her domain. In short, she is everywoman, a treasure and a princess, reduced to playing the role of a slave beyond her father's gates.

Though her name Nnu Ego, "moneybags," and her mother's, Ona, "jewel," indicate how precious they are to their fathers (Emecheta, with tongue in cheek, also hints at their value as property), their wealth does not buy them free of the oppression that comes with the territory. In recapitulating the stories of enslavement already narrated in *The Slave Girl* in *The Joys of Motherhood,* Emecheta preserves intertextual links to demonstrate that very little has changed in the status of women and the country in three generations.

Ona is the prototype of the "male daughter." Though uneasy about being tossed between her father and her lover, she enjoys some liberties denied female daughters. However, she too is oppressed, as she has no rights to exercise her personal choices like a male son, a point Amadiume (1987, 32) underscores in her study of virilized women. This accounts for Ona's deathbed request that Agbadi, her lover and Nnu Ego's father, should allow Nnu Ego to make her marital choices, a freedom that was denied her.

Thus, even the "feminist" freedom to remain unmarried enjoyed by Ona is fraught with limitations, as we never really know what she actually wanted. Not only is she controlled by her father's wishes, which turn her into a part-male or a neuter, she also suffers under the power struggle between her and her lover. The injured Agbadi rapes her to show that, weakened though he might be, he is still in control. He demonstrates the male desire to oppress woman and to be seen to do so. Ona enjoys being raped, for his desire for her marks her superiority to the other women in Agbadi's household. She is a marginal figure in the text; like the writings on the margins of a book, she is an aside, as she belongs neither to the male world nor to the female, losing the advantages of each group. This creates an identity crisis for her. In spite of Emecheta's attempts to romanticize Agbadi's and Ona's lovemaking, Ona's potential remains unexplored; she is a tragic figure in not being her own person, bound as she is by tradition.

With the next generation, Nnaife's servitude is not limited to his degrading duties. References to him as a *boy* abound in the text. He hungrily eats a mango like a schoolboy, picks balls for white men golfing as if he were a student, and wrongly assumes he is the one referred to as "old boy" by the golf players. Colonialism thrives on the premise that the colonized are childlike and undeveloped. Handicapped by such self-fulfilling prophecies, how does a man father his children? The difference between the men who stayed on in Ibuza, such as Agbadi or Nnu Ego's first husband, and those who left to work with whites, such as Nnaife, is not fortuitous. The encounter with whites mutates the been-to into a has-been, no longer able to run home and country efficiently. As the only models their children have to emulate, the issues become infinitely compounded.

Like a woman, Nnaife waits for his master's return as Nnu Ego would wait for his return from World War II. While he thus becomes gradually feminized, his white counterpart becomes progressively divinized. Nnaife's fate is sealed when he is abducted into the master's army with its reminiscences of the slave past when people were caught and taken to an unknown destination. Fighting in World War II over issues the conscripted soldier knew nothing about ironizes the position of the native fighting for other people's liberation.

Colonized men, particularly the urbanized rather than the rural dwellers, are slaves and prisoners as much as the wife and mother is. Later in the novel, Nnaife's second-class citizenship is further confirmed with his imprisonment after a trial with a European jury. His life in Lagos gradually deteriorates; it ends ignominiously in prison for his daring to act as a macho father when he violently defends his daughter's honor, albeit with Nnu Ego's matchete. Obviously, it is quixotic for an unarmed urban dweller to venture to protect his daughter or to control her destiny. Jeopardized, Nnaife's attempt at playing big daddy experiences its final pangs and is stillborn. Nnu Ego grasps this fact intuitively; in a touching, midwifely gesture of affirmation and cooperation, she embarrassedly covers the laboring Nnaife's nakedness by readjusting his *lappa*, which almost flies open during the confusion of his arrest for delusively fighting for his daughter. A woman protects a man, delicately. Emecheta thereby affirms the need for mutual reinforcement as men and women parent together for the full benefit of family and country.

Susan Andrade (1990, 100) observes of *The Joys of Motherhood* that "Emecheta's act of writing this narrative draws attention to the ironic status of *Efuru* as the "mother" text of (anglophone) African women's literature, thereby signifying on Nwapa again. By so doing, *The Joys of Motherhood* appropriates the male purview of the production of texts by conflating it with the female production of children." Since the novel is Emecheta's grieving for her disloyal daughter, Chiedu, who, tragically and coincidentally, later dies, the speed with which she accomplished the writing expresses her psychological need to replace the displaced child with a text she could control in a way a re-calcitrant child can never be.[13] Nnaife, Nnu Ego, and their creator Emecheta thus bow to the exigencies of parenthood.

Nnu Ego and Nnaife, as the parents of the *ogbanje*, Oshiaju, endure more hardships than most. As Oshiaju's name indicates, the forest, that is, the grave, has rejected him, a sign that he has come to stay. The power struggle between Oshiaju and his parents is therefore very interesting and is an eye opener, as their commitment is hardly reciprocated. His Western education makes him skeptical of their beliefs in medicine men, whom he views as quacks. Oshia buys his freedom through intelligence, education, and, as one would expect of an *ogbanje*, travel to another world. He abandons the enslaved fold to become a been-to, returning from the alien world of the Americas only to bury his mother.

Oshiaju and his brother escape the hazards of the polygynous household with all its emotional violence. Thus, children are better off than women, who are placed under a male who is not worthy of the authority, as Nnu Ego blurts out in the court scene. Polygyny in an urban setting is devastating, for "She and her husband were ill-prepared for a life like this, where only pen and not mouth could really talk" (Emecheta 1979, 179). Dumbfounded in their illit-erate existence, they remain slaves to the end, while their educated sons become liberated to some degree but remain out of touch.

In addition, the polygynous household is the home front where Nnu Ego and her co-wife Adaku are embroiled in combat. Nnu Ego "fought the war too here in your family" (183), the men inform the newly returned soldier Nnaife. Co-wives are soldiers on active duty in an undisclosed or openly declared warfare. The debilitating effects of the engagement leave Nnu Ego battle weary, hungry, and crazy.

She strikes the reader as the prototype of the sweet mother superimposed upon the embittered wife. She is a martyr whose sainthood remains unac-knowledged and unrecognized by her husband and sons. As Gillespie and Kubitschek (1990, 30) comment on such female propensity, "Women gener-ally cannot articulate . . . degenerative aspects of caring because caring consti-tutes the whole social definition of their being good; they are psychically un-able to forego social approval and to imagine alternatives which are 'not good.'" They continue, "But the traditionally good woman expects something

---

13. Emecheta wrote the manuscript to work out her anxiety about the position of a mother in a grown child's life.

for all that she has given up" (32). Nnu Ego's self-destruction is Emecheta's lesson to woman to raise her self-esteem, to love, cherish, and empower her self in the community rather than live in expectation of a reward from children.

As Adaku had the attributes of the "bad woman" whom Amadiume (1987, 92) describes as somebody "who enjoyed wrongdoing and her aim was . . . to break up her husband's household," Nnu Ego is cast in the stereotype of the "good woman" who, Amadiume stresses, "looked after her husband, never refused him food and made sure that things worked out well in the household. She looked after her children, fed them, kept them clean and gave them good home training. She usually helped her husband financially through her own efforts" (93). Emecheta then punctures these images, dramatizing their displacement and irrelevance in an urban milieu by making the "bad" Adaku with her two daughters sophisticated and a big success while the "good" Nnu Ego with her numerous progeny remains an embarrassing failure. It is Adaku who experiences the joys of motherhood, not Nnu Ego; it no longer pays to be "good" in this fast-changing world.

Adaku's move out of her absent husband's house is a daring enterprise, an unspeakable course of action in the 1940s, as well as now. To contain women with such disruptive ideas, the Igbo refer to a free woman in this unattached state as *ajadu* (a prostitute), although she might not be actively soliciting men for economic or sexual gratification. So incensed are the Igbo at the thought of such a woman that *igba ajadu* (prostitution) is synonymous with *igba akwuna kwuna*, a phrase whose onomatopoeic echoes are meant to convey the horror and repetitiveness of the condition, further ostracizing the single woman. Hence, women rarely separate from their husbands, to say nothing of divorcing them. In disparaging herself by referring to her carefully orchestrated move as prostitution, Adaku may be a new woman, but, in a way, she is still a daughter of her times, naturally retaining vestiges of her oppression.

In her summation of some of the criticism on Emecheta, Cynthia Ward (1990, 86) comments that in many "'essentialist' readings of Emecheta," critics reproduce "an image of the African woman as 'essentially oppressed.'" With Nnu Ego, such critics have chosen to accent the slave part of her *Chi*, ignoring her royalty as a princess. Nnu Ego is the deracinated female, subject to the abject, colonized male, her husband Nnaife, literally the father of something unspecified, though it should read Nnabuife, "father is priceless." That lack of specificity in his naming underscores the insubstantiality of his role as father or husband. As a slave and a princess, Nnu Ego remains eternally ambiguous in her duality: her natal beginnings with an absent mother who did not marry her father and who passed away in childbirth, her awkwardness in the Lagos metropolis, and her difference when she revisits rural Ibuza make her a perpetual outsider.

She is recognized as a first wife, and she particularly cherishes the adulation and the reflected glory of having educated sons, who could have mediated between her and the increasingly confusing westernization of her world were they not absent. Riding home first-class in the lorry on her final journey back to Ibuza ironizes the would-be been-to's declassification. Her self-perception about her unbelonging eventually degenerates into madness.

The family's been-toism fragments the extended family. Driven by poverty, Nnu Ego advocates the process with her hostility toward Nnaife's traditional duty to look after his deceased brother's family. Imbued with her philosophy and following her example, in that she hardly kept in touch with her own father, her sons repeat her mistakes; as they move up in status by marrying white women (no longer serving them like their father), they concentrate on their nuclear families, to her chagrin. Their big funeral for her marks the end of a phase and the beginning of another when she becomes apotheosized. In the ritual celebration, they cut the umbilical cord linking them to her, which she did not want severed. Her sons and their white wives do not need to pray to her for children. Nnu Ego, alive or dead, is irrelevant, as most mothers invariably become in the Western world.

The dead child she starts her childbearing career with, after the initial barrenness, denotes the stultifying atmosphere of colonialism. The child who had made a woman out of Nnu Ego and a man out of Nnaife dies, to show that colonialism had dealt their vital part a deathblow. She ends her childbearing phase with a stillbirth, the thwarting of their dreams. If life under the colonial master/mistress is deadly and cause for suicide for Nnu Ego, life with numerous children and an absent husband is financially and emotionally crippling.

The alcoholic Nnaife hardly fares better. A would-be musician without talent, the eagle-eyed Nnu Ego sees through him. From the powers conferred on him by leviratic practice, he acquires his brother's wives, since women, once married, become family heirlooms. Though he can control women in his victimhood, his power continues to erode with Adaku's challenge and his twin daughter Kehinde's elopement.

In spite of the limitations, Nnu Ego achieves what her husband cannot. She brings up their children practically single-handedly, with little or no help from their impecunious father. Nnu Ego and her *Chi* express her split personality: the cosmopolitan wars with the rural, the rebel with the conservative, as she longs to be an only wife, though she was the product of a liaison that killed her mother's rival. An example of the sacrifices entailed in motherhood, in death she repudiates it, like Uhamiri. Now a genuine social mother and an ancestor, Nnu Ego protects women by not granting them requests for children, because they do not realize the ramifications of their prayers. By deriving the title of the novel from the last page of Nwapa's novel, Emecheta joins Nwapa in conveying the need for a renaissance for Efuru's and Nnu Ego's progeny.

The poverty-stricken Nnu Ego, cynically named, and Adaku, "the daughter born into wealth," are two sides of an Emechetan coin, one conservative and the other progressive. Adaku's rebellion leads to money-making and liberation, while Nnu Ego's conservatism leads to anxiety, madness, and eventual death. These two contradictory impulses form the essence of Emecheta's contribution and challenge others to address unresolved issues in the palaver. The anxiety about parenthood in the text parallels Emecheta's anxiety about her own nuclear family as well as about her role as mother and daughter. With the challenge she was facing from her daughter Chiedu's disloyal return to her father after all the years of his abandonment, Emecheta realized that behind every successful woman is her self, not husbands or sons or daughters, for children are also part of the female predicament.

Adaku, now an ex for all intents and purposes, dares to become a "prostitute" by withdrawing from an unsatisfactory marriage; like Emecheta, she thrives. In this celebratory return to woman's first profession, prostitution, like writing, liberates, for, like the author's relationship with her male characters, woman can determine the terms of her relationship with the opposite sex through it. In finally parting from her husband, the old Nnu Ego, like Efuru, joins the select band of bitter wives without husbands. In this state, woman's vision is rarefied and beneficial to other women. If books are children, then children are like books. Nnu Ego's letting go of her children can be read as the separation of the artist from her published work. Emecheta thus acknowledges that the text and the child, like the *ogbanje*, must necessarily lead a separate existence from the author/mother/parent; the joys of parenthood lie hidden in knowing when to let go of the child. A healthy parting of the ways ensures that each journeys on unencumbered.

Destination Biafra: Humpty-Dumpty and Daughters-of-the-Soil

I am a woman and a woman of Africa. I am a daughter of Nigeria and if she is in shame, I shall stay and mourn with her in shame.

Buchi Emecheta, *Destination Biafra*

The failure to communicate meaningfully in the palaver in Nigeria resulted in the civil war. In *Destination Biafra* (1983a), the second war novel to be written by a Nigerian woman, Emecheta envisages women's roles in a Nigeria divided by warring men to be multiphasic and cooperative. A diverse group of women as *omunwa*/mother (public and private), warrior, power broker, peacemaker, healer, and wife undertake a hazardous journey to Biafra, the secessionist enclave, on a quest for safety, peace, and an ideal. The novel has the makings of picaresque fiction, while the journey from one fractious world to another conflates images of birth, death, rape, pillage, and hope in its *ogbanje* surrealism.

The novel depicts the emotional trauma and violence experienced particularly by women and children during the 1967–70 civil war in Nigeria. Critics have questioned Emecheta's right to write about the war, since, unlike Nwapa, she was not physically present in Nigeria when it took place. Emecheta's decision to tell the women's perception of the war raises issues about aesthetics and the role of the exile in the palaver. For example, how many combatants actually write war novels? What part does the writer's imaginary play in creativity? Are Emecheta's gestures from the symbolic Trafalgar Square and Sandhurst utterly irrelevant to the war, internationalized by the politics of oil?

In the author's foreword, Emecheta claims that the original first part of *Destination Biafra,* dealing with the Sandhurst section of the book, disappeared mysteriously while the manuscript was with the editor. The manuscript must have posed a serious threat to whoever effected this sabotage. After the terrible experience she had with the burning of her first manuscript, it is curious that Emecheta does not take precautions with her manuscripts. However, the cause of that conflagration appears identical to the reason for the disappearance of the later manuscript: the need for patriarchy to silence women. Since this section was on Sandhurst, the center of conventional British militarism, any intrusion into its labyrinths by a female outsider had to be steamrolled.

In her characteristic fashion, Emecheta beat a quick retreat. She writes, "I felt as if my bank manager had told me that he had lost my money" (vii). When the metaphor for the manuscript changes from the child to monetary investment, one realizes that she is hinting at the moneys connected with the battle for oil that underlay the civil war.

In spite of the banking image, Emecheta retains the image of the text as child in the novel. Indeed, she must have had a foreboding of disaster as she fills the text with miscarriages, stillbirths, monstrosities, and a high infant mortality rate. Twelve years after the cessation of hostilities, she was undoubtedly apprehensive about the reception of the work, which turned out to be gripping even though it was poorly edited.[14]

The protagonist is the woman army officer, Oritsha Debbie, *orisa de bi* in Yoruba, "the deity was here." Her divine presence suffuses the novel, imposing some order on the Nigerian dystopia. Debbie is also an acronym for destination Biafra, the idyllic state that this romantic and quixotic officer-turned-foot-soldier dreams of, for Biafra holds the "key to freedom" (119). The name Oritsha (the Itsekiri word for *orisa*) ushers in the Osun dimension: Debbie is the lone female soldier among men, sent to make things right in the chaotic world. Though an officer, like Osun, she is disrespected and raped by fellow officers; the nation will continue in disarray until they do right by women. This stresses Emecheta's ethical concern, which centers on the nature of corruption and disorder, their pervasiveness in Nigeria and Biafra, and the position of women in such a dystopia. As a romantic, Debbie yearns for a wholesome Nigeria without ethnic or gender sectionalism. Her journey toward Biafra therefore doubles as a collective dreamscape, a movement toward a utopia—that is, nowhere.

The spirit of a fragmented Nigeria is exposed in the Dickensian battle of the clothes that takes place in the cathedral between Mrs. Odumosu and Mrs. Durosaro, the wives of two political rivals. Ostensibly in *aso ebi,* both attend the ceremony identically clothed through coincidence, not by design. Mrs. Odumosu orders her rival to go back home and change. Unaware of the battle for autonomy raging in his cathedral, the Bishop praises the two warriors for coming to church in *aso ebi* as a sign of kinship and reconciliation. This gross misreading of tyranny and resistance would be hilarious if the ripple effects were not so tragic. The church battle is followed by "a battle of words going on in the Western region" (36); they precede the bloody war. The novel is replete with power tussles in a country still indirectly ruled by the British, ceremonially represented by her erstwhile colonial officers who control the army and ammunitions.

14. Nineteen-eighty-two was a busy year for Emecheta, when she produced *Destination Biafra, Double Yoke,* and *Naira Power.* She had spent 1980–81 in Calabar, teaching creative writing at the University under unsettled and, what she considered, unsatisfactory conditions. Such situations bring out the writing spirit in her, but she wrote too quickly, as evidenced by some flaws in these three texts.

Like many educated compatriots, the been-to Debbie, who was educated in Britain and has an English lover, Alan Grey, stands for change in Nigeria. However, she is compromised by her been-toism and a corrupt father, wealthy enough to provide his family with gold shoes for the independence ceremony. By joining the army, Debbie intends to fight several battles. First and foremost, she dissociates herself from her father by giving her loyalty to the future of a country free from corruption.

She confronts the issue of gender and the distribution of power between armed men and unarmed men and women. Moving from the helpless position of civilians and women to the self-empowerment that the military enjoys, Debbie attempts to feminize the army. She exiles herself from the softness of her father's palace to the hardness of the soldier's barracks, meting out violence instead of being protected from it. When this virilized woman leads her troops to eliminate some Igbo officers, she performs a soldierly duty, indirectly avenging her father's death like a male daughter.

However, when Debbie is gang raped by other soldiers, she is put back in her place. Higgonnet (1986, 74) comments that "If woman is taken to be a commodity, rape means total devaluation: reified, then stolen, she has no essence left to justify her continuing existence." If the civil war is "our very first war of freedom" (Emecheta 1983a, 160), Debbie's fight against people ostracizing her because she had been raped and rendered "worthless" in their eyes is a personal battle she must win for all rape victims. She moves on the road to success by first accepting herself, fighting "a personal war for her womanhood" (174), hitting back when another rapist, Salihu Lawal, slaps her for being "dry," her "juice" already expressed by previous male attackers. Debbie's rape is a metaphor for the violation of women, the weak, the poor, the illiterate, and minorities in Nigeria by those who are stronger, most especially the educated and the military. Since Osun survived, so will her progeny.

An officer who cannot defend herself is not worthy of the post. Exchanging her gun and uniform for pen, paper, *lappa*, and a baby, Debbie recovers her dignity as a westernized African woman. She continues her march toward Biafra as a member of a community of women and children. Part of her struggle now involves documenting her story as a female participant in the war, particularly as most of the stories told by men exclude women and the home front. Like Adah, her predecessor, Debbie is a writer and, therefore, Odu's daughter. Emecheta's keen interest in the role of the woman writer in the palaver urges her to project herself into these women writing on the side. Debbie is destined to revise the war novel by uncovering its secrets. Her manuscript consists of "yellowing scraps of paper" (223). Unfortunately, "most of the incidents were written down in her personal code which only she could decipher. If she should be killed, the entire story of the women's experience of the war would be lost" (223–24). Fortunately, she is not killed. Daringly acting the male role of the *babalawo*, Emecheta decodes it to make it accessible to the public.

The secrets cover rape, birth, death, surviving, caring, encouraging others, and looking after the children for a future after war. It needs a woman to stress that war is not only about killing and dying but also about living, loving, reproducing, and sacrificing. Debbie's manuscript is meant to heal, not exacerbate, emotions. The destructive power of Debbie's gun is replaced by the creativity of her pen. Since Debbie is *Destination Biafra*, she has indelibly inscribed herself into the text. Out of the trauma of war she reproduces this unique text of a woman's many-pronged battle for a decent society, totally revising the male war novel, exemplified by Eddie Iroh's *Forty-eight Guns for the General* (1976).

The women's war contrasts with the violent male war raging in the background. Her story extends to ordinary people, rural and analphabetic women whose potential for leadership men always ignore to their loss. It is noteworthy that, for many women, "to struggle against militarism *is* to struggle against patriarchy and male violence against women" (hooks 1984, 125). Debbie gradually combats it in Nigeria, Biafra, and Britain.

In *Destination Biafra*, eighteen people set out from Nigeria to Biafra, but only two women and four children live to tell the tale. The war half of the story stems from the group's ordeal on the road to the Biafran utopia. This community of women and children invariably suffer calamity when they encounter men, usually soldiers. Some of the women are as courageous as soldiers, while others are also as frightened as soldiers can be. These working-class women struggling for their very lives differ remarkably from the bickering, frivolous politicians' wives. The courage displayed by their hostess at Agbor shows the selflessness of poor women in a state of crisis.

A sisterhood emerges as strong as that in a nunnery. This is buttressed by the care and concern shown by the dutiful Irish nuns who sacrifice their lives to save others. The Mother Superior is indeed a superior mother who lays her life on the line to help all the children who cross her path. Throughout the text, social motherhood is pitted against militarism. "To Nigerians, in marriage the male partner was superior and the female must be subservient, obedient, quiet to the point of passivity," Emecheta comments (1983a, 43). However, in a state of war, when most of the men are absent or dead, the woman has to fend for herself and for the children left in her care, or else the nation will collapse.

Mother Earth protects her own with the thick vegetation that she proffers as cover for the weary travelers. The men try to depopulate and defoliate her with bombs and chemical weapons. The man-made road turns into a place for slaughter, whereas the natural river and the air provide safer routes for escape and survival.

Though the birth of the boy named Baby Biafra kills his mother, it also rekindles hope for the future. When the baby also dies, the country Biafra can be read as something immature, a utopia, a mortuary, a dead end. As deadly as Nigeria, Biafra has no moral basis for continued existence. Debbie attacks those like the rebel leader Abosi, who have put their personal ambitions before the interests of the people. The war between the two leaders, the Biafran Abosi and the Nigerian Momoh, is a clash between the educated and the half-educated, the rich and the upstart, the been-to and the stay-at-home. Significantly, Mrs. Abosi keeps miscarrying, while Mrs. Momoh gives birth to a hideous creature after a tedious pregnancy, clues that the leaders have nothing tangible to offer. Where one man fails to make Biafra viable, the other turns Nigeria into a monstrosity.

Emecheta's ultimate view of the civil war as a personal duel between two feuding megalomaniacs, is, however, reductive. Marie Umeh (n.d., 11–12) captures this limited aspect of the war in *Destination Biafra* succinctly: "*In allegorical fashion then, Debbie represents sacrifice and goodness. The allusion of Gowon's and Ojukwu's betrayal of countless Nigerians at the center of their power struggle reinforces the negative. The myth of male superiority is, of course, dismantled; at the same time the redemptive role Debbie is to act out, exalted. Thus, women . . . are superior to men,*" even if they are not liberated. Since the Biafran dream was for political and economic liberation from Nigeria, implicit in the civil war is the desirability for women to be liberated, too. The men on the Nigerian and Biafran sides, as well as the British, refuse to entertain the idea, creating an ironic undercurrent throughout the text.

Debbie starts off on her journey as a soldier but ends up in Biafra as a mother of two orphans. On reaching Biafra, or what is left of it, Debbie kisses the ground, like Bessie Head's Elizabeth in *A Question of Power*. By thus declaring herself a daughter-of-the-soil, she affirms her womanhood and Nigerianness. Yet her nationalism is at odds with her association with the imperialist, her British lover Alan Grey. When he recoils from her in horror at her tale of rape, she reaffirms her wholeness, knowing fully well that she can have no meaningful relationship with somebody who perceives her as soiled. Though her destination was Biafra, which had died as prematurely as Baby Biafra had on her back, the future lies before her, and she is in control.

Debbie's quest is ideological, and her changing attires are telltale signs of her metamorphosis. Her beautiful clothes at Abosi's wedding and at the beach make her self-conscious and uncomfortable, the budding capitalist. Her ill-fitting soldier's uniform marks her out as a would-be feminist, an outsider in the Nigerian army. After the rape, with only one *lappa,* she is forced to forget her pain and act as a mother, but she is unable to tie the baby on her back unaided. "What type of women is Africa producing?" asks a disgusted male soldier (Emecheta 1983a, 190). Debbie is a new type of woman who needs help to care for the children, for she will not be limited to childbearing like her mother's generation.

Full of contradictions, Debbie is the would-be Marxist sporting gold shoes—the spoils of a corrupt capitalist father. She is Nigeria, with Biafra in her heart. She is the victimized woman and the ostracized minority turned savior. She is the soldier with peaceful intentions. She is the nationalist with a British accent and a been-to experience. In sum, Debbie is as paradoxical as Nigeria.

Double Yoke: Double Yolk and Yokefellows

Here feminism means everything the society says is bad in women. Independence, outspokenness, immorality, all the ills you can think of so even the educated ones who are classically feminist and liberated in their attitudes and behaviour, will come round and say to you, 'but I am gentle and not the pushful type.'"

Buchi Emecheta, *Double Yoke*

Double Yoke (1982a) was Emecheta's second novel to appear in 1982. It is a critical exercise to transform the patriarchal Nigerian university into a national agency to disseminate the gospel of a brotherhood and sisterhood without crippling hierarchies. Palava sauce can now be read as a yoke. Extending the pun, it is the equally nutritious but cholesterol-laden yolk. Its doubling ensures the viability of an emergent community conscious of its oppressive agencies.

The text was prompted by Emecheta's return for a one-year stint as creative writing professor at the University of Calabar, after being away in England for about eighteen years. Home was anything but sweet, and reminiscences of that traumatic return can be read into *Kehinde* (1994). In spite of the culture shock, her prolonged absence enables her to look dispassionately at her subject with fresh eyes. Occasionally she appears estranged, an outsider watching the capers of a strange people. With this been-to dissociation, writing from the margins of society not only as a woman but as an educated, disgruntled nationalist has its advantages, except that those who remained behind to muddle on are irritated by criticisms from those who were not patriotic enough to stay. The been-to writer has to confront this palava of not fully belonging.

In *Double Yoke*, the visiting Miss Bulewao, the creative writing teacher, Emecheta's alter ego, is determined to instill in her students a new national vision. As teacher, mentor, and mater, Miss Bulewao soon realizes the complexity of her task when her class is plunged into darkness because of a power outage. Emecheta thus narrows the problem down to power plays at the university, a microcosm of the Nigerian society. The challenge of darkness where there should be light in an institution of higher learning indicates the pervasive nature of the issues. Keeping people in the dark contradicts the spirit of education. Ete (the Efik word for Brother) Kamba, a student prepared for the occasion, starts his evangelical work of establishing a progressive brotherhood when he produces a torchlight. However, its power is weak, unlike electricity. Being an outsider, Miss Bulewao has no basic survival skills, for, in her ignorance, she had scheduled classes to take advantage of the cool evenings, forgetting that the power supply cannot be guaranteed. Reading and writing in the dark epitomize the dilemma of the Nigerian elite.

Also, a society in which the majority of the people are not provided for, in which pedestrians have to battle against heavy and dangerous traffic because there are no sidewalks, is an oppressive one. That oppression rears its head in other facets of life. When Ete Kamba, in trying to do his creative writing assignment, puts "his biro onto a clean sheet of paper" (13), and one hundred and forty-three pages later has completed his "essay," ostensibly the writing of *Double Yoke*, we realize that the creative process is a matter of ingenious shifting in this stultifying atmosphere. Importantly, for the first time Emecheta uses a man as her artist character.

Unfortunately, Emecheta's ingenuity surprisingly fails her in this novel. If she wanted Ete Kamba to write the novel (not an essay), he has obviously learned little from Miss Bulewao's creative writing class. Henry James would have been distressed at Ete Kamba's manipulation of point of view: Ete Kamba writes about himself as if he were somebody else. To be charitable, this failure to write himself into the text can be read as a problem of identity as his new self evolves. Occasionally, he switches codes as an omniscient narrator, confusing fiction with nonfiction in the most elementary manner. The use of flashbacks "remembering" what he could not have known creates a disjunction that Emecheta has to accept the blame for, rather than Ete Kamba.

Another way to view this technical aspect of the novel is to say that Emecheta did not commit a flaw, but acted deliberately: she makes Ete Kamba write a story ineptly, producing a raw draft, which he fails to edit in his careless Nigerian fashion. Or perhaps she wants to show how duplicitous a man can be. Not only can Ete Kamba not produce a child of his own, as his girlfriend Nko can, but he also cannot write a text of his own, stealing Emecheta's text only to pretend he wrote it. Whichever way we look at it, something is wrong. His writing assignment on what an ideal Nigeria should be demonstrates Emecheta's anxiety about gender relationships in contemporary Nigeria and the state of the country.

The oppressive university environment is her main concern. The sexist environment is exacerbated by faculty intimidating students. For women, the yoke is multiple, as they juggle the responsibilities of womanhood, motherhood, wifehood, academic life, and tradition. Men too bear their own burden of double-consciousness in the intricate balancing of their Nigerian and Western heritage.

Operating in this oppressive milieu, Ete Kamba wants his girlfriend Nko to be seen as a Madonna; her simple clothes and nunlike scarf preserve the look of innocence that he desires. He is bitterly disappointed that she may not be a virgin, a point that Emecheta deliberately leaves unclarified to destroy the obsessive image of the mother as a virgin. She reiterates the issue of the double-standard morality by indicating that Ete Kamba is not a virgin, yet he has the temerity to batter Nko for not being one. As a feminist mentor, Miss Bulewao quickly deals a deadly blow to his machismo.

Nko's feminist sisterhood is rooted in the question of virginity. She debunks the myth that women must be virtuous but not men. She affirms her new slant in morality and gender relationships by declaring that men turn women into prostitutes. Nko was admitted into Unical on the basis of intellectual equality with men. She strives for equality in other spheres of gender relations. In growing assertive, she counters sexism with "bottom power," like Nwapa's Amaka, using Professor Ikot, who sexually harasses his female students.

Ikot tricks Nko into going with him to Kwa Falls, to her fall. The road is hazardous and hardly motorable, a sign of the dangerous journey that Nko is undertaking. The Mephistophelian Ikot predictably rapes Nko. Refusing to play the role of the helpless victim, she boldly demands from him the highest grade for her work, thereby attempting to dismantle the power structure. To restore his manhood for Ikot's appropriation of Nko, his property, Ete Kamba and his friends feminize Ikot in a bashing that shows how vicious men can be when it comes to their women. Ete Kamba castrates the older man "So that he can never perform again" (151). The humiliated Ikot is left naked to walk the streets to his house like a madman; indeed, as a preacher and a professor, he is out of his senses to play games with people's spiritual and academic lives. When Ikot reverses the situation by adroitly claiming that he had been attacked by armed robbers, Emecheta establishes the morass of troubles in the leadership of the country. That the students are imaged as armed robbers presents a bizarre situation that compromises the future generation.

While Ete Kamba obtains emotional support for his masculinist actions from his friends, the female community sustains Nko. Miss Bulewao turns confessor to Ete Kamba, persuading him to reverse his double standard by accepting Nko, impregnated by Professor Ikot. If a man can have a child out of wedlock and is able to bring the child into a new marriage, the same privilege should be extended to the virilized Nko, who has decided not to have an abortion. The work ends with a womanist vision as Nko, helpless because of her father's death, receives support from Ete Kamba, who prevents her from committing suicide. His decision to unite with her demonstrates enlightenment. His weak torchlight, hardly piercing the darkness of the small classroom, grows into a bright idea that can alter the course of the palaver.

Double Yoke is thus a sexual-political romance intriguingly written by the male student, Ete Kamba. He envisions a modern, womanist Nigeria with radical changes in gender relationships that even Osun would approve. Furthermore, his spirit of compromise is exemplary of what the new Nigerian man should be. Instead of the double yoke with its changing standards, we have a double yolk in which a feminized man and a virilized woman come together to produce a better society. By dealing with the troublesome issues of female virginity and legitimizing a woman's outside child, Emecheta has courageously touched a sensitive point in gender relationships. In her scheme, she crushes the multiple yoke under which men and women operate and invalidates the religious evangelism that maintains the status quo to the disadvantage of women. In the final analysis, *Double Yoke* reads as an academic response to the problems that destabilize Nigeria.

The Family: Uncovered Secrets

But do you marry your daughters? . . . The man in the story had committed an incest with his daughter and, according to the culture of the land, the women of the village executed the man. And if the man had not been caught, he would have been killed by thunder. . . . And a father who had any sexual urge towards his daughter had offended the Earth.

Buchi Emecheta, *The Family*

In *The Family* (1990), Emecheta extends her already encyclopedic range by treating the controversial subject of incest. Shrewdly located within an international context to escape bashing by Nigerian masculinist critics, her subject is Jamaica, Nigeria, and England in a proliferative triangular relationship. By ending Nigerian women's silent grief for this offensive side of sexuality in the black family, Emecheta dares to throw some light on the darker side of rape, thereby moving beyond *Destination Biafra*. As only a been-to disturbingly can, she counters one taboo with another, by tapping the forbidden power of speech. Nonetheless, exploring the unspeakable subject of sexual and emotional abuse within a Jamaican family rather than a Nigerian one is hardly a sisterly move for a writer reaching out to the African diaspora to claim kin. Only a trouble maker would arrogate such Pan-Africanist powers of kinship in another world.

The Family belongs to a recognizable black fiction tradition merely hinted at in some African texts.[15] In the novel, Emecheta revises such predecessors' works as Ralph Ellison's *Invisible Man*, James Baldwin's *Just Above My Head*, Maya Angelou's *I Know Why the Caged Bird Sings*, Toni Morrison's *The Bluest Eye*, Gayl Jones' *Corregidora*, and Alice Walker's *The Color Purple*. With the continued erosion of black power in a racist universe and the consequent sociopolitical chaos, black women writers present incest as a ripple effect of black historical disenfranchisement in the public domain. Incest manifests itself as the internalization of the despicable: a tragic, inward turn through which the black man misuses his paltry power, expresses his rage by preying on his weak daughter, violates boundaries, and betrays her trust. Moving from the abstractions of rape as a metaphor for the invasion and breakdown of black patriarchy from slavery through colonialism to the contemporary miasma, Emecheta gives incest a face and a name. She insists that incest produces female victims who withstand the stresses of a vicious war. One can grapple with this postulate by rereading the power play in the subtext of the myth of Osun; violated by her brother *orisa* during colonization, she flourished for her tale to be incorporated into the Odu.

In Igbo proverbial discourse, incest is *nso ani,* a "taboo against the land or Ani," Mother Earth. Faulty fathering thus destroys the essence of womanhood, to restore which the erring male must be reprimanded by the Earth goddess, that is, a maternal force (sometimes the woman writer herself), using natural means (oftentimes the writer's control of the story line) to ritually cleanse the polluted land for a wholesome life. This privileges female spiritu-

---

15. See, for example, *Song of a Goat,* J. P. Clark's play mentioned earlier; *The Broken Calabash,* a play by the Nigerian playwright Tess Akaeke Onwueme; Bessie Head's *A Question of Power;* and Rebeka Njau's *Ripples in the Pool,* among others.

ality, as *nso ani* entails a bloody sacrifice for the return to normalcy. The African religious concept of communal involvement for the communal good embedded in *nso ani* displaces the Christian notion of individual guilt and atonement.

Incest boils down to a question of power. Unable to exercise meaningful authority in the public domain, the incest perpetrator, with his low self-esteem, typically turns against his daughter, over whom he has total control. However, in yielding to the temptation of appropriating power so grossly, the perpetrator loses it. The adult male who has no power even in his own household is dead; thus, committing incest is suicidal.

Incest speaks to issues raised in the model of equal parenting by father and mother proposed by Chodorow (1978) and Dinnerstein (1976). Janet Jacobs (1990, 514) confirms their theoretical standpoint when she writes: "Rather, in recognizing and addressing the child's perspective on power relations within the family, it becomes painfully clear that as long as children are exclusively nurtured by women, the victimizers will not be held accountable for their actions," a conclusion that is slightly at variance with fiction by black women. They *do* blame the victimizer, in spite of extenuating circumstances.

The woman writer also blames the mother for her faulty mothering, a crucial point also noted by Jacobs in "Reassessing Mother Blame in Incest." The traitorous mother is an extension of the treacherous nation. The incest survivor serves as a paradigm for political disenchantment, highlighting the absence of the maternal principle in public life. On the personal level, the incest survivor needs a new family to nurture her back to health. Emecheta explores the possibility for renewal in *The Family,* following a remarkable meeting.

According to Emecheta, the gathering of ten women in her hotel room after a talk she gave in Preston, England, serves as a pre-text for the novel. The fact that eight of the women had been sexually abused highlighted the enormity of the female sexual predicament. The ten formed a genuine family, a sympathetic community and sisterhood within which the women who had been violated could open up and feel a sense of belonging. Though the emotional outburst and understanding commemorate and celebrate a sexual-political moment and might be short lived, they are liberating. Emecheta prolongs the moment as she emphasizes the healing function of writing for both the writer and the reader. It is important to note that, although the women are excluded from the text, in one's mind their temporary but meaningful coming together contrasts with the chaos of the families that Emecheta depicts in the ironically titled novel. Renamed *The Family* by her American publishers, it was first published under the title *Gwendolen* in England, the two titles expressing conflicting emphases on the community and the individual.

The protagonist in *The Family* is the little girl, Gwendolen, whose name no one in her family can pronounce correctly. As Yoruba children are, she is known severally: as Juney-Juney, June-June, Grandalew, and Gwen (is this after Charles II's mistress, for this is her name at school in London?), she is a multiple personality, seen differently by each person she encounters. Clearly, she is inscrutable. Gwendolen, also referred to as Grandalee (is she a magdalene?), and her friends Shivorn (is she Chiffon, light and consumable?) and Cocoa (is she dark and consumable, too?) are in sexual jeopardy. As in fairy tales, they wait for the magical moment to be rescued from the crippling poverty and devastating barrenness of Granville Hills in Jamaica. Their budding sexuality is their bane.

The Family depicts the tragic failure of the characters to achieve a sense of family at different levels—nuclear, extended, communal, racial, national, or international. However, Emecheta closes with a positive vision of a new world order, odd but stabilizing. She subversively deflects attention from the male offender turned tragic hero, in the epigraph to this section, to concentrate on the incest survivor. For the women, preoccupied with justice, fail to provide solace for the female victim, who is invariably ostracized. *The Family* creates new myths and, with them, the beginnings of a tradition of the new.

We eventually arrive at a ritual moment of motherhood when woman and her child become the center and objects of worship, forming *the family*. This happens for Gwendolen, who, in her mother Sonia's absence, serves as daughter, sister, and, incestuously, wife in her family. Her womanish role culminates in motherhood when she gives birth to her daughter-sister, Iyamide. The wise women, the changing Sonia and her Nigerian friend Mrs. Odowis, reluctantly come to pay their obeisance to the trio—the Madonnalike Gwendolen, who had been impregnated by the father; Emmanuel, her Greek friend and the baby's surrogate father; and Iyamide. Gwendolen's *siddon look* tactics of acting without appearing to act has improved her chances in life. This new trinity displaces the two unwholesome triangular relationships involving Gwendolen, her grandmother Naomi, and her surrogate grandfather, Uncle Johnny, on the one hand, and Gwendolen and her two parents, Sonia and Winston, on the other.

True incest between father and daughter is so horrific that many writers make the offender a surrogate father, as in *The Color Purple* and *I Know Why the Caged Bird Sings*. Emecheta revises these, and she modifies Morrison's tragic concept of the incest victim as a childless, crazy survivor in *The Bluest*

Eye. To encourage the sufferers seeking a way out of their psychic pain, Emecheta leads the maddened Gwendolen to recovery and lets her bear her father's child and thrive in the process.

The journey is not easy for the pregnant Gwendolen. Her aimless walk away from her London home into the night of despair is treated as criminal and insane. It lands her at the police station and in an asylum. This response to her rebellion against her father is indeed maddening. Her new family affords her maternal power. In the three generations covered in the text, at the center of each family is a daughter—Sonia, Gwendolen, then Iyamide.

Commenting on the appropriateness of Iyamide as the baby's name, Ama, the Ghanaian nurse says, "I know the Yorubas of Nigeria and the Ibos use the word 'Mother' to mean best woman friend, a woman's saviour. Of course, a mother and even a husband can call a woman 'Mother,' but never 'Baby' like they do in the West" (Emecheta 1990, 210). Meanwhile, Sonia degenerates into a "Baby" to her opportunist lover, James Allen, while Iyamide becomes a "Mother" to Gwendolen in an interesting role reversal that speaks to Sonia's parenting.

By naming the baby Iyamide (Yoruba for "my mother has arrived"), Gwendolen criticizes the countries (Jamaica and Britain), the African continent, and the adult women who failed to nurture her as mothers, abandoned her to her pain and confusion, and then dared to blame her. Through the nature of her story line, Emecheta ironizes and subverts Yoruba patriarchal practice of using the naming of a child to commemorate paternal history, which suppresses the mother's story. Once Gwendolen loses contact with her biological parents, she must construct a new history through her daughter. The yarn is twisted with Iyamide's resemblance to Winston. The duplication feminizes their father, thereby knitting the feminine and the masculine strands of their story and giving it a wo/man's face.

Family is, however, not restricted to clear blood ties. Women bond over traumatic experiences, especially those stemming from male oppression. Young people also suffer from reckless power displayed by adults. These groups come together to form families. For the exiled Jamaicans and Nigerians, family is inventing a mother country of one's own, with a shared emotional language, history, values, and experiences in a foreign land. The emergence of an Afro-English colony in England blurs national lines and enables Emecheta to give an essentially Nigerian story a Jamaican outfit.

Indeed, as a spokeswoman for the black been-to family, Emecheta appropriates West Indian life, even though she had never been to Jamaica. Using her imaginative power and her long association with Caribbeans in England, she captures her sisters' stories from that part of the black family. Her yarn signifies extensively on the harsh family life in Joan Riley's Caribbean novel, *The Unbelonging*.

Thus, Gwendolen's story, grounded in a triple heritage, is the tale of every black girl in England. The arch villains of the piece are Uncle Johnny, who sexually assaults her from age nine in Jamaica, and her father, the stammering Winston Brillianton, who also keeps raping her in England until her pregnancy betrays him as a sinner. Through Uncle Johnny, who typically replaces Gwendolen's absent father and late grandfather, and Winston, Emecheta conjures up, as in all her texts, the black fatherless condition. Women counter this pass with their obsessive preoccupation with motherhood. The burden of such writing is too strident for men's ears. Yet, men are the eye of the problem in more senses than one.

Among the predominantly illiterate in Granville, Uncle Johnny serves as their eye, reading their letters to them. His not being trusted compounds reception. Thus, Sonia always cross-checked Uncle Johnny's free readings of her letters with a paid Indian letter reader/writer. This raises important aesthetic points. Why does she not trust his reading yet depend on the Indian's? Issues arising from Western education, communication, and reception are here compounded with those of race and gender. When the woman author talks rather than writes, and she listens as a reader rather than sees, with a man mediating between her and the text, misreadings abound. We see this in the London section of the novel, when another letter reader, the Nigerian landlord Aliyu, deliberately misreads a telegram. Aliyu's intention was to protect his illiterate listeners, the Brilliantons, from the unpleasant news of Grandma Naomi's death. In typical Yoruba fashion, by reading her death as an illness, he, as the unwilling bearer of bad news, dissociates himself from the news to manipulate reception. The intimacy of the oral-aural medium and the distancing in the writing-reading dimension demarcate the people involved in writing and receiving a text and emphasize their disparate needs.

Additional problems of communication arise. Gwendolen fails to report the assaults to her Granny Naomi, though the psychological consequences are there for her grandmother to read. Granny Naomi, however, is an unwilling reader. Gwendolen codes her report in bed wetting until she escapes to her paternal grandmother, who also fails to grasp the meaning of Gwendolen's running to her for refuge. On her return to her maternal grandmother, Gwendolen tells her story in plain words. Her audience's mixed reception, ranging from sympathy to silence to disbelief to blame to ex-communication, underscores the predicament of the rape victim. This is why a community of survivors forms a more dependable family for the sufferer.

To add to the confusion, Granny Naomi appears jealous of Gwendolen, who has unwittingly deprived her of a lover and provider. The older woman, including Sonia later, fears displacement by the younger woman, and responds incongruously in this community, which has lost the traditional African way to react to rape and incest through immediate, punitive measures, as the epigraph clearly states.

Emecheta introduces this discord in the mother-daughter relationship, to demonstrate family dissonance, exacerbated by sexism, poverty, separation, and, most importantly, acculturation. The unwholesome ménage à trois in Granville gives way to another in England. The older women privilege their relationship with the men, at the expense of the mother-daughter connection. Under the tutelage of her Nigerian friend, Gladys Odowis, Sonia gradually moves from relying on men to a new sisterhood that reserves a special place for daughters. Journeying from Granville to Kingston to claim her place as daughter, the dark-skinned Gwendolen had also encountered the color problem. The "Yellow niggers" snub their darker relations, bewildering Gwendolen further. Her light-complexioned paternal grandmother refuses to keep this dark daughter. From Kingston Gwendolen flies to England, where color takes a more bizarre form, and the "moder kontry" coldly receives the adopted daughter, nearly murdering her.

There are too many silences when people should talk. "Sonia could bully him [her husband] into silence" (113), for Winston finds it difficult to communicate. His stammering is the result of a stressful childhood as a dark child raised by a light-complexioned, rejecting mother. In spite of his brilliance, as his surname Brillianton suggests, he violates his daughter as he had been violated. Stammering his way through life, he bequeaths to Gwendolen impotent silence.

Gwendolen's and her parents' inability to read or write or to speak the Queen's English renders the family dysfunctional. Her inability to scream, because Uncle Johnny had forcefully silenced her by covering her mouth during the rape, and her failure to make a lot of palava after the event are consonant with her socialization. They express the lack of dialogue on gender issues in the black world. Gwendolen's acquiescing to rape for many years is a violence to the self. Victimization on gender and/or age lines shows the complexity of oppression and the fact that the oppressor can sometimes make the victim an accessory to his crime through powerful thought control. Later, when Winston berates Gwendolen for not being a virgin, we witness once more the male double standard that continues to befuddle gender relationships as he adds insult to the sexual and psychological injury.

The women's role vis-à-vis their victimized daughter is telling. Aliyu's confusion of Granny Naomi's death with sickness epitomizes female disorder. Alive, she was really dead as she failed to protect Gwendolen, who was constantly raped in the same room where she slept. Dead, she is believed to be alive, creating another opportunity for Gwendolen to be raped by her father on her mother's departure, ostensibly to look after Naomi. To Emecheta, one has to read one's text for one's self to avoid misreading or lying or misinterpretation. In other words, cultural interferences in communication can be remedied by information, just as illiteracy and its drawbacks can be remedied by learning to read, for people to function optimally.

As a sociologist, Emecheta is also concerned with the place of nurturing in life. Sonia becomes mentally destabilized at her mother's death, conscience stricken because she had not cared for her mother who had helped her parent Gwendolen when she needed such support. With her stillborn child, she has reached a dead end. The been-to Sonia overstays her return to Granville and fails to communicate with her family in England because she is unable to write or keep track of the passage of Western time. Her prolonged absence extends Gwendolen's duties beyond that of mother to her siblings to that of wife to her father, hence Winston's pained confession as shown in the epigraph, oddly phrased as a question, whether a man could marry his daughter.

As her father's housewife, Gwendolen "felt like a child who kept on stealing money from her mother's purse, but knew that one day, just one day, she would be caught" (147). This monetary image is further developed when Sonia becomes maddened at the thought of sharing with Gwendolen the money that accrues to them on Winston's death. With its Emechetan touch, Winston's death in a gas explosion propels him into a drum where he is baptized in tar. This doubly tarred baby turns into trash when Sonia buries the knife with which she intended to kill Gwendolen in a rubbish bin, which she refers to as Winston Brillianton. Winston and his disruptive sexuality are toxic waste that must be buried. In death, he has neither lips nor ears, those oral-aural parts of the anatomy that he had never made use of appropriately in life and through which he committed more sins with his hypocritical sermons.

Emmanuel replaces him in Gwendolen's life. When asked why she brought in the Greek boy to act as Gwendolen's lover and teacher, Emecheta retorted that it was not so much that redemption lay for troubled blacks through whites but that the modern family is beginning to take different forms among less racially conscious youths. An artist and a carpenter by trade, Emmanuel is the messianic figure who brings order into Gwendolen's life. Although Gwendolen tells him, "So many tings you no understand, white boy" (156), their relationship is built on cooperation, far different from the hostility between Nigerians and their colonial masters in Ulasi's *Many Thing You No Understand*. In a womanist conclusion that takes care of the racial dimension in the background, Emecheta has Emmanuel and Gwendolen communicating meaningfully. He succeeds in teaching her how to read, revealing to her the power of the black woman's printed word. She, in turn, encourages him to stick to his trade in a reciprocity that strengthens their troubling relationship originally built on deception.

Emecheta's final statement is bold and disquieting. She moves fiction and ethics to another realm by insisting that one's daughter should be one's sister (literally) and mother (metaphorically). The image of Gwendolen as a single, liberated, self-sufficient, healthy mother is too pat and at odds with the profoundly disturbing image of the fatherless black child or the commonplace wandering madwoman.

Emecheta makes adroit use of Sonia's postpartum dementia and Gwendolen's prenatal blues, which uncannily coincide with their respective losses of a mother and father. As a subtext, madness, short lived in both instances as in many black women's texts, is linked with the (pro)creative process and the separation, through death, of parent and child. The pain of the double parting in birth and death is as disorienting as the throes of producing a creative work, for Emecheta conceptualizes the creative process as a state of temporary insanity, using Gilbert and Gubar's (1987) paradigm of the nineteenth-century madwoman writer. Since Emecheta considers her books as her children, in *The Family* she neatly ties together the familial links between writing, madness, giving birth, and dying, each process an *ogbanje* movement from one world to another. The bereaved Emecheta, grieving for her late daughter, Chiedu, projects her loss onto Sonia and Gwendolen, writing their been-to stories to make sense of her life and heal herself.

Kehinde: Bintu and the Search for a Home

A woman whose face I cannot see comes towards me. She holds her palm frond across my path to stop me. She has with her a little girl whom I immediately recognise. My Taiwo. "No," she says, "go back. I have this one." The woman indicates the little girl, who does not smile. "Your father was coming to you, but you sent him back. He was coming to look after you because he feels guilty about not looking after you the last time. But you have refused to receive him. He wants you with him, but you have to go back. You have to learn to live without him."

Buchi Emecheta, *Kehinde*

In her latest novel, *Kehinde* (1994), Emecheta locates woman's anguish in the insecurities, from the womb to the grave, of not being assured a home or a place she can always call her own. Dislocation forces woman to become a frequent traveler, an *ogbanje/abiku*, restlessly searching for a home, while agonizingly learning to live without significant others. That is the destiny of the novel's been-to protagonist, Kehinde, who is everywoman. As with *Gwendolen*, once more Emecheta inscribes female authority in the text by naming it after a woman, as Nwapa had done with Efuru and Idu.

Strategically placing her Igbo twin in a Yoruba space, Emecheta broadens the scope of her work, moving the Nigerian novel by women beyond the limits set by Nwapa in her figurative use of twins in *One Is Enough*. By prioritizing Kehinde, a Yoruba cognomen, which is reserved for the second twin to appear and which is not gender specific, Emecheta subverts the Yoruba concept of twinhood and its power dynamic. She deconstructs the myth of the less-powerful Kehinde (read "woman") by virilizing her protagonist and endowing her with twin authority. Thus, joining the ranks of those who believe that Kehinde is more powerful for being circumspect and in control, Emecheta characteristically kills off Taiwo, making her serve Kehinde as *Chi*, in a relationship based on cooperation instead of rivalry. Without any doubt, as when men and women help one another, together twins constitute a formidable force for good.

In this politics of naming, further complicated by Kehinde's Catholic upbringing, which earns her the name Jacobina, after Jacob, Emecheta signifies on the biblical tale of inheritance, thereby placing the female and postcolonial particular in a religious and international frame. The metaphor of twinhood, especially as realized in the absent-present Taiwo, implies, conflictingly, fracture and double sightedness. The two split halves occasionally functioning at best as one, wander through changing worlds where they remain permanent outsiders perpetually gazing inward.

Emecheta's protagonist, Kehinde, is even more powerful than usual because of her multiple heritage. She is a genuine Nigerian because she has a Western education, was born in an unspecified place, has Hausa connections (since her natal family is located in Sokoto in the north of Nigeria), is Igbo by origin, and is raised in Yorubaland. She is the girl "Who has the *chi* of three great women in her" (82)—hers and her twin's and her mother's, both of whom died to give her life. Her deep spiritual ties with these affirmative Igbo sources empower and stabilize her. In addition to her Catholicism, she also has Islamic connections through her best friend, Moriammo. Thus deeply endowed, protected, and broadly etched on gender, national, international, and religious grounds, the been-to Kehinde-Jacobina is also the Nigerian nation in the diaspora.

The enigmatic Kehinde is constructed in relation to absences: she is the twinless twin, the parentless child, the husbandless wife, the childless mother, the friendless friend, the nationless exile, an *ogbanje/abiku* who characteristically turns wombs into tombs, her mother's and hers. In a fascinatingly imaginative sweep designed to capture Kehinde's perspective while in the womb and with a technique that reminds us of the best of Ben Okri's *The Famished Road,* Emecheta writes:

> Together we fought against the skin that kept us captive. We wanted to burst out and escape into the open. We did not know what lay out there in the world, but anything, anywhere was better than where we were. We communicated with each other by touch and by sounds. Sounds which only we could understand. Then one day, we laid siege on the skin wall that kept us enclosed. Frustrated, we banged and we shouted; and we kicked and cried in our limited space. Exhausted, I fell asleep. I felt even in sleep the cessation of the rhythmical movements I was accustomed to. I felt around me in the now warm thickening water for my sister, but she had become just a lump of lifeless flesh. . . . I cried for her in my now lonely tomb. . . . As she dried, I had more space. . . . But I did not eat my sister, as they said I did. (18)

Casualties in a war of resistance, the abelian twist and the nagging question of cannibalism speak to Nigerian consumerism and its fatal postcolonial consequences. Despite this limitation, throughout life, Kehinde, perpetually a "half-person" (59), has to learn that she is the better half. This knowledge will keep her going. For a writer of Emecheta's stature, it is disappointing that such exciting writing is not fully sustained.

Thus, she experiments, but only to a limited degree, with travel in spirit land, the protagonist's conversation with her *Chi,* switching from the omniscient to the first person narrative with ease. Moving beyond the constraints in *The Family,* where she failed to capture the flavor of Jamaican patois, she experiments with Nigerian pidgin. The dialogue between Kehinde and Moriammo is a case in point:

> "*What situation* you dey *mumble* about? Abi, you don begin talk to your second now in old age? Dem say twins sabi talk to demselves plenty, plenty time."

Kehinde laughed lightly to cover her embarrassment. "No, I just dey say we never *depend* on our husbands *financially. At least* my Mama *never did.*"

"How you know? Your Mama die when you be small pikin. Go home, go relax. Be a been-to Madam. *Put your feet up. Be a white woman.* Make you enjoy the sunshine. There go be plenty of servants too. So *what's your trouble,* enh?"

"So wetin you tink say I be? I no be Igbo woman?"

"I know who you be. Igbo woman who no go happy until she dey work and work and carry the burden of the whole world. All that work, work dey give us power?" (52; my emphasis)

As the italicized words indicate, Emecheta's pidgin is overly anglicized, revisiting problems raised with Ulasi. However, in this crucial passage, Emecheta cryptically thrashes out gender issues in the fine tradition of Zora Neale Hurston. Like Hurston's Janie, Kehinde inherits her marital home as a reward for her labor.

In this one-hundred-and-forty-one–page novel, with its encyclopedic potential, Emecheta flits through numerous subjects, teasing the reader. In the chapter interestingly titled "Kehinde and Albert," Emecheta discusses the twins cramped in the womb, an indication that Kehinde's husband, Albert, is the Taiwo of this marriage, and we know that Kehinde as a twin will not be bested. As usual, Emecheta uses sexuality to comment on power relationships. Kehinde's newfound sexuality moves from the passivity of watching "naughty" movies (significantly interrupted by Moriammo's crying son, Olumide) and being propositioned by the Arab as a sexual object to the rebellious activity of sex with her Caribbean tenant, a complication her son Joshua repudiates. However, these two phases of Kehinde's self-assertion counter Albert's humiliatingly polygamous liaisons on his return to Nigeria. Foucault's comment on human behavior and sexuality is germane in this conflict: "Of the three possible modes of [sexual] behavior—hiding it entirely, hiding it while revealing it, or flaunting it—all can appear as a result of sexuality, but I would say that it is related to a way of living. It's a choice in relation to what one is as a sexual being and also as a writer. It's the choice made in the relationship between the style of sexual life and the work" (1986, 183–84). By making their untoward choices, Kehinde and Albert claim their independence. The liberties of a double life and an adulterous existence hardly seem worthy of a midlife rebellion; unfortunately, been-to thinking seems reduced to equality in sexual promiscuity.

Signifying on Bedford's *Yoruba Girl Dancing*, Emecheta's been-to existence is riddled with its undecidability and overlapping configurations. Not at home anywhere but somehow managing to survive, Kehinde, the been-to, claims several homes: the womb turned tomb; her natal home, which is exchanged for Aunt Nnebogo's; and Nigeria, which she replaces with England, Lagos with London.

Yet the controlling metaphor in London is abortion and rejecting the repentant absent father, as indicated in the epigraph to this section. Emecheta exploits her interlingual facility as a technical shortcut to drive her point home: abortion by a woman whose favorite sister is Ifeyinwa, "there is nothing comparable to a child," and one of whose mothers is Nnebogo, "mother is a gift," is a statement that goes against the Nigerian grain. With its rejection of her father, Onuorah, "everyone's voice," Kehinde moves herself from the affirmative *kwenu* position in the national discourse, settling for a separate peace by tying her tubes in been-to fashion and acquiescing to Albert on the abortion. With its additional negative images of the stolen pram and hungry, Thatcherian children deprived of milk, London is hardly child friendly. Racism and mindless jobs make it a hostile, unproductive world.

Lagos equally kills the spirit with its maternal absences, memories of the stillbirth, lies, evasions, in-lawism, sexism, sororal dissonance, religious hysteria, corruption, and anarchy. Albert ruins Kehinde's homecoming by becoming polygynous, turning Kehinde into a mummified (she resents the Nigerian habit of being called mummy), asexual outsider with younger, more attractive, and better educated co-wives. As home is so overwhelmingly devastating to the been-to woman who has kept away too long, Kehinde, rejected by family at birth and once more ignored by family in mid-life, prefers the ills of London to the insecurities of Lagos. In flying back to London's waiting arms, Kehinde figuratively reenacts her life story of orphanage and making do with substitute mothers. Emecheta boldly challenges the Nigerian myth that children do not mind being raised by women who are not their biological mothers. The tropes of Lagos and London as mothers and hometowns thus has a tragic postcolonial twist. Self-preservation demands that this abandoned twin flee from and abandon mother Africa, which has degenerated into a killing field. Nonetheless, using the mysterious Caribbean, Mr. Gibson, as Kehinde's solace and substituting him in her life for the thoughtless Albert hardly cuts it. Emecheta's goal to establish the true meaning of polygamy is obvious in Kehinde's declaration of liberation to her son Joshua: "It's not a crime to love [Mr. Gibson]. Your dad has taken two other wives in Nigeria, and I'm not complaining. That's one of the beauties of polygamy, it gives you freedom. I'm still his wife, if I want to be, and I'm still your mother. It doesn't change anything" (Emecheta 1994, 138). Read in another way, a woman's life is always on the edge.

Nigerian London spites her as *femme sole*. She also encounters hostility from the Muslim world in Tunde, Moriammo's husband, who severs their long-standing relationship. The Muslim twist comes to a head when Kehinde, despite being now a London graduate, is objectified by the stereotyped, unnamed wealthy Arab, who predictably demands kinky sex. Emecheta gives short shrift to Islam and its sexism by killing off Tunde in a car accident.

In another development, Kehinde's son, Joshua, becomes petulant and shadows her. She bests him in twin fashion, stands up for her lover from the diasporan pool, and claims the family house for her very own. This is an aggressive, confrontational, Thatcherian world, where a woman must make choices, even unpopular ones. Nonetheless, like his biblical namesake, Joshua is billed as Kehinde's successor. Part of her still reaches out to Nigeria, where the daughter she abandoned, Bimpe, has chosen to live, because of her boyfriend Elijah. This new world of multiple choices accents the state of Nigeria and the Nigerian diaspora, especially woman's determination to stake her claims in the commonwealth. More than a mere survivor, Kehinde is the new black woman. Her story is about the other world, about separations, losses, gains, and starting again. The *ogbanje* enigma conflates with the been-to phenomenon in the duality of Kehinde, the character and *Kehinde* the novel. With this happy fusion, Emecheta optimizes her multiple heritage.

In spite of some limitations, *Kehinde* has substantially contributed technically, thematically, and ideologically, to Emecheta's writing. Overall, what strikes the reader is Emecheta's energy and her boldness in questioning established ideas. As a result, her contribution to the palaver is unsettling. The bite of her palava sauce, with its been-to spices, jolts one to see that she is not proffering food for a peaceful closure but is supplying food for continuous thought. Without any doubt, her oeuvre is at the cutting edge of the Nigerian novel by women.

Chapter Six
Fakunle, Okoye, Alkali, Eno Obong, Bedford: *Siddon Look*

Only cowards beat their wives because it is a cheap means of silencing a woman. And cheats beat their wives because they know that [they] will have an easy win.

Funmilayo Fakunle, The Sacrificial Child (1978)

Nobody is the government, so you can't talk of cheating the government.

Ifeoma Okoye, Men Without Ears (1984)

A woman who takes a husband for a father will die an orphan.

Zaynab Alkali, The Stillborn (1984)

Simply to be part of that creation [of the garden house]. To fashion out the essentials of modern living from the natural substances of the earth. To build where nature left off, without changing the grain. That would be true creativity—a masterpiece that would graft unto the original without any ripples.

Eno Obong, Garden House (1988)

We were a miniature village, thirty people lived in our house. Grandpa lived on the top floor and was attended by his own servants. He and Grandma had been effectively separated for fifteen years [because of his "outside" wife]; he never came downstairs. Even so he ruled us all, his word was law and his power was absolute. . . . My grandmother . . . ruled the rest of the household from her sitting room, which served as another courtyard inside the house. . . . I loved Grandma, she was fat and marvellously comfortable to sit on.

Simi Bedford, Yoruba Girl Dancing (1991)

Sweet Mothers: The Younger Generation

By the nature of their calling, writers sit down and look on, but not idly. In a dire situation, *awon iya wa* too practice a similar, magical, contemplative art with their *siddon look* tactics. In their different ways, Flora Nwapa, Adaora Ulasi, and Buchi Emecheta have used this tradition. They have urgently staked their claims as mothers and daughters by opening up the palaver in the Nigerian novel to incorporate a legitimate female perspective. They set distinct patterns for the next generation of postwar women writers to develop further.

Their works validate women's role in Nigeria and ensure the emergence, for the first time, of women novelists from other parts of the country: the Yoruba, Funmilayo Fakunle and Simi Bedford; the Northerner, Zaynab Alkali; and the Ibibio, Eno Obong. The Igbo Ifeoma Okoye is another newcomer. Together, they have produced a textual *aso ebi* with their repetitions, modifications, and individual signatures, clearly indicating that they belong together.

These are writers on the frontier of literature, competing in a man's world at a moment when Nigeria is in deep crisis. Since Osun implanted in women the notion that the first female among males is an endangered species, especially at a critical juncture in the community's existence, each knows the risks that the radical black feminist runs in being ostracized by black men and called a "goddamn traitor to the race," as Calvin Hernton (1984) so graphically summed up the analogous African-American wo/man palava.

The hostile reaction of black males to Ntozake Shange's *for colored girls* (1975), Michelle Wallace's *Black Macho and the Myth of the Superwoman* (1979), and Alice Walker's *The Color Purple* (1986) is instructive for Nigerian women. Zora Neale Hurston, in 1937, had preceded these writers in the hot seat, fending off black male anger at *Their Eyes Were Watching God* (1978), which, to the myopic, "shamed" the race instead of uplifting it. Curiously, Morrison, writing as an older woman, has been spared such aggravation. Hernton's remark that the recent hostility to women writers "came from all sectors of the black population: the press, the literary and scholarly journals and magazines; on black and white college campuses and in the ghettos as well" (1984, 140) sums up the dilemma of the black woman novelist who prioritizes gender over a more global black perspective as Morrison skillfully does.

The backlash predictably produced Shahrazad Ali's seemingly alien response in her book *The Black Man's Guide to Understanding the Black Woman.* Ironic in her stereotypically matriarchal thrust, she in part authorizes the black man to batter his assertive woman into silence. By acquiescing, the men unintentionally give this older woman authority over them, turning her into Big Mama whose word is law. Ali's verbal facility and imposing figure in television programs served as a perfect model of the aggressive woman she wants slapped and silenced. As she continuously deconstructed her position by her very presence and dogmatic pronouncements, I wondered why enraged women bothered to attack her when she is really a living example of how a woman can thrive by carefully orchestrating a controversy.

In keeping with Osunian principles, woman must thrive by any means necessary, in spite of a predominantly masculinist ethos. The Nigerian response has produced writers who exhibit the Osunian syndrome of the "sweet mother," a phenomenon Ogundipe-Leslie finds offensive. As I indicated earlier, the sweet mother is a complex, sometimes manipulative, figure, who will do what she has to do for the benefit of her family/nation. As an archetype in the texts, she has a crucial role in the palaver, not just as cook to prepare the palava sauce, but as wise woman playing a complementary role to the man.

If the sweet mother were an inane configuration, she would not be feared. She is a hybrid of the Woolfian Angel in the House and the matriarch who can criticize and discipline her ward when circumstances warrant it. In a speech delivered in January 1931, Virginia Woolf described the Angel-in-the-House phenomenon thus: "She was intensely sympathetic. She was immensely charming. She was utterly unselfish. She excelled in the difficult arts of family life. She sacrificed herself daily. . . . [I]n short she was so constituted that she never had a mind or a wish of her own, but preferred to sympathize always with the minds and wishes of others. . . . [S]he was pure" (1979, 59). The sweet mother has many of these qualities. However, unlike the Angel in the House, she must have her own wishes, since her sphere necessarily extends beyond the domestic. As the head of her small unit, she must exercise emotional, mystical, educational, and/or economic power. In public, her responsibility is cut out for her. The female characters are projections of the writers themselves, who, in spite of their sweetness, have an acerbic side that can pinpoint whatever is injurious to the individual or community. There is nothing sweet in their critique of society, though their desire for harmony is sweetness itself. To participate meaningfully in the palaver, the sweet mother has a mind of her own as she suggests ideas rather than impose her will on the listener or put herself in an awkward position to be imposed on.

In the novel, therefore, the writer's preoccupation is, typically, with national ills, since Nigeria's status as the world's most populous black nation makes remedying them crucial for black progress. The women's agenda is intricately woven into the national one and serves as an important subtext for reconciliation and healing. For their labor, two of these sweet mothers have won awards by the Association of Nigerian Authors: Okoye in 1984 for *Men Without Ears* and Alkali in 1985 for *The Stillborn*. Eno Obong received honorable mention from the Noma Prize Committee in 1989 for her first novel, *Garden House*.

Although acclamation was not total, this auspicious reception was perhaps possible because the men, out of embarrassment during the United Nations' decade of the woman, wanted to prove that, though there were men without ears, many men *had* ears, and were willing to listen to the women's side of the palaver.[1] In this period of military regimes, army wives were beginning to give the military a human face. The oil boom left a dream of what money can do and the post-oil-boom period showed the chicanery of financial deals. These were the days when the strains of Prince Nico Mbarga's "Sweet Mother" and Uwaifo's "If You See Mammywata" dominated the air waves. The popular songs and the continuous playing of them were calls to women to mother the nation and to act as problem solvers, as indicated in the troubled Mammywata tune.[2]

The female literary response to this open male invitation to the palaver was swift. In difficulty, people go to their mothers, who quickly turn to religion for insight into the dilemma. To Mammywata, whose maternal waters have a cooling, cleansing, calming effect in times of deep trouble, they turned. The national predicament has propelled each of these writers toward spirituality, relying on the Mammywata archetype at the center of the text to effect a desirable outcome to the crisis. This deep need for superhuman intervention for the individual and the nation expresses people's desire for coexistence rather than confrontation in the post–civil war period. Like the Egyptian Isis, the writers try to put together that which warring parties continually pull apart.

Their concept of the Mammywata contrasts with the African-American "tragic mulatto." Mammywata is the magic mulatto who brings the good things of life to the believer. The Nigerian and the European come together in her to produce a dependable mother figure, since cultural harmony is a must in a multicultural Nigeria. Sabine Jell-Bahlsen's film "'Mammy Water,' In Search of the Water Spirits in Nigeria" (1991) graphically presents the impor-

1. Acclamation was not total; see note 1 to the Introduction.

2. Victor Uwaifo's lyric goes:

> If you see Mammywata o,
> If you see Mammywata o,
> Never, never, you run away, ee, ee
> Never run away. . . .

As I stated above, Prince Nico Mbarga's tune has endured because it touches a Nigerian, even an African, cord. Tellingly, it is more widely recognized than the Nigerian national anthem, and I wish that it were the national anthem, because of its ability to draw people together. It is still used at parties, regardless of generational differences. The following are some of the ad-libs:

> You fit get another wife, you fit get another husband, but you fit get another mother? No!
>
> My mother is great . . . greater than the world!
>
> Sweet mother, I will never forget you for the suffer you suffer for me, . . . and if I should forget you, therefore, I forget my life, the air I breathe in.
>
> And then on to you men, forget, verily, forget your mother, for if you forget your mother, you've lost your life.

tance of Mammywata in achieving spiritual healing while ensuring health and wealth for the devotee. The writers try to convey this crucial element in the transcendence of suffering in Mammywata worship.

The most important distinction of this generation of writers is the shift from the colonial to the contemporary world, the rural to the urban, the illiterate to the educated, as they inscribe their selves in their texts. No longer are they compelled to tell the sagas of their ancestors, as Emecheta deemed necessary, since their three predecessors have accomplished that duty. The cogency of the contemporary validates the palaver, moving the discourse away from fruitless abstractions.

Fakunle uses her maiden name and Eno Obong her given name as pen names, while Okoye and Alkali retain their married names. These choices demonstrate the constraints and freedoms that have colored women's attitudes. Where nineteenth-century British women writers used male pseudonyms as a self-protective strategy to ensure fair criticism, these Nigerian writers' choices send out different signals: belief in fatherhood, selfhood, and the family. Their novels provide clues as to the continued need for more sophisticated ways that the educated/gifted woman should adopt to advance her course as daughter, wife, mother, and responsible citizen. Their shift in focus to the educated woman is politically sound: once she is genuinely free, there is hope for her mothers and the rest of the country.

Writing in a postwar era, the prevalence of orphaned children in these four writers' texts, especially girls without mothers, comes as no surprise. It is symptomatic of the effects of a violent and violated nation, adrift, with an uncommitted military leadership and an increasingly unscrupulous and ungovernable population. These writers wisely emphasize what women have in common with civilian men rather than stress those issues that keep the sexes apart. As public mothers, they grapple with problems and seek a resolution, often through mediation and propitiation.

Their concerted effort has culminated in a growing awareness and the emergence of women's collective literary power in Nigeria. The West has produced Fakunle. True to her name, *Ifa kunle*, "Ifa's halo suffuses the household," her texts are secrets from the Odu matrix. Her novels, *The Sacrificial Child* (1978), *Chasing the Shadow* (1980), and *Chance or Destiny?* (1983), were produced by her father's press. Fakunle claims that she takes after her father, who worked tirelessly producing school texts. Like Ifa religious verse, her works are at once facile, profound, oracular, and teacherly texts. Fakunle has been joined by Bedford, whose 1991 novel *Yoruba Girl Dancing*, by its very title, stakes a claim for Yoruba women's moves. Okoye has emerged in the east with

Behind the Clouds (1982) and *Men Without Ears* (1984), preacherly texts denouncing the straits in which the family and the nation find themselves. The north has produced Alkali, whose apocalyptic *The Stillborn* (1984) and *The Virtuous Woman* (1987) are prophetic writings on the sands of Nigerian historical time. Eno Obong is from the southeast. Her *Garden House* (1988) is clearly a Mammywata text that celebrates sacrifice, celibacy, and self-control; these, as well as the discriminating use of power in all spheres, are vital for the development of the beneficial principles of Mammywata. Her dual consciousness is essential for progress and the emergence of a new world order in Nigeria, as exemplified by the new capital, Abuja. Eno Obong's dream is a pastoral Nigeria, a garden house, solidly constructed by a people's cooperative using durable, indigenous material in place of untested imports.

The writers' recourse to the vernacular is in the tradition of seeking oracular voices for guidance in troubled times. The media frenetically reproduced a panicked population, as myriads of desperate women and men embraced (and still do) Christianity, Islam, and/or different traditional religions, in an unprecedented quest for a quick fix or cure-all. The spiritual energy released would miraculously erase the collective experiential anguish of unending indifferent military rule. Priestesses of a literary cult for national rehabilitation, the writers too had to resort to different religions to counter the insidious pressures of military regimes, during which the population at large learned violence osmotically. Together, these women writers, their readers, and the anonymous participants in religious rituals have opened up an expansive place, national and international, where the national disaster is played out in public view. In the anarchy, their duty is maternal, sororal, filial, and uxorial, as they try to locate the mystical essence in the palaver.

Like most African-American women current in contemporary politics, these Nigerian writers "realize that feminist theory, feminist organizing, woman's conferences, and women's studies courses generally lack an ideological philosophy capable of systematically encompassing the histories, experiences, and material needs of black and working-class women" (Joseph 1983, 136). Their approach is, consequently, womanist, as they reach out to black men in a collaborative effort to help correct not just the gender imbalance but other crucial issues that plague black people everywhere. The spirit of compromise is vital for a meaningful palaver. Palavering with womanist intentions to heal is vernacular and workable for Nigerians and black people elsewhere.

In sum, the dominant aspect of the women's writing is nationalistic, exploring the turbulent course that the country has taken and the need for a spiritual revolution. The women's agenda is muted, serving as one symptom of the larger problem. The conflation of the womanist spirit and the palaver in these women's novels can be expressed in the prudent words of the Nigerian woman playwright 'Zulu Sofola:

> In the African world view, the emphasis is . . . on harmony and communion. There is no need to destroy another creature in order for one to exist. Nor is there any need for a system to be destroyed simply because one aspect of creation deems himself the only one fit to exist. "There is room for many or more," says a Black American spiritual. This is reminiscent of Yoruba and Igbo sayings. In the former it is said that the sky is wide enough for all the birds to fly without hurting each other. And in the latter the saying goes thus: "Let the kite perch; let the eagle perch; that which does not allow the other to perch, may his wings break." It is not just the survival of the fittest, but the survival of all. (1988, 79)

To this end, women's novels must continue to be recognized, as the Association of Nigerian Authors has done, and must be made part of the required reading in schools, to enable boys and girls to participate in the discourse. The aim is to change people's desire to oppress and the victims' acceptance of oppression; also, the sexes must see that they are interdependent.

Martina Nwakoby's novel, *A House Divided* (1985), which I will discuss only briefly, voices the concern for nationhood and woman's role in it. Zaynab Alkali's epigraph to this chapter captures succinctly the disappointment and pain that the Nigerian woman experiences as her marital expectations are frustrated, to the detriment of family and country. Yet, the obverse of Alkali's statement holds true, for, more often than not, a man who takes his wife for a mother will grow to live a full life, and both will build a home together. The lack of reciprocity in gender relationships has increasingly baffled the present generation of young women, who balk at being mistreated. They work out ways to contain man's power and, yet, use it.

Fakunle, Okoye, Alkali, Eno Obong, and Bedford have as their constituency emergent, educated women whose attitude toward men differs from that of their mothers.[3] Writing after Nigerian independence and the civil war, and concentrating on these historical periods that have had a tremendous impact on women's thinking account for their political consciousness and restive-

---

3. Eno Obong has taken her given name, which is one word, and split it into two words, with Obong doubling as a surname. She makes a powerful statement about owning herself through this mark of identity. Chinweizu now has a sister.

ness. Having married and with children, they understand the unease and even terror under which the wife operates in her husband's household; they give free rein to women's thoughts, to steer the palaver onto solid ground.

Enervating as the battle of the sexes can be, they have tried to avoid making it the sole issue, parleying for a sensitivity to the general cause, over and above those sectionally grounded. Eno Obong's enchanting phrase "garden house" captures this ideological position of women's civic responsibility. Garden house stands for an edenic, womanist vision of a new Nigeria, for Nigerian women and men, built on Nigerian soil, with Nigerian materials and tools, by Nigerian workers from all walks of life and all sections of the country, with diasporan good will. These five writers' visceral reaction to such a vision is compellingly made in their preferred closure: a coming together to heal the wounds left by sectional or gender infighting. As *Chi na eke*, they attempt to reproduce men and women, sharing out the largesse fairly and consistently. Their spirit thus has nothing saccharine about it, for, as Aidoo informs us with one of her titles, there is "no sweetness here." Their sweetness is balanced with firmness and judiciousness—the attributes of the sweet mother.

For all their surface sweetness, these women are not politically distant from their three predecessors. All seem to agree with the most outspoken of them, Emecheta, in a tough womanism. As Osun's daughters, this implies, to reiterate, that they will parley with their men, even play games, to ensure that they forge ahead together without too much acrimony. They will not repeat men's mistake of using aggression to exclude or exile those different, since it has generated the present impasse. These writers show courage, emboldened by the safety in large numbers, with so many women writing novels while others produce texts to bridge the gaps created by the neglect of the female perspective in academia and national politics.

The appearance of autobiographies by women and biographies of women, with all the fanfare of launching them, has resulted in greater visibility of educated women since the 1980s.[4] Dynamic, intelligent, and, at the same time,

4. Besides Emecheta's autobiography, 1986 and 1987 saw the launching of one other autobiography, Rose Adaure Njoku's *Withstand the Storm,* and two biographies, *An African 'Florence Nightingale': A Biography of Kofoworola A. Pratt,* by Dr. Justus A. Akinsanya, and *A Lady: A Biography of Lady Oyinkan Abayomi,* also by a man, Folarin Coker. The women involved took center stage at the ceremonies, making women visible. It is memorable that, during the launching of Rose Adaure Njoku's book in Lagos, her husband, Colonel Njoku, sat in the audience weeping as his wife described a cavalcade of her actions that showed she was the soldier in their household during the civil war.

Just as blacks are nauseated by the stereotypical "Uncle Tom" in American literature, reading the character as a symptom of white complacency and condescension toward blacks, so feminists

fashion conscious, the sophisticated Maryam Babangida introduced a new dimension to female leadership. As the first First Lady to take an intellectual and political interest in gender aspects of labor and economics, claiming that a soldier's wife contributes invaluably to the military family, she has brought fresh insight to sexual and national politics in Nigeria. Without meaning to flaunt it, she demonstrates in *Home Front* (1988) that the military are in firm control because they are tightly knit and disciplined and their women support them. With her interest in rural women, she ingratiated herself with them to gain their support while creating an atmosphere conducive for the intellectual deliberation of women's issues. Producing novels or discussing them in this seemingly receptive atmosphere gives a tremendous boost to women's political consciousness, even if Maryam Babangida's agenda was, in the final analysis, self-serving.

While husbands in the generation of the first three writers faced the agonizing task of battling with colonialism and its aftermath, husbands in the era of these five women have the equally mortifying task of dealing with civilian inadequacies in a military regime. The men naturally take out their frustrations on women. With these political uncertainties, writing imposes order and proffers a modicum of power to the woman writer. Dealing with A disjointed outer world that has reproduced dysfunctional families and exacerbated male-female relationships, these five writers have followed the tradition set by their predecessors. The belief in the corrigibility of man binds them together in a truly womanist vision.

Since Nigerians frown on divorce, the fact that women have to tolerate the intolerable in marriage has created, on the negative side, frustrated and pretentious wives. These have grown into a nation of tough women who have no other place to go, so they remain in their homes, intent on rebuilding them instead of absconding and letting everything they have worked for come to naught. This is far from Kehinde's been-to, separatist ideology. That tenacious, Nigerian spirit binds women and the writers to establish the idyllic gar-

---

find the idea of the ideal woman as an angel or "sweet mother" irritating. Nigerian women do not necessarily consider it so. For example, the late nonagenarian, the childless Lady Oyinkan Abayomi, was fêted as a sweet mother par excellence by the children, now successful adults, she had fostered. The present Alaafin of Oyo, Oba Lamidi Adeyemi, is one of her children; he launched the book with royal pomp and pageantry at the University of Ibadan, where she was regaled for her maternal qualities as nurturer and disciplinarian.

I reviewed the manuscript of the autobiography of Dr. Irene Ighodaro, the first Western - trained female doctor in West Africa and a wonderful role model; I recommended it for publication by Heinemann at Ibadan.

den home. The task is certainly as tedious as keeping Nigeria one, but it must be done.

They, too, have heard and heeded Nigeria's call to duty, responding in their own way. As full-fledged members of the Nigerian family, they are not willing to look on idly while history is being made. That five of the eight writers considered using their fathers' names and personal names as pen names is noteworthy as a declaration that they too are legitimate heirs in the household, that they are daughters-of-the-soil. They have no intention of letting men deprive them of their heritage.

Funmilayo Fakunle: Opening the Secrets in the Calabash

Funmilayo Fakunle's tragic vision, like Emecheta's, stems from the starkness of a social science background. In her novels, she examines life through the dynamics of marriage and family, while concentrating on socialization practices, problem solving, and the rituals and religious aspects that distinguish the Yoruba. By opening Odu's calabash to reveal life from a Yoruba woman's perspective for the first time, Fakunle plays the novel role of the *iyalawo* (my coinage for the female counterpart of the *babalawo*), thereby introducing another dimension to the palaver.

To her, the Yoruba marriage is a war that man seems to win "because he is always right" (1978, 70). Wife battering, in-law meddling, infidelity, and polygyny create a dysfunctional family. Yet, through socialization, both sexes have come to expect them, creating a state of anomie in women. Many women have, therefore, taken the offensive in urban centers, turning into sharks to counter masculinism. These are Amaka's sisters, and each of the five writers portrays such characters this way as a warning. To clarify her point, Fakunle also contrasts them with sweet women.

Fakunle's first published novel, though not the first to be written, is *The Sacrificial Child* (1978). In it she shows the extent to which misogyny has eaten into the Yoruba fabric, turning marriage into a war zone. This outlook affects the general view of women, leading them to feel exiled. Wives, divorcees, prostitutes, educated women, and any woman who dares to resist is disgraced.

For reading on the journey, the undergraduate female protagonist, Nike, arouses the ire of the "motor boy." Young and illiterate though he is, he has already learned to express contempt for women, especially literate upstarts. A woman reader, inevitably open eyed, is a fearful thing to behold, so she must be put in her place. Encouraged by the cab driver, the boy verbally abuses Nike by singing Ebenezer Obey's popular tune, which captures male fear of women's education and its liberatory potential. Hers is the petrifying stare of the

293

Medusa, which can paralyze men or make them impotent. (See Newman 1990, 1031, for a parallel analysis of the gaze of the Victorian woman.) Therefore, men and, unfortunately, illiterate women want educated women controlled.

To convey the deep-seated distrust men have for women, Fakunle figuratively uses the juju, *magun* ("don't climb"), an invisible chastity belt, that a suspicious husband places on his wife, unbeknownst to her, to make her lover somersault, once he climbs upon her. Thus, the married woman becomes a hill or mountain that no other man can climb or conquer, once she belongs to a husband. Enforcing the unwritten law with a vengeance, he stakes a claim to his property by magically writing on the woman in invisible ink. Invariably, she reads the signs belatedly, as does a minor character in the novel, to her eternal mortification. Yet, her jealous husband enjoys his own infidelities untrammeled, once he secures women not written on.

Fakunle diligently and graphically explores the politics of the extended family and the machinations of the polygynous household. For the wife, life is hazardous in such militarized zones. Man sets his women at each other, while he escapes into the waiting arms of some other feckless woman.

Signifying on *Efuru*, Fakunle presents man's insensate need to feel superior to his wife. When this is not the case, as in Sina's and Nike's marriage, he invariably beats her into submission. Wife battering as an unfailing means of control is accepted as legitimate by both men and women. When a woman has the courage to attack it and/or to defend herself effectively, she is immediately construed as a witch out to kill her husband. Equality between the sexes entails death for man, metaphorically speaking, for he has to kill something in himself for it to occur; hence his fear. Sina, Nike's husband, lies constantly, then graduates to battering her, for "He would no longer wage a war of words against Nike. He was going to fight a battle of physical strength" (Fakunle 1978, 66). He wisely changes his tactics, as a woman invariably wins a verbal war but loses a physical confrontation.

The Sacrificial Child is thus an anatomy of a Yoruba marriage plagued by ethnocentrism and sexism. If courtship is the period when a man courts a woman, marriage is the time when a woman courts a man and his extended family. The horrors of wifehood might be alleviated by the joys of motherhood. Women therefore worship their children as Nike does her daughter Ayo, the "joy" which softens the blow of her disastrous marriage, which was initially a love match.

At stake is the desirability of building a new home where the couple can lead a wholesome existence. Many problems stand in their way. Ethnocentrism and in-lawism take their toll. When the Olori, Sina's stepmother and head of the women in the palace, comes to live with them, she brings with her the complex politics of the traditional, polygynous household of the *kabiyesi*, Sina's royal father. Sina and Nike's monogamous household is incomprehensible to the Olori and the illiterate wives in the extended family. Compounding the situation are Olori's ignorance about Nike's westernized child-drearing practices. In the generational and cultural clash among the women, the Olori resents Nike's authority as an educated woman, authority of a kind that she, an older woman and a queen in postcolonial Nigeria, has never experienced. Nike's control of her home, which stems from her strong professional standing, arouses the envy of Ronke, an illiterate sister-in-law denied such privileges. These differences, which are similar to those between the been-to and the stay-at-home, throw the female ranks into disarray, leaving Nike alone and enervated, under siege.

To heal the wounds inflicted in the battle between the male and the female, between the traditional woman and the westernized, and between one ethnic group and another, Fakunle sacrifices Ayo, hence the title of the novel. With Ayo's death, predictably brought about by Olori's (inadvertently) poisoning her, Sina finally realizes that this old enemy, cast in the stereotype of the wicked stepmother and the dangerous mother's co-wife merged together, has literally taken the joy out of his marriage.

It is ironic that the incompetent Olori comes from Ondo. According to Abiodun, in a telephone conversation, Ondo is recognized for its traditional progressiveness; its first ruler, Pupupu, was a woman, and the Olobun—the powerful woman who controls the market—still has a crucial role in installing any ruler. As the leading woman in charge of women's destiny in the palace back at Ondo, it is sad that the Olori cannot function effectively by at least acting the Big Mama in her stepson's modest abode. Like an Ifa text, the novel has a concealed meaning. By spotlighting the modern extension of the Ondo kingdom, Fakunle is concerned with contemporary, ethnic infighting and women's lack of solidarity in Nigerian politics.

Fakunle makes Sina play a leading role in restoring order when he initiates reconciliation with the disenchanted Nike in a womanist closure. Fakunle's exploration of marriage from the viewpoint of a newly married couple in *The Sacrificial Child* contrasts with the middle-aged couple in the next novel. Like Emecheta, she has mapped out the lines of a contemporary saga of Nigeria. In *Chasing the Shadow* (1980), she moves the national saga into the subtext beyond the ethnic squabbles that precipitated the civil war, to zero in on the war itself as epitomized in the fall and rise of a family.

According to Fakunle, though *Chasing the Shadow* is the second novel to appear, it was the first to be written. It explores marriage from the perspective of a middle-aged couple. Fakunle's proclivity toward analyzing her works in her introduction and wishing the reader a "happy time" is reminiscent of eighteenth- and nineteenth-century writers. She is obviously conscious of the role of the reader and the problems of reception.

In *Chasing the Shadow,* she takes up the cause of Grace Aiyeduru, who, literate in Yoruba though not in English, is thoughtlessly treated by her husband, Dapo Aiyeduru. Although Grace is not professionally trained like her husband, early in the marriage she had supported him financially by dint of hard work. This prevented her from improving herself educationally, making her inferior because he has risen to managerial status in the bank. However, he mismanages every aspect of his life.

The book opens with Grace's nightmare in which her right arm is amputated without anesthetics and her house burns. The images of amputation and conflagration point to a grim prognosis for her marriage, at one level, while establishing the violence of a civil war at another. Dapo's subsequent abandonment and replacement of Grace figuratively turns Grace into an amputee, destroying the home she built. This is obviously a common story, and the laws of retribution reinstate the disgraced woman.

Portrayed in the sweet mother stereotype, Grace is "tongue-tied" when her husband banishes her from their house and twenty-five-year marriage, having acquired a younger, prettier, and more socially acceptable wife, Kofo Smith. The exiled Grace, with her *siddon look* strategy, is grounded in a place—Surulere—for her "patience," while Kofo is associated with another place, Olorunsogo, a sign of a new breed of vampiric Lagos women, ready to grab all they can from any man, destroy him, and then carelessly move on to the next victim. In the grim battle of the sexes, the feminist can understand such a woman, but Fakunle prefers the sweet mother, Grace, alias Mama Rotimi, named for her loyalty in graciously standing by her husband in spite of his cruelty. She is rewarded when she returns home to restore peace. Meanwhile, she pleads her case verbally and writes to her husband in Yoruba, begging to be reinstated. He ignores her writing to his peril, as people who disregard women's orature and writing discover.

Together, Kofo and Grace make up the Madam-madonna archetype. When Kofo replaces Grace in the House of Peace, woman is no longer tongue-tied. Turning the home into a house of war, Kofo lies and nags, and, gradually virilized, she refuses to cook or keep house, and she commits adultery, fleecing Dapo of all his money. Her symbolic burning of his first marriage album produces the ashes of their marriage, for Dapo's macho response is to batter her. However, she wins in the verbal battle, as he grows progressively tongue-tied, like Grace. As the relationship deteriorates, he is financially handicapped, like a woman in the throes of an unpleasant marriage. In thus feminizing him, Fakunle makes him experience what Grace's life had been. The House of Peace turned into a house of war epitomizes the Nigerian situation. Gender war is a civil war where both sides are bound to be losers.

Kofo's feminism is as trite and Western as her name, Smith, indicates. Playing a deadly game of in-law politics, Dapo's old mother compliments Kofo for being westernized (unlike Grace) by referring to her as *oyinbo*, "white person." One of Mammywata's degenerate daughters, Kofo is a mermaid with velvety skin acquired from eating expensive fish (Fakunle 1980, 40). Her infidelities, disloyalty to her "husband," frivolity, restaurant and hotel crawling, fast life, and fashion consciousness are all signs of her liberation. These are the shadows of feminism that many urban Nigerian women are chasing, according to Fakunle. To cope with the unexpected attack on his manhood, Dapo batters Kofo viciously, precipitating the birth of twin daughters. Fakunle doubly "punishes" Dapo with the birth of two daughters. Such internalized self-deprecation in a woman writer is quite troubling.

The lack of female solidarity in the struggle against men is reiterated in this text. Grace's mother-in-law abandons her when Grace appeals to her to intervene. During Kofo and Dapo's sham wedding, women in the extended family play an active part, disrespecting their co-wife, Grace, who has been so ignominiously displaced. The illiterate wives are proud to refer to themselves as the "slaves" in the family. Women vie for positions as number-two wives or as girlfriends to married men without thinking of the hardships their predecessors faced. The horror scene in the labor ward, with heartless nurses unwilling to help women in labor, is a sign of women's internalized self-hate.

The sordidness of life in the capital, Lagos—with its corruption, immorality, meanness, and aimlessness, and with people party crawling and spraying money—epitomizes the national decadence. As Lagos and its artificial values are gradually interiorized in the rural areas, there is hardly any sense of honor left anywhere. This is the national tragedy.

Fakunle resolves the sexual-political impasse moralistically by killing off all the "bad" people: the feminist Kofo dies suddenly in a car accident; the sexist Dapo dies slowly and excruciatingly from an ulcer, the cankerworm in society. Fakunle sentimentalizes his illness in her customary deathbed scene, in an attempt to win the reader's sympathy for the repentant sexist.

She ends the novel by introducing a real *oyinbo* in the form of Rotimi's white wife, Sylvia. As one fake *oyinbo* chased Grace out of the house, this genuine *oyinbo* remains by her side to reestablish the House of Peace.[5] This is Nigeria and her Western alliances both before, during, and after the civil war. Reconstruction is grounded in the strengthening of the Western connection with Sylvia's biracial son, Babatunde, "father has returned." Dapo is happily reincarnated through his grandson. If Rotimi is what Fakunle refers to as a "carbon" copy of his father, Dapo, then Babatunde (the future generation) is a lighter copy of his grandfather. This process of bleaching and replication, like *aso ebi,* maximizes similarity and difference. Though Babatunde's light skin is a source of concern for some characters in the book, Fakunle seems to imply that only been-to Nigerian males can treat women fairly. This is in keeping with her conclusion in *The Sacrificial Child,* where she reproduces gender parity in a family that has become nuclear and westernized. It appears peace can only be restored through the *grace* of an increased Western sensibility, following the inevitable human sacrifice. Ifa must undergo a sea change and go West, or is it North?

With such an ending to *Chasing the Shadow,* it appears that Fakunle herself is ironically chasing a shadow; but perhaps not. By imposing a Western ambience at the tail end of a book so steeped in Yoruba culture, spiced with curses, incessant prayers, and philosophical sayings, she hastily weaves these two strands together to form a texture remarkable for its oracular ambiguity. Nigeria/Yorubaland must be democratized through alien infusion.

In an attempt to refine and Nigerianize her thinking, thereby clearing herself of being overly anglicized, she replaces the biracial child with the albino in her next novel, *Chance or Destiny?* (1983), a prophetic piece which questions the Yoruba reading of the albino as mystic and its impact on creativity and Yoruba life.[6] Fakunle's use of children in all of her texts—sacrificing Ayo to restore order in *The Sacrificial Child,* introducing Babatunde as a recuperative gesture in *Chasing the Shadow,* and utilizing albino children to plumb the occult in *Chance or Destiny?*—is strongly grounded in Yoruba hermetism.

Trinh Minh-ha's comment about the position of the writer is germane to this context: "The writer is necessarily either God or Priest. . . . The Priest's role

5. The union of the white woman and the black woman reminds us that Fakunle studied Race Relations for her master of science degree. Emecheta's *The Family* has a comparable ending with the friendship of Gwendolen and Emmanuel. Been-to social scientists understandably include whites in their womanist havens.

6. Interestingly, each of the novels includes a different photograph of Fakunle, in a studied pose, with hair processed, in a flamboyant Western outfit. It is unusual for a Yoruba woman to be dressed up formally in Western clothes instead of the customary *buba,* "loose top," *iro,* "big lappa," *gele,* "headtie," and *iborun,* "shawl."

is to transcribe and/or explain as truthfully as possible God's confiding voice. The closer to this voice s/he claims to stand, the more weight her/his vision or opinion is likely to carry" (1989, 29). In her role as priestess or *iyalawo*, Fakunle's revelation of two *orisa*'s secrets is as abstruse in her third novel *Chance or Destiny?* as Ulasi's in *The Man from Sagamu.*

By postulating the title in an exclusionary form and as a question, Fakunle, as writer, presents a conundrum. Her resisting protagonist, Bose, a born-again Christian, tragically refuses to read her life from the inclusionary Yoruba framework of chance *and* destiny. Willy-nilly, Bose is intimately connected with Osun, the *orisa* in charge of *Ori*, "*destiny*," clearly echoed in the title of the novel. As the mother of two albino boys, she also comes under the auspices of Orisanla/Obatala, the Yoruba creator deity. Orisanla's *chance* handiwork, which deviates from the norm or is not aesthetically pleasing, should, ideally, be tolerated, indeed, respected and protected. Unfortunately, Bose is a reluctant mother of albino children; she refuses to accept a mystic role, a stance that speaks to hostile reception of the child/text.

Abiodun rationalizes the Yoruba attitude of tolerance in reception thus:

> Of immediate relevance here is the Yoruba saying *Mo iwa fun oniwa,* literally, 'Recognize existence in respect of the one existing,' or, idiomatically, 'Concede to each person his or her own particular character,' which may not be like yours or pleasing to you. From this statement, it is clear that the Yoruba respect this category or level of the aesthetic and acknowledge it. This would explain the Yoruba admiration of divinities like Sonpona [in charge of small-pox], Sango [who controls thunder and lightning], Ogun [whose jurisdiction is war and metallurgy], Esu [the trickster], Iku [who manages death], all of whose characters or behaviors may be perceived as immoral in human terms. The hunchback, the albino, and other deformed persons—all the handiwork of Obatala—receive their "license" or right to be respected and admired by virtue of their relationship with their creator, the cause of their existence, as shown in the saying *Owo Orisa l'aafi wo Afin,* 'We perceive the honor [divinity] of Orisa [the sculptor divinity] in the albino.' (1987a, 69–70)

Rather than revere the divinity in her albino children, Bose berates divine sanction, seeks to change it, and succumbs for going against the grain.

The basic philosophy in Yoruba aesthetics, willing us to recognize and respect identity, individuality, and difference in life and in works of art, problematizes the adversarial and closed nature of Western attitudes and literary studies. Writing her anguish of a silent reception into *Chance or Destiny?*, Bose's two albino boys can be likened to Fakunle's first two novels. The third novel is prophetic and full of despair, for Fakunle envisages the end of her career as a writer. Her text, deeply steeped in Yoruba culture, turns out to be her last; her silence parallels Bose's death after the birth of her black daughter, following a *babalawo*'s cryptic prediction. This daughter is Odu herself, whose incarnation brings about the mother's death. Bedeviled by contemporary uncertainty, Fakunle entwines her destiny with Bose's.

Commenting on the dilemma of uncertainty, Clara Odugbesan (1969, 202) observes: "Ifa is regarded not as a deity to be worshipped, but as an oracle from which people try to obtain certainty from uncertainty in any human problem ranging from the choice of a . . . husband or wife . . . to the request for the gift of a child." *Chance or Destiny?* is an Ifa puzzle on the nature of problem solving in Yoruba society, a dimension the sociologist Fakunle is keenly interested in.

Chance or Destiny? dramatizes the human desire for certainty and the Sisyphean need to avert an ineluctable fate. These very human motivations propel the characters, especially Bose and her sweet mother-in-law, to run from pillar to post, seeking an end to albinism. Instead of going to Ifa, since they cannot appeal to Orisanla, their Christianity leads them to seek help from Alagba, the head of the Aladura sect; Alagba transforms Christianity into an indigenous, oracular source. Dissatisfied with the vagueness of Christianity, they go to Islam, represented by the Afaa, the charismatic Alhaji. They avail themselves of other options with the Western-educated doctor, finally having recourse to the *babalawo* Baba Idogo. Though a teacher, Bose has failed to learn that the assurances she seeks, they cannot genuinely give. Wanting answers where there are none and demanding predictions that one is not really willing to accept represent the modern existential crisis. Further, Bose ignores genuine, indigenous resources to her peril. Retaining Ifa's propensity for conundrum, Fakunle leaves the titular question unanswered, because it is presumptuously phrased, and Ifa's opinion is never sought. Resisting three Yoruba divinities is foolhardy.

The work opens with an unforgettable scene, delineating the humiliation and rage that polygyny arouses in some women, while their husband is left unscathed and in control. Aside from the dangers in this household, Bose's mother-in-law, with only one son to her credit, is afflicted with the *abiku* problem. However, Bose and Jide's monogamous household is not more conducive to happiness, since they are also afflicted by the scourge of the whiteness of their albino offspring. In spite of their love, Bose dies, and, for the third time,

Fakunle uses death conveniently for closure. The births and deaths in her texts show her desire for the death of the old and the birth of a new way of life. Without the intensity of Bose's fruitless search to alter her destiny, her black daughter and two albino sons are raised in a wholesome household, guided by a disciplined, grieving father and grandmother.

Bose's original offense is in recoiling at the sight of her albino son, followed by her deep-seated rejection, which she camouflages with a surface love. Although she later appears to accept him, she is further traumatized when she has another albino son. Her frantic search for a solution, which takes her to four radically different sources of help, belies whatever love she displays for the children.

People's stares at this black mother with two albino sons and children's ostracizing of the boys are in themselves the sins of exclusion, of exile. Even as they make Bose more susceptible to the trauma of difference, such intolerance accounts for the violence of modern life. By not genuinely accepting to mother these special gifts, unpleasing though they may be, she exacerbates her situation, incurring the wrath of Orisanla. She never learned any lessons from her mother-in-law's final acceptance of her destiny as the mother of *abiku* children, who refused to stay. Bose's death is, therefore, predictable.

Another textual reading is possible. Bose's resistance to albinism is a lament against the westernization of Nigerian culture, a process that she finds tragic and alarming. Yet, she is a teacher and a Christian and goes to a Western-trained doctor for help. Having a black child in her thinking would be an affirmation of her culture, yet she cannot decipher the Afaa's or the *babalawo*'s predictions. Her attitude speaks to Nigerian cultural ambiguity, the double consciousness that confuses her and ultimately brings about her death. Signifying on Soyinka's *The Interpreters,* Fakunle sees the albino as a profound interpreter of contemporary culture, the enigma of blacks in white skin.

Like Alkali, who interprets Nigerian life through school children, through whom one transmits cultural values, Fakunle is also interested in the future generation, by exposing the ills in Nigeria from the 1960s to the 1970s. Her examination of the family, its socialization processes, the psychological impact on women and children of polygyny, and sexist practices reveals some of the problems in society. By depicting the "thorny road" ahead for albinos, Fakunle (1983, 57) recognizes the difficulties of multiculturalism.

She makes Jide an *abiku* to demonstrate, through his mother's hardship, that woman's artistic problems are linked with the myths of infant mortality. In the birth and rebirth cycle involved in the *abiku* syndrome, she proffers an analogue for the creative process involved in writing, rewriting, and revising until one arrives at the final version, which remains permanent, like Jide. Writing is therefore a process as agonizing as child birth and child care, though the end product can be finally fulfilling.

Through Bose's religious and quasi-medical journey, Fakunle explores the psychodynamics of a Yoruba family faced with an intractable problem, seeking quick solutions along several avenues. The different answers they receive are a lesson in the complexity of interpreting Ifa divination, life, and literature. The Yoruba know that

> Today's divination
> May not be valid tomorrow [that is, in the future].
> This is the reason Babalawo [Yoruba diviners]
> Must divine repeatedly every five days
> [that is, once in each four-day week].
> (Abiodun 1987a, 63)

Obviously there are no quick solutions in life. One has to experience the benefits of quiet contemplation, because tragedy is a "natural occurrence in human life, just as happiness [is]" (Fakunle 1983, 137).

Fakunle believes, with Odugbesan, that "Sacrifice is probably the most significant aspect of Ifa divination, for one's request is not granted without some kind of offering" (Odugbesan 1969, 203). Just as Nike in *The Sacrificial Child* has her daughter sacrificed to overcome ethnocentrism, misogyny, envy, and sexism, and as Dapo and Kofo are killed off to restore the House of Peace, so Bose dies in the "sacrificial role of women." Thus Fakunle's final vision is steeped in the mysticism of Yoruba religious beliefs and practices. As *orisa*, priestess, *iyalawo*, and writer, she contributes cryptically to the Nigerian palaver by demanding that children, men, and women make sacrifices for the good of family and country.

Ifeoma Okoye: Maladies, Malaise, and National Recovery

On the cover of Ifeoma Okoye's *Behind the Clouds* (1982), her first novel written for adults, there is a picture of a healthy baby on the back of a woman. We do not know the sex of the baby, as there are no telltale signs to indicate this. Indeed, there is no need to know, for in this novel, having a child is vital. What is intriguing is that the woman has no head in the photograph. This figurative decapitation aptly conveys woman's headless position in the Nigerian consciousness. As Emecheta puts it in *The Family*, woman is a "baby machine"; if the country believes that woman does not need her head for her role as mother, something has gone very wrong. To advance creatively as woman and mother, she has to put on her thinking cap by having her head firmly fixed where it should be, for these are difficult times.

In revisiting the theme of childlessness, Okoye does just that in *Behind the Clouds,* as she revises J. P. Clark's *Song of a Goat* along the lines of Nwapa's Ojiugo in *Idu.* As Soyinka observed in *Myth, Literature, and the African World,* Clark's story of the tragedy of male infertility was problematic for Western audiences, who did not understand why Zifa's impotence could not be medically treated. Such a simple Western solution ignores the very essence of the Nigerian man's tragedy, emanating from a masculinist ego that prevents him from admitting the truth of his impotence. This denial is central to the Nigerian dilemma. Through Ojiugo, Nwapa diagnosed the Nigerian malady, and woman, refusing to wait, openly sought its remediation. In her own two novels, Okoye, as daughter-of-the-soil and as *omunwa,* uncovers Nigeria's shortcomings, as any responsible mother would, to ensure stability.

To this end, Okoye boldly states that what lies behind the clouds in Nigeria is not a silver lining, but a lack, a defective leadership, male impotence which men and women, old and young, are unwilling to address. Silence tears the national fabric apart, and until women speak out in different ways in *Behind the Clouds,* there is no way to mend it. As a mother rounding off her story and using every means at her disposal to effect a cure, Okoye resolves the problem matter-of-factly by giving her plot a Western twist. The male-sterile Dozie, cocky in his ignorance, is brazenly told by his pregnant mistress that he is not the father of her child, a truth lovingly confirmed by his wife Ije, the protagonist. With the ménage a trois dismantled, Dozie and Ije can start a new life after his medical treatment overseas. The saving grace on this occasion has been the enlightenment that education has conferred on Dozie, aptly named for the reparative role he plays in the text. An architect, he will supervise the rebuilding of his family and society after his own rehabilitation. Operating with a consensus on the nature of the problem, recuperation based on complementarity follows conciliation. Okoye's point is simple: Nigerian recovery must be based on a cooperative effort across gender lines; men must examine themselves, for they cannot go it alone. Offended by her off-putting, female position, Charles Nnolim (1989, 34) complains about "the lack of subtlety in execution" in Okoye's novels. True, the ingredients in Okoye's palava sauce are obvious for a purpose; men must also be able to see them and cook them up. More *omunwa* than a critic's writer, she merely seeks a radical but simple solution to a complex problem. With Okoye responding to her predecessors, childlessness as a Nwapan trope for literary barrenness ceases to have any validity, especially as female texts proliferate in Nigeria.

While concentrating on the nature of marriage in the Igbo community, Okoye is able to examine its sexist aspects and the difficulties that the lack of female solidarity causes. The problem of the other woman who, over the years, has grown so brazen as to move into her rival's home to keep the husband to herself, has been thrust into the urban consciousness. From that angle, the 1982 *Behind the Clouds* is a variation of two 1980s texts: Fakunle's *Chasing the Shadow*, and Ba's *So Long a Letter*. This coincidence emphasizes the pressures on the urban marriage and the impending collapse of the family. Besides the intractable problem of the other woman, female in-lawism is also a bane. The embittered wife often makes a wicked mother- or sister-in-law. The stereotype of the cruel mother-in-law drives home the point of female disunity. These vicious cycles should be instructive about woman's destructive self-hate, for it means that woman has suffered everything and has learned nothing in her marital journey to benefit the younger generation.

In tackling modes of problem solving, Okoye uses her central character, Ije, to traverse the same ground as Soyinka in the farcical Jero plays and Fakunle in *Chance or Destiny?* The recourse to a new type of religious leader in the Pentecostal churches and the fact that he is usually a fake whose visions are clouded by his sins of deception is terrifying. These writers underscore the point that the population, severed from its religious traditions, revels in a foreign form of worship that holds no deep spiritual meaning; thus, they emphasize the nature and extent of urban deracination and desperation. Though not a biological mother, Ije is drawn in the archetype of the sweet mother, solicitous for the welfare of her mother-in-law (who, unfortunately, fails to reciprocate), her husband, and her maid. Her nurturing extends to the outside world. Though she has been sorely tried, she is still able to resist committing adultery with the church leader to achieve her desire to have a child. That is the ultimate in goodness, since others have fallen in their desperation.

Her name Ije, "journey," reiterates the point that life and marriage are difficult undertakings. It also emphasizes woman's tortuous relationship with man and the extent she has journeyed on the road to taking control when man is out of line. To maintain her dignity and sanity, the childless Ije, with the firmness of the sweet mother, moves out of her hellish polygamous household, worsened by her child-obsessed mother-in-law, to live by herself. When she is vindicated by Dozie's painful stumbling into self-knowledge, she is reunited with her husband, now made whole in a fairy-tale ending. The abandoned house that they were building together can now be completed. This house symbolizes a new type of family and indeed a new healthy nation of enlightened men and women working together for the good of all.

Okoye's prize-winning second novel, *Men Without Ears* (1984), focuses on the national malaise—corruption, expensive and lavish lifestyles, the artificiality of relationships in oil-rich Nigeria, and anarchy. As *omunwa*, worried about national decadence, Okoye is still concerned with home building at the familial and macrocosmic levels. Her winning a prize for dealing with this aspect of the palava means that men are listening to women's contribution to the palaver.

Chigo, the protagonist, is the only man with ears in *Men Without Ears*. By contrast, his brother Uloko is up to his ears in the type of wheeling and dealing that has crippled Nigeria. He uses books such as *Easy Way to Riches* and *How to Be a Millionaire* as primary texts. The atmosphere of graft pervades private lives, public clubs, and business offices. Borrowing money for lavish parties and grandiose schemes is commonplace, a parallel to the escalating national debt, with nothing substantial to show for it. Okoye uses Chigo and Uloko allegorically to represent good and evil in Nigeria. Since the Nigerian Chigo was born and bred in Ghana, educated in England, and worked in Tanzania, he is a been-to. His cosmopolitan experiences permit him to view with horror the depths to which the Nigerian society from Lagos to Enugu, from the rural to the urban, has degenerated. Indeed, the entire story is seen through his been-to eyes.

The use of the first-person narrative is refreshing, as we see everything from the *korokoro* eyes of the newly arrived Chigo, who is filled with consternation and disgust at the horror that passes for sophistication in Nigeria. Though the people he meets are jacks-of-all-trades making money unscrupulously, he has a Pan-African vision, and is concerned about Nigeria's leadership role in the continent. While using a male character as a mouthpiece, Okoye feminizes Chigo, who has ears to hear, eyes to see, and a mouth and pen to criticize the people who offend his sensibility. His name is not gender specific. His role is, therefore, maternal and instructive in its corrective posture; he is a sweet but acerbic mother.

The society that Okoye depicts has gone to the dogs. The men, bedecked with jewelry, wear laces as if they were women or chiefs. Whatever the motivation, their nicknames, such as Young Millionaire, and their outfits define a people in a crisis of identity. The need for the nouveaux riches to display their wealth in the form of cars, lavish parties, and unnecessary celebrations is troubling. They crudely donate money for different causes as a publicity stunt.

Their conception of time is African, with a firm determination not to be controlled by Western notions of time. Okoye humorously criticizes the general practice of not starting events off on time and the inability to make and keep to schedules. Thus, Young Millionaire invites Chigo, Uloko, and his wife to dinner at his house, but when they arrive he is not at home. The cocktail party held by Uloko on Chigo's behalf starts almost two hours late. Okoye implies that a people for whom time means nothing are a people who have fallen out of time. If one is out of time, then one is lost, and these people are lost because they do not belong to past time, present time, or future time. Uloko later finds out that there are tragic repercussions in existing in limbo.

Okoye scoffs at Nigerian predilection for using titles and boasting about their professions. Referring to a character as "Engineer Akah" as if Engineer were his first name, Okoye satirizes the degeneration of professionalism. Though hilarious, her account of the scramble for the plane at the beginning of the novel shows that the corruption and disorder in Nigeria are perpetrated by the educated in urban centers. Her humor is her greatest strength, mollifying the intensity of her criticism that those who should know better are the very ones committing the atrocities.

Okoye also satirizes the Nigerian work ethic, with women converting their offices into trading bases at the expense of the jobs they are paid to do. Cheating, tardiness, fraud, and irresponsibility are so widespread and brazen that they have reached epidemic proportions, to the detriment of the country's economic growth. Okoye comments on the uncommitted nature of work in the public sector, *olu oyibo*, "white work," conveying a feeling of impending disaster.

Unfortunately, the disorder is so widespread that it has stretched its tentacles into the rural areas. Okoye sensitizes the reader to the need for urgency to avert total anarchy. When his rural kinsmen ostracize Chigo to side with Uloko in their sibling rivalry, we realize that Uloko's money talks so loudly that the deaf inevitably hear the wrong things. Uloko's plan to kill Nweke, Chigo's servant, in the village, as part of the ritual to make money, establishes the loss of the ethics that the countryside was cherished for. To institute order, Okoye kills off Uloko. He dies of hypertension, having been comatose with his blood pressure running high, just as he and his ilk have let the tensions in Nigeria rise to an unprecedented level by their careless existence. In Okoye's predictably neat ending, death awaits men without ears. Nigeria will survive with attentive people like Chigo, who will improve the old homestead.

Okoye's theme of national survival and renewal is echoed in a popular song by a female artiste, "Nigeria go survive." Okoye's contribution to the palaver is straightforward: pinpoint the trouble spots without quibbling and set about writing (righting) them. Hers is a simple, maternal, salvational vision that might work, if only it were widespread and not countered by cynicism.

Zaynab Alkali: Salts and Preservation

I spent my entire life dreaming, I forgot to live. . . . But it is also important to remember that like babies dreams are conceived but not all dreams are born alive. Some are aborted. Others are stillborn.

Zaynab Alkali, *The Stillborn*

It is becoming so that every other person you talk to has been affected one way or another by a road accident. Why! by God, it's becoming an epidemic. . . . God has other priorities than to help a nation that is bent on destroying itself.

Zaynab Alkali, *The Virtuous Woman*

Zaynab Alkali, the first woman novelist from the northern part of Nigeria, arrived on the literary scene with a resounding welcome by the Association of Nigerian Authors: they awarded her the 1985 prize for her first novel, *The Stillborn*. On joining the exclusive club, Alkali announced that she was not a feminist, as Omolola Ladele (1988, 327–28) informs us. A sweet woman whose pen can occasionally be acerbic, her criticism of Nigerian society is as forthright as Okoye's. Her political acuity emerges quite clearly in an interview with Odia Ofeimun, in which she expresses her vision of woman's role in Nigeria. She zeroes in on her first novel, whose "message," she maintains, "is not for the womenfolk alone but for the menfolk as well. I suppose, I am trying to say that we've got a job at hand and that of nation building and I would like not only the men to take up the responsibility of building the nation but to encourage the women to help in the process" (Ofeimun 1985). Her work is suffused with this cooperative ideal.

From this perspective, *The Stillborn* (1984) can be read as an allegory of the Republic of Nigeria when it was administered as three regions. These are represented by the three young couples in the novel. The three men and three women meet on the outskirts of Hill Station, which, with its European residents, represents Britain. Atop the hill, the couples declare their independence. Full of promise, they intend to march forward to form a new, integral whole. *The Stillborn* images each couple's disastrous outcome—that is, the disintegration of the three regions in the bitter, internecine struggles that plagued Nigeria shortly after independence. The men are ravaged by alcoholism and an easy urban lifestyle, while the women are left to play a salvational role to build a new family.

Hill Station is noted for its stone houses, a mark of its unresponsive nature. Its asbestos poisons the environment, while its generator shatters the peace of

307

the quiet village whose mud huts stand for its vulnerability to the colonial intruders. As "overlord" (2), it domineeringly looks down on the village, casting the distant electric light from the distance on the village dwelling in darkness. The contrasting images of foreign technology and local practice, the urban and the rural, form the core of the novel. The former gradually encroaches on the latter, corrupting it.

The novel opens with a journey from school in a vehicle recklessly driven on a dusty road, Nigeria's tedious and hazardous journey in learning how to govern, manage democracy, and gain self-control by its men. However, the central character is the dynamic woman, Li. The unbearable heat and Li's benumbed legs during the journey foreshadow the period of the protagonist's adulthood, when she waits in vain to enjoy her conjugal rights from her absent husband, Habu Adams. How long can a woman wait for a man without exercising her options?

Alkali's vision of Nigeria, symbolized by Li's mud family house, is disconcertingly grim. The extended family remains united for a period through Baba the father, a disciplinarian, and Kaka the grandfather, tenacious and tradition bound. The limitations of those in authority can be inferred from Baba's "abnormal behaviour" and the incongruity of his reading a book, *Teach Yourself How to Read* (8). The literate and gifted Li predictably rebels against her father, a beginning reader. Sule, the first son, who could have taken over from the fragile Baba, absconds, abandoning a daughter born out of wedlock for his sisters to mother. The family house attracts the alcoholic headmaster. The remaining two men, Garba and Habu Adams, wretched womanizers, become lost in the entanglements of city life. Thus, the men are overly authoritarian, weak, absent, or reckless.

Male irresponsibility is reiterated during the symbolic climb by the three girls to fetch firewood from the hilltop, while the three boys lie in wait to scare them. Faku, one of the girls, disappears from the scene in fright; in adult life, overwhelmed by her situation, she turns into a prostitute. The reaction of Li's sister, Awa, is to lie prostrate on the ground; later in life, she appears passive, playing the role of the sweet mother in touch with the earth. She bears the burden of caring for all the children of the household, including her alcoholic husband. The third girl, the "stubborn" Li, reacts differently. Legs firmly apart in a masculinist pose, she holds up her cutlass, ready to take the offensive for the good of home and country.

Alkali's portrait of the she-men and the "he-woman," as she refers to the indefatigable and virilized Li, signifies on Nwapa's *Efuru*. The image of women as builders and men as destroyers is troubling, even if it is valid. It raises an aesthetic problem: what should a woman writing in a country that has continuously been in a state of anarchy through male misrule write about? How does a woman writer separate so-called negative, black male stereotypes from genuine concern? If, in this respect, *The Stillborn* resembles Ntozake Shange's *for colored girls who have considered suicide when the rainbow is enuf,* and Alice Walker's *The Color Purple,* it is because the texts emanate from the same source and express a genuine anguish for change on the part of men. Stereotyping stems from a committed response to a nagging problem.

Furthermore, misogyny and male self-centeredness appear to widen the gap between men and women, according to Alkali. She encapsulates this aspect with her vignette on Manu the hunchback, a "woman-hater turned woman-lover" (53). Echoing Okoye's concern in *Behind the Clouds,* Alkali makes Manu impotent. Although he knew he was impotent, he still went ahead to marry, with disastrous and embarrassing consequences. Such yoking epitomizes the inequities of a sexist society. Power must be earned and not be regarded as man's inalienable right; better still, a couple have to work closely together with the true knowledge of each other's shortcomings.

Through her portrait of Baba, Alkali also attacks Islam's oppression of women. She prefers the freedom entrenched in the "heathenism" of indigenous Nigerian religions, as represented by the old grandfather, Kaka. Li makes a hole through the fence that her father has built to restrict the women, figuratively destroying the wall that incarcerates women in Islam. Through purdah, or the veil and the enveloping clothes that woman is forced to wear because man cannot control his desire, Muslims keep women apart so as not to pollute men. This apartness, this exile, Alkali posits, destroys the communal effort necessary for building the home and nation. Making a hole instead of climbing over the fence leaves a subversive sign. When Li lies to her father about the hole, implying that a dog might have made it, she is referring to woman's existence in Islam as a dog's life.

"Heathenism," by contrast, is liberating, though Grandma's fourteen marriages to men she had met in the marketplace are troubling. They emphasize Grandma's dynamism and the lackluster nature of men as well as the liberty that women associate with the marketplace. From this place of exchange, Grandma satisfies her "quest for modern living coupled with a foreign culture, a thing that was sweeping the whole community like wildfire" (25).

Li inherits from her stepgrandmother the basic desire for freedom but not the means of achieving it. Li compromises and soils herself by accepting ten shillings from Habu Adams in the market. Monetary exchange marks the doom of their marriage because he has bought her. With a name like *Adams*, the only English name in the novel, Alkali conjures up negative Adamic notions of shirking one's duties and prevaricating; Habu Adams fits the slot perfectly. Marriage to such a man is a dead end, destroying the progress of home and country.

Drawn in the archetype of Mammywata, Li's portentous birth and her resemblance to a "river goddess," "with the head of a woman and the tail of a fish" are signs of her superiority. As Uhamiri's daughter, she is a doer and not a passive woman. Throughout the novel, Alkali, like Nwapa, is concerned about the position of gifted women in marriage to inferior husbands. While Li waits for her husband, as Efuru had done before her, she rebuilds her father's collapsed house on a stronger foundation, using more durable materials. Li's dreams, like Efuru's, are of a promising future.

In her outspokenness, Li is an alter ego of Alkali herself. Li is controlled only by her grandfather, who refers to her as "mother." As ancestral guide, he asks her to wait for her absent husband, in spite of his shiftlessness. Womanist to the core, she waits patiently for him. When Habu Adams lies crippled and helpless in the end, Li goes to assist him. To her sister Awa she remarks, quite sweetly, though to our incredulity, "I will just hand him the crutches and side by side we will learn to walk" (105). Tottering together they will set out on the journey to nationhood. This calculated, slow walk contrasts with the reckless abandon of the driver of the motorized vehicle Li was traveling in at the beginning of the book. Rather than have a man driving her, she now is in control, as Jane Eyre is in control at the conclusion of Brontë's novel. A woman should not waste time waiting for male assistance, for the men are hardly in a position to help. In her womanist closure, Alkali affirms that national strength lies in conciliation and cooperation between the sexes.

The three school girls in Alkali's second novel, *The Virtuous Woman* (1987), remind us of the three girls in the preceding book. They also echo Nwapa's composite heroines in *Women Are Different*, making it clear once again that Alkali is dealing with nationalist issues allegorically. She uses the biblical idea of the virtuous woman to conceptualize Nana, the protagonist. If a reader had missed the link between Alkali (Alka-Li) and the character Li, she makes the self-projection into her second protagonist clearer by naming her Nana Ai (I). This is author-identified because Alkali projects her feelings of insecurity about her position as an author from Northern Nigeria into the crippled and orphaned Nana.

The Virtuous Woman is a picaresque novel centered on a tedious and hazardous journey by lorry and train undertaken by three girls setting out to school. Through the experiences of the picara on the road, the author represents those in authority, criticizing the way they waste time talking rather than doing in a time of crisis.

As the story takes place in 1964, its historic specificity captures the chaos after Nigerian independence. The picaro is named Abubakar and his close companion, Bello, after the first prime minister of Nigeria, Sir Abubakar Tafawa Balewa, and the first premier of Northern Region, Sir Ahmadu Bello, the Sardauna of Sokoto, respectively. Journeying south, that is, the northern attempt to integrate with the south to form a united country, is a move fraught with dangers. Yet, it must be made.

The Virtuous Woman is in some ways a fictive and simpler realization of the subject matter of Soyinka's *The Road*. Since Soyinka had overlooked women as characters in his play, as if Ogun does not slaughter his daughters on the road, too, Alkali concentrates on three girls as her central characters, to right this oversight. Though Nana Ai's left leg is crippled by polio, this sign of her "obvious disability" as a woman does not prevent her from participating meaningfully during the journey. She performs her role as a leader and surrogate mother to her two companions, who are going to school for the first time. She also mothers one of the twin children during the journey.

Alkali makes three lorries travel southward heedlessly. They represent the three regions of Nigeria in 1964, heading toward the disaster and carnage of the civil war. "It seemed as if the journey had bound them into one being with a single destiny" (35), and so indeed it had, because all Nigerians had become embroiled in the issues. Led by the young drivers, that is, the coup plotters, whose giddiness turned out to be the beginning of a hideous bloodletting, the disaster was man-made not ordained. Nana's grandfather, Baba Sani the diviner, had seen the bloody handwriting in the sand. However, he was reluctant to divulge the horror to the young Nana, since from that gory road accident was going to emerge the long-awaited prince, Bello, who would rescue her so that they can march forward together.

On the literal level, Alkali uses the road accident to criticize the criminally reckless drivers who ply Nigerian roads, causing the daily, preventable carnage. Metaphorically, it stands for the inexperienced leadership and governments that Nigeria has been plagued with. Their irresponsibility has caused the country a bloody civil war and irreparable loss of untold proportions in human and material resources. Woman's role following the disaster is palliative.

The girls have to be circumspect in reaching their goal. Traveling in the

311

lorry, named "Hakuri" for the patience that women exercise, they move safely and wisely to arrive at an illuminating destination—a school for girls. The other two lorries are ironically named "Allah Sarki" (Allah is King) and "Allah Kiyaye" (Allah protects). Both become entwined in a gory destiny following their juvenile rivalry. Immature competition between leaders with ethnic support systems ends in tragedy, as Nigeria's political experience has proved. The common people who do not protest against such leadership are partly to blame, and they suffer for remaining silent or for foolishly encouraging unnecessary competition. Allah remains king and will not deign to protect foolish people, hence the fatal accident.

Alkali succinctly states the painful point that Nigeria has not learned much from past disasters. Dwelling on repetitions, she provides a vignette in which a twin who survives the road accident is handed over to his uncle. The scene replays Baba Sani's taking over of Nana at the death of her entire nuclear family in a car crash. Baba Sani's mystic power is unable to curb the gory appetite of the road, for the fault is not the earth's but that of the people who treat her with careless abandon as they drive roughshod over her.

The rapport between Nana and the mother of the twins during the road journey demonstrates the importance of female solidarity in a time of crisis. The woman mothers Nana, who in her own turn acts as surrogate mother to one of the woman's twins. The woman supplies the group with calabash to make music, thereby bringing harmony where there was discord. Woman's role is therefore vital in Alkali's vision; both the educated and illiterate, young and old, must pull their resources together to aid in home/nation building. These are some of the characteristics of the virtuous or sweet woman.

The train journey that follows the disaster on the road is an experience with mixed blessings. The trio find it difficult to board the train, a comment on the tardiness in starting off a female revolution necessary to rehabilitate the country. An army officer aids them in a military intervention that appears romantic but later turns out to show his power. Whether military rule is paternalistic, as Alkali envisions it here is debatable. However, of all the people who have authority over the girls on their frightening journey through life, the officer is the most altruistic. In this society, adult men invariably act recklessly: the secretary in charge of the girls' welfare wants to seduce them, in true picaresque tradition; they have to care for their sick male escort, in a role reversal that emphasizes the healing role of women in facilitating the building of a healthy nation.

These virtuous women are supported by some prudent men who play strategic roles in the novel. Such a character is the sagacious Baba Sani, steeped in traditional lore. Androgynous, he has his ears pierced like a woman and has a lion tattooed on his chest as a sign of his virility (86–87). Alkali appears to agree with Chodorow's precepts about the necessity for developing a maternal streak in men; his ability to mother Nana makes him complete, and he shows that men like him have a crucial role to play in an emerging society.

Bello is his son, not only as the long-awaited grandson-in-law, but as a young man possessing the admirable qualities that Nigeria needs for rehabilitation. Nana cries twice in the novel, at the beginning of the journey while parting from the old man and at the end during her temporary parting from Bello, showing her close relationship to these two men. Nana's daydreaming, her heritage of divination inherited from her grandfather, unites with Bello's sterling qualities to assure woman that she need no longer weep for the absence of responsible men. The romantic plot and the political statement merge in the coming together of these two spiritually attuned couple, Bello and Nana.

Alkali's utopian vision is of a country made up of androgynous types, where the men are she-men and the women he-men. Together, they establish a womanist haven for the good of all. Her ideology is thus strongly nationalistic—the rebuilding of a Nigeria by responsible men and women. She appeals to the women not to wait idly but to work together with the men, crippled though they may be, to accomplish the vital duty of reconstruction. Nana Ai knew her herbs and could become a doctor, like her father and her grandfather. Alkali identifies woman's role, especially the writer's, as one of reconciliation and healing rather than confrontation. She is clearly Nwapa's daughter, and the womanist connection is visible in their approach to the Nigerian palaver.

Eno Obong: Mammywata to the Rescue

Eno Obong, a newcomer to the women's literary scene, has dazzled her readers with her consciously crafted *Garden House* (1988). That it did not win the Noma award can be attributed to the fact that 1989 was remarkable for its crop of new talents.

She has raised profound issues of women's naming and identity by refusing to be identified by her married name, Regina Johnson, or by her maiden name, Atta, as a writer. In a move that reminds us of Malcolm X, she has declined to append an English name to an African text; neither will she use the male surname that also makes her an appendage to her father. Escaping from the position of the subaltern as a daughter, a wife, and a neocolonial woman, she has reinforced her self-esteem by using only her given name. By breaking the name into two, she has created a self-identity that is compatible with the

313

thrust of the novel. Eno Obong uses her given name as a pen name because, as someone facetiously put it, a married Nigerian woman can hardly speak against patriarchy. Casting off the patriarchal links symbolized by the names liberates her to explore perspectives that the very notion of her being subjected to patriarchy obscures. *Garden House* is dedicated to her three daughters "with hope," as she puts it, that girls will thrive in the garden house/country that she fictionally envisages.

In the novel, a new, collaborative beginning develops on firm, indigenous, simple foundations in Abuja, the new heart donated to the country as a capital in a radical surgery aimed at a quick national recovery. It replaces Lagos, the old, diseased heart. With its foreign orientation, Lagos is a complex establishment that has collapsed from the tensions arising from the conflicting plans originally intended to lead her to recovery.

Mayen, the protagonist, envisions the new capital/country metaphorically as "A garden house. . . . A wide crystal garden house. The sun pouring in. And blossoms sprouting at my feet" (114). The building of the garden house is linked with the symbolic progression to the new place, Abuja, comparable to Emecheta's Biafran ideal, except that Eno Obong's Abuja is vibrant where Biafra is a dead end. Abuja's pristine beauty stems from its crystal clearness, with the sunshine illuminating and bleaching everything pure. Blossoms abound in this Eden, unlike Mayen's baby, named Blossom, whose sacrificial death literally turns her mother into an ex, making a fresh start possible.

Eno Obong moves beyond Okoye's *Men Without Ears,* locating Nigerian corruption in an international context and concentrating on the scandalous spending spree in the oil-boom days. She quickly establishes her thesis for a new world order by using subtle contrasts, for she is not one to engage in a raucous palaver: the simple Mayen, Abuja bound to construct her garden house, with the garish Alhaja Sherifat, an out-and-out Lagosian bogged down as a landlady; the androgynous and protean Keki Tovu with the masculinist and sly Captain Iweme; the architect and geologist Wande Adebo with the wheeler-dealer Kabiri. Skeletonized, the story has a moralistic plot in which the "bad guys" are killed off and the good ones drive off to the sunny Abuja.

Garden House is a *Bildungsroman* featuring Mayen, whose name many mispronounce. Who, then, is Mayen? As Eno Obong is identified in different ways, so Mayen is known severally as Mmayen, Maya (Angelou?), Maria, Mum, mermaid, and Mammywater. Her beauty and fluid movements in combing her long, thick hair mark her out as Mammywata incarnate. Indeed, her "survival and continued growth [after she was orphaned] was regarded as a special favour from the goddess [Mammywater], whose mark she was said to carry in the thick mob of hair that sprouted abundantly from her head" (13).

Signifying on Nwapa, Eno Obong presents Mayen's fate as a variant of Efuru's and the myth of the water deity, Ogbuide/Uhamiri. Constantly keeping watch on the sea as she helplessly waits for her drowned, unmourned parents to sail home, Mayen establishes a lasting bond between land and sea, in her unbounded vision. Orphaned in these mystical circumstances, she is forced to live with her terrified aunt, who turns her into an outcast, in accordance with their indigenous religion and in response to the people's dread at this survivor. To preserve the village, she is finally exiled to a Roman Catholic convent. Thus, in her first two abodes, the little girl has experienced death, without its being named, and emotional abandonment. Her first six abodes mark her initial powerlessness, but they shape her religious, spiritual, and political development. A woman shapes a home, and a home shapes a woman. In the magical seventh and final home, everything falls into place, and she is able to realize her dream of a garden house by collecting the materials and creating the artifacts necessary for building it after she had performed a spiritual expiation.

With the white nuns' connivance, the young Mayen is raped by a white man in her third abode, the convent in her pristine Nigerian village, Ibino. Keki Tovu, the Nigerian soldier-teacher, rescues her and, as her mentor, nurses her back to health. However, the emotional and physical keloid grows; it will take a prince charming in the form of Wande Adebo to finally cauterize it.

To ensure that she remains one of them, the nuns exile her to Ireland, where she is imprisoned in a nunnery, her fourth place of abode. In a clash between Catholicism and Islam, the Muslim, Kabiri, rescues her through some devious means that later boomerang. Hibernating in an English cottage with a blossoming garden, her marriage to Kabiri remains unconsummated for three years, because of the trauma of the rape and because she has betrayed her own indigenous faith and the teachings of Keki Tovu. However, like the flowers around her, she undergoes a metamorphosis into womanhood as she experiences maternal stirring in her love for her stepson, Bamidele. As his name indicates, he has to accompany Mayen, his new mother, on the journey home to Nigeria. Her yearning and love for Bamidele, "spawn of the diaspora" (13), affirms Mayen's growing, mystical knowledge of the sea and the Nigerian links with the Caribbean within a black, international, been-to context. Yet, the jet set she mixes with draws her farther away from the (inter)national calling that Keki Tovu had prepared her for.

315

In the next phase of her growth, she moves to the concrete monstrosity in Ikeja, Lagos, where she and Kabiri sleep on a waterbed, a sign of their marital instability, with Mayen's liberating waters reduced to confinement in plastic. In the increasingly Islamic atmosphere of her marriage, she becomes a biological mother, only to face the trauma of the sickness and loss of her daughter, whose faulty genetic engineering shows that her mother has betrayed her cause.

Having flirted with Catholicism and Islam, she moves full circle, back to Ibino, her mystical beginnings, to a magical beach house where she recuperates, reassesses her options, and becomes initiated into her Mammywata calling, which she had unwittingly resisted. To end her watch over the sea, Wande Adebo, the charming prince, rescues and anchors her, completing her healing and training by initiating her into the unfathomable world of sex. After her return to Mammywata, she becomes spiritually charged to go north with him to their garden house, Abuja. If Mayen stands for Nigerian womanhood, Eno Obong clearly envisions woman's role as that of a social mother who dares to dream dreams about rehabilitating the country and puts her dreams into action through a cooperative effort.

Three men—Keki Tovu, Kabiri, and Wande—come into her life at crucial points in her growth, as men did with Efuru and Jane Eyre. Thus, houses and men help to shape Mayen's development, which is closely tied to her calling to establish a stable indigenous home/nation, as she has been taught by Keki and Mama Saro—who is appropriately from Freetown, Sierra Leone—to work for this cause. This womanist ethos thrives with the collaborative efforts of committed men and women. Eno Obong's use of flashbacks, the civil war background, and the constant movements in time and space capture the ripples of an unsettled, chaotic country. The dream house, that is, the ideal condition, will be realized with Mayen's and Wande's collaborative guidance.

To achieve her womanist ends, Eno Obong weaves an intricate *lappa* that covers characters from different parts of the country and the international community, so as not to isolate Mayen/Nigeria. Indeed, she shows that the children of the diaspora, like the ex-isled Bamidele, have a technological role to play in the new Nigeria. Religious, ethnic, and sexual differences; the rural, the urban, and the cosmopolitan dimensions in Nigeria; and the international economic axis represent the formidable forces that one has to battle with to achieve the goal.

Mayen turned weaver with a modern loom serves as Eno Obong's mouthpiece. Each weaves an elaborate net and, as a fisherwoman and Mammywata, catches a wide variety of fishes. The result is that *Garden House* is not claustrophobic, as its internationalism expresses Eno Obong's aesthetic principles. She seeks to draw Mayen-Nigeria away from the murky and crude past to a crystal-clear future that will earn her a respectable place among women and in the committee of nations.

In the pattern that emerges, Mayen serves as the woof that links the disparate parts. Her rape in the Catholic convent contrasts with Keki Tovu's brutal castration during an Islamic uprising. Keki grows mystical, ultimately becoming a savior, able to ward off evil. The magical power of his name, once uttered, saves Mayen from being raped again by Kabiri. By following Keki Tovu's precepts, Mayen grows spiritually. At last, she escapes from the materialistic, corrupt, and vicious, international business world of decadent Lagos, seeking respite by fleeing to the simple, indigenous world of Ibino. Here she is finally able to take the best out of Catholicism, merging it with Mammywata worship to form a new religion. Her other mentor, Mama Saro, who taught her to cherish things African, would have approved of the new religion, as it frees her from positions inimical to the emergence of the new woman/nation.

Other patterns emerge in further contrasts between the spiritually developing Mayen and the worldly wise and manipulative Alhaja Sherifat. The forthright, androgynous Keki Tovu sharply breaks from the devious path of Captain Nwoko Iweme. Wande Adebo, an architect by vocation, inherits Mayen, since her husband, Kabiri, enthralled in the money-making world, dies in the ruins of his foreign-based garden house with Iweme.

Lagos serves as a war zone because soldiers are in power. General Shaba's lack of control of his numerous children from different liaisons is symptomatic of the moral climate of the city and the country. His home front is a battleground, with his vengeful wife, Nkoyo, acting as the commanding officer. However, she brings a modicum of order into his chaotic life. As Mayen's relation, Nkoyo serves as an example that Mayen must not emulate, since Nkoyo's agenda of vengeance for civil war wrongs is so limiting and self-serving, a far cry from Mayen's (inter)national political plan.

Eno Obong starts off the novel ritualistically, respectfully calling to the sea to guarantee a fruitful voyage and a safe return, as an experienced storyteller should before telling a tortuous tale. Mayen is closely linked with the sea, an expanding symbol for birth and death, nurture, cleanliness, and moral uprightness. In this context, Mayen is Efuru's daughter. As Mammywata's favorite, Mayen attracts wealth to her husband, but she has the usual child-bearing problems. Like Efuru, Mayen's only daughter dies to make way for a new life. Mayen returns to her aquatic source, to cleanse herself from the corrupting contact with Lagos.

317

In her journey toward genuine Africanness, Wande Adebo is her male half. When they meet for the first time, like twins, both are identically dressed in safari suits, whose greenness marks their closeness to nature. Their *aso ebi* identifies them as belonging together, as two of a kind. Wande, an architect like Okoye's Dozie, also studied geology and so understands the African soil, knowledge denied Kabiri. Solidly grounded, Wande complements Mayen's water-centered identity. Eventually, he anchors the "wandering mermaid," to make her settle down in the final abode. Therefore, he has to rescue her from the up-and-down waterbed on which she and Kabiri act out a dreadful marital existence. The sickle-cell anemic child of that unfortunate union epitomizes the sickening association. The child's death not only marks the end of the union, but severs Mayen's association with Lagos and Alhaja Sherifat, after whom her child is named.

Wande and Mayen project Eno Obong's artistic vision as they design their own garden house and, in the process, make *Garden House* an aesthetic reality. As Mayen *talks* to Wande about the house, inspiriting it, Wande *records* her words by sketching her ideas. This unique artistic collaboration turns words into drawings; it proffers a new aesthetic dimension, which conflates the power of the spoken and written word with architectural vision. This fusion of a dream, its artistic conceptualization, and its realization in praxis establish the functional limits of African aesthetics. Eno Obong's perception of African art is one in which men and women must collaborate to produce a simple, functional, genuinely African artifact.

By contrast, Kabiri's garden house is grandiose and foreign. It is destined for destruction, just as Naira House, which serves as a lighthouse to the money-minded Kabiri, is gutted by fire in preparation for the purificatory closure. By burning Naira House, that is, the scheming monetary basis of the country, Eno Obong shows her disgust for money's corrupting influences. She draws attention to the rotten foundation of Kabiri's garden house by having the dead child, Blossom, buried in the garden. Since the house stands for neo-colonialism and its negative forces, its foundation on swampy soil indicates that it is not permanent. Built in Lagos, geographically near the shoreline and on the periphery, it will no longer be permitted to dominate the rest of the country, hence its collapse with the unscrupulous Kabiri and Iweme in it.

Wande and Mayen's garden house, the new Nigeria, is built on solid ground in the center of the country at Abuja. It is furnished with indigenous artifacts made of products from the Nigerian sea and land by Nigerian people from different walks of life. Women, like the divorcée Amina, black children from the diaspora like Bamidele, who has lived up to his name and returned home, and the outcasts of Lagos society, ordinary citizens, like Mayen and Wande, come together to form a force to establish a livable society. They are imbued with Mama Saro's womanist ideology that affirms freedom in engaging in African culture. Mama Saro dies in Freetown, free from the shackles of neocolonialism. As an ancestor and a pathfinder, she guides Mayen's destiny, before she died, ordering her back to Ibino.

The incident in the sea following Mayen's return to Ibino confirms her rebirth. She meets her parents in the whirlpool, which serves an amniotic function. After the labor to prevent herself from drowning, she is born, naked as a babe, her clothes lost in the undertow. Once again her Aunt Ime rescues her, this time with a difference. No longer abandoning her, together, they create a new religion by fusing tolerable aspects of Christianity with the local Mammywata worship. The reborn Mayen spins material from the sea, weaves it, sews it, and sends the finished product to Abuja for interior decoration. She connects Ibino with Abuja culturally, the drifting back and forth in rhythm with the sea refrain. Her sewing collective in the beach house reminds one of Alice Walker's *The Color Purple,* with Celie sewing not only to make a living, but for self-affirmation.

Eno Obong celebrates Mammywata, using Mayen as the village mascot, to underscore the fecundity of this phase of Mayen's existence. The religious festival brings all the villagers together in a memorable aquacade that signifies on Paule Marshall's carnival scene in *The Chosen Place, The Timeless People* (1984). The fertility festival ends appropriately with a sexual ritual, as Wande and Mayen consummate their relationship. Mammywata apparently approves, blessing them with a child. Wande's double-A genotype fuses with Mayen's defective gene to beget the healthy children who will dwell in the garden house, that is, Abuja/Nigeria/Africa/the black world.

In her subplot, continuing Nwapa's attack on Roman Catholicism in *One Is Enough* and Alkali's on Islam in *The Stillborn,* Eno Obong confronts both religions in a two-pronged onslaught, to bring down these bastions of female oppression. Her uneasiness about Alhaja Sherifat's Lagos-style feminism is demonstrated in having armed robbers beat her before the gates of her house. She survives, but walks with a limp, like Esu, her trickster self exposed to the naive and trusting Mayen.

Alhaja Sherifat and Amina, Mayen's friend, are two different faces of women in Islam. Amina, turned into a ghost of her real self by the sexist demands of Islam and hidden behind her clothes and veil, is neither seen nor heard. Though invisible, like oppressed Muslim women in Saadawi's novels, she has eyes through which she observes the inequities of the religion. Gradually, she begins to gain human form as she becomes infatuated, unfortunately, with Captain Nwoko Iweme, the first available male. Next, she learns to write. By inscribing herself in a letter to Mayen, she assumes a form with feelings. When, in that gripping scene between Amina and her husband Audu, she presents herself naked before him, melodramatically attired for his patriarchal role as defender of the Islamic faith, the reader remembers the Muslim fanatics who castrated Keki Tovu. The patriarchal Audu acts appropriately as the son of an Emir by protecting Islam from female corruptibility. His unwillingness to face her nakedness is Eno Obong's way of criticizing the religious praxis. He cannot stand the stench emanating from her private parts, wracked and torn apart during parturition, because he, as a fundamentalist, would not permit the only available doctor, a male, to attend her difficult labor.

Audu's repudiation of Amina is meant to be the ultimate insult from a husband turning a wife into an ex. In a subversive move, Amina too deals his ego the ultimate blow by declaring that she is a "left-over" from an affair with Iweme. Is Audu's heir Iweme's son? Although in Islam the child belongs to the marriage bed—that is, to the husband, even if he did not father him—the writer's silence on the question of bastardy is designed as a coup de grâce against religious fundamentalists and jihadists. It frees Amina.

Amina in purdah is akin to Mayen in the convent. Islam and Roman Catholicism fail to grasp the idea that man and woman were made to mate, yet can exercise self-control. The power of the word magically rescues both women: the mere idea of marriage opens Mayen's prison doors in the convent, just as the notion of adultery springs Amina's prison gates wide open. Through Amina, Eno Obong symbolically frees the women in purdah and heals women, even child brides, whose private parts have been ripped open by callous rapists and difficult births that make them stink from urinary incontinence.

The indigenous religion also undergoes a sea change. As I noted, the harsh aspect of that religion prevents people from mourning those lost in the sea and extending love to the orphaned Mayen. Restitution is made when, in the end, the love that is an implicit part of Christianity becomes part of the indigenous religion, enabling Mayen to become reintegrated into the society that had expelled her. The new religion is marked for its inclusiveness as it welcomes men, women, children, and outsiders.

Eno Obong's political thrust is based on cooperation across gender lines, economic independence, self-sufficiency, and freedom from corrupting postcolonial links. Her dream is to have a country with sweet mothers like Mayen, sweet freedom fighters like Amina, sophisticated children like Bamidele, reliable men like Wande, committed people like those recruited from Lagos, and economic and cultural links between the villages and the center; this is a womanist haven. Eno Obong's utopian garden house appears optimistically at the end of a line of women writers who deeply wish that Nigeria will develop into a position of strength, enabling her to liberate black men and women all over the world. Wande knows the "bedrock formations throughout the country"; in short, Africa's children know her very well and realize that the way to free all her peoples is to use progressive, indigenous methods to build the continent on solid foundations. For a first attempt, Eno Obong's *Garden House* is a solid realization of the womanist dreams passed down by her predecessors, Nwapa, Ulasi, Emecheta, Fakunle, Okoye, Alkali, and many others in the African continent and the diaspora. Yet, she too now lives in exile in the United States.

Simi Bedford: Home as Exile and Exile as Home

Simi Bedford's *Yoruba Girl Dancing* (1992), published in 1991, is a welcome addition to the Yoruba women's corpus in particular. It neatly ties up the textual/textile strands of the Nigerian novel by women, establishing itself as a part of the national *aso ebi*, with its own characteristic motifs. The novel is an excruciating search by an African girl, Remi Foster, for a place of her own in the world, while coping with the insecurities caused by the presence/absence of her fathers and mothers during her development.

As a descendant of former slaves who returned to Nigeria, and with a distinctive English surname to prove the historical British connection as well as a Yoruba given name entitling them to claim a place in Nigeria, like Eno Obong's Bamidele, Remi represents this special, *abiku* Nigerian community that straddles two cultures. In this capacity, she is a been-to par excellence. Surviving under Nigerian and British fosterage, as her last name clearly demonstrates, these descendants' multiculturalism is indicative of a deeply rooted ambivalence, manifest in their dual status as insiders and outsiders. Further, as a girl with the attendant gender limitations, Remi's painful lot is exacerbated by simultaneously (un)belonging, the perpetual longing to be in another place, and the feeling of being out of place or of belonging to several places at once. Thus, she is constantly searching for security. Occasionally, this is provided by sitting on the lap of her Grandma, who rules her household from her rocking chair in her courtyard, or by gossiping with her Grandpa at a breakfast table heavily laden with assorted fruits in his section of the house, or by scampering around in the company of her playmates in the main courtyard with its fruit trees. These Nigerian havens swiftly become memorialized when the little girl tries to find a special place on the *Ariel,* without another child on board, as she is magically transported from the Foster home to foster homes and school in England. Bundled off at age six, away from the relatives she knows, she has to bear the trauma of this cruel and unusual separation. She finally finds a home when her natural mother settles in England, her father having purchased a house for his entire nuclear family, as they rebarbarize the center in a countermove to colonize Britain.

By joining this new group consisting of Africa's and Britain's foster children, all remarkable for their bilingual names, Remi's political consciousness peaks. Now an adult narrator, she observes: "Yes, all of us from Lagos, and that includes some gorgeous men. You remember all those boys we used to know, Akin Williams, Olu Thompson, Wole Grant: they've all grown up. The girls are here too of course, Ayo Smith, Dele Hopkins, Alaba Jones, all in London" (Bedford 1992, 181). Carrying on synergetically in the place they have found for themselves, these offspring of former slave returnees, known in some Yoruba dialects as *Olukunmi,* shortened to *Lukumi,* "Beloved" (compare Cuban *Lucumi* and midwest Igbo *Onukwumi,* diasporan Yoruba still living among the Igbo in Delta State), form a formidable group with other displaced people of color from around the globe. Home is where they find themselves collected lovingly. As *abiku,* they claim a place of their own in Britain while being reassured that the other world, that is Africa, is also up for grabs.

For the first time in the Nigerian novel by women, a child serves as a first-person narrator, and, powerful griotte that she is, Remi tells her story effectively by contextualizing it geographically and historically. Writing from the perspective of this beloved girl's chatter, Bedford relays her gossip: "She says that the food in England have plenty magic, because Sisi Bola only stick out de back when she go, but she stick out the fron too like a elephant when she come back" (5). This graphically conveys the innocent child's ignorance of the politics of premarital pregnancy and its confusion with overeating in this text that is preoccupied with consumption. What one takes in, in the form of food or knowledge, becomes problematized throughout the text. Remi's continuously shifting perspective is fascinating as she starts off her story in Nigeria as a little girl in a large extended family. Shipped off at six to England, she continues to narrate her story up until her days as a law student in Britain. Trinh asserts cryptically in theorizing the first-person narrative position, "I am not I can be you and me" (1989, 90); this notion demonstrates the ramifications of Bedford's textual/textile project that include herself, her fictional character, and the reader, especially the westernized African woman. Bedford problematizes the geopolitical notion of the African woman by introducing Estelle Matthews, the white girl from South Africa, only to establish that, since Africa is synonymous in white minds with savagery and dark skin, Estelle cannot qualify to be African. But South African racialized politics is an aside in this ambitious book that flirts with different global issues.

At stake in all this is how to educate the Nigerian woman. To modify Nwapa's Nigerian Pidgin English adage: to go England no hard, na return. Bedford's novel is therefore addressed to the Nigerian nouveaux riches who think it fashionable and progressive to ship their children off to England at an early age without considering the psychological damage done to the children, not to mention that the few of them who return to Nigeria are usually maladjusted. Bedford dialogues with Dillibe Onyeama's *Nigger at Eton,* that autobiographical account by a Nigerian judge's son about his harrowing experience in the expensive and exclusionary English public school system. Unfortunately, Onyeama's saga has not made any difference in the thinking of rich Nigerians, since people in this class rarely read, busy as they are wheeling and dealing to amass wealth corruptly and be seen consuming it.

Where Remi's ancestors were sold into slavery, thereby bequeathing her with empathy for the Israelites and a mixed heritage of horror and pride for having survived exile and thrived, her tyrannical father voluntarily returns her into the status of the slave dependent by shipping her off to cold Britain to be schooled. She becomes transformed into an "Englishwoman," even acknowledged as such by English people. However, as a "darkie" with a skin color that the schoolchildren believe might tragically rub off on them, no extent of sophistication can ever make her racially acceptable to some of the teachers, boys, and, especially, to post–World War II Germans whom she visits.

Yoruba Girl Dancing affirms the notion of the palaver with the Germans as talking trivialities. Remi knows no German and her hosts know no English, so they can only communicate in single, choice words from a dictionary through which the old woman in the house finally manages to tell her, with the affirmation of the entire household, that she is black, *and* (not *but*) she is beautiful. For Bedford, who was a model, such affirmation is not only aesthetically progressive, it is psychologically reassuring. For Remi, however, it is unfortunately a setup, for one of the men of the house invades her privacy, feeding her chocolate in a sexually suggestive atmosphere. Bedford thus signifies on Aidoo's *Our Sister Killjoy,* while deconstructing the notion of Remi's status as an Englishwoman, as Remi believed she was. The Germans' actions confirm her place as "darkie," the ex-slave from "darkest Africa," in spite of Helene

323

Cixous' counterclaim; Remi is, therefore, sexually available. Other reminiscences of World War II resonate in this story set in the 1940s, preventing Remi's Jewish friend, Phoebe, from going on the trip to Germany. The long, checkered *abiku* Jewish history, partly recorded in the Bible that served as Remi's primer, helps her to empathize with the Jewish ostracism that intersects with hers. With the global sweep of the novel, the hostility maps out her position geographically and historically.

Remi's role as child-mediator amid the friendly fires of the dyarchic factions of her grandparents' household parallels Bedford's role as writer. Ogundipe-Leslie defines such a role succinctly when she observes that

> African writers are, in fact, caught in a double-faced fastness. Not only are they writing in a capitalist universe, they are writing in a colonial and neo-colonial one with all its attendant problems. Not only are they fighting the values of the ruling elite in their country, they are also fighting foreign influences. Yet as mentally colonised and alienated persons, they are often unconsciously judging their society by Western standards and imposing foreign values while at the same time trying to sell their indigenous values, their Africanity, to the West. For these reasons, they are writing in a foreign language, talking to the West while claiming to forge the uncreated consciousness of their race. And it is this African image presented by the African writer that is ironically the view of the Western world of Africa. (1994, 48)

Sometimes, Bedford's role does seem to be to bleach "darkest Africa" in order to make it acceptable to Europe and Remi's increasingly whitened eyes and thoughts. To this end, Bedford deconstructs continuing nineteenth-century notions of African mental incapacity, what we now refer to as the infamous findings of the Bell Curve, by making Remi a very bright student. Predictably, this does not alleviate the racism of her teachers, who expect only mediocrity or failure from her.

To further her purposes, Bedford therefore confines the Nigerian section of her novel to remnants of a Victorian Lagos in this fascinatingly doubly conscious household where Yoruba and English customs compete and overlap. She provides us with an occasional foray into the Nigerian interior into Enugu. Slight reminiscences of other uphill locations can be gleaned through such characters as the Muslim servant Nimota. She brings in "heathenism" (Bedford 1992, 17) by successfully visiting the lower-class Jankara market to consult the charismatic Mama Ibeji (mother of twins) for juju to ensure that she secures her sought-after boyfriend, Kemi, as husband. Remi accompanies Nimota for that crucial walk/work. From that initiation, Remi naturally obtains the talismanic protection to negotiate the palava terrains that await her in Europe as the following extract attests:

> As the old boy [Remi's English literature teacher] loves to point out, there's no written culture in my [Remi Foster's] country. I'm sure he thinks I'm using some kind of voodoo to woo the language to me in the same way Brabantio accused Othello of using spells on Desdemona. . . . Othello was destroyed . . . because his marrying Desdemona was seen as an attempt to become a Venetian, and the Venetians could not tolerate this in a black man. It has become increasingly obvious to me that if I do the same thing by trying to become one of you, I am likely to receive the same type of treatment. All this time I've been living in a fool's paradise and now I don't know who I am. It's a tragedy. (172–73)

By dealing with deeply entrenched racism that dates back to Shakespeare with its self-fulfilling, prophetic tones, Remi locates her place in religion, history, as well as literature, while prioritizing the problems that she faces as a black girl who should be dating in a hostile white country. Learning from Othello's marital tragedy, she must somehow transform the latest place of exile into a productive home. She succeeds through the magic of words by writing herself into the text. Mammywata's daughter sans long hair, which was shorn preparatory to going to England since the English would not know how to care for it, she magically closes the text by dancing as she had danced as a child at the beginning of the book while celebrating a wedding. She celebrates the finding of a prospective partner with the surprising, "I fell in love with Akin Williams at once" (182), and, as she dances, she gives the novel a somewhat Victorian ending that overlaps a happy Yoruba construct.

This last dance brings the story full circle. Not only does it remind us of the first dance to celebrate a Yoruba wedding with the pregnant Sisi Bola at the beginning of the novel, it contrasts sharply with the stiff waltz, quickstep, and uncoordinated rock-and-roll that pass for dance in Europe. An English wedding sans supple dance resembles a funeral; the only English dance that comes near to being comparable with the Nigerian needs alcohol to get it moving. Using stereotypes to deconstruct and build her case as she creates a narrative space, Bedford uses creative dance symbolically to portray a community at peace with itself. The marriage of the young and the old in the newly formed colony in England of people of color from different parts of the globe, with particular reference to the migratory habits of been-tos, affirms Remi's prospects. Her reacquainted boyfriend, Akin, remarks, "We have survived, and very soon we can all go home" (185); perhaps. The final words of the novel move us to the beginning while creating an end and a new beginning: "How we danced. The music poured through our veins and we flowed with the beat. The wheel had come full circle. We wound and unwound our bodies seamlessly as if we had no bones. Is there a sight more beautiful, the older women said, than a Yoruba girl dancing?" (ibid.). The rhetorical question grapples with the stereotype of blacks and dancing while affirming its ritualistic, spiritual purpose.

Remi represents the whole of West Africa with a Fante princess as her paternal grandmother, the son of returnees as a paternal grandfather, superimposed on Sierra Leonean and Gambian matrilineal connections. They are all grounded in Nigerian soil. Furthermore, one stepgrandparent is from the British working class—Bigmama, who prefers to be called "Aunty," in an effort to dissociate herself from her black in-laws. Remi's favorite mother, Grandma, is really a stepgrandmother, who becomes apotheosized and acts reassuringly as her *Chi* and comforter (83, 95) in the lonely, dreary days of her arrival at school in England, where she is emotionally motherless. In her narrative, Remi presents a world of sharp contrasts between Lagos/Nigeria and England. Her palatial ancestral home with its courtyards, the men's section marked off from the women's, differs remarkably from the tiny working-class houses and cold schools that become her abode in England. The latter generate insecurity because they are forever shifting, based as they are on an economics of affection. Surplus food in Lagos gives way to the rationing of postwar England. Here, her favorite dishes, such as the Sierra Leonean plasas—"crain crain"—that is the Yoruba *ewedu,* can only be remembered. Another favorite, rice and soup, masquerades as rice pudding, with its milk and sugar, that her white foster parent, Aunty Betty, produces in an attempt to please her. The lack of an English palava sauce poses a great deal of culinary problems for Remi's palate and growth; with a lot of palava, she is inevitably transformed into an Englishwoman. In the end, her inefficient mother begins to cope with housekeeping, and we smell the stews cooking in their new kitchen as Remi gradually becomes detoxified from being an Englishwoman and blossoms, like the many flowers in one of her schools, into an Afro-Englishwoman.

During her metamorphosis, clothes also perform an important function. "Serious jewellery" (18) and clothes form the center of middle-class, Yoruba women's lives, with the *aso ebi* playing a significant role. Clothes therefore abound in the Yoruba section of the text, with fabrics from different parts of the globe, to hand-woven Yoruba *aso oke,* worn in full regalia. By contrast, Remi is always badly clothed in England. Her oversized raincoat, the "tortoise house" or "rubber house" (60, 68), chosen by her white Bigmama, encases the ashy, flaky skin of the black girl—this white woman, despite having brought up black stepchildren, still does not know how to care for a black child's toilet in the harsh British weather. Remi's unfashionable swim wear and tasteless, hand-me-down uniforms complete the grim picture. Where her Nigerian mothers are flamboyant in their profusion of clothes, her English foster mothers are remarkable for their lack of taste. The rock-like Aunty Betty is encased in corsets, mortifying both her flesh and her spirit. Her white foster mothers thus have no clue as to the aesthetics of presenting a Yoruba girl for possible dancing nor do they dress her appropriately for enjoying the essence of life.

In spite of her Dickensian humor and reminders of aspects of Soyinka's *Ake,* Bedford's text signifies on Ama Ata Aidoo's *Our Sister Killjoy,* while Bedford is in turn signified on by Emecheta in *Kehinde.* Deviating from Aidoo, Bedford and, later, Emecheta have their been-to characters opt for colonizing England instead of making a firm return to Nigeria. As the last writer to come out in *aso ebi,* Bedford ties the motifs all together very neatly, establishing a sense of belonging with all these writers. Like the others, she deals with deeply rooted problems such as racism, sexism, classism, the relationship between fathers and daughters, and the establishment of a respectable place for the African in the world.

In her woman's struggle against these sites of oppression, Remi tackles the concept of Africa invented by the *National Geographic* magazine (163) and the notion of Britain as "civilized" by constantly using animal images for blacks and whites as a sign of our mammalian classification. Whites are referred to somewhere as "porcine" (78), "giant turtle" (102), "shelled crabs" (110), "huge bear" (113), with Tarzan, no less, living with chimps/monkeys (90). Africans, particularly Remi, hardly fare better. Besides being a tortoise, Remi is also growing into a "wild animal"/"baboon" (128), "the Gorilla" (165), while foster children get replaced like "shark's teeth" (9).

However, the child-friendly, welcoming, open spaces of Nigeria with its many willing mothers, public and private, contrast sharply with the child-hostile, cold, cramped spaces of England. The now emotionally motherless Remi, fostered by preoccupied white women, has to learn to negotiate the racist terrains with the traditional trickster tortoise as teacher. At the heart of this discourse is the nature of the African child's education. Is it to her advantage

327

to become anglicized? Remi resists this process, even as she temporarily succumbs to its polarizing notion when she is paradoxically referred to by the
adults as either an Englishwoman or an African. Dismantling this, she finally sees herself as both African and English. Remi had already learned a lot
before leaving Nigeria, an informal education that withstands all the emotional battering that she receives in her English schools and communities. She
turns out to be an unwilling learner in the British system, her resistance
punctuated by unheard screams at the beginning of her initiation into British
mysteries which obviously are not psychologically and culturally sound for
an African. The images of containment aboard the *Ariel,* the terror of being
drowned, with the image of women's struggle with the uniformed and tyrannical Miss Smith, are prelude to what lies ahead for her. Being thrown into icy
waters and wallowing in mud during one memorable English vacation underscore her displacement.

To survive in this game, she has to deconstruct the stereotypes of barbarism
implicit in Tarzanism, while stressing the cruelty of the white gaze (86) and
speech for the black girl. To survive, she has to employ *siddon look* tactics like
her embattled Grandma; temporarily she belongs neither to the English world
nor the now distant, erstwhile familiar Nigerian world:

> As I would not be drawn and continued as it were to *play dead,* I
> soon ceased to be of interest, and general conversation was re-
> sumed. I sat with the other two new girls in contemplative silence.
> . . . Instead of wishing I could be back at home, I only wanted to be
> back safely behind the door of the junior sitting room.
>
> Grandma would have been disappointed—she would have ex-
> pected me to speak up for myself—and Yowande would have been
> scornful. It was easy for them, they were safe *at home.* (87; my em-
> phasis)

By playing the *abiku,* she manages to remain safe in England through accessing the Nigerian cultural imaginary. Her friend Jessica unwittingly plays the
role of Mammywata, as a "watersprite," "whose hair gleamed silver and
whose white skin shone green in the hollows of her elbows and knees. . . . From
the very first night . . . she had given every indication in sidelong looks and
glances, and an interest in everything I had to say, that she was as fascinated
by me as I was by her" (88). This mutual fascination of two Mammywata figures aids Remi to overcome the trauma of being outside her elements. Stereotypically, with her athletic feats, her "*apotheosis* was completed on Sports Day
at the end of summer term" (95; my emphasis), though it becomes overshad-

owed by the embarrassment of having a white, working-class foster mother visit her in her upper-class, private school. However, her inability to sing like Paul Robeson, though she is black and all blacks are supposed to be able to sing, deals a curious blow to Western, fixed categorizations of blacks.

In Bedford's games with the traditional assignment of place to people, the novel opens by emphasizing the oral dimension: "Africans can talk oh!" (1). Of course, she counters the idea by accessing a scribal heritage by *writing* the novel. In the writing, she makes use of the four languages she had acquired in the Nigerian household: her Yoruba, her Nigerian Pidgin English, her Nigerian English, with its "towering Nigerian vowels," which her elocution teacher, Miss Clifford-Broughton, "successfully razed to the ground" (101) in order to anglicize her, and her King's English. The talk is, of course, punctuated by necessary silences, as Remi continually plays the eavesdropper and the voyeur in order to have titillating information to pass on to the reader.

The tragedy of her English education becomes patently clear at the point when Remi receives two gentlemen as visitors. Though one of them is her father, she fails to place them. This inability of the Western-educated woman to identify and place the father speaks to the problem that womanism has tried to address: the fact that black women also need to study their fathers as an essential part of their curriculum for wholesomeness. Unfortunately, Remi's father, Simon Foster, is not only tyrannical with his authority to imprison people as Lord Chief Justice in Nigeria, he has no sense of direction, as is evidenced by his constant inability to negotiate English terrains, a metaphor for his ignorance of what an English education and life are really about. His laughter while (proudly or embarrassedly) exclaiming about his daughter, "She has become an Englishwoman," only for Remi to comment, "But they would never know what it had cost me" (131), addresses the point of male ignorance of the female perspective. The lack of understanding and a united front complicates the wo/man palava. For one who administers law to so delegitimize his daughter by banishing her to his parents because of her wrong gender, then seemingly favoring her by sending her off to school in England, his parenting is criminal. Its conflicting signals show that, as a father, he has violated his daughter in the name of education.

The constant confusion of her gender, as she is mistaken for a boy, is a problem that Remi faces in addition to the racism in European societies. Thus the gender aspect intersects with the racial dilemma of being an African in appearance, though European by acculturation. What is wrong with being an African in Europe? How does a black woman with short hair negotiate the sexual divide? These are some of the questions that Bedford raises. The answer for Remi on her visit to Germany is the characteristic Fanonic nervous condition: "It was a great relief to spend a few hours recuperating at the farm before the return journey when the road users behaved in precisely the same way [coming out of their cars to stand and stare at her], so that I went to bed that night suffering from acute paranoia" (166–67). Later, her host, Herr Schofbeck, creeps through the "*french* window" (167; my emphasis) to molest her with unwanted sexual attentions.

Fortunately for the reader, like Tsitsi Dangarembga's Tambu and Nyasha in her novel *Nervous Conditions* (1988), that "acute paranoia," which, also for Emecheta, inspires and drives the author into a state of urgency that makes the writing or talking of a text possible, is what compels Remi-Bedford to tell this harrowing story of the consequences of exile. The resulting text can be considered "serious jewellery" for its preciousness. Not having the luxury of independence that Aidoo's Sissie possesses, however, Remi makes do with England, now that her biological mother and othermothers have come to watch her, and others like her, study and, especially, dance. Dance in this context implies leading a life controlled by the poetry of motion. The final dance doubles as a public exorcism of European devilry; as such, it is a sign of recuperation. It reinforces the fact that the been-to/*abiku* has chosen somewhere to stay with the psychological support of her African mothers, literal and literary.

I can only say to Simi Bedford, welcome to the fold: so wide is the Nigerian *lappa* as a spread that it can cover us all. We must also remember that the palava spread doubly refers to the untying of our mothers' tongues preparatory to eating and speaking out.

•

As the palava grows more complicated and professional Nigerians flee the country in great numbers, the question of gender inequities is almost irrelevant in the face of national disintegration and the hardships and suffering every Nigerian, except a select few, face. The palava is not whether people should be liberated, for that point is taken for granted by the writers' courage in tackling different manifestations of oppression of women, men, and children. The moot points are how to free the children from the trauma of racism and ethnicism, stem the terror of militarism, totalitarianism, and political chaos, tackle the poverty engendered by international economics, and eliminate the waste in human resources resulting from sexism. The writers have advanced the palaver to the stage where we must not only dream but must use women's texts to deliver more formidable blows for political, social, and psychosexual liberation. The audience should respond to make the palaver productive and constructive. Helen Chukwuma (1988, 38) recognizes the responsibility of the audience, and she affirms it with the pun in the pithy Igbo saying: "*Anu akaghi, na egbu okenye; aka anughi, na egbu nwata.* Hearing and not talking kills an elder; but talking and not heeding kills a child."

Holding Fire: For Home and Country

Nigeria, Athena-like, popped out of Lord Lugard's head without the would-be Nigerians participating in the birthing process. In the absence of the patriarch, the result has been a monstrous polygynous household, incapacitated with petty rivalries, perpetually at war with itself. What is called for at this juncture of our dilemma is to play out the politics of the polygynous household, with a mother in charge of each small unit; this means decentralization and the establishment of a womanist essence at each center with the units' collaboration, because we know that, if the big household collapses, we go with it. If we play our politics shrewdly, as men and women, we can live to honor our mothers and encourage fathers, who conveniently absent themselves for a while when there is trouble, to accept responsibility. This is homecoming time; we must put the house we inherited in order.

This book is, therefore, dedicated by me in hope and good will to my siblings, especially my brothers, in Nigeria and beyond, still reading in the dark. May I remind you of a cryptic remark by Zora Neale Hurston, who conjured up metaphors, hoodoo, and, in desperation, introduced a gun to defend a woman in *Their Eyes Were Watching God* while handling a debacle similar to ours: "YOU HEARD HER, YOU AIN'T BLIND" (1978, 123; my emphasis).

My mother, Dora Mgbolie Chikwenye Okocha Okonjo, wove the traditional Ogwashi-Uku white cloth, which she ritually gave to each of her seven children as part of a heritage. I lost all my *lappa* during some of the six burglaries I endured at the University of Ibadan campus, before I escaped into exile, to the safety of Amherst College and Sarah Lawrence College. By this time, my mother was too old to weave another set to replace what was stolen. However, she viewed the experience philosophically, commenting that perhaps whoever finally got to own the stolen goods desperately needs them to complete the reading of the lines on their palm, to establish their destiny. Thus, I have some unknown "relatives" clandestinely sharing my heritage. They are welcome to the circle, in the hope that they will learn to respect it. I also lost another priceless possession, a set of Akwete cloth woven by the mother of one of my students. I tried to replace these by purchasing textiles similar to them, but they have never meant the same sentimentally, because the weavers were anonymous. With time, I have come to accept these unknown women also as mothers who have helped me to get over a horrendous period of my life. With the writing of this book, I deal with my disappearing heritage; I have tried to reciprocate by weaving them and other invisible mothers like them into this text to prepare me for sojourn not just in my father's house, like Appiah, nor yet in my mothers' house, with its separatist subtext, but, with a womanist zeal, in our parents' house. Here we can continue our palaver, because I expect some response to this book in the form of words and action, if we are to avert another Algeria, Kenya, Sudan, Ethiopia, South Africa, Liberia, Somalia, Rwanda, Zaire, Haiti. . . . We must dare to look into the haunting eyes of our children from these countries and others, then search our soul. Siblings always have some palava; my hope is that our house will be salvaged, to establish a womanist ethos after the community partakes of the ritualistic peace offering, my palava sauce and all those by women writers that made mine possible. Together, brothers and sisters, we can cook up more nurturing recipes at home, for us and all the children. How long must we play the fool in front of everybody?

NDI B'ANYI, KWENU.

Works Cited

Abanime, E. P. 1986. Ideologies on Race and Sex in Literature: Racism and Anti-Racism in the African Francophone Novel. *College Language Association Journal* 30 (2): 125–43.

Abel, Elizabeth, ed. 1982. *Writing and Sexual Difference*. Chicago: University of Chicago Press.

Abiodun, Rowland. 1987a. The Future of African Art Studies: An African Perspective. *African Art Studies: The State of the Disciplin*. Paper presented at a symposium organized by the National Museum of African Art, Smithsonian Institution, Washington, D.C. September 16.

———. 1987b. Verbal and Visual Metaphors: Mythical Allusions in Yoruba Ritualistic Art of *Ori*. *Word and Image* 3 (3) (September): 252–70.

———. 1989. Woman in Yoruba Religious Images. *African Languages and Cultures* 2 (1): 1–18.

Achebe, Chinua. 1958. *Things Fall Apart*. London: Heinemann.

———. 1976. Chi in Igbo Cosmology. Pp. 131–45 in *Morning Yet on Creation Day*. New York: Anchor Books.

———. 1988 [1987]. *Anthills of the Savannah*. New York: Anchor Press.

Acholonu, Catherine. 1989. Ogbanje: A Motif and a Theme in the Poetry of Christopher Okigbo. Pp. 103–11 in *Oral and Written Poetry in African Literature Today*, vol. 16, ed. Eldred Durosimi Jones, Eustace Palmer, and Marjorie Jones. Trenton, N.J.: Africa World Press.

Aidoo, Ama Ata. 1985 [1970]. *Anowa*. Burnt Mill, Harlow, UK: Longman.

———. 1985 [1965]. *Dilemma of a Ghost*. Burnt Mill, Harlow, UK: Longman.

———. 1977. *Our Sister Killjoy, or Reflections from a Black-eyed Squint*. Burnt Mill, Harlow, UK: Longman.

———. 1981. Unwelcome Pals and Decorative Slaves—Or Glimpses of Women as Writers and Characters in Contemporary African Literature. *Medium and Message: Proceedings of the International Conference on African Literature and the English Language*, vol. 1, 17–37. Calabar, Nigeria: University of Calabar.

———. 1992. The African Woman Today—An Overview. Keynote Address delivered at the First International Conference on Women in Africa and the African Diaspora: Bridges Across Activism and the Academy. University of Nigeria, Nsukka, July 13–18.

Akinsanya, Justus A. 1987. *An African 'Florence Nightingale': A Biography of Kofoworola A. Pratt*. Ibadan: Vantage.

Ali, Shahrazad. 1990. *The Black Man's Guide to Understanding the Black Woman*. Philadelphia, Pa.: Civilized Publications.

Alkali, Zaynab. 1984. *The Stillborn.* Lagos: Longman.

———. 1987. *The Virtuous Woman.* Lagos: Longman.

Amadi, Elechi. 1986. *Estrangement.* Ibadan: Heinemann.

Amadiume, Ifi. 1987. *Male Daughters, Female Husbands: Gender and Sex in an African Society.* London: Zed Books.

Andrade, Susan Z. 1990. Rewriting History, Motherhood, and Rebellion: Naming an African Women's Literary Tradition. *Research in African Literatures* 21 (1) (Spring): 91–110.

Anozie, Sunday O. 1984. Negritude, Structuralism, Deconstruction. Pp. 102–25 in *Black Literature and Literary Theory,* ed. Henry Louis Gates, Jr. New York: Methuen.

Anyidoho, Kofi. 1982. Kofi Awoonor and the Ewe Tradition of Songs of Abuse *(Halo.)* Pp. 17–29 in *Toward Defining the African Aesthetic,* ed. Lemuel A. Johnson and Mildred Hill-Lubin. Washington, D.C.: Three Continents Press.

Appiah, Kwame Anthony. 1992. *In My Father's House: Africa in the Philosophy of Culture.* New York: Oxford University Press.

Armstrong, Robert G. 1979. The Public Meeting as a Means of Participation in Political and Social Activities in Africa. Pp. 11–26 in *Socio-political Aspects of the Palaver in Some African Countries.* UNESCO.

Awe, Bolanle. 1985. The Humanity of the Yoruba Goddess Osun: An Introductory Note. Paper presented at the Institute of African Studies Seminar series, University of Ibadan. April 17.

Awkward, Michael. 1989. Appropriative Gestures: Theory and Afro-American Literary Criticism. Pp. 238–46 in *Gender and Theory: Dialogues on Feminist Criticism,* ed. Linda Kauffman. Oxford: Basil Blackwell.

Ba, Mariama. 1981. *So Long a Letter,* trans. Modupe Bode-Thomas. Ibadan: New Horn Press, 1981. Originally published in French as *Une Si Longue Lettre* (1980).

———. 1986. *Scarlet Song,* trans. Dorothy S. Blair. Burnt Mill, Harlow, UK: Longman. Originally published in French as *Un Chant Ecarlate* (1981).

Babangida, Maryam. 1988. *The Home Front: Nigerian Army Officers and Their Wives.* Ibadan: Fountain.

Baines, Elizabeth. 1986. Naming the Fictions. Pp. 175–77 in *Feminist Literary Theory: A Reader,* ed. Mary Eagleton. Oxford: Basil Blackwell.

Baker, Houston A., Jr. 1984. *Blues, Ideology, and Afro-American Literature: A Vernacular Theory.* Chicago: University of Chicago Press.

———. N.d. 'There Is No More Beautiful Way': Theory and the Poetics of Afro-American Women's Writing. Manuscript.

Banyiwa-Horne, Naana. 1986. African Womanhood: The Contrasting Perspectives of Flora Nwapa's *Efuru* and Elechi Amadi's *The Concubine.* Pp. 119–29 in *Ngambika: Studies of Women in African Literature,* ed. Carole Boyce Davies and Anne Adams Graves. Trenton, N.J.: Africa World Press.

Barrett, Michele. 1986. Feminism and the Definition of Cultural Politics. Pp. 160–63 in *Feminist Literary Theory: A Reader,* ed. Mary Eagleton. Oxford: Basil Blackwell.

Barthes, Roland. 1977. The Death of the Author. Pp. 142–48 in *Image—Music—Text,* trans. Stephen Heath. New York: Hill and Wang.

Bascom, William. 1991. *Ifa Divination: Communication between Gods and Men in West*

Africa. Bloomington and Indianapolis: Indiana University Press.

Bedford, Simi. 1992 [1991]. *Yoruba Girl Dancing.* New York: Penguin.

Beier, Ulli. 1980. *Yoruba Myths.* Cambridge: Cambridge University Press.

Beauvoir, Simone de. 1972. *The Second Sex,* trans. and ed. H. M. Parshley. Harmondsworth: Penguin.

Bennett, Paula. 1993. Critical Clitoridectomy: Female Sexual Imagery and Feminist Psychoanalytic Theory. *Signs: Journal of Women in Culture and Society* 18 (2) (Winter): 235–59.

Benstock, Shari, ed. 1987. *Feminist Issues in Literary Scholarship.* Bloomington and Indianapolis: Indiana University Press.

Berg, Maggie. 1984. Song of Lerwins. London: Heinemann.

———. 1991. Luce Irigaray's "Contradictions": Poststructuralism and Feminism. *Signs: Journal of Women in Culture and Society.* 17 (1) (Autumn): 50–70.

p'Bitek, Okot. 1984. *Song of Lawino* and *Song of Ocol.* London: Heinemann.

Bloom, Harold. 1973. *The Anxiety of Influence: A Theory of Poetry.* Oxford: Oxford University Press.

Braxton, Joanne M., and Andree Nicola McLaughlin, eds. 1990. *Wild Women in the Whirlwind: Afra-American Culture and the Contemporary Literary Renaissance.* New Brunswick, N.J.: Rutgers University Press.

Bryce, Jane. 1988. A Feminist Study of Fiction by Nigerian Women Writers. Ph.D. diss., Obafemi Awolowo University, Ile-Ife.

Brown, Elsa Barkley. 1989. Womanist Consciousness: Maggie Lena Walker and the Independent Order of Saint Luke. *Signs: Journal of Women in Society and Culture* 14 (3) (Spring): 610–33.

Brown, Lloyd. 1981. *Women Writers in Black Africa.* Westport, Conn.: Greenwood Press.

Busia, Abena P. B. 1988. Words Whispered Over Voids: A Context for Black Women's Rebellious Voices in the Novel of the African Diaspora. Pp. 1–41 in *Studies in Black American Literature, vol. 3: Black Feminist Criticism and Critical Theory,* ed. Joe Weixlmann and Houston A. Baker Jr. Greenwood, Fla.: Penkevill Publishing.

Callaway, Barbara J. 1976. Women in Ghana. Pp. 189–201 in *Women in the World: A Comparative Study,* ed. Lynne B. Iglitzin and Ruth Ross. Santa Barbara: Clio Books.

Callaway, Helen. 1987. *Gender, Culture and Empire: European Women in Colonial Nigeria.* London and Basingstoke: Macmillan.

Caskey, Noelle. 1986. Interpreting Anorexia Nervosa. Pp. 175–89 in *The Female Body in Western Culture: Contemporary Perspectives,* ed. Susan Rubin Suleiman. Cambridge, Mass.: Harvard University Press.

Chinweizu, Onwuchekwa Jemie, and Ihechukwu Madubuike. 1983. *Toward the Decolonization of African Literature.* Washington, D.C.: Howard University Press.

Chodorow, Nancy. 1978. *The Reproduction of Mothering: Psychoanalysis and the Sociology of Gender.* Berkeley and Los Angeles: University of California Press.

Christian, Barbara. 1989. The Race for Theory. Pp. 225–37 in *Gender and Theory: Dialogues on Feminist Criticism,* edited by Linda Kauffman. Oxford: Basil Blackwell.

Chukwuma, Helen. 1988. Aspects of Style in Igbo Oral Literature. Pp. 31–52 in *Introductory Readings in the Humanities and Social Sciences,* ed. Gloria Chukukere.

Onitsha: University Publishing.

Cixous, Helene. 1976. The Laugh of the Medusa, trans. Keith Cohen and Paula Cohen. *Signs: Journal of Women in Culture and Society* 1 (4) (Summer): 875–93. Reprinted in *Feminisms: An Anthology of Literary Theory and Criticism,* ed. Robyn R. Warhol and Diane Price Herndl, 334–49. New Brunswick, N.J.: Rutgers University Press, 1991.

Clark, John Pepper. 1964. *Three Plays: Song of a Goat, The Masquerade, The Raft.* London: Oxford University Press.

———. 1988. Abiku. In *A Selection of African Poetry,* introduced and annotated by K. E. Senanu and T. Vincent, 205. Essex, England: Longman.

Coker, Folarin. 1987. *A Lady: A Biography of Lady Oyinkan Abayomi.* Ibadan: Evans Brothers.

Conde, Maryse. 1972. Three Female Writers in Modern Africa: Flora Nwapa, Ama Ata Aidoo, Grace Ogot. *Presence Africaine* 2:136–39, 143.

Crowder, Diane Griffin. 1983. Amazons and Mothers? Monique Wittig, Helene Cixous and Theories of Women's Writing. *Contemporary Literature* 24 (Summer): 117–44.

Cudjoe, Selwyn R. 1988. *R. V. S. Naipaul: A Nationalist Reading.* Amherst: University of Massachusetts Press.

d'Almeida, Irene Assiba. 1986. The Concept of Choice in Mariama Ba's Fiction. Pp. 161–71 in *Ngambika: Studies of Women in African Literature,* ed. Carole Boyce Davies and Anne Adams Graves. Trenton, N.J.: Africa World Press.

Dangarembga, Tsitsi. 1988. *Nervous Conditions.* Seattle: Seal Press.

Dateline. December 27, 1993–January 9, 1994. *West Africa* 3979:2355.

Dathorne, O. R. 1975. *African Writers in the Twentieth Century.* London: Heinemann Books.

———. 1976. *African Literature in the Twentieth Century.* Minneapolis: University of Minnesota Press.

Davies, Carole Boyce. 1986. Introduction: Feminist Consciousness and African Literary Criticism. Pp. 1–23 in *Ngambika: Studies of Women in African Literature,* ed. Carole Boyce Davies and Anne Adams Graves. Trenton, N.J.: Africa World Press.

Davies, Carole Boyce, and Anne Adams Graves, eds. 1986. *Ngambika: Studies of Women in African Literature.* Trenton, N.J.: Africa World Press.

Davis, Angela Y. 1983. *Women, Race and Class.* New York: Vintage Books.

Dinnerstein, Dorothy. 1976. *The Mermaid and the Minotaur: Sexual Arrangement and Human Malaise.* New York: Harper and Row.

Diong, Bakomba Katik. 1979. The Palaver in Zaire. Pp. 77–93 in *Socio-Political Aspects of the Palaver in Some African Countries. UNESCO.*

Donovan, Josephine. 1987. Toward a Women's Poetics. Pp. 98–109 in *Feminist Issues,* ed. Shari Benstock. Bloomington and Indianapolis: Indiana University Press.

Drewal, Henry John, and Margaret Thompson Drewal. 1990. *Gelede: Art and Female Power among the Yoruba.* Bloomington: Indiana University Press.

Driver, Dorothy. 1982. Feminist Literary Criticism. Pp. 203–13 in *An Introduction to Contemporary Literary Theory,* ed. Rory Ryan and Susan van Zyl. Johannesburg: Ad Donker.

Eagleton, Mary, ed. 1986. *Feminist Literary Theory: A Reader*. Oxford: Basil Blackwell.

Echeruo, Michael J. C. 1977. *Victorian Lagos: Aspects of Nineteenth Century Lagos Life*. London: Macmillan.

Ekwensi, Cyprian. 1976. *Survive the Peace*. London: Heinemann.

———. 1979. *Jagua Nana*. London: Heinemann.

Elugbe, B. O., and A. P. Omamor. 1991. *Nigerian Pidgin: Background and Prospects*. Ibadan: Heinemann Educational Books.

Emecheta, Buchi. 1972. *In the Ditch*. London: Allison and Busby.

———. 1977. *The Slave Girl*. New York: George Braziller.

———. 1979. *The Joys of Motherhood*. New York: George Braziller.

———. 1980a. *The Bride Price*. Glasgow: Fontana Books.

———. 1980b. *Second-Class Citizen*. Glasgow: Fontana Books.

———. 1982a. *Double Yoke*. London and Nigeria: Ogwugwu Afor.

———. 1982b. A Nigerian Writer Living in London. *Kunapipi* 4 (1): 116–17.

———. 1982c. *Naira Power*. London: Macmillan.

———. 1983a. *Destination Biafra*. London: Fontana Books.

———. 1983b. *The Rape of Shavi*. New York: George Braziller.

———. 1986a. *Head Above Water*. London: Fontana Books.

———. 1986b. *A Kind of Marriage*. London: Macmillan.

———. 1990. *The Family*. New York: George Braziller.

———. 1994. *Kehinde*. Portsmouth, N.H.: Heinemann.

Emenyonu, Ernest N. 1988. The Rise and Development of Igbo Literature. Pp. 33–38 in *Perspectives on Nigerian Literature*, ed. Yemi Ogunbiyi. Lagos: Guardian Books.

Enekwe, O. O. 1988. Interview with 'Zulu Sofola. *Okike: An African Journal of New Writing* 27/28 (March): 56–66.

Evans, Mari, ed. 1983. *Black Women Writers (1950–1980)*. New York: Doubleday.

Evans, Martha Noel. 1985. Writing as Difference in Violette Leduc's Autobiography *La Batarde*. Pp. 306–17 in *The (M)other Tongue*, ed. Shirley Nelson Garner, Claire Kahane, and Madelon Sprengnether. Ithaca, N.Y.: Cornell University Press.

Fakunle, Funmilayo. 1978. *The Sacrificial Child*. Oshogbo: Fakunle Major Press.

———. 1980. *Chasing the Shadow*. Oshogbo: Fakunle Major Press.

———. 1983. *Chance or Destiny?* Oshogbo: Fakunle Major Press.

Farwell, Marilyn R. 1988. Toward a Definition of the Lesbian Literary Imagination. *Signs: Journal of Women in Culture and Society* 14 (1) (Autumn): 100–118.

Fayemi, Olufunmilayo. 1981. Placing Mabel Segun in the Proper Perspective. *The Guardian*, March 5, p. 37.

Felman, Shoshana. 1993. *What Does a Woman Want? Reading and Sexual Difference*. Baltimore: Johns Hopkins University Press.

Foucault, Michel. 1977. What Is an Author? Pp. 113–38 in *Language, Counter-memory, Practice: Selected Essays and Interviews*, ed. Donald F. Bouchard; trans. Donald F. Bouchard and Sherry Simon. Ithaca, N.Y.: Cornell University Press.

———. 1986. *Death and the Labyrinth: The World of Raymond Roussel*. Translated by Charles Ruas. Garden City, N.Y.: Doubleday.

Frank, Katherine. 1984. Feminist Criticism and the African Novel. *African Literature Today* 14:34–48.

———. 1987. Women Without Men: The Feminist Novel in Africa. Pp. 14–34 in

Women in African Literature Today, no. 15, ed. Eldred Durosimi Jones, Eustace Palmer, and Marjorie Jones. Trenton, N.J.: Africa World Press.

Friedan, Betty. 1965. *The Feminine Mystique.* Harmondsworth: Penguin.

Friedman, Susan Stanford. 1991. Creativity and the Childbirth Metaphor: Gender Difference in Literary Discourse. Pp. 371–96 in *Feminisms: An Anthology of Literary Theory and Criticisms,* ed. Robyn R. Warhol and Diane Price Herndl. New Brunswick, N.J.: Rutgers University Press.

Gallop, Jane. 1987. Reading the Mother Tongue: Psychoanalytic Feminist Criticism. *Critical Inquiry* 13 (2) (Winter): 314–29.

Gardiner, Judith Kegan. 1982. On Female Identity and Writing by Women. Pp. 177–91 in *Writing and Sexual Difference,* ed. Elizabeth Abel. Chicago: University of Chicago Press.

———. 1985. Mind Mother: Psychoanalysis and Feminism. Pp. 113–45 in *Making a Difference: Feminist Literary Criticism,* ed. Gayle Greene and Coppelia Kahn. London: Methuen.

Garner, Shirley Nelson. 1985. "Women Together" in Virginia Woolf's Night and Day. Pp. 318–33 in *The (M)other Tongue,* ed. Shirley Neslon Garner, Claire Kahane, and Madelon Sprengnether. Ithaca, N.Y.: Cornell University Press.

Garner, Shirley Nelson, Claire Kahane, and Madelon Sprengnether, eds. 1985. *The (M)other Tongue: Essays in Feminist Psychoanalytic Interpretation.* Ithaca, N.Y.: Cornell University Press.

Gates, Henry Louis, Jr. 1988. *The Signifying Monkey: A Theory of Afro-American Literary Criticism.* New York: Oxford University Press.

———, ed. 1984. *Black Literature and Literary Theory.* New York: Methuen.

Giddings, Paula. 1992. The Last Taboo. Pp. 441–65 in *Race-ing Justice, En-gendering Power: Essays on Anita Hill, Clarence Thomas, and the Construction of Social Reality,* ed. Toni Morrison. New York: Pantheon Books.

Gilbert, Sandra M., and Susan Gubar. 1987. *No Man's Land: The Place of the Woman Writer in the Twentieth Century,* vol. 1: *The War of the Words.* New Haven: Yale University Press.

Gillespie, Diane, and Missy Dehn Kubitschek. 1990. Who Cares? Women-Centered Psychology in *Sula. Black American Literature Forum* 24 (1) (Spring): 21–48.

Gleason, Judith. 1987. *Oya: In Praise of the Goddess.* Boston and London: Shambhala.

Greene, Gayle, and Coppelia Kahn, eds. 1985. *Making a Difference: Feminist Literary Criticism.* London: Methuen.

Gubar, Susan. 1985. "The Blank Page" and the Issues of Female Creativity. Pp. 292–313 in *The New Feminist Criticism,* ed. Elaine Showalter. New York: Random House.

Halliburton, Karen, and Valerie A. Canady. 1994. Parenting: Double the Fun. *Essence* 25 (3) (July): 106, 109.

Hammond, Dorothy Bramson, and Alta Jablow. 1970. *The Africa That Never Was: Four Centuries of British Writing About Africa.* New York: Twayne.

Head, Bessie. 1974. *A Question of Power.* London: Heinemann Educational Books.

———. 1977. The Collector of Treasures. Pp. 87–103 in *The Collector of Treasures and Other Botswana Village Tales.* Oxford: Heinemann International

Hernton, Calvin. 1984. The Sexual Mountain and Black Female Writers. *Black American Literature Forum* 18 (4) (Winter): 139–45.

Higgonnet, Margaret. 1986. Speaking Silences: Women's Suicide. Pp. 68–83 in *The Female Body in Western Culture*, ed. Susan Rubin Suleiman. Cambridge, Mass.: Harvard University Press.

hooks, bell. 1981. *Ain't I A Woman: Black Women and Feminism*. Boston: South End Press.

———. 1984. *Feminist Theory: From Margin to Center*. Boston: South End Press.

———. 1990. *Yearning: Race, Gender, and Cultural Politics*. Boston: South End Press.

Hudson-Weems, Clenora. 1992. Africana Womanism and Feminism, Black Feminism, Africana Womanism. Papers presented at The First International Conference on Women in Africa and the African Diaspora: Bridges Across Activism and the Academy. University of Nigeria, Nsukka, July 13–18.

Hull, Gloria, Patricia Bell Scott, and Barbara Smith, eds. 1982. *All the Women Are White, All the Blacks Are Men, But Some of Us Are Brave: Black Women's Studies*. Old Westbury, N.Y.: Feminist Press.

Hurston, Zora Neale. 1978 [1937]. *Their Eyes Were Watching God*. Urbana and Chicago: University of Illinois Press.

Idowu, E. Bolaji. 1962. *Olodumare: God in Yoruba Belief*. London: Longman.

Iglitzin, Lynne B., and Ruth Ross, eds. 1976. *Women in the World: A Comparative Study*. Santa Barbara, Calif.: Clio Books.

Iroh, Eddie. 1976. *Forty-eight Guns for the General*. London: Heinemann.

Jacobs, Janet Liebman. 1990. Reassessing Mother Blame in Incest. *Signs: Journal of Women in Culture and Society* 15 (3) (Spring): 500–514.

James, Stanlie M. 1993. Mothering: A Possible Black Feminist Link to Social Transformation? Pp. 44–54 in *Theorizing Black Feminisms*, ed. Stanlie M. James and and Abena P. A. Busia. London and New York: Routledge.

Jardine, Alice. 1985. *Gynesis: Configurations of Woman and Modernity*. Ithaca, N.Y.: Cornell University Press.

Jehlen, Myra. 1981. Archimedes and the Paradox of Feminist Criticism. *Signs: Journal of Women in Culture and Society* 6 (4) (Summer): 575–601.

Jell-Bahlsen, Sabine. 1991. "Mammy Water," In Search of the Water Spirits in Nigeria (59 min.). Film shown at the conference "Queens, Queen Mothers, Priestesses and Power: Case Studies in African Gender." The Schomburg Center for Research in Black Culture, April 8–11.

Johnson, Barbara. 1984. Metaphor, Metonymy and Voice in *Their Eyes Were Watching God*. Pp. 205–19 in *Black Literature and Literary Theory*, ed. Henry Louis Gates, Jr. New York: Methuen.

———. 1991. Apostrophe, Animation, and Abortion. Pp. 630–43 in *Feminisms: An Anthology of Literary Theory and Criticisms*, ed. Robyn R. Warhol and Diane Price Herndl. New Brunswick, N.J.: Rutgers University Press.

Joseph, Gloria L. 1983. Review of *Women, Race and Class* by Angela Y. Davis. *Signs: Journal of Women in Culture and Society* 9 (1) (Autumn): 134–36.

Kahane, Claire. 1985. The Gothic Mirror. Pp. 334–51 in *The (M)other Tongue: Essays in Feminist Psychoanalytic Interpretation*, ed. Judith Kegan Garner, Claire Kahane, and Madelon Sprengnether. Ithaca, N.Y.: Cornell University Press.

Kaplan, Ann. 1974. Feminist Criticism: A Survey with Analysis of Methodological Problems. University of Michigan Papers in Women's Studies, no. 1.

Katoke, I. K., and D. K. Ndagala. 1979. The Palaver in the United Republic of Tanzania. Pp. 61–76 in *Socio-political Aspects of the Palaver in Some African Countries*. UNESCO.

Keohane, Nannerl O., Michelle Z. Rosaldo, and Barbara C. Gelpi, eds. 1982. *Feminist Theory: A Critique of Ideology*. Brighton: Harvester Press.

Kolodny, Annette. 1985. A Map for Rereading; or, Gender and the Interpretation of Literary Texts. Pp. 241–59 in *The (M)other Tongue: Essays in Feminist Psychoanalytic Interpretation*, ed. Judith Kegan Garner, Claire Kahane, and Madelon Sprengnether. Ithaca, N.Y.: Cornell University Press.

Ladele, Omolola. 1988. Zaynab Alkali. Pp. 327–32 in *Perspectives on Nigerian Literature: 1700 to the Present*, vol. 2, ed. Yemi Ogunbiyi. Lagos: Guardian Books Nigeria.

Lilienfield, Jane. 1981. Where the Spear Plants Grew: The Ramsays' Marriage in *To the Lighthouse*. Pp. 148–69 in *New Feminist Essays on Virginia Woolf*, ed. Jane Marcus. Lincoln: University of Nebraska Press.

Lindfors, Bernth. 1985. The Famous Authors' Reputation Test or The Poet Calling the Cattle Black. Paper presented at a Colloquium at Universität Bayreuth, West Germany, June. Published in 1988 as The Famous Authors' Reputation Test. *Kriteria: A Nigerian Journal of Literary Research* 1 (1) (February): 25–33.

Lindsay, Beverly, ed. 1980. *Comparative Perspectives of Third World Women: The Impact of Race Sex and Class*. New York: Praeger.

Literature and the English Language, vol. 1. 1981. Calabar, Nigeria: University of Calabar Press.

Lorde, Audre. 1978. *Uses of the Erotic: The Erotic as Power*. Trumansburg, N.Y.: Out and Out Books.

Lyonga, Pauline Nalova. 1985. Uhamiri, or, A Feminist Approach to African Literature: An Analysis of Selected Texts By Women in Oral and Written Literature. Ph.D. diss., University of Michigan.

Magona, Sindiwe. 1991. *To My Children's Children: An Autobiography*. London: The Women's Press.

Mann, Kristin. 1991. Women, Landed Property, and the Accumulation of Wealth in Early Colonial Lagos. *Signs: Journal of Women in Culture and Society* (Women, Family, State, and Economy in Africa) 16 (4) (Summer): 682–706.

Marcus, Jane. 1981. Introduction. Pp. xiii–xx in *New Feminist Essays on Virginia Woolf*, ed. Jane Marcus. Lincoln: University of Nebraska Press.

———. 1982. Storming the Toolshed. Pp. 217–35 in *Feminist Theory: A Critique of Ideology*, ed. Nannerl O. Keohane, Michelle Z. Rosaldo, and Barbara C. Gelpi. Brighton: Harvester Press.

———, ed. 1981. *New Feminist Essays on Virginia Woolf*. Lincoln: University of Nebraska Press.

Marshall, Paule. 1984 [1969]. *The Chosen Place, The Timeless People*. New York: Vantage.

———. 1983. *Praise Song for the Widow*. New York: Penguin.

Mba, Nina Emma. 1982. *Nigerian Women Mobilized: Women's Political Activity in Southern Nigeria, 1900–1965*. University of California, Berkeley: Institute of International Studies.

McConeghy, Patrick M. 1987. Woman's Speech and Silence in Hartman von Ane's *Erec*. Publications of the Modern Language Association 102 (5) (October): 772–83.

Miller, Christopher L. 1990. *Theories of Africans: Francophone Literature and Anthropology in Africa*. Chicago: University of Chicago Press.

Modleski, Tania. 1987. Rape Versus Mans/laughter: Hitchcock's *Blackmail* and Feminist Interpretation. Publications of the Modern Language Assocation 102 (5) (October): 304–15.

Moers, Ellen. 1976. *Literary Women*. Garden City, N.J.: Doubleday.

Mojola, Yemi. 1988. Adaora Ulasi. Pp. 178–84 in *Perspectives on Nigerian Literature: 1700 to the Present*, vol. 2, ed. Yemi Ogunbiyi. Lagos: Guardian Books.

———. 1989. The Works of Flora Nwapa. Pp. 30–36 in *Nigerian Female Writers: A Critical Perspective*, ed. Henrietta C. Otokunefor and Obiageli C. Nwodo. Lagos: Malthouse Press.

Morrison, Toni. 1983. Rootedness: The Ancestor as Foundation. Pp. 339–45 in *Black Women Writers (1950–1980)*, ed. Mari Evans. New York: Doubleday.

———. 1987. *Beloved*. New York: Alfred A. Knopf.

Mudimbe, V. Y. 1988. *The Invention of Africa: Gnosis, Philosophy, and the Order of Knowledge*. Bloomington and Indianapolis: Indiana University Press.

———. 1991. Letters of Reference. *Transition: An International Review* 53:62–78.

Nasta, Susheila, ed. 1992. *Motherlands: Black Women's Writing from Africa, the Caribbean and South Asia*. New Brunswick, N.J.: Rutgers University Press.

Newman, Beth. 1990. "The Situation of the Looker-on": Gender, Narration, and Gaze in *Wuthering Heights*. Publications of the Modern Language Association l05 (5) (October): l029–41.

Njau, Rebeka. 1975. *Ripples in the Pool*. London: Heinemann.

Njoku, Rose Adaure. 1987. *Withstand the Storm*. Ibadan: Heinemann.

Nnolim, Charles. 1989. The Writings of Ifeoma Okoye. Pp. 30–36 in *Nigerian Female Writers: A Critical Perspective*, ed. Henrietta C. Otokunefor and Obiageli C. Nwodo. Lagos: Malthouse Publishers.

Nwachukwu-Agbada, J. O. J. 1988. Oral Literature and History: Examples from Igbo Proverbs. Paper presented at the Department of English, University of Ibadan, April 12.

Nwakoby, Martina. 1985. *A House Divided*. Enugu: Fourth Dimension Publishers.

Nwapa, Flora. 1966. *Efuru*. London: Heinemann Books, 1966.

———. 1970. *Idu*. London: Heinemann Books.

———. 1971. *This Is Lagos and Other Stories*. Enugu: Nwankwo-Ifejika.

———. 1975. *Never Again*. Enugu: Nwamife Publishers.

———. 1981. *One Is Enough*. Enugu: Tana Press.

———. 1984. *Wives at War and Other Stories*. Enugu: Tana Press.

———. 1986. *Women Are Different*. Enugu: Tana Press.

———. 1991. Priestesses and Power Among the Riverine Igbo. Paper delivered at the conference on "Queens, Queen Mothers, Priestesses and Power: Case Studies in African Gender." April 8–11. The Schomburg Center for Research in Black Culture, New York.

Nwoga, Donatus Ibe. 1984. *The Supreme God as Stranger in Igbo Religious Thought*. Ahiazu Mbaise: Hawk Press.

Obong, Eno. 1988. *Garden House.* Ibadan: New Horn Press and Heinemann.

Odugbesan, Clara. 1969. Femininity in Yoruba Religious Art. Pp. 199–211 in *Men in Africa,* ed. Mary Douglas and Phyllis M. Karlberry. London: Tavistock.

Ofeimun, Odia. 1985. Zaynab Alkali: An Interview. *The Guardian,* March 27.

Ogunbiyi, Yemi, ed. 1988. *Perspectives on Nigerian Literature: 1700 to the Present.* 2 vols. Lagos: Guardian Books.

Ogundipe-Leslie, Molara. 1987. The Female Writer and Her Commitment. Pp. 5–13 in *Women in African Literature Today,* vol. 15, ed. Eldred Durosimi Jones, Eustace Palmer, and Marjorie Jones. Trenton, N.J.: Africa World Press.

———. 1994. *Re-creating Ourselves: African Women and Critical Transformations.* Trenton, N.J.: Africa World Press.

Ogunyemi, Chikwenye Okonjo. 1985. Womanism: The Dynamics of Black Female Writing in English. *Signs: Journal of Women in Culture and Society* 11 (1) (Autumn): 63–80. Reprinted in *Mit Verscharftem Blick,* 1989. Also in *Revising the Word and the World: Essays in Feminist Literary Criticism,* ed. Vévé A. Clarke, Ruth-Ellen Joeres, and Madelon Sprengnether, 231–48. Chicago: University of Chicago Press, 1993.

Ojo-Ade, Femi. 1991. Of Culture, Commitment, and Construction: Reflections on African Literature. *Transition: An International Review* 53:4–24.

Okonjo, Kamene. 1976. The Dual-Sex Political System in Operation: Igbo Women and Community Politics in Midwestern Nigeria. Pp. 45–58 in *Women in Africa,* ed. Nancy J. Hafkin and Edna G. Bay. Stanford, Calif.: Stanford University Press.

Okoye, Ifeoma. 1982. *Behind the Clouds.* London: Longman.

———. 1984. *Men Without Ears.* London: Longman.

Okpewho, Isidore. 1971. *The Victims.* Garden City, N.J.: Anchor Books.

———. 1976. *The Last Duty.* London: Longman.

———. 1989. African Poetry: The Modern Writer and the Oral Tradition. Pp. 3–25 in *Oral and Written Poetry in African Literature Today,* ed. Eldred Durosimi Jones, Eustace Palmer, and Marjorie Jones. Trenton, N.J.: Africa World Press.

Okri, Ben. 1991. *The Famished Road.* London: Vintage.

Ola, V. U. 1981. Flora Nwapa and the Art of the Novel. Pp. 91–111 in *Medium and Message: Proceedings of the International Conference of African Literature and the English Language.* Calabar: University of Calabar Press.

Olney, James. 1973. *Tell Me Africa: An Approach to African Literature.* Princeton, N.J.: Princeton University Press.

Onwuteaka, V. C. 1965. The Aba Riot of 1929 and Its Relation to the System of Indirect Rule. *Nigerian Journal of Economic and Social Studies* 7 (3) (November): 273–82.

Onyeama, Dillibe. 1972. *Nigger at Eton.* London: Leslie Frewin.

Osundare, Niyi. 1989. The Poem as a Mytho-linguistic Event: A Study of Soyinka's "Abiku." Pp. 91–102 in *Oral and Written Poetry in African Literature Today,* vol. 16, ed. Eldred Jones. Trenton, N.J.: Africa World Press.

Otokunefor, Henrietta C., and Obiageli C. Nwodo, eds. 1989. *Nigerian Female Writers: A Critical Perspective.* Lagos: Malthouse Press.

Pathak, Zakia, and Rajeswari Sunder Rajan. 1989. Shahbano. *Signs: Journal of Women in Culture and Society* 14 (3) (Spring): 558–82.

Perry, Alison. 1984. Meeting Flora Nwapa. *West Africa* (June 18): 1262.

Petersen, Kirsten Holst. 1985. Unpopular Opinions: Some African Women Writers. Pp. 107–20 in *A Double Colonization: Colonial and Post-Colonial Women's Writing*, ed. Kirsten Holst Petersen and Anna Rutherford. Oxford: Dangaroo Press.

Petersen, Kirsten Holst, and Anna Rutherford, eds. 1985. *Kunapipi* (Special Double Issue on Colonial and Post-Colonial Women's Writing) 7 (2) and 7 (3).

Pheterson, Gail. 1986. Alliances Between Women: Overcoming Internalized Domination. *Signs: Journal of Women in Culture and Society* 12 (1) (Autumn): 146–60.

Porter, Mary Cornelia, and Corey Venning. 1976. Catholicism and Women's Role in Italy and Ireland. Pp. 81–103 in *Women in the World: A Comparative Study*, ed. Lynne B. Iglitzin and Ruth Ross. Santa Barbara: Clio Books.

Register, Cheri. 1982. Motherhood at Center: Ellen Key's Social Vision. *Women's Studies International Forum* 5 (6):599–610.

Rich, Adrienne. 1977. *Of Woman Born: Motherhood as Experience and Institution*. New York: Bantam.

———. 1980. *On Lies, Secrets, Silence: Selected Prose 1966–1978*. London: Virago Press.

———. 1986. Compulsory Heterosexuality and Lesbian Existence. Pp. 22–28 in *Feminist Literary Theory: A Reader*, ed. Mary Eagleton. Oxford: Basil Blackwell.

Riley, Joan. 1985. *The Unbelonging*. London: The Women's Press.

Robinson, Lillian S. 1991. Treason Our Text: Feminist Challenges to the Literary Canon. Pp. 212–26 in *Feminisms: An Anthology of Literary Theory and Criticisms*, ed. Robyn R. Warhol and Diane Herndl. New Brunswick, N.J.: Rutgers University Press.

Saadawi, Nawal El. 1983 [1975]. *Woman at Point Zero*, trans. Sherif Hetata. London: Zed Books.

Said, Edward. 1978. *Orientalism*. New York: Pantheon.

Schor, Naomi. 1981. Female Paranoia: The Case for Psychoanalytic Feminist Criticism. *Yale French Studies* 62:204–19.

Shange, Ntozake. 1989 [1975]. *for colored girls who have considered suicide when the rainbow is enuf*. New York: Collier.

Showalter, Elaine. 1982. Feminist Criticism in the Wilderness. Pp. 9–35 in *Writing and Sexual Difference*, ed. Elizabeth Abel. Chicago: University of Chicago Press.

———. 1985. Introduction: The Feminist Critical Revolution. Pp. 3–17 in *The New Feminist Criticism: Essays on Women, Literature, and Theory*, ed. Elaine Showalter. New York: Random House.

Showalter, Elaine, ed. 1985. *The New Feminist Criticism: Essays on Women, Literature, and Theory*. New York: Random House.

Slemon, Stephen. 1988. Magic Realism as Post-colonial Discourse. *Canadian Literature* 116:9–24.

Smith Esther, Y. 1986. Images of Women in African Literature: Some Examples of Inequality in the Colonial Period. Pp. 27–44 in *Ngambika: Studies of Women in African Literature*, ed. Carol Boyce Davies and Anne Adams Graves. Trenton, N.J.: Africa World Press.

Smith, Sidonie. 1987. *A Poetics of Women's Autobiography: Marginality and the Fictions of Self-Representation*. Bloomington and Indianapolis: Indiana University Press.

Sofola, 'Zulu. 1988. African Society and the Concept of Freedom. *Okike: An African Journal of New Writing* 27 (28) (March): 74–82.

Solberg, Ralph. 1983. The Woman of Black Africa, Buchi Emecheta: The Woman's Voice in the New Nigerian Novel. *English Studies* 64 (3) (June): 260–61.

Soyinka, Wole. 1976. *Myth, Literature, and the African World.* Cambridge: Cambridge University Press.

———. 1988. Abiku. In *A Selection of African Poetry,* introduced and annotated by K. E. Senanu and T. Vincent, 189. Essex, England: Longman.

———. 1989 [1981]. *Ake: The Years of Childhood.* New York: Vintage.

Spillers, Hortense J. 1985. Three Women's Texts and a Critique of Imperialism. *Critical Inquiry* 12 (1) (Autumn): 243–61.

———. 1987. A Hateful Passion, A Lost Love. Pp. 181–207 in *Feminist Issues in Literary Scholarship,* ed. Shari Benstock. Bloomington and Indianapolis: Indiana University Press.

Spivak, Gayatri Chakravorty. 1981. French Feminism in an International Frame. *Yale French Studies* 62:154–84.

———. 1990. *The Post-Colonial Critic: Interviews, Strategies, Dialogues,* ed. Sarah Harasym. New York: Routledge.

Steady, Filomina Chioma. 1981. *The Black Woman Crossculturally.* Cambridge, Mass.: Schenkman Publishing.

Steihm, Judith. 1976. Algerian Women: Honor, Survival, and Islamic Socialism. Pp. 229–41 in *Women in the World: A Comparative Study,* ed. Lynne B. Iglitzin and Ruth Ross. Santa Barbara: Clio Books.

Stimpson, Catharine R. 1971. "Thy Neighbor's Wife, Thy Neighbor's Servants": Women's Liberation and Black Civil Rights. Pp. 452–79 in *Woman in Sexist Society: Studies in Power and Powerlessness,* ed. Vivian Gornick and Barbara K. Moran. New York: Basic Books.

———. 1982. Zero Degree Deviancy: The Lesbian Novel in English. Pp. 243–59 in *Writing and Sexual Difference,* ed. Elizabeth Abel. Chicago: University of Chicago Press.

———. 1987. Introduction. Pp. 1–6 in *Feminist Issues in Literary Scholarship,* ed. Shari Benstock. Bloomington and Indianapolis: Indiana University Press.

Stratton, Florence. 1994. *Contemporary African Literature and the Politics of Gender.* London and New York: Routledge.

———. 1988. The Shallow Grave: Archetypes of Female Experience in African Fiction. *Research in African Literatures* 19 (2) (Summer): 143–69.

Sudarkasa, Niara. 1987. The "Status of Women" in Indigenous African Societies. Pp. 25–41 in *Women in Africa and the African Diaspora,* ed. Rosalyn Terborg-Penn, Sharon Harley, and Andrea Benton Rushing. Washington, D.C.: Howard University Press.

Suleiman, Susan Rubin. 1985. Writing and Motherhood. Pp. 352–77 in *The (M)other Tongue: Essays in Feminist Psychoanalytic Interpretation,* ed. Shirley Nelson Garner, Claire Kahane, and Madelon Sprengnether. Ithaca, N.Y.: Cornell University Press.

Suleiman, Susan Rubin, ed. 1986. *The Female Body in Western Culture: Contemporary Perspectives.* Cambridge, Mass.: Harvard University Press.

Sutherland, Efua. 1967. *Foriwa.* Accra: State Publishing Corporation.

Taiwo, Oladele. 1984. *Female Novelists of Modern Africa*. London: Macmillan.

———. 1986. *Ngambika: Studies of Women in African Literature.*

Terborg-Penn, Rosalyn, Sharon Harley, Andrea Benton Rushing, eds. 1987. *Women in Africa and the African Diaspora*. Washington, D.C.: Howard University Press.

Thiam, Awa. 1986. *Black Sisters Speak Out: Feminism and Oppression in Black Africa*, trans. Dorothy S. Blair. London: Pluto.

Tlali, Miriam. 1979. *Muriel at Metropolitan*. London: Longman.

Trinh T. Minh-ha. 1989. *Woman, Native, Other: Writing Postcoloniality and Feminism*. Bloomington and Indianapolis: Indiana University Press.

Tutuola, Amos. 1984 [1952]. *The Palm-wine Drinkard*. New York: Grove Press.

Ubesie, Tony. 1977. *Juo Obinna*. Ibadan: Oxford University Press.

Ulasi, Adaora Lily. 1971. *Many Thing Begin for Change*. London: Michael Joseph.

———. 1973 [1970]. *Many Thing You No Understand*. London: Michael Joseph.

———. 1974. *The Night Harry Died*. Lagos: Educational Research Institute Nigeria.

———. 1978a. *The Man from Sagamu*. Glasgow: Fontana.

———. 1978b. *Who Is Jonah?*. Ibadan: Onibonoje.

Umeh, Marie. 1987. The Poetics of Thwarted Sensitivity. Pp. 194–206 in *Critical Theory and African Literature*, ed. R. Vanamali, E. Oko, A. Iloeje, and Ernest Emenyonu. Ibadan: Heinemann.

———. N.d. Buchi Emecheta. *Fifty African and Caribbean Women Writers*, ed. Anne Adams. Westport, Conn.: Greenwood Press, forthcoming.

UNESCO. 1979. *Socio-political Aspects of the Palaver in Some African Countries*. Paris: UNESCO.

Valenzuela, Maria Helena. 1991. The Military Regime, Women and Dictatorship in Chile. *Alternatives: The Food, Energy, and Debt Crises in Relation to Women*, 1:97–108. Organizers: Neuma Aguiar and Thais Corral, DAWN—Development Alternatives with Women for a New Era. Rio de Janeiro: Editora Rosa dos Tempos LTDA.

Van Allen, Judith. 1976a. "Aba Riots" or Igbo "Women's War"? Ideology, Stratification, and the Invisibility of Women. Pp. 59–85 in *Women in Africa*, ed. Nancy Hafkin and Edna G. Bay. Stanford, Calif.: Stanford University Press.

———. 1976b. African Women, "Modernization," and National Liberation. Pp. 25–54 in *Women in the World: A Comparative Study*, ed. Lynne B. Iglitzin and Ruth Ross. Santa Barbara: Clio Books.

Viera, Carol. 1982. The Black Man's Burden in Anticolonial Satire. *College Language Association Journal* 26 (1) (September): 1–22.

Vogely, Nancy. 1987. Defining the "Colonial Reader": *El Periquillo Sarmiento*. Publications of the Modern Language Association 102 (5) (October): 784–800.

Walker, Alice. 1992. *Possessing the Secret of Joy*. New York: Harcourt Brace Jovanovich.

———. 1984. *In Search of Our Mothers' Gardens: Womanist Prose*. London: The Women's Press.

———. 1986. *The Color Purple*. Boston: G. K. Hall.

Wallace, Michele. 1979. *Black Macho and the Myth of the Superwoman*. New York: Dial Press.

Wambui wa Karanja. 1987. "Outside Wives" and "Inside Wives" in Nigeria: A Study of Changing Perceptions in Marriage. Pp. 247–61 in *Transformations of African*

347

Marriage, ed. David Parkin and David Nyamwaya. Manchester: Manchester University Press.

Ward, Cynthia. 1990. What They Told Buchi Emecheta: Oral Subjectivity and the Joys of "Otherhood." Publications of the Modern Language Association 105 (1) (January): 83–97.

Warhol, Robyn R., and Diane Price Herndl, eds. 1991. *Feminisms: An Anthology of Literary Theory and Criticisms.* New Brunswick, N.J.: Rutgers University Press.

Weixlmann, Joe and Houston A. Baker, Jr., eds. 1988. *Studies in Black American Literature,* vol. 3: *Black Feminist Criticism and Critical Theory.* Greenwood, Fla.: Penkevill Publishing.

Wilentz, Gay. 1992. *Binding Cultures: Black Women Writers in Africa and the Diaspora.* Bloomington and Indianapolis: Indiana University Press.

Willis, Susan. 1985. Black Women Writers: Taking a Critical Perspective. Pp. 211–37 in *Making a Difference: Feminist Literary Criticism,* ed. Gayle Greene and Coppelia Kahn. New York: Basic Books.

Woolf, Virginia. 1979. *Women and Writing.* London: The Woman's Press.

The World Bank. 1992. *World Development Report 1992: Development and the Environment.* New York: Oxford University Press.

Wright, Richard. 1945. Black Boy; A Record of Childhood and Youth. New York: Harper and Brothers. Reprinted 1966 by Harper and Row in the series, A Perennial Classic.

Index

Index